D1193909

During the Reformation period many of the fiercest debates centred on the nature of authority. These covered every aspect of Christian faith and life. The authority of Scripture; the authority on which disputed points of faith and order could be decided; the authorising of ministry in the Church; the efficacy of the sacraments, were all contested. Such issues are shown by the author of this study to remain ecumenically significant, both because it proved impossible to resolve them at the time to everyone's satisfaction, and because they continued for many generations to represent the focus of mutual hostility between the separated churches. Dr Evans aims here to piece together underlying connections in the theology of the Reformation period, as a contribution to ecumenical dialogue. By looking at the ideas about language and reasoning which influenced and shaped the debates, she seeks to draw ecumenical lessons.

PROBLEMS OF AUTHORITY
IN THE REFORMATION DEBATES

PROBLEMS OF AUTHORITY
IN THE REFORMATION DEBATES

G. R. EVANS
Lecturer in History, University of Cambridge

CAMBRIDGE
UNIVERSITY PRESS

Published by the Press Syndicate of the University of Cambridge
The Pitt Building, Trumpington Street, Cambridge CB2 1RP
40 West 20th Street, New York, NY 10011-4211, USA
10 Stamford Road, Oakleigh, Victoria 3166, Australia

First published 1992

Printed in Great Britain at the University Press, Cambridge

A catalogue record for this book is available from the British Library

Library of Congress cataloguing in publication data

Evans, G. R. (Gillian Rosemary)
Problems of authority in the Reformation debates / G.R. Evans
p. cm.
Includes bibliographical references.
ISBN 0 521 41686 8 (hardback)
1. Authority (Religion) – History of doctrines – 16th century.
2. Reformation. 3. Christian union. I. Title.
BT88.E92 1992
262'.8'09031–dc20 91-33100 CIP

ISBN 0 521 41686 8 hardback

FW

Contents

Preface

It became evident in the later Middle Ages and more urgently in the early sixteenth century that something was wrong with both the doctrine and the practice of authority in the Church in the West. Persistent patterns of dissent appeared. There was clear evidence of corruption, financial and spiritual, in the running of the institution of the Church. A great deal of scholarly effort was devoted at the time to trying to understand the nature of the problem and to suggesting remedies, but on the whole it was a piecemeal endeavour. No-one succeeded in providing a comprehensive account of the complex of 'authority' questions which were being raised about absolute divine sovereignty, the centrality of Christ, the primacy of Scripture, the necessity of grace, temporal, social and governmental structures, the ordering of the Christian community, although there were some bold and wide-ranging attempts.

Throughout the debates runs a preoccupation with 'power', under-stood by both sides as primarily a 'power over' or 'dominion'. The reformers pointed to an 'imposition', or 'usurpation' of a power which properly belongs only to God, but which was in their view being exercised by a privileged few in the Church over the faithful. The result was a power-struggle, a confrontation of claims to authority which made it impossible in the end for both sides to sit down together and work out a resolution of the conflict of understanding in which they had become entangled, because it was also a combat of strength. Order in the Church was put under intolerable stress. The crisis reached such proportions that before the end of the sixteenth century the Church in the West was fragmented.

In this study I have tried to piece together underlying connections and habits of thought in the huge collective endeavour of the theology of the Reformation period; they enable us to glimpse the shadow of a systematic theology of authority and to begin to see why the sixteenth-century attempt to find a theological resolution which all sides could recognise was not successful. I cannot claim to have provided all that is said here with its full context of political, social and intellectual reference, and little is said about the question of moral authority, except insofar as it arises in connection with the debate about the Church's internal problems and structures of authority, and not about the fundamental missionary task of the Church. But authority is a notoriously vexed and complex subject, and I hope these omissions may be excused in what is already a long book. I am conscious too that such a study cannot, of its nature, do full justice to the slow and subtle processes by which the thought of individuals among the reformers evolved, and those who have made a special study of Luther or Calvin and the others may complain that I have misrepresented them in this way. It is necessary, too, for a study of this kind to take grand strides backwards and forwards across the centuries from time to time. I have not been able to see how to avoid these difficulties and at the same time present a coherent picture of the authority problems of the sixteenth century as both local and temporal, and also perennial. And that has seemed the most important thing to attempt in the interests of any ecumenical usefulness this study may have for today.

Today's concerns about power and the abuse of power are equally strong but rather different. They have been particularly evident recently in the discussions of the World Council of Churches. It may be that something is to be learned from the sixteenth-century failure to resolve differences and to quiet anxieties. It is already evident as a result of ecumenical conversations of the last few decades that what once seemed immovable problems are now beginning to be resolved. I have tried to build on their beginnings, and this study is offered as a contribution to that ecumenical endeavour.

Acknowledgements

Although my work on this complex of questions began many years ago, this book owes its completion to the generous gift of time afforded by a British Academy Readership in 1986–8. It is also in no small measure indebted to the opportunities of drafting and redrafting in consultation which have come my way in working on some of these topics with the Faith and Order Advisory Group of the Church of England's Board of Mission and Unity, and the Archbishops' Group on the Episcopate. To members of these groups and to many friends I owe a great debt. I am also most grateful to Alex Wright of Cambridge University Press, the typesetter Fiona Wilson, and Ann Mason, who copy-edited the text, for their goodwill and patience, and for their generous and friendly expenditure of their professional skills.

This book is cousin to two others. The first is *Authority in the Church: a challenge for Anglicans* (Norwich, 1990), which was written as a result of the same Readership and under the stimulus of the same discussions. The second is *Christian Authority: Essays Presented to Henry Chadwick* (Oxford, 1988). This study took the germ of its present form as a paper to be included in that volume, but it grew much too big. Perhaps it may be offered to him now as an appendix.

Abbreviations

Acta CT	*Acta Concilium Tridentinum*, 13 vols. (Fribourg, 1901–38)
A–L	Anglican–Lutheran Conversations, in *Growth*
A–R	Anglican–Reformed Conversations: *God's Reign and our Unity* (London, 1984)
ARCIC I	Anglican–Roman Catholic International Commission, Final Report, in *Growth* (AI, AII are the texts on Authority)
ARCIC II	*Church as Communion*: an agreed statement by the Second Anglican–Roman Catholic International Commission (London, 1990)
BEM	*Baptism, Eucharist and Ministry*, Lima Report of the World Council of Churches, in *Growth*
B–R	Baptist–Reformed Conversations, in *Growth*
Calvin, *Antidote* to Trent	in *Opera, CR* 35
Calvin, *Institutes*	*Institutes of the Christian Religion*, in *Opera, CR* 29–30
C. Cath.	*Corpus Catholicorum*
CCSL	*Corpus Christianorum Series Latina*
CHLMP	*The Cambridge History of Later Mediaeval Philosophy*, ed. N. Kretzmann, A. Kenny and J. Pinborg (Cambridge, 1982)
Collatio	Lorenzo Valla, *Collatio Novi Testamenti*, ed. A. Perosa (Florence, 1970)
Confessio Saxonica	Melanchthon, *Confessio Saxonica, Werke*, VI, ed. R. Stupperich (Gütersloh, 1955)
CR	*Corpus Reformatorum*, ed. C. G. Bretschneider *et al.* (Brunswick, Nova Scotia, 1834)
CSEL	*Corpus Scriptorum Ecclesiasticorum Latinorum*
Decades	J. Bullinger, *Decades*, ed. T. Harding (Parker Society, Cambridge, 1849–52), 4 vols.

Defence	William Fulke, *A Defence of the Sincere and True Translations of the Scriptures into the English Tongue* (London, 1583), ed. C. H. Hartshorne (Parker Society, Cambridge, 1843)
De Iustitia et Libertate Christiana	Seripando, *De Iustitia et Libertate Christiana*, ed. A. Forster, *C. Cath.* 30 (Münster, 1969)
D–RC	Disciples – Roman Catholic Conversations, in *Growth*
Eck, *Loci*	Johannes Eck, *Enchiridion Locorum Communum*, ed. P. Fraenkel, *C. Cath.* 34 (Münster, 1979)
Elegantiae	Lorenzo Valla, *Elegantiae de Lingua Latina* (Lyons, 1501)
Erasmus, *Letters*	in *Collected Works* (1–), ed. and tr. R. J. Schoeck *et al.* (Toronto, 1974–)
Growth	*Growth in Agreement: Reports and Agreed Statements of Ecumenical Conversations on a World Level*, ed. H. Meyer and L. Vischer (Geneva, 1984)
Language and Logic I, II	G. R. Evans, *The Language and Logic of the Bible*, vol. I (Cambridge, 1984); vol. II (Cambridge, 1985)
Laws	Richard Hooker, *The Laws of Ecclesiastical Polity*, ed. W. Speed Hill (Cambridge, Mass., 1977)
Louvain	Articles of the theologians of Louvain, 1544, WA 54.416–22
L–RC	Lutheran–Roman Catholic Conversations, in *Growth*
MGH Epp.	*Monumenta Germaniae Historica Epistolae*
More, *Responsio*	Thomas More, *Responsio ad Lutherum*, ed. J. M. Headley, *Complete Works*, vol. 5 (London/Yale, 1969)
Paris Articles	Articles of the theologians of Paris, 1544, *CR* 35
PL	*Patrologia Latina*
Pollet	*Correspondance de J. Pflug*, ed. J. V. Pollet (Leiden, 1969–82), 5 vols.

Remains	Hugh Latimer, *Sermons and Remains*, ed. G. Corrie (Parker Society, Cambridge, 1844–5)
Repastinatio	Lorenzo Valla, *Repastinatio Dialecticae et Philosophiae*, ed. G. Zippel (Padua, 1982)
Resolutiones	Luther, *Resolutiones Disputationum de Indulgentiarum Virtute*, ed. O. Clemen, *Werke* (Berlin, 1950)
R–RC	Reformed–Roman Catholic Conversations, in *Growth*
Smalkald Articles	Luther, Smalkald Articles, 1537, in Tappert
ST	Aquinas, *Summa Theologiae*
Tappert	*The Book of Concord*, ed. T. G. Tappert (Philadelphia, 1981)
Trent	Decrees and Canons of the Council of Trent (roman figures refer to Sessions of the Council)
Vera Eccl. Ref. Rat.	Calvin, *Vera Christianae Pacificationis et Ecclesiae Reformando Ratio, CR* 35
VSS	Wyclif, *De Veritate Sacrae Scripturae*, ed. R. Buddensieg (London, 1905)
WA	Luther, *Werke* (Weimar edition)
WA Briefe	Luther, *Briefwechsel* (Weimar, 1930–83)
Zwingli, *Defence*	Zwingli, *Defence of the Reformed Faith,* 67 Articles of 1523, *Werke* I
Zwingli, *Werke*	Zwingli, *Sämtliche Werke, CR* 88–101

Principal collections of articles and theses mentioned in the text

Introduction

The confession of Christ as Lord is the heart of the Christian faith. To him God has given all authority in heaven and on earth. As Lord of the Church he bestows the Holy Spirit to create a communion of men with God and with one another. To bring this *koinonia* to perfection is God's eternal purpose. The Church exists to serve the fulfilment of this purpose when God will be all in all.[1]

Christian authority is Christ's authority. The debates on authority which rent apart the Church in the West in the sixteenth century turned again and again on whether Christ's sovereignty was being set at risk in the Church's life; and whether his Word, Holy Scripture, was being disregarded or overridden by those in authority in the Church.

The chapters which follow look first at sixteenth-century concerns over the authority on which Christians believe matters of faith. As textual scholarship investigated Greek and Hebrew and raised the possibility that there ought to be emendations, Scripture itself could no longer be looked upon, in an uncontroversial way, as a text to which one could simply point. The testimony of the authorities other than Scripture with which everyone in the West had been familiar for generations, ceased to be uncontroversially acceptable to many Protestants, and qualifications hedged about the use even of the Fathers. Proof by reasoning, which had reached a high point of sophistication in the late Middle Ages, and in which there had normally been embedded authorities to support propositions, underwent revolutionary attack.

These are in part epistemological matters, in part critical and methodological, and they must stand behind any enquiry into the content of a theology of authority in salvation and its relationship to authority in the Church. We have both the advantage of hindsight to help us judge whether a difference of sixteenth-century opinion was merely about language; and the disadvantage that we cannot now enter into the sixteenth-century situation without making some effort of intellectual fellowship. But if we have been quarrelling even in part about the

---

[1]   ARCIC I, Authority I.1.

1

interpretation of words and the implications of arguments, there can be no more essential task than to try to understand the doctrine of logic and language with which sixteenth-century thinkers were working when the Protestants' Confessions and the Decrees and Canons of the Council of Trent were framed.

In succeeding chapters we come to a series of areas of major concern throughout the sixteenth-century Church in the West. By what authority can the Christian know himself to be accepted by God, and forgiven for his sins? Has he any power to help himself? Is authority vested in some way in the Church to help him? Does the Church have authority to 'bind and loose', to 'reconcile' the penitent to God when he falls into sin again and again, and repents, or to deny him reconciliation if he does not repent? What authority does baptism carry in God's eyes? Is it necessary for salvation? What happens in the Eucharist? Does the priest who says the words of consecration have authority to make the Eucharist effective on behalf of those who are present? Of those they love who are not present? How is authority to be understood and exercised in the day-to-day running of the Church? Who has authority to make someone a minister to others? Is authority in the Church properly hierarchical? Ought there to be one minister with authority over the whole Church, and if so, exactly what are his powers and responsibilities? Who has authority to make decisions about matters of faith and order? How can decisions be made when the Church is divided?

All these are intimately interconnected areas of authority. They form a single system. That must be so if Christ is Lord and communion his purpose. The difficulty, in the sixteenth century and today, is to see them as a unity.

i. THE AGENDA

The Lutheran theologian Martin Chemnitz (1522–86) spent a period in his thirties as ducal librarian at Königsberg. This gave him an opportunity which had not come his way before as a university lecturer to sit down at his leisure with a good library and take stock of his habits of study. He says that he began by reading the books of the Bible through in order, comparing 'all the various versions and expositions, old and new, that were in the library'. This sort of textual criticism, involving the comparison not only of interpreters, but also of differences in readings and translations, was something relatively new. Chemnitz's method was to make a note of 'anything that seemed memorable or remarkable', 'on paper arranged for this purpose'. Secondly, he read the writings of the Fathers, and again he noted what caught his attention. Then he 'diligently read' more recent authors, those who drew attention to 'fundamentals' of doctrine as 'purified' by the reformers. He concentrated, he remarks, chiefly on those who wrote 'polemical treatises on the controversies of our time'. (He specifies the arguments of the 'Papists, Anabaptists, Sacramentarians'.) He made notes of the ways their explanations and solutions were arrived at and tried to determine for himself 'what solutions were the best'.[2] Here, as in his study of the Bible, new possibilities were added to the old, and Chemnitz was consciously trying to work his way from foundation texts to the conclusions of modern scholarship.

He tried to reduce the mass of material to manageable working matter by systematically making extracts, with a scholarliness only perhaps Robert Grosseteste matched among the mediaeval compilers of *florilegia*.[3] He was influenced, as earlier generations had been, by contemporary fashions in theological debate. In the commentaries written on Peter Lombard's *Sentences* generation by generation since the twelfth century, such changes of fashion are apparent not only in the opinions which are advanced and the terms which attract particular notice, but also in the topics which receive special attention. Similarly, when Martin Chemnitz was struck by a sentence or two in his reading, or by a particular argument, he was noting matters of topical concern for his generation, and looking out for 'purified doctrine', as Lutheran scholarship had come to understand it.

He did so on the basis of two sets of ideas, one perhaps more consciously in his mind than the other. The first was a mediaeval heritage. The general shape of the syllabus of 'systematic theology' had been more or less settled in the first hundred years or so of theology's formal study as an academic discipline in the new universities of Europe. In the mid-twelfth century Peter Lombard had arranged his *Sententiae* from the Fathers in a topic order; a century later Thomas Aquinas produced a *Summa Theologiae* which was to outrun its rivals in use as a standard textbook by the end of the sixteenth century.

Aquinas' method was to begin by considering the nature of theological

---

2   Tr. A. L. Graebner, 'An Autobiography of Martin Chemnitz', *Theological Quarterly*, 3 (1899), 472–87.
3   See R. W. Southern, *Robert Grosseteste* (Oxford, 1986) on the *dicta*. Also see collections in Cranmer, *Miscellaneous Writings and Letters*, ed. J. E. Cox (Parker Society, Cambridge, 1846) for a more closely contemporary comparison.

subject-matter and the methods appropriate to it as a discipline, and then to examine questions about the existence and attributes of God; unity and Trinity, the creation, and within it angels and humankind and their mode of knowledge of God; then human right living, the effect of sin and God's work of redemption. The *schema* was, in outline, much the same as that of Hugh of St Victor, Peter Lombard's older contemporary, in his *De Sacramentis Ecclesiae*, and of Peter Lombard himself, whose *Sentences* were always studied as part of a theologian's training throughout the later Middle Ages. This theological framework was devised before the developments of the later Middle Ages had begun to pose questions about authority in the Church so serious and comprehensive as to require systematic treatment in their own right. Aquinas is inclined to deal piecemeal with those which were apparent to him, as they arose within the existing framework.

Chemnitz's notion of what was 'fundamental' was, then, in part determined by the *schema* of systematic theology as he knew it. But he also had a sense that Luther and others in the reforming communities were rediscovering truths which were 'essential to salvation' and which had somehow become obscured, distorted or cluttered with extraneous matter in the teaching of the late mediaeval Church. It was in this spirit that when Melanchthon advised the Elector Maurice on the Interim document drawn up in 1548 to try to bring about peace in the war in Germany, he stressed the differences between essentials and inessentials, *res necessariae et non necessariae*.[4] These seemed to the participants to be debates in which everything was to be lost or won, the salvation of individuals and the salvation of the world.

Except among the radicals and Socinians, the essentials and fundamentals at issue[5] were not the Trinitarian and Christological dogmas debated in the first Christian centuries and set out in the Creeds. The credal formulations commanded almost universal acceptance. Indeed, Luther rehearses them in Part I of the Smalkald Articles (1537) in order to underline that they 'are not matters of dispute or contention, for both parties confess them'. A great deal was amicably agreed at the Colloquy of Ratisbon in 1541 before protestant and Catholic negotiators came to a stop in mutual suspicion. Calvin was able to say 'Amen' to a number of the Decrees and Canons of Trent. But the Creeds are exceedingly brief on the doctrine of salvation and the Church, and what had come to seem fundamental in the sense Chemnitz means was a series of non-negotiable

[4]   Vatican, MS. Barb. Lat. 806, fo. 244.
[5]   Cf. A–L Pullach (25), *Growth*, p. 17.

central principles in this area on which a great deal was now seen to turn, and which appeared to the reformers to be the key to the whole theological system. Chief among these were 'Christ-centredness', justifying faith, the acceptance of no ultimate authority in matters of faith but that of Scripture.

Luther more than once points out the ramifications of error to which misunderstanding of such basic principles could lead. Those who hold fast to 'the chief article of Jesus Christ' have, he argues, remained secure in the true faith. 'All error, heresy, idolatry, offence, misuse and evil in the Church originally came from despising or losing sight of this article of faith in Jesus Christ.' He says that the idea that we must make satisfaction for sins committed after baptism is the 'source and origin of all monasteries, masses, pilgrimages, invocations of the saints and such, with which people try to make satisfaction for their sins'.[6] He thinks that the Mass is a 'dragon's tail' which has 'brought forth a brood of vermin and the poison of manifold idolatries' such as purgatory; vigils; pilgrimages; fraternities, those 'monasteries, chapters and vicars' which 'have obligated themselves to transfer by legal and open sale' Masses for the benefit of the living and the dead; relics; indulgences.[7]

Luther's picture of things running away at a gallop, once first principles have been lost sight of, conflates a number of ideas which he did not himself always clearly separate. Uppermost in his mind was the threat to the faith of simple people, who were in danger of believing that the purchase of indulgences assured their salvation; they were putting all their trust (*tota fiducia*) not in Christ but in a bit of paper with a wax seal, in the mistaken belief that indulgences brought forgiveness and effected a reconciliation between themselves and God.[8] Here the issue was not strictly whether the theology was mistaken, but the perennial problem of popular misunderstanding. This was coupled, as it has been in every Christian century, with the persistent tendency of uneducated people to turn to magic and the help of local and familiar spirits in their troubles. When Luther speaks of a trail of implications of abuse arising from failure to keep to Christ, he is referring in part to muddle of this sort. But he came to believe that the Church had gone along with popular misunderstanding, even fostering it for its own pecuniary ends, and encouraging the faithful to put their trust in all the aids and apparatus the penitential system and

6 *WA* 39ⁱ.111.
7 Smalkald Articles II.2.
8 Ninety-Five Theses, 32 and 38, *Resolutiones*.

the system of indulgences now afforded. His own grasp of the theology of indulgences was imperfect in the period when he compiled the Ninety-Five Theses, as he later acknowledged in 1545 in writing *Against Hanswurst*.[9] Melanchthon comments that the theology of penance was confused until Luther came to grips with it.[10] There is some truth in the view that the theology underlying indulgences at least was still not quite clear. As we shall see, the practices connected with the granting of indulgences in the later Middle Ages preceded the development of the theology which explained and justified them.

We have, then, a number of factors in the upheaval of early sixteenth-century theology: an existing order and syllabus of 'systematic theology' as studied in the universities, which could not fully accommodate the theological issues which had been raised by the developments of the last mediaeval centuries; a longstanding custom of the adoption of certain topics for fashionable debate from time to time in the schools; the perception that something was wrong pastorally and practically within the life of the Church, partly as a result of corruption, but also because neither the full syllabus of theological studies nor the topics of current academic interest were encouraging systematic thinking about what was wrong; a sense of 'emergency' among the reformers.

If we are to see how the agenda of debate was drawn up, and how difficult it was to perceive at the time the importance of the task of approaching systematically the problems of authority which were being raised, we must try to capture the freshness of his insights as they appeared to Luther himself. In the period from about 1516, he was beginning to think in an orderly way about the nature and process of personal salvation, to find the kinds of question put in academic teaching of theology unhelpful, and to read the Bible afresh for himself. The result was a creative ferment in his mind, and a sense of high discovery. The driving force was not merely his own sense of intellectual dissatisfaction. It was also strongly pastoral. As he discusses the theology of indulgences and the abuses connected with contemporary practice, Luther begins to discover a number of important principles. First, it cannot be overemphasised that indulgences cannot bring salvation.[11] The popular assumption that they can, leads to distortions of emphasis which obscure

9   *WA* 51.462ff.
10 *Apologia* for the Augsburg Confession, Art. 12, Tappert, p. 183.
11 Ninety-Five Theses, 23, 29, 49, 52, 89.

the great simplicities of our redemption;[12] because in preaching about indulgences ministers push the Word into the background, or omit reference to it altogether,[13] these simplicities are not brought before people's minds. The cross put up by the indulgence-seller when he speaks is thought by the people to have a power equal to that of the Cross of Christ itself.[14] In truth this cross and the indulgences it promises are very insignificant graces in comparison with the true Cross.[15] The real message of the Cross is that we are to take it up in a lifetime of repentance,[16] and follow Christ through pain, death and all the sufferings of this life.[17] The 'theologian of the Cross' – that is, the true theologian – teaches that sufferings, crosses borne and death are the treasure (*thesaurus*) of all that is most precious, and that the Lord of this theology consecrated and blessed them not only by the touch of his most holy flesh, but also by the supremely holy embrace of his divine will; and he left them here to be kissed, sought after and embraced by us.[18]

Luther is seeking to emphasise in these Theses that good works and willing acceptance of suffering are not mere machinery. There had come to be a strong sense of the mechanical in performing a set action. (Praying at a particular shrine and giving alms won an indulgence of 4,000 years at Halle in 1521.[19]) It was only too easy to slip from asking for an outward act as a sign of penitence making the relief of indulgence appropriate, to seeing the act as being in itself enough to make reparation. What was fair practice in feudal relations or in business between man and man seemed proper between man and God too. Indulgences were regarded as a fair transaction. One got what one paid for.

Luther argues first that doing good works and performing acts of piety (and their converse the willing acceptance of suffering) are worthwhile.[20]

12 In a letter to Albert of Mainz written in October 1517, Luther tried to draw the bishop's attention to the belief of many of the faithful that when they have bought a letter of indulgence they are assured of salvation, and that the grace obtained by indulgences is so great that there is nothing which cannot be forgiven in this way.
13 Theses 53, 54, 55, 62, 78.
14 Thesis 79.
15 Thesis 68.
16 Thesis 1.
17 Thesis 94.
18 Thesis 58.
19 See Luther's diatribe *Against the Spiritual Estate of the Pope and the Bishops, falsely so-called*, on the festival of relics in the new cathedral at Halle in 1521, *WA* 10[ii].95ff.
20 Thesis 32.

Such actions are better than buying indulgences.[21] But their value lies not in their capacity to satisfy or pay for our sins, but in their tendency to encourage us to grow in love and holiness. Love grows by works of love and thereby becomes better, but no-one actually grows by buying an indulgence.[22] Such growing, Luther is sure, continues until the soul enters Heaven; it is possible for souls in purgatory to grow – indeed, that is what they are there for.[23] If we think we are making satisfaction by our actions, or by substitute indulgences, we shall lose a necessary fear, the *timor dei*, the fear of death, of judgement, of Hell, of pangs of conscience.[24] It is a fear of which not even souls in purgatory ought to be free.[25] (Luther is against this form of assurance.) Pain and fear are our true Cross; they help us.

Unpacking the implications of his initial criticisms, Luther begins to see his way. Confidence in our own works, or in bought 'works', leads to the error of seeking to be justified through our works (*per opera nostra*) and through our own righteousness (*nostra iusticia*) rather than through faith.[26] It is faith in Christ which justifies, not our works or even our repentance. Even if you do not believe yourself to be sufficiently contrite – and you can never be sure that your contrition is sufficient – nevertheless, if you believe in him who says, 'He who believes and is baptised will be saved,' you are saved. What you have depends on your faith: *Tantum habes quantum credes.*[27] There is no confidence of salvation (*fiducia salutis*) for us in anything but the one Jesus Christ, and no other name given under Heaven by which we are to be saved.[28] Thus Luther contrasts the simplicity of justification by faith with the anxious nagging and worrying of seeking salvation by personal effort.[29]

Luther must not be allowed to bulk too large in this story. In the Ninety-Five Theses and the supporting arguments Luther soon supplied to go with them, we have a text to which much significance has been attached because of their importance in setting in motion a chain of events in

21 Theses 41, 42, 43.
22 Thesis 44.
23 Thesis 18.
24 Theses 14, 15, 16, 17.
25 Theses 17, 19.
26 *Resolutiones*, p. 124.37–9.
27 Thesis 38, *Resolutiones*, p. 105.9–19.
28 Thesis 32.
29 Acts 15.11, *Resolutiones*, pp. 37–8.

Luther's own life which made him a leader of reform.[30] But the Theses were no more than a conspicuous event in more widespread developments. Zwingli found a similar complex of difficulties of a theological and practical sort clustering round the controversy about baptism which was stirred up by Anabaptist preachers. These presented what seemed to him, too, a danger of leading the simple faithful astray.[31] In his *Defence of the Reformed Faith* in 1523, Zwingli claims to have been preaching for a good five years on topics closely similar to those which were exercising Luther. Like Luther, but apparently more or less independently,[32] Zwingli had come to place an emphasis upon the sovereignty of God, the centrality of the Gospel, man's dependency on the efficacy of Christ's Passion for forgiveness in the sight of God.

Zwingli's *Defence* covers a wider span of topics than Luther had yet encompassed. There were significant differences of emphasis, over the Eucharist in particular. Zwingli did not share Luther's antinomianism, and he regarded 'doing good' rather differently as to its place in the Christian life. But as he began to read Luther's works he came to recognise that they were responding in substantially similar ways to the same perceived abuses, although he acknowledges in correspondence with Rhenanus that he found Luther spiky reading (*echinus*) at first.[33] Both were responding as pastors to the signs they saw, in the lives of the faithful, of incompleteness and some incoherence in the Church's teaching about salvation.

Luther and Zwingli were voicing criticisms which were already in the air and which had, in some cases, been there for a long time. Some of their ideas struck old chords of resentment about the Church's teaching on authority, chords which had been sounding at intervals since at least the twelfth century, and which had been heard again more recently among Lollards and Hussites. But the force and persistence with which Luther in particular brought certain questions to prominence encouraged an unprecedented shaking up of the framework within which the topics of

---

30 For a bibliography of the debate about the posting on the Church door at Wittenberg, see K. Aland, *Martin Luther's Ninety-Five Theses* (St Louis, Miss./London, 1967), pp. 99–100 and see, too, K. Honselmann, 'Wimpinas Druck der Ablassthesen Martin Luthers 1528 (nach einem der 1517 von Luther ausgegebenen Texte) und Luthers frühe Ausssagen zur Verbreitung seiner Ablassthesen', *Zeitschrift für Kirchengeschichte*, 97 (1986), 189–204.
31 W. P. Stephens, *The Theology of Huldrych Zwingli* (Oxford, 1986).
32 *Ibid.*, pp. 45–6.
33 Zwingli, *Werke* VII.152, Letter 67, and p. 175, Letter 79.

systematic theology had been considered, since the *summae* of the twelfth and thirteenth centuries had suggested an appropriate order. We can see the impact at a glance by contrasting the agendas of the Fifth Lateran Council of 1512–17 and of the Council of Trent.[34] The Lateran Council had on its list one or two matters of faith and order. It decided against the neo-Aristotelian doctrine of the soul which some theologians had been putting forward; it made a decree on usury; most importantly in Session IX (1516), it endeavoured to establish clearly the relationship of the authority of a Pope to that of a Council. In its condemnation of heretics and its directives on preaching it looked back to the disturbances of the fifteenth century, particularly the aftermath of the Hussite revolution. But its chief preoccupation was with matters of internal order, with the repair of structures of authority and decision-making within the Church which had been put under strain by the conciliar movement, and especially by recent moves in France to hold in royal hands the nomination to bishoprics. The Council of Trent (1545–63), by contrast, found it necessary to set out in detail clear rulings on large areas of Christian doctrine. Enormous questions of faith and order had been forcibly opened up in the half century between.

Interested enquirers were already asking for a map in the first quarter of the sixteenth century.[35] Melanchthon published the first version of his *Loci Communes* in 1521. Martin Bucer and Thiébaud Schwartz sent a list to Matthew Zell in September 1523 in answer to his request for advice on what he should accept and what he should reject in the current controversy (a list not of course necessarily representing Bucer's mature thought). The most important point, they say, is that everything should be tested against Scripture, and what contradicts Scripture utterly rejected. There is a question how far the Church should be obeyed in matters of faith. This is the *vestibulum*, the point of entry into all controversies. It can be stated with confidence that the Scriptures speak of nothing but Christ the Saviour; that resolves 'that greatest controversy' (*maxima illa controversia*) whether we are justified by faith not works; that is, by

---

[34] It is also instructive to note the topics of Pico della Mirandola's *Apologia* of the 1480s: Christ's descent into Hell; mortal sin; adoration of the Cross; whether Origen is saved; freedom of belief; three Eucharistic questions (*Opera Omnia*, ed. C. Vasoli and repr. Hildesheim, 1969 from edition of 1557–73, vol. I, pp. 114ff.).

[35] For comparison with earlier preoccupations, see A. Hudson, *The Premature Reformation* (Oxford, 1988), p. 389, for a 'Lollard' list.

Christ, not by our own merits. It follows that salvation and righteousness are not to be sought from the sacraments, from the merits of the saints, from one's own confession or satisfaction. It is asked what sacraments are attested in Scripture, what is the Lord's Supper and what benefits it brings to minister or people, what benefits are to be expected from the cult of saints, whether confession is allowed by Scripture, what it is to make satisfaction, and under that head, what prayers and fasting are for. Indulgences are condemned. It is asked what is the power of binding and loosing; what is excommunication; what is the value of blessing water, salt and other things; whether vows should be permitted, particularly monastic vows; what of human traditions; what of images and processions and anointing; what of the authority of magistrates, the ministers of the Church, the Pope; what of tithes? These topics had already been taken up by Luther with greater or lesser thoroughness, and Bucer recommends vigorous defence of *doctrina sana* and sharp contradiction of error.[36]

It is striking that a list which begins so firmly at the *vestibulum* and proceeds at first in a logical way, unfolding implications of taking up certain positions, should fall so quickly into disorder. Comparatively small matters such as the blessing of water are interspersed with large questions about civil and ecclesiastical authority; there is a good deal of repetition. This is a pattern which tends to recur elsewhere. Old grievances which can be found in the popular anticlericalist movements from the twelfth century reappear alongside the relatively new preoccupations with certain aspects of the doctrine of salvation. Radical claims about authority (all Christians may administer the sacraments; there is no authority in the Church over matters of faith, but only in Scripture) mingle with concern over matters which touch ordinary people's lives directly (what shall I do to be saved?). If we take one of the major markers of progress in reforming thought, the Augsburg Confession of 1530, we find something of the same order in disorder. The Articles begin with God, like a mediaeval *summa*, and continue with original sin and Christology. The fourth article covers justification, the fifth the ministry of the Church, with a series of following articles on ecclesiology. A ninth article on baptism is followed by Article Ten on the Lord's Supper. Confession and repentance follow, then the use of the sacraments,

---

[36] Bucer, *Correspondance*, ed. J. Rott (Leiden, 1979), pp. 200–3, no. 49. On Schwartz, see no. 68, n.2.

ecclesiastical order, rites, civil affairs, the Last Judgement, free will, the cause of sin, faith and good works and the cult of saints. The final articles are separated off as giving an account of abuses which have been corrected by the reformers; the topics are: communion in both kinds, the marriage of priests, various practices in the saying of Mass, confession, rules about forbidden foods, and their implications for the place of human tradition, monastic vows and ecclesiastical power.

In 1531, Hugh Latimer, who had come under suspicion in England for Lutheran sympathies, was required to subscribe to articles stating that there is a place of purgation for souls after this life, where souls are helped by Masses, prayer and alms-deeds; that the saints mediate by praying for us in Heaven; that pilgrimages have merit; that the keys of binding and loosing 'given unto Peter, doth remain to his successor bishops, although they live evil; and they were never given for any cause to laymen', that 'the images of the crucifix and saints are to be had in the church, in memory, honour, and worship of Jesus Christ and his saints'.[37]

Individual topics were compelling, and their interconnectedness perceived to be so various and complex that again and again we find the same group of subjects treated in different orders. At Ratisbon in 1541, with three protestant and three Catholic representatives, the meeting considered the Fall, free will, original sin; then justification, the jurisdictional authority of the Church, penance, the teaching authority of the Church, the sacraments, the relationship of ecclesiastical authority, ecclesiastical discipline. When the faculty of theology at Paris produced its list of Articles in 1544, they began with the assertion that baptism is necessary to salvation even in infants, went on to free will, penance, the necessity of good works, then to transubstantiation, the sacrifice of the Mass, and communion in both kinds; then to the question whether anyone but a priest duly ordained may validly administer the sacraments; then to points concerning miracles, prayers to the Blessed Virgin and the saints, shrines, pilgrimages, the adoration of the Cross and of images; then to purgatory; whether the Church on earth is visible; whether definitions in matters of doctrine may be made by the visible Church in circumstances of controversy; to the place of tradition; excommunication; the authority of Councils; obedience, conscience, the making of vows. Cardinal Seripando, one of the chief architects of the Trent pronouncements on justification, compiled a collection of texts for reference in which lists of key points reflect Luther's preoccupations. Is purgatory Scriptural? Are souls in purgatory beyond 'meriting' or sinning, and do they have assurance of their salvation? Do indulgences remit *culpa* or *poena*? If they remit *poena*, is it temporal or eternal penalty? If temporal, is it as imposed canonically, or as imposed by divine justice? Do the saints have merit to spare for the 'treasury'? If contrition, confession and absolution do not involve a fresh application of Christ's merits, how can it be of help for indulgences to draw on the infinite store of Christ's merits? And so on.[38]

At Trent itself the Council considered, in order over nearly twenty years, the Creeds, the relationship of Scripture and tradition, original sin, justification, the sacraments, penance, communion in both kinds, the sacrifice of the Mass, orders, marriage, purgatory, saints, relics and images, monastic vows, indulgences. During this period the Church of England's Thirty-Nine Articles, which had begun to evolve from a set of six articles of 1536, the Bishops' Book of 1537, the Six Articles of 1539, the King's Book of 1543, were maturing into the Forty-Two Articles of 1553 and a more definitive series of Articles of 1563. They were to undergo some final revision before they were issued in 1571. In their scope fall all the main topics of controversy and there is an attempt, at least in the first few, to impose a systematic order.

The reformed theologian Gisbert Voetius (1589–1676) was still struggling with the problem of putting all these elements in order in the next century. He tries to pick out principal corruptions as he sees them: false doctrine on the merit of works; false teaching concerning auricular confession and absolution, concerning the 'application' of actions and prayers and hymns to other people's benefit, the possibility of freeing and helping souls after this life by 'human satisfaction', papal indulgences and dispensations, and all the exactions and procedures of the penitentials and the apostolic chancery.[39]

These common difficulties in settling on a useful and generally acceptable working order for dealing with this complex of questions reflect the heat of the debate of the sixteenth century. The combatants repeatedly perceived interconnections and entailments which had not been apparent to the predecessors of Aquinas, to Aquinas himself in compiling his *summa*, or to his immediate successors in their *summa*-making. It seemed

[38] Vatican, MS Vat. lat. 80, fos. 94–5 and 73–5.
[39] J. Beardslee, *Reformed Dogmatics* (Oxford, 1965), p. 271.

to Melanchthon that their underlying presence was already creating strains in the theology of the later Middle Ages. His sketch of the situation in relation to the doctrine of penance is prejudiced but not inaccurate.

> All good men ... even the theologians, admit that before Luther's writings the doctrine of penitence was very confused. The Commentaries on the *Sentences* are full of endless questions which the theologians could never explain satisfactorily. The people could grasp neither the sense of the matter nor the chief requirements of penitence nor the source of the peace of conscience. Let any one of our opponents step forward and tell us when the forgiveness of sins takes place.[40]

A good deal of theological ground was covered in the sixteenth-century attempts to deal with this agenda in its various forms. Progress was made with many problems. But in some areas polemic drove the disputes into blind alleys or ran them up against blockages and intransigence. We have, as it were, the minutes of the discussions and a number of preparatory papers and correspondence; there are some interim settlements. But we do not have a systematic theology of authority from the period of the Reformation and Counter-Reformation in which the concerns of both sides are given their place. No real endeavour was made to draw the threads together in that way; it would not have been possible in the circumstances. Nor could anyone at the time take stock of the context of anterior abuses and resentments with any degree of coolness, or with the perspective which only the passage of time makes possible.

ii. THE INSTRUMENTS OF CHRISTIAN SCHOLARSHIP

The vitality of the scholarship of late fifteenth-century and early sixteenth-century Europe was the product of cross-breeding of influences, the introduction of new blood into the old stock. Nor is it possible to separate 'arts' and 'theology' here. Lorenzo Valla's *Repastinatio Totius Dialecticae* of the 1440s is best known as a pioneering textbook of the new 'humanist' approach to grammar, logic and rhetoric. The reader comes away with a strong impression of the contribution the book seeks to make to the reform of the *artes* envisaged as an end in itself. But the opening chapters address as a matter of priority a wide range of problems which arise in connection with

---

[40] *Apologia* for the Augsberg Confession, Art. 12, Tappert, p. 183.

theological language. Valla speaks to theologians. These *recentes theologi*, he says, are full of empty Aristotelian ideas (*locupletes inopibus*). They make a god of Aristotle. Yet they have no real expertise either in what Aristotle says about language, or in the Latin (or Greek) language itself.[41]

It remained as true for the sixteenth century as it had been during the Middle Ages that the *artes* were the handmaids of theology. There are little logical jokes in this connection in Shakespeare as there were in Langland or Chaucer. Every thinker brought to the study of Scripture and to speculative theology a basic equipment of ideas and assumptions about the behaviour of language. It is this profound and subtle networking of fundamentals and habits of thought which defeats classification and makes it valuable to approach the question of the instruments of Christian scholarship at the level of the minutiae of language-study.

When Luther, disturbed by the abuses he saw in the penitential practices of the Church in Germany, tried to get back to first principles, he studied the way the word *poenitentia* is used in the Bible. He could have set about that by using one of a number of aids. Bible dictionaries or concordances were available from the late twelfth century, and one of these would have given him a list of passages where the word occurs. But he read texts *in extenso*, letting the fuller context of the discussion make its mark. He found himself in the midst of a *iocondissimus ludus*. He felt as though the words were playing with him, tossing him about on all sides (*verba undique mihi colludebant*).[42] His preconceptions were shaken up, and what had always seemed a 'bitter' word began to seem 'sweet' to him. He began to perceive a contrast between *poenitentia*, 'penance' (which he understood as a laborious process), and *poenitentia* as 'repentance', the simple and liberating change of heart which it seemed to him was described in Paul's words.[43] This approach by word-study came naturally because of Luther's training in the three arts of the mediaeval trivium, grammar, logic and rhetoric, a grounding he shared with all the scholars we shall meet, although there was great variation in the details of their knowledge and in their attitudes to their early education.

In a letter to Hess in Erfurt, written in 1523, Luther expresses with some vehemence his own view, as a reformer, of the place of the arts of language in Christian education – clearly with an awareness that

---

41 *Repastinatio*, I, Proemium, p. 7.16ff.
42 *WA* 1.525.
43 *Ibid.*

contemporary scholars were facing Jerome's classic dilemma. Luther sees no conflict between being *Christianus* and being *Ciceronianus.* On the contrary, he says,

> I am persuaded that there can be no sound theology (*sincera theologia*) without expertise in the arts of language (*sine literarum peritia*) ... I see that there has never been a notable (*insignis*) opening up of the Word of God, except where languages and letters have sprung up and flowered like so many John the Baptists to prepare the way. I do not wish ... young people to be denied the opportunity to study poetry and rhetoric ... These studies make them able first to grasp holy things, and then to treat of them skilfully and felicitously. So I pray you ... if my request carries any weight, to ensure that your young men practise as industriously as possible in poetry and rhetoric (*ut strenue et poetentur et rhetoricentur*). As Christ lives, I am often furious that I was not allowed to study poets and orators sometimes at that age ... I would have given much for a Homer so that I could learn Greek.[44]

Luther speaks with particular feeling here about the need for the study of languages and for the value of reading ancient literature, perhaps because his own training had concentrated elsewhere. But the trivial arts, grammar, logic and rhetoric, in different proportions, had formed the basis of his education, too, as they had for every educated man since late Roman times. Calvin, too, speaks with approval of the value of such a training. He describes how the grammarian trains a boy and then hands him over to someone else, who polishes him in the higher disciplines. Rhetorical skills, he says, are 'noble gifts of God' which men receive from the Holy Spirit to put to good use in their common life.[45]

A good preacher needs 'Logick to divide the Word aright, Rhetoricke to perswade, School Divinity to perswade Gainsayers, knowledge of many Tongues to understand Originals and learned Authors'. The English Calvinist bishop John Hacket (1592–1670) felt as free as any metaphysical poet among his contemporaries to mix old and new thinking and to make use of mediaeval and modern traditions alike as he saw fit. Here he puts his finger on the great strength of scholastic method, its effectiveness in assembling arguments for and against and determining where the truth lies. But he also takes it for granted that the theologian

---

44   *WA* 3.49.
45   On 1 Cor. 1.17, *CR* 49.320ff., cf. on Gal. 3.24.

needs to know not only Latin but Greek and Hebrew and perhaps more, so that he can read his sources and above all Holy Scripture in the original. His preacher stands in equal need of a training in clear thinking ('to divide the Word aright'), and skills of persuasion.[46] In this catalogue of educational requirements lie embedded assumptions about the value of the long tradition of the study of the trivium which had formed the staple of teaching, without a break, if with varying emphases, since classical times. These arts of language were often studied in a superficial way or patchily; but in the hands of the most able they proved to be capable of leading to profound understanding of the nature and functioning of language, to be durable through changes in pedagogical fashion, and to be adaptable as the focus on theological and Scriptural language shifted to new quarters.

The early Christians established a sometimes uneasy relationship with a contemporary philosophical system which set a high value on reason as the distinguishing mark of man.[47] It continued to be necessary, both in the formative early period and in subsequent centuries, for Christian scholars to be conscious of their debt to the culture and scholarship of the secular world, and to find a *modus vivendi* in relation to it. In every period the strains of the tension between trained but 'natural' reason, and a 'given' revelation, have made themselves felt. Origen (*c.*185–254) explained the matter in terms of the Holy Spirit's work as instructor of the reason and illuminator of the soul. Augustine (354–430) thought that man's reason had been so damaged by sin that without help from God he could not even begin to think straight, and that the task of revelation was to set reason right; but he also trusted that reason could, if used in a disciplined way, make sense of revelation with the help of an illuminating grace. Aquinas (d. 1274) asks what was a commonplace question in his day, whether there is a place for the application of reason in the study of matters of faith. He points out that just as in other sciences argument is not directed towards establishing the first principles of the science, which are self-evident, but to using those principles to prove other things within the area covered by that sphere of knowledge, so it is with *sacra doctrina*.[48]

---

[46]   H. Davies, *Like Angels from a Cloud* (San Marino, Calif., 1986), p. 143, and see John Plume's introductory biography to John Hacket's *A Century of Sermons*, p. xxxviii.

[47]   See *The Cambridge History of Later Greek and Early Mediaeval Philosophy*, ed. A. H. Armstrong (Cambridge, 1967), for a survey.

[48]   *ST* I q.1.a.8.

Struggling with the same fundamental question, Galileo says in a letter to Father Catelli, written in December 1613, 'It is the office of wise expositors to strive to discover the true meanings of passages in the Bible which agree with ... conclusions which rest on necessary demonstrations.'[49] That is, right interpretation ought to accord with reason, and with a reason educated and formally exact.

In the period of the Reformation debates the instruments available to Christian scholars had never been so sophisticated or so plentiful. Mediaeval language-theory and logic were still in use, alongside all that was new in Renaissance learning. Melanchthon speaks of a *ludus litterarius*, a dance of the *artes*, in which the three chords of the muses Polymnia, Euterpe and Melpomene ought to harmonise. At the same time, the profound and complex difficulties which had arisen earlier about the ways in which human intellect could properly be applied to the study of Scripture and to the framing of statements of belief were vastly compounded by the reformers' call for a return to 'Scripture alone', and by the controversies about the authoritativeness of Hebrew, Greek or Latin texts; of the Fathers; of the Church's official pronouncements; of private judgement. We begin with these matters because they form the background and the context for all that follows. Questions of logic and language, less or more formally treated, pervade the sixteenth-century debates on every aspect of the question of Christian authority.

Nowhere perhaps is this influence more important than in the theory underlying the framing of the numerous sets of 'articles' or 'commonplaces' produced by the reformers and their opponents.[50]

A science has two definitive characteristics for Aquinas. It must be the study of a distinctive subject-matter or area of knowledge (as natural science or mathematics). It has first principles which are self-evident to reason, or which are derived by reason from such *per se nota*. These are ideas to be found in Aristotle's *Posterior Analytics*, and they rest on certain assumptions about the nature of knowing and the knowable. If we ask whether *sacra doctrina* is a science of this sort, the evidence seems to Aquinas to be conflicting. On the one hand, theology starts not from *per se nota* but from articles of faith (*articuli fidei*); these, by definition, are not conceded by everyone, so they are not first principles in the same

---

49 Galileo, *Dai Carteggio e dai Documenti*, ed. F. Flora (Milan, 1953), pp. 154–5.
50 See further on all this the section on 'Authority in debate' below (Chapter 3.iii).

way as those of other sciences. Moreover, it deals with particulars of a historical and revealed sort, such as the stories of Abraham, Isaac and Jacob, and a true discipline ought not to be concerned with anything but general truths. On the other hand, as Augustine says, there is no other science which deals with the subject-matter of saving faith (*fides saluberrima*), so it seems that *sacra doctrina* must be a science,[51] because that is certainly a distinct area of knowledge.

This kind of thinking about the proper spheres and methods of the sciences persisted as a commonplace, so that one might make a little jest about it in the confidence of being understood. Luther, for example, asks in a letter to Spalatin whether he ought to be speaking like a grammarian or like a theologian (*ut Theologus*; *ut Grammaticus*).[52] But it was also a matter of continuing serious philosophical concern. Melanchthon discusses the concept of the *doctrinae genus*.[53]

This brings us into the vastly complex area of the mediaeval theory of 'topics', and its implications for sixteenth-century scholars endeavouring to prove the truth of *articuli fidei*. The art of drawing arguments from 'topics' was in familiar use in the academic and ecclesiastical disputations of the mid-sixteenth century. But the heritage of ancient and mediaeval work on topics was far more subtly interfused and important in its sixteenth-century implications than this sort of easy identification of a 'topic' would at first suggest. Theologians refer to *articuli*, *aphorismi*, *veritates*, *assertiones*, *regulae*, *loci communes*, *conclusiones*, *propositiones*,[54] *theses*. In different ways these are all *loci*, topics, and we need to get a picture of their relationship to the theory of topics, if we are to see what kind of claims are being made, methodologically and as truths, for the 'articles' in such confessional documents as the Augsburg Confession of 1530, or the Thirty-Nine Articles of the Church of England, or for Luther's various *theses*, Melanchthon's 'commonplaces' or even the topics of Calvin's *Institutes*.

The common idea in all sorts of 'topics' is of a memorable, compact entity, a point, or a mental index card which can easily be referred to and brought into use. Memory was one of the five parts of rhetoric in the

---

51 *ST* I q.1.a.2.
52 *WA* 1.133, *Werke* 6.8.
53 *De Philosophia Oratio*, *CR* 11.282.
54 It should be borne in mind that a proposition used as a premiss in a syllogism is often supported by an argument of which it itself forms the conclusion. Propositions and conclusions differ not in their status as truths but in their position in the syllogism.

classical tradition. A trained and stocked memory was indispensable to the orator. It provided him with a resource of illustrative material and a store of arguments which he could call upon in framing his discourse, what Cassiodorus describes as *collectiones argumentorum*.[55] The conception of orderly storage of material in abbreviated form underlies both the ancient notion of the way the memory is constructed (Augustine's idea of a treasury from which ideas and images could be brought out at will), and the formal techniques of memorisation which were taught in the schools of rhetoric. From mnemonic 'places'[56] topics (*loci*) derive their name, and the term *locus* and its fellows thus covered both stories, illustrations, examples, similitudes, analogies; and stock arguments or principles which are the 'places' where arguments start.

The notion of 'placing' arguments ready-made in a store prompts Cicero to speak of *sedes argumenti*.[57] Bartholomew Latomus in our period prefers another image of Cicero's, used in the *De Oratore*, when he compares the *locus* with a little house or dwelling-place (*domicilium*; *habitaculum*). From it, he says, the argument is drawn and derives its force of proof (*vis probandi*).[58] The *locus* is thus something more than a pigeon-hole when it serves to hold an argument. It came to be thought of as a self-evidently valid logical form, an identifiable type of argument, so that if any given instance can be shown to be drawn from it, that particular argument can be seen to be valid as being of that type. This is already a well-developed notion in Cicero. Cicero lists a number of these types.[59] Rudolph Agricola explains for sixteenth-century readers that these 'common' arguments embrace all the particular arguments which may be advanced from them, and that is why they are called 'places'; they are *reposita* in which lie all those things which are capable of winning belief (*faciendae*

---

55 Cassiodorus, *In Psalmos*, *CCSL*, 97, p. 19.
56 The art of memory was, the classical story went, devised by Simonides who developed the trick of locating items to be remembered in places about the room, so that he could recall them at will by thinking of their positions. Even when the teaching of this art of memory died out with the decay of rhetoric in the late Roman world, the notion of 'placing' persisted. We find Hugh of St Victor in the first half of the twelfth century teaching his students to memorise the Psalms by thinking of the coloured initials which mark their beginnings. See Francis Yates, *The Art of Memory* (London, 1969) and G. A. Zinn's forthcoming study on Hugh of St Victor.
57 *Topics* II.8.
58 *Ennarrationes B. Latomi in Topica Ciceronis* (Strasbourg, 1539), p. 11.
59 *Topics* X.46ff.

fidei instrumenta). One must find the right general type of argument to apply to the case in hand, by looking in the correct 'place'.[60] The 'place' might be, for example, the *genus* to which the subject of discussion belongs, so that one might say that Socrates is mortal because he is a man. Ernolao Barbaro notes in a letter to Pico della Mirandola that contemporary rhetoricians know how to use these topics; they can readily identify an argument *a toto* or *a genere*.[61]

Aristotle's *Topics* was not read in the mediaeval West until the twelfth century, but Cicero and later Boethius drew ultimately upon Aristotle in framing their accounts.[62] For Aristotle a topic is not only a strategy of argumentation but also a principle. He sees dialectical topics as forming a distinct group, and he places 'rhetorical' topics in a separate class as helps in constructing rhetorical arguments; and mnemonic topics in yet another class, as helps in recollection. Boethius sees a topic both as a principle, or major premiss, and as a foundation for a genre of argumentation. In its first sense, it may be a *communis animi conceptio*, a self-evident truth, in the Euclidean and Boethian sense. Seripando, one of the outstanding theologians of Trent, was familiar with the notion and its link with geometrical *theoremata*. He speaks in his treatise on *Righteousness and Christian Freedom* of geometrical postulates which need no proof because as soon as anyone hears and understands them, they are recognised to be true.[63]

But claims made by our sixteenth-century authors for the manifest rightness of their arguments do not necessarily imply a claim that the maxims or principles involved are self-evidently or necessarily true.[64] As

---

60   Rudolph Agricola, *De Inventione Dialectica Lucubrationes* (Cologne, 1539), I.ii, pp. 7–8; I.xx, p. 167, cf. Cicero, *Topics* II.8.

61   *Epistolae, Orationes et Carmina*, ed. V. Branca (Florence, 1943), I.103.

62   Cicero, *De Oratore* II.38.160ff. See *CHLMP*, chapter 14, especially p. 114 and note p. 115 on the relationship of Cicero's *Topics* to Aristotle's *Topics*.

63   *De Iustititia et Libertate Christiana*, p. 58: *statim cum quisque audierit, quidque vocabula significent, intellexerit*; cf. Boethius, *De Hebdomadibus, Theological Tractates*, ed. H. F. Stewart, E. K. Rand and S. J. Tester (London, 1973).

64   It is important to be clear here about the difference between self-evident or necessary truth in the propositions – the question of subject-matter – and necessary connection between premisses and conclusion. We may have such *necessitas consequentiae* without arriving at a necessary conclusion (*necessitas consequentis*). What gives demonstrative argument its force, as Ockham explains, is dependence on prior necessary propositions (*ex propositionibus necessariis prioribus*); that causes all doubt to disappear (*qua habita cessat omnis dubitatio*) and there remains no question about the conclusion (*quaestio circa conclusionem*) (Ockham, *Opera Philosophica*, 1, *Summa Logicae*, ed. P. Boehner (New York,

Aquinas points out, truths of faith cannot be held to be *per se nota* without ceasing to be objects of faith. But their reliability is important. It can be claimed that they depend on Scripture and therefore carry Scripture's authority. Articles 22, 24, 32 of the Thirty-Nine Articles of the Church of England say so explicitly. Among the theses of his Heidelberg Disputation of 1518 Luther gives both 'reasons' and 'authorities', and in some cases supporting arguments. Pico della Mirandola thought it appropriate to include Greek, Arabic and modern *auctoritates* in his *Conclusiones*, as well as Biblical and patristic ones.[65] Eck gives authorities in his *Enchiridion* of *Loci Communes*. In the background is a preoccupation with the status of these theses or *loci* as principles. Conrad Neobarius explains that *communes rerum notae* are things generally known with which people can make comparisons so as to judge whether what they are being told is true.[66] Melanchthon says, no doubt with the discussion of the division of the sciences in the *Posterior Analytics* (I.i–ii) in mind, that 'in each field of study there are certain *capita* or heads, under which the subject-matter is divided' and that these are *loci communes*, 'common themes' or the 'common forms of all'.[67]

This preoccupation was fostered in part by the high status the demonstrative method had enjoyed since the late twelfth century. Demonstrative proof is discussed by Aristotle and Boethius, and employed with unmatched elegance by Euclid in his *Elements*. The *Posterior Analytics*, Boethius' *De Hebdomadibus* and the *Elements*, were all being studied seriously for the first time in the Middle Ages in the schools of the

---

1974), Part III², chapter 19, p. 536.6–8; *ibid.*, chapter 18, pp. 534–6). Whatever its formal structure, whether 'Euclidean', 'Boethian', or a single argument taking a syllogistic form, the necessary argument contains or ultimately rests upon a *communis animi conceptio*, a self-evident truth (the phrase *communis animi conceptio* is used by Boethius in the *De Hebdomadibus* and in twelfth-century translations of Euclid). Martin of Dacia shows that certain propositions are *per se nota* because if there were no such propositions it would be necessary either to resort to infinite regress to prove any truth, or to prove *a* by *b* and *b* by *a*, which would clearly be unsatisfactory. Such *per se nota* need and are susceptible of no proof or demonstration (Martin of Dacia, *Quaestiones super Librum Topicorum Boethii* (Copenhagen, 1961), Q.1. v–vi, pp. 320–4; *ibid.*, Q.2, pp. 325–6).
65 Pico della Mirandola, *Conclusiones*, ed. B. Kieszkowski (Geneva, 1973).
66 Conrad Neobarius, *De Inveniendi Argumenti Disciplina Libellus* (Strasbourg, 1536), definition of *locus*.
67 Melanchthon, *De Locis Communibus Ratio*, CR 20.695ff.

twelfth century.[68] There appears to be a broad distinction in structure already in the twelfth century between those treatises whose authors build up a system of theorems in the manner of Euclid (Nicholas of Amiens), and those who give a string or stream of principles derived more or less from one another (Alan of Lille).[69] Matthew de Janova (d. *c*.1393) attempts the more difficult Euclidean pattern. He begins by setting out four basic rules or axioms supplied by divine revelation. The first is the written law God gave on Mount Sinai. Then he adds three *regulae speciales* by which false prophets can be distinguished from true prophets (Deuteronomy 13.1–9; 18.6–9). With the aid of these four rules, this *quadruplex doctrina regulativa*, he explains, everyone can judge for himself whether what he is told is the teaching of the Holy Spirit. This is done by deriving further rules from the first four, and by testing one's conclusions by these rules: Is this in harmony with God's law and precepts? Is it derived from God and his *sacramenta*? Does it lead us away from the love of this world? Does it point to right faith and is it conducive to salvation?[70] Matthew de Janova uses the demonstrative method in this way to try to bring to the exercise of private judgement a means of checking that the conclusions drawn are right and thus he seeks to resolve one of the major difficulties which arise if there is no ecclesiastical *magisterium* to refer to.

The simpler structure, involving no more than a loosely related series of principles, is frequent. Thus we find series in which one thesis is shown to follow from another. Luther uses the pattern in the theses for a disputation. No authority after Christ is to be equated with that of the apostles and prophets (1); The apostles had a sure promise of the Holy Spirit not only as a group, but as individuals (3); Only those who had a responsibility for handing on the articles of faith are called the *fundamentum ecclesiae* (4); None of their successors had this promise as individuals (5); Therefore it cannot be argued that because the apostles were able to do so their successors can do the same (6); The successors of the apostles must follow them and accept their authority (7); If they do not do so they are heretics or Antichrists (11); So bishops in council can err as anyone else can, if they do not follow the authority of the apostles (12); If they

68 *Theological Tractates, De Hebdomadibus.* See the *Metalogicon* of John of Salisbury, ed. C. C. J. Webb (Oxford, 1929).
69 See my *Alan of Lille* (Cambridge, 1983), Appendix I.
70 Matthew de Janova, *Regulae Veteris et Novi Testamenti*, ed. V. Kybal (Prague, 1908), I.2, pp. 25ff.

do not err that is not due to the authority of their congregation (13).[71]

In all this the universal respect for the demonstrative method was an important factor in encouraging scholars to use it. Dante experiments with it in his *Monarchia*. Luther several times stresses the dependence of one conclusion on another in his Ninety-Five Theses, as does Fisher in his Confutation of Luther.[72] Hooker places reason under Scripture in a graded list of proofs in order of 'firmness', dividing reason's endorsements into 'intuitive beholding', that is, the recognition of self-evident truth; 'strong and invincible demonstration' to which 'the mind doth necessarily assent because it rests upon self-evident truths; probability.[73]

But there was also a school of thought which associated topics with merely 'probable' arguments. Boethius explains a method of locating the middle term which links the two terms of a syllogism's conclusion. He classifies all possible types of middle term (those which are taken 'from a part' of other terms, for example, or 'from a whole'). A knowledge of these *differentiae* or *genera* of middle terms will enable the student to find the middle term he wants in any particular syllogism. The topic expresses only the general relationship (*habitudo*) of one thing to another (*rei ad rem*). Thirteenth-century authors emphasise this probability of topical arguments, distinguishing extrinsic topics, which can give only uncertain and weak conclusions, and intrinsic topics, which can give stronger conclusions. This assumption that topics is the art of the probable is taken up by Lorenzo Valla in the 1440s and by Agricola (1444–85), with approval for the flexibility topics give the orator in constructing his argument. Sixteenth-century scholars maintain the distinction. 'I am a philosopher. I desire to "demonstrate" the truth. I leave the rest to orators.' 'You say that not everything can be demonstrated. There is a place for probable arguments.'[74]

Boethius failed in his attempt in the *De Differentiis Topicis* to settle satisfactorily for his successors the question of the difference between 'dialectical' and 'rhetorical' topics. The theological *loci* and *articuli* of the sixteenth century are framed as a rule in the context of a predominantly dialectical style of disputation. To take two examples: in his *Antidote* to

---

71   *WA* 39ⁱ.184ff., *De Potestate Concilii.*
72   John Fisher, *Assertionis Lutheranae Confutatio, Opera Omnia* (Würzburg, 1697 repr. facsimile, 1967), col. 287, no. VI, *constat haec ex praecedenti.*
73   *Laws* II.vii.5.
74   Ernolao Barbaro, *Epistolae*, I.103.

Trent we find Calvin pronouncing with heavy irony such axioms as 'No man is to see what every man sees',[75] and 'Of a truth the horned and mitred herd are worthy of such a privilege'.[76] These are *loci* of a sort and they typify the freedom of form and use orators had long liked to claim for themselves in argument, in contrast to the dialecticians. Cicero distinguishes in his *De Inventione* between arguments which work on the mind by pointing out a resemblance between the thing to be proved and something to which experience compels assent; and the forms of deductive or syllogistic reasoning. Thomas Bricot, author of a number of standard textbooks in use in the early sixteenth century, identifies the *argumentationes rhetoricae* in a broadly Ciceronian way.[77]

In periods when rhetoric was in the ascendancy over logic the freedom and flexibility of argument the orators allowed themselves was a matter of pride in a higher art. We find such sentiments being expressed by sixteenth-century humanists who argue that dialectic is all syllogisms and not a proper study in depth for the orator.[78] A person who wishes to 'draw the listener's mind to his opinion'[79] must use argument. But plain argument does not touch the feelings.[80] It is rhetoric which lends the *perspicuitas* which is given by figures and ornament,[81] carries the mind outside itself,[82] teaches, persuades and moves,[83] touches the *affectus*. John Buridan had already suggested in the fourteenth century that in ethics it is necessary to use a special logic, arguments which would appeal to human beings capable of being swayed by passion.[84] Rudolph Agricola rehearses the old commonplaces with a new conviction; he goes further; he returns to something of the old arrogance of classical rhetoric. Just as in grammar we have a starting-point for correct speaking and writing, and only in rhetoric a guide to the finer points, so in the art of argument logic gives the bare bones of a training – with an emphasis upon the crude and mechanical syllogism – and rhetoric makes it possible to

[75] Calvin, *Antidote* to Trent VI, Canon 33.
[76] *Ibid.*, VII, Canon 3.
[77] Thomas Bricot, *Textus Totius Logices* (Basle, 1492), opening.
[78] *CHLMP*, p. 804.
[79] Agricola, *De Inventione Dialectica*, II.ii, p. 196.
[80] *Ibid.*, II.iii, p. 198.
[81] *Ibid.*, II.ii, p. 196.
[82] *Ibid.*, II.iii, p. 199.
[83] *Ibid.*, II.v; cf. Augustine, *De Doctrina Christiana*, IV.
[84] Buridan on Aristotle's *Ethics*.

deploy arguments with refinement and subtlety and make them convincing not only to the reason but also to feeling and experience.

A contrast is being made here between syllogistic and topical approaches. Cicero said that the proper province of the orator was the discovery of arguments (*inventio*), that of the dialectician the judging of arguments to see whether they were valid and thus to determine where the truth lay. Finding arguments in their resting-places is the art of topics; judging them is a task of syllogistic.[85] Just as in the high Middle Ages the *studium sacrae Scripturae* had given rise to points of theological controversy out of which had evolved a fully systematic theology once they had been articulated and debated, so now Melanchthon found that his study of Romans suggested the need for a series of topically arranged brief treatments of key points. He began work on his *Loci Communes*. In a *prima adumbratio*, about 1520, he was exploring definitions – of 'grace' and 'faith' and so on – by comparing authorities.[86] He identified three main topics in Romans: justification, predestination, the living of a right Christian life. He wrote in a prefatory letter to the first edition of the *Loci* of his wish to make the Pauline line of argument (*disputationis argumentum*) clear by explaining briefly (*paucis verbis*) those things upon which Christian doctrine depends (*e quibus ... summa Christianae doctrinae pendeat*). These *loci* are not, he stresses, to be regarded as an object of study in isolation; they are not to lead people away from the study of Scripture, but rather encourage them to deeper reading.

The theologians of the sixteenth century who arranged their material under topic-headings, or who offered a statement of their position in the form of a series of *loci* or *articuli* or *theses* were drawing upon this complex tradition. Topic-headings such as Melanchthon employs in his *Loci Communes* are a way of providing pigeon-holes for the discussion. The articles of the Augsburg Confession or their like are intended to be self-evidently valid compact arguments, or principles, and where they need support that is provided in various ways. At Trent the *articuli* of the heretics were listed and each theologian chose those on which he wished to comment.[87] In the Decrees and Canons of the Council of Trent the Decrees provide a full discussion and the Canons summarise the key points which are to be used for reference as a means of checking on

[85] Cicero, *Topics* II.6.
[86] *CR* 21.59.
[87] E.g. *Acta CT* 9.7ff.

orthodoxy. The Canons take the form, 'If anyone says ... let him be anathema.' This makes a frame within which to set an 'article'.

We can see something of the flexibility of the method in the Thirty-Nine Articles of the Church of England. Some of the Articles take the form of theses. 'The Old Testament is not contrary to the New' (7); 'The three Creeds ... ought thoroughly to be received and believed' (8); 'The cup of the Lord is not to be denied to lay people' (30). A proof by reasoning or authority is sometimes added to support the thesis: 'for both in the Old and New Testament everlasting life is offered to mankind by Christ ...' (7); 'for they may be proved by most certain warrants of holy Scripture' (8); 'for both the parts of the Lord's Sacrament, by Christ's ordinance and commandment, ought to be administered to all Christian men alike' (30). Other Articles begin with a thesis and go on to develop its implications. 'Original sin standeth not in the following of Adam (as the Pelagians do vainly talk); but it is the fault and corruption of the Nature of every man ... whereby man is very far gone from original righteousness, and is of his own nature inclined to evil ...' and so on (9). 'Not every deadly sin willingly committed after baptism is sin against the Holy Ghost, and unpardonable. Wherefore the grant of repentance is not to be denied to such as fall into sin after baptism ...' (16). The same use of 'wherefore' or its equivalent is found in Articles 13, 17, 20, 31, 32.

A number of these articles are miracles of compression, packing together all the checks and balances of much longer sequences of argumentation to be found elsewhere in contemporary literature, in such a way as to place the thesis accurately in its place in relation to the controversy. 'The condition of man after the fall of Adam is such, that he cannot turn and prepare himself, by his own natural strength and good works, to faith, and calling upon God: Wherefore we have no power to do good works pleasant and acceptable to God, without the grace of God by Christ preventing us, that we may have a good will, and working with us, when we have that good will' (10). Articles 26 and 27, which deal with the unworthiness of ministers and with baptism, respectively, are outstanding examples of this type of article which is itself a miniature resolution of much disputation, though not all the articles are methodologically so elegant.

There is variation, too, in the ways in which the sets of articles, theses, canons are related to one another not only structurally but in subject-matter. The Thirty-Nine Articles represent a full span of 'topics' of systematic theology, rather as a mediaeval *summa* was designed to do in its questions and articles. The Augsburg Confession concentrates chiefly on matters of current 'topical' interest.

The fact that one may use the vocabulary of 'topics' advisedly in both connections is of significance. The study of topics in the mediaeval period and in the sixteenth century embraces a wide range of aspects, is sometimes contradictory and often confusing to contemporaries, and remains fundamentally unclear to modern scholarship.[88] The word *locus* is notably various in its connotations. Yet the frequent choice of the title *Loci Communes* by reformers who wanted to write manuals of systematic theology, and the pervading habit of using 'articles', makes it plain that the heritage of 'topic' studies is immensely important for our purposes.

The method proved a natural choice for Luther when he wanted to challenge malpractice over indulgences; he published a series of theses for debate. When the Protestants in Germany were seeking peace, acceptance and Imperial approval they framed a Confession in twenty-eight articles (Augsburg, 1530). In 1541, at Ratisbon, six theologians met, three protestant and three Catholic, to debate a set of articles in the hope of reaching agreement. The Louvain faculty of theology produced thirty-two Articles in 1544 in which they attempted to give a coherent account in German, at a level ordinary people could understand, of the Catholic position on the questions the Lutherans had raised. The Council of Trent began by collecting *articuli et errores* and discussing them *separatim*, then produced canons in the form of condemnatory 'articles' on the key points of dispute under each broad heading discussed. The Church of England drafted and redrafted the series of articles which found their final form in the Thirty-Nine Articles. Not all these are articles of the same sort but they and the many other examples which survive from the period have in common the attempt to reduce complicated and inter-connected questions to manageable units for discussion and to list the essentials.

Articles and commonplaces were, then, deemed to have authority for more than one reason. Some had the intrinsic power to convince which belongs to the self-evident truth, or to the truth derived from it. Luther made only modest claims for his collection of academic *theses*. These 'propositions', he says, have seemed worth collecting and publishing so that those who want to refer to them may have a *breve memoriale*, a compact reference book. Nevertheless, they appear to him to amount in

[88] On the *status quaestionis*, see the chapters on 'topics' in *CHLMP*.

sum to the 'principal articles of the Gospel' (*articuli principales Evangelii*), without which, truly understood and *pure tractis*, the Church of Christ cannot subsist.[89] There is clearly a sense here that these are the first principles of a body of knowledge, a science of theology, and authoritative in that way and for that reason. A third sort of authoritativeness is implied in the collections of articles in which a Church set out its fundamentals – as in the Thirty-Nine Articles of the Church of England and their continental counterparts. Here there is, as it were, an ecclesial 'issuing authority', often in co-operation with the authority of prince or state. While an academic thesis might be open to disputation – indeed that was in part its purpose – an article might require subscription as a condition of ordination or of the granting of title to the clergy; or even as a condition of Church membership.

If we turn from 'articles' to the use of words we come upon a similar pattern of underlying technical complexity, for in logic and language studies lay the powerhouse of the intellectual activities of the age. Skills in the arts of argument and a concern with the behaviour of words are as apparent in the Reformation debates as they had been in the later Middle Ages. The combination could lead to what seemed only sophisticated games-playing. But when Melanchthon complained that at Worms (1540–1) Eck, who acted as spokesman for the Catholic party, played games and performed tricks like a magician (*praestigiae*) with words, tossing about the words *crimen, culpa, peccatum* and disputing like a Socrates full of sophistries, disguising his own view the better to attack his adversary, he was accusing him of irresponsibility in the use of the instruments of serious Christian scholarship.[90]

In such a climate one could not say that a dispute was 'only' about words. 'These and similar monstrosities show sufficiently that the controversy between us and them is not only a matter of a word, as certain dismal conciliators now assume', says Luther, arguing that those who say that the directives in Matthew 5 are 'commands' not 'counsels' are not merely making a verbal distinction.[91] 'Let us not raise a quarrel about a word', says Calvin in the *Antidote* to the Canons of Trent, raising just such a quarrel, and pressing for careful definition.[92] The question whether what

---

[89] *WA* 39i.2–4.
[90] *CR* 4.725.
[91] *WA* 39ii.189, Theses 36, 37.
[92] *CR* 35.495.

is at issue is 'only a matter of words' is raised again and again in the disputation for the licentiate examination of Schmedenstede in 1542.[93] The controversy is not a matter of words when we say that everything in Matthew 5 is 'command' but our opponents say these are 'counsels', argues Luther.[94] It is because talk of words is not merely talk of words, and there are *reales controversiae* beneath the *verbales*, that there can be no easy reaching of agreement,[95] said the protestant side at Ratisbon in 1541. But Seripando, discussing *iustitia* in the context of the Trent debates, asks whether it is necessary to break the Church apart over one little word (*propter unam voculam*), to which a sense can be given which both sides will accept.[96]

From his vantage-point as a Greek scholar, Valla notices that a variant reading of 1 Corinthians 15.52 seems to bring the text into conflict with John 5.29, and he compares other passages to try to arrive at a reading in accordance with a right doctrine of resurrection.[97] We find Melanchthon pointing to *nota vocabula* in the *Confessio Saxonica* of 1551. The scholars of the Council of Trent compare definitions, weigh a 'proper' against an 'improper' sense of 'merit', for example,[98] and exclaim over how much can turn on a word: *renascentia, illuminatio, fides, iustitia, iustificatio*, and so on.

Certain aspects of this preoccupation with words proved particularly important. In the doctoral disputation of Hieronymus Weller in 1535 we meet the frequent contention of reformers that words not in the Bible, and those too technical to be understood by ordinary people, ought to be avoided. 'In theological disputations words must be used which are familiar and clear.' The bad examples given are the scholastic expressions: *fides acquisita, fides infusa, charitas formata, fides informis, fides explicata.*[99] In the climate of discussion of the first half of the sixteenth century, the lingering of Latin scholastic vocabulary with its insistence on what seemed to Luther and Calvin and others a number of false distinctions, made this a heated issue, and they pressed for the use of strictly Biblical terms in theological discussion, because these alone were incontrovertibly authoritative.

[93] *WA* 39ⁱⁱ.187.203.
[94] *WA* 39ⁱⁱ.189, Thesis 37.
[95] *CR* 4.256–7.
[96] *Acta CT* 12.668.
[97] *Collatio*, pp. 213ff.
[98] *Acta CT* 12.314.
[99] *WA* 39ⁱⁱ.53.

The problem was that debates about words could not be made to go away. Yet to keep to words used in Scripture and avoid theological neologisms was not a practical possibility, as the framing of the Creeds demonstrates. Those who attempted translation into the vernacular in our period are sometimes quite frank about the difficulty. Miles Coverdale, aware that his rendering will be compared with Tyndale's, warns his reader not to be 'offended' at differences in their choice of words. It should be no stumbling-block, he says, to find 'scribe' in one version and 'lawyer' in another. 'Thou shalt find no more diversity between these than between four pence and a groat', he promises. But Coverdale himself selected words for a purpose where he thought a theological point needed making. He says that he has deliberately sometimes used 'penance', sometimes 'repentance', to meet the difficulties which attach to the word *poenitentia*.[100] Gregory Martin of the English College at Rheims published in 1582 a criticism of the many 'corruptions' of the Holy Scriptures for which the 'English Sectaries' were responsible, and accused them of making 'partial and false translations' to the advantage of their heresies. In reply, William Fulke put up a defence, saying that the translations were 'sincere and true'. He was aware that the reformers often chose their words with exegetical intent, or in implied criticism of the late mediaeval Church. He explains, for example, that the word 'bishop' may be misleading to ordinary people, who will think of 'a great lord only, that rideth about in a white rochet'. That is why, in his view, the translation must attempt to show that 'the name of a bishop describeth his office', that is, 'to be an overseer of the flock of Christ committed to his charge'. Similarly, 'martyrs' must not be 'taken only for them that are tormented and rent in body … Here it is needful to show, that the saints that suffered for Christ had their name of their witness or testimony, not of their pains and torments.'[101]

A second major area of preoccupation was with the longstanding issue of the relation of words to things. Augustine asks in the *De Magistro* what the word 'nothing' can mean. He has been arguing that every word must signify in order to be a word at all, and now he tests the principle where

---

100 Coverdale, *Remains*, ed. G. Pearson (Parker Society, Cambridge, 1846), Prologue to the Reader. On *poenitentia*, see Chapter 8.ii below.
101 *Defence*, p. 218, and cf. p. 386 on 'justification'.

it seems weakest.[102] The assumption that to 'signify', a word must stand in a relationship to some 'thing' underlies all mediaeval epistemology. The Stoic heritage insisted that there is a natural correspondence between words and things. Varro looked for the 'natural' origins of words in his etymologies and the same sometimes absurd enquiries recur in Isidore's seventh-century *Etymologies*. Discussions of the relation of words to things depended a good deal in the mediaeval West upon Augustine's account of the matter in the *De Doctrina Christiana* (I–II), but increasingly with reference to the epistemological explorations of grammarians and logicians. Some contend that a word can signify a thing only if it is subordinated to a mental 'term'.[103] It was argued that signification is the creation of understanding in the mind of the hearer ('sense'),[104] by linking his concept both to the word and to the 'thing', the created or divine reality which is signified. The problem of the meaning of the word *chimaera*, which refers to a thing which might exist but never has, was of compelling interest in the fifteenth and early sixteenth century,[105] because it seemed to challenge that assumption. One late mediaeval commentator suggests that the difference between the nominalist and realist approaches lay in the concern of one with the properties of terms (words) and of the other with the nature of things.[106]

It is within this tradition of thinking in terms of words and things that Conrad Neobarius, writing a handbook of dialectic, divided the *disserendi ratio*, the art of argument, into the interpretation of words and the comprehension of things.[107] Erasmus (*c*.1466–1536) begins his *De Ratione Studii* of 1511, which he intended to be a Christian equivalent of

[102] Augustine, *De Magistro*, II.3, and for mediaeval discussions, see D. P. Henry, *The Logic of St Anselm* (Oxford, 1967), p. 207.
[103] E. J. Ashworth, *Language and Logic in the Post-Medieval Period* (Dordrecht, 1974), pp. 42–4.
[104] E.g. Thomas of Erfurt, *Grammatica Speculativa*, in Duns Scotus, *Opera Omnia* (Louvain, 1639), chapter 54.
[105] See Ashworth, *Language and Logic*, p. 47 and bibliography.
[106] Conrad Villoslada, 'La Universidad de París durante los estudios de Francisco de Vitoria, O.P. (1507–33)', *Analecta Gregoriana*, 14 (Rome, 1938), pp. 88–9, and see Du Plessis d'Argentre, *Collectio judiciorum de novis erroribus* (1755), I.ii.286–8 on the effect of the edict of 1473–4 by which Louis XI forbade the teaching of nominalism at Paris.
[107] Conrad Neobarius, *Compendiosa Facilisque Artis Dialecticae Ratio* (Strasbourg, 1536), definition of *disserendi ratio*.

Quintilian, from the starting-point of Augustine's introduction to the *De Doctrina Christiana*. Knowledge, he says, is of two sorts, that which is concerned with things and that which is concerned with words. Knowledge of things is obtained only by speaking about them in words, so a person who is not skilled in language will be short-sighted, deluded and unsound in his knowledge of things.[108] Luther, writing on Deuteronomy, seeks to distinguish between words and things in the Bible's history books. 'These are truly called sacred histories not because those things were done by holy men, but because they were accomplished according to the holy Word of God, which hallows everything; ... the proud and carnal are deceived by the simplicity of things in the Scriptures, for they take no notice of the Word of God and value only the things.'[109] Are we talking about a word or a thing? asks Calvin, when he discusses justification by faith.[110] The theologians of the Council of Trent asked what justification is, *quoad nomen* and *quoad rem*. It was argued that even if there is diversity of terminology (*quamvis in verbis discrepent*), everyone agrees about the thing itself (*omnes in re conveniunt*).[111]

Thirdly, we come to the complex of meaning and reference which so preoccupied mediaeval scholars. The mediaeval scholar asked, 'What does this word mean?'; 'What does this word mean in this context?' and sometimes, towards the end of the Middle Ages, 'What does this phrase or sentence mean if we take it as a whole?'[112] This is still the natural approach in the sixteenth century, and nowhere more importantly than in discussions of Scriptural and theological usage. Reformers and Counter-Reformers alike are alert to mistakes about meaning and ready to accuse one another of errors. Calvin castigates the scholars of the Middle Ages for their mistakes.[113] Luther explains that one of the reasons why it is necessary to study the Biblical languages of Latin, Greek and Hebrew (cf.

108 Erasmus, *De Ratione Studii*.
109 *WA*, 14.566–8.
110 Calvin, *Vera Eccl. Ref. Rat.*, *CR* 35.594. Calvin, *Antidote* to Trent, col. 443; *Vera Eccl. Ref. Rat.*, *CR* 35.598.
111 *Acta CT* 1.603; 5.261 (22 June 1546); 5.279.
112 On the *complexe significabile*, a notion put forward by Gregory of Rimini in the fourteenth century and revived in the sixteenth by Juan Dolz and Fernando de Encinas, see *CHLMP*, pp. 794–5.
113 On John 11.1, *CR* 75.255.

John 19.20) is so that no 'foolish meanings' will be introduced.[114] Those who have no experience of the language, he says, 'pull the meanings of the words to pieces and cause ambiguities and confusion'.[115] The Council of Trent reflected on the way some 'heretics' torture and twist the meanings of the words of Scripture.[116]

We shall see these preoccupations with the behaviour of words repeatedly coming into play. Although in many respects they belong to the late antique and mediaeval world at least in their technical expression, they are nevertheless necessary anxieties, for two main reasons. First, they often touch on epistemological fundamentals or upon the deepest principles underlying a theological concept. That is to say, they bring us to basics again and again. And secondly, it is still often suggested in ecumenical discussion that one side or the other is playing games with words, constructing a fair-seeming statement which is merely a cover for foul play beneath. If that objection is to be got out of the way, it is as important now as in the sixteenth century for everyone working on these problems of authority to do so in the fullest possible possession of the language and its ways.

---

[114]   *WA* 43.247 and 389.
[115]   *WA* 44.39.
[116]   *Acta CT* 5.92 and 268 (1546).

PART I

Authority for the truth of the faith

1. The authority of the text

It was Luther's contention that the Church could play a part in the salvation of the individual only through her ministry of the Word, and that the ministry of the sacraments stood under that ministry and was salvific only by the power of the Word. He and other reformers were trying to redress an imbalance which had made the sacramental ministry of the Church in the later Middle Ages so prominent as almost to obscure the ministry of the Word altogether.

This had been a matter of practice, not dogma. The saving power of Scripture was a commonplace of mediaeval discussion. Peter Lombard, for example, in his preliminary discussion of those signs which not only 'signify' but also 'justify' in his twelfth-century *Sentences*,[1] considers the question of the relationship of the Church's ministry of the sacraments to the ministry of the Word. The opening question of Aquinas' *Summa Theologiae* a century later is whether the study of 'holy learning' (*sacra doctrina*) through Scripture is 'necessary to salvation'.[2] For the majority of mediaeval authors there was no question of separating Scripture from the Church in its saving work. The ministry of the sacraments could not take place outside the community of the Church; the ministry of the Word belonged there in the same way.

Yet in practice that ministry came to be somewhat neglected in the late mediaeval Church. Stephen Langton's Constitutions of 1222 require parish priests 'to feed the people with the Word of God', but local priests rarely preached, and many were insufficiently educated to attempt it. It ceased to be usual to include a sermon in the celebration of Mass. From the thirteenth century, the work of preaching tended to devolve upon the friars. The result was some disjunction between the itinerant and occasional ministry of the Word on the one hand, and the pastoral and local sacramental ministry on the other. It was thus a notable feature of reform in many German towns in the early sixteenth century that local clergy were seeking to bring preaching back into their ministry, give it a regular and central liturgical place, and stress its importance as a means of bringing people to a saving faith.

Our concern here is not so much with this matter of the regular use of Scripture, as with questions of 'authority' in the Church's ministry of the

---

[1] Sent. I, Dist. 1, c.1.1.1.
[2] *ST* I q.1.a.1.

Word. There were two broad areas in which these were important in the reforming thought of the sixteenth century. The second, which concerns the structures by which the Church exercises authority in matters of faith, must wait for later chapters. The first is the matter of the very identity of Scripture itself and the nature of its relationship to other textual 'authorities' (such as the Fathers, decrees, canons); and to the Church acting as its 'witness and judge';[3] and to proofs and demonstrations which rest on reasoning; in short, the problem of the Bible's authority as a living and working text in the community of the faithful.

i. THE TRUE TEXT?

The study of Scripture as we have it in the Canon is the study of a written text, from which oral tradition and the possibility of adding, altering or subtracting are explicitly excluded.[4] That fact above all governs the debate about the authority of Scripture in its sixteenth-century form, because it creates unendurable tensions when it comes to saying precisely which words, and in which order, make up that text. Scholarship was at work on Greek and Hebrew as well as Latin. The Bible was also being made available to ordinary people in the vernaculars. Since Jerome's translation of the Bible had come into more or less standard use in the West from the fifth century,[5] there had been no pressing need for this sort of discussion about what constituted the text of Scripture. In practice the Vulgate was treated not as a translation derived from the original, but as though it had itself been given directly by God; upon its words it seemed perfectly proper to build up a body of literature, commentary, speculative theology and legislation embodying Vulgate terms and phrases. There was precedent for looking at a translation in this way, in the tradition that the Septuagint Greek version of the Old Testament was itself directly inspired, and the translators prophets;[6] but in the case of the Vulgate the reason was perhaps primarily practical. Few Christian scholars in the

---

[3]   Cf. Thirty-Nine Articles, 20.
[4]   Both the content of the Canon and the question of the status of oral tradition were, however, major topics in the debates of the Council of Trent.
[5]   The Old Latin versions seem to have survived in at least fragmentary use in quotation.
[6]   Jerome's thinking is outlined in W. Schwarz, *Principles and Practice of Biblical Translation* (Cambridge, 1955), pp. 27–8. He came to have doubts on this score.

West after the sixth century could have read the Scriptures in the original languages. That continued to be the case for nearly a thousand years. The first requirement, then, before Biblical scholarship could begin systematically to embrace the study of the Greek and Hebrew text, was the establishment of a reasonably widespread knowledge of these two original languages of Scripture. Augustine of Hippo lived at a time when the knowledge of Greek was already becoming less commonplace in the West; he himself had difficulty with the language. From the separation of the Eastern and Western halves of the Roman Empire until late in the Middle Ages, few in the West knew Greek, and few Christian scholars knew Hebrew. Those who dabbled in either language at first tended to restrict themselves to enquiries about the meanings of individual words, rather than attempting to learn the language as a whole. (There are accounts of Christian scholars consulting Jews in this way in the twelfth century.)

As early as 1312, under pressure from Ramon Lull, the Council of Vienne decreed that chairs of Greek, Hebrew and Biblical Aramaic (Chaldean) should be established at the universities of Paris, Bologna, Salamanca and Oxford. In fact it was not until the end of the century when Manuel Chrysoloras was brought to Florence that Greek was taught seriously in any part of Europe.[7] In the late 1490s Cardinal Ximenes, Archbishop of Toledo and one of the most influential churchmen of his day, lent his patronage to the endeavour.[8] He formed the plan of founding a new university where Greek and Hebrew would be taught as well as other languages. Building was begun in 1502 near Madrid at Alcalá (Complutum), and the university was teaching by 1508. The three languages were being taught at the Trilingual College in Louvain from 1517. Yet for much of the period when pioneering work was being done on the text of Scripture in the original languages individual scholars were finding their own way. In a letter to Erasmus in 1517 William Latimer says that he finds it a slow and difficult task to learn Greek, especially to attain any fluency in it.[9] Guillaume Budé claimed to be self-taught,

---

    Augustine defended the Septuagint's inspiration (*ibid.*, p. 40).

7   See B. Bischoff, 'Das griechische Element in der abendländische Bildung des Mittelalters', *Mittelalterliche Studien* (Stuttgart, 1967), II.246–75, and M. W. Herren (ed.), *The Sacred Nectar of the Greeks* (London, 1988).

8   M. Bataillon, *Erasmo y España*, tr. A. Alatorre (2nd ed. Mexico City, 1966), pp. 1–71.

9   Erasmus, *Letters*, Letter 520, 4.201–2.

although he had had help it seems from John Lascaris, an Italian Hellenist in Paris, brought to France by Charles VIII. Erasmus could also claim to be *automatheis*. Both had some experience of the failings of rascally Greeks, who promised teaching, often for large fees, but who proved to be incompetent instructors, or to have no real grasp of the written language.[10] Although instruction was to be had for the determined, there were thus considerable obstacles of a practical sort in the way of learning either Greek or Hebrew even in the early sixteenth century. Things were still not sufficiently settled in language studies for either Luther or Calvin to be able to study Greek or Hebrew without making special arrangements. Calvin learned Greek during his time at Bourges (1529–30), Luther after he had begun teaching at Wittenberg. Greek and Hebrew studies were never exactly parallel. There had been a tendency for those individual scholars of the Middle Ages who made forays into the learning of either language to concentrate on one rather than the other. Robert Grosseteste in the early thirteenth century was a Greek scholar; Nicholas of Lyre (*c.*1270–1340), one of the pioneers of systematic work on the Hebrew Old Testament, knew virtually no Greek. Johannes Reuchlin (1455–1522) was unusual in being able to offer both languages. Erasmus found it impossible to master both languages at the same time, and even after him few could claim equal knowledge of both.

It was in this climate of experimentation in the study and teaching of the sacred languages that Melanchthon set about devising textbooks and a syllabus for the teaching of Greek. He wrote to Spalatin in December 1518, describing the two courses of public lectures he was giving, one on grammatical principles (*res grammatica*) and the other devoted to the reading of authors with his pupils. He begins with Plato's *Phaedo*, thinking the *Symposium* unsuitable for 'innocent ears'; he wonders about including Thucydides.[11] This had been the broad pattern of grammatical teaching in Latin throughout the Middle Ages; grammar and authors; and it continued to be the model for sixteenth-century university teaching of the sacred languages. At Vienna in 1554, for example, Hebrew was taught in this way, grammar alternating with the reading of some Old Testament

---

[10] D. McNeil, *Guillaume Budé and Humanism in the Reign of Francis I* (Geneva, 1975), pp. 10–11, and D. Geanakoplos, *Greek Scholars in Venice* (Cambridge, Mass., 1962), p. 4.

[11] *CR* 1.56, 16 Dec. 1518.

book, although Hebrew grammars were scarce;[12] and for Greek the grammars of Theodore of Gaza and Chrysoloras were used, with Aristophanes, Demosthenes, Isocrates, Libonius and Dio read in the first year, and Homer and Epigrams in the second.[13]

The work of the philologists of the fifteenth and early sixteenth centuries was directed in the first instance to checking and correcting the Vulgate text. Valla's work was put into print by Erasmus in 1505. He defended Valla against the accusation that he had done no more than correct 'a nodding translator's plainly inadequate renderings of the meaning' and what is 'plainly corrupt'. But he himself was prepared to go further. If Valla merely examined points which raise difficulties of reading or rendering and showed a reference for the Vulgate text which makes him infer in places that there ought to be a correction in the Greek where it disagrees with the Latin, Erasmus attempted something altogether bolder. He made a new Latin translation, printing the Greek text alongside, so that readers could see for themselves the evidence on which he based it (1516). Erasmus' first concern was to get the Latin text right; the provision of the Greek was a secondary matter.

Erasmus found that what he was doing was no less controversial than Valla's exercise. It raised a number of questions of authority. Valla had been accused of taking on himself a task which in Jerome's case had been entrusted to the translator by a Pope. Erasmus seems to have done the same. But, as he protests in a letter of 1516 to Henry Bulloch, there was no preliminary authorisation of Jerome's work by a General Council. It was 'published first and approved ... thereafter'.[14] His own version should surely be allowed to find its place in the same way, to be read without prejudice and judged on its merits? That was allowed to Jacques Lefèvre d'Étaples in his work on St Paul. He 'did some time ago for St Paul what I have done for the whole New Testament. Why should certain people wait until now to rise in their wrath as though this were something

12 See Schwarz, *Principles*, p. 66.
13 R. Kink, *Geschichte der Kaiserlichen Universität zu Wien* (Vienna, 1854) 1 January 1554, pp. 380–4. The stimulus to compose new grammars carried over into work on the vernaculars too. See G. A. Padley's second volume of *Grammatical Theory in Western Europe*.
14 Erasmus, *Letters*, Letter 456, 4.44–5.

new?' asks Erasmus.[15] The problem Erasmus had come up against was not simply that of the official authorising of published work on the Bible, but of the 'official' character of the authority of the Vulgate itself.

Erasmus complains that opinion is 'most foolishly against him' because he subjects 'Christ's words to the rules of Donatus'. Here he makes a deliberate reference to Gregory the Great's comments in his prefatory letter to the *Moralia* on the book of Job that the Bible is not to be held answerable to the ordinary rules of grammar. The learned climate was different in Erasmus' day, but the problem substantially the same one as that which faced Gregory: of the degree to which Scripture could legitimately be practised upon by critical skills developed in the study of the formal arts of language. But Erasmus makes a distinction between what he is prepared to say about the Vulgate text and what he is prepared to do with the Greek. The Greek, whatever its stylistic faults, is sacrosanct to him. 'As it is known that the Apostles wrote Greek, though not very correctly, I have not changed a single letter in the language they used; much less have I wished to bring Christ's words under the rule of [grammatical] law.'[16] On the basis of this distinction between the sanctity of an original and a translated text, Erasmus asks whether his opponents can seriously be arguing that no change at all is possible in the Latin? If so, 'what will they make of those passages in which the existence of a corruption is too obvious to be denied or overlooked?' He protests that he has set out not to 'undermine' the text but to 'restore' it, to give Christians 'the text they love' in a form which they could 'read more accurately and understand more correctly'. That is no more than plain scholarliness.[17]

What seemed to Erasmus' critics to be at stake was not a mere translation, but the authority of one of the principal Fathers of the Western Church. One way of sidestepping this difficulty was to cast doubt on Jerome's authorship of the Vulgate, or of parts of it, and thus to save his face. Valla and d'Étaples did so. Erasmus raises the possibility. He is emboldened to accuse the hypothetical unknown translator of bad usage, solecisms, inconsistent renderings, omissions of material found in the Greek text, additions to the Greek text, failure to convey the nuances of the Greek.

This device would not do. Not only Jerome's reputation but the whole Western exegetical tradition was at stake, and the possibility that for more

[15] Letter 456, 4.47.
[16] Letter 843, to Martin Lips, 6.7, 1518.
[17] Letter 456, !4.46.

than a thousand years the Church had been 'deluded' into thinking his text reliable, 'that General Councils had erred … and that many learned Fathers and most holy men who interpreted it had laboured in vain'. The General of the Carmelites argued in the debates of Spring 1546 of the Council of Trent that all this 'seemed incompatible with reason'.[18] Those who were prepared to concede that corruptions were present[19] suggested compromises. Perhaps we can make a distinction between trivialities and those things in Scripture which 'pertain to faith and morals', and remain confident that their transmission has been protected by the Holy Spirit so that no soul might be led astray; but that is a slippery road. Perhaps we may regard the corruptions as having arisen in transmission, and as being therefore not Jerome's fault; then there would be something to be said for collecting as many *antiqui translatores* as possible and making comparisons, 'not because we are in doubt about the translation of Jerome … but so as to purge corruptions'. Perhaps we may argue that though it was appropriate for Jerome to go back to the Greek and Hebrew manuscripts, because in his day there were so many Latin versions that the *diversitas* and *varietas* was disturbing to the faithful, now that is not necessary. All that would be achieved would be some very minor corrections, and even those might not be right; and there would be the risk of stirring up uncertainty among the faithful about the reliability of the words of Scripture.

Deep and serious questions about both the authority of the text of Scripture itself and that of the Church as 'witness and keeper' of Scripture[20] were thus raised by these first endeavours to check and correct the Vulgate. They made the very study of the sacred languages controversial. The foundation of the Collegium Trilinguum at Louvain prompted Latomus (Jacob Masson) to publish an attack to which Erasmus and others produced a riposte, the *Dialogus Bilinguum ac Trilinguum*. A number of those who ultimately took the conservative side on certain points, but who were themselves linguists, found their position none too certainly, and perhaps attacked Erasmus on some points the more fiercely for that reason: Latomus; Frans Tittlemans in Louvain; Petrus Sutor; Noel

---

18   *Acta CT* 12.509 (cf. the same sentiments in Maarten Dorp's letter to Erasmus, Letter 304, 3.21).

19   Isidore Clarius, bishop of Foligno (b. 1495), made a full comparison with the Hebrew text and found over eight thousand errors in the Vulgate text, a figure which stuck in protestant minds (see Fulke, *Defence*, p. 62).

20   Thirty-Nine Articles, 20.

Beda; members of the Paris Faculties; Stunica of the Complutensian team which was working on the Polyglot Bible; Sancho Carranza also in Spain.

Erasmus wrote to John Colet in 1504, to report on the progress he had made in the work on the Bible Colet had inspired him to begin when he visited him in England.[21] Three years earlier, Erasmus had finished four volumes on Romans at a rush. He would have gone on, but for a number of distractions of which, he says, 'the most important was that I needed the Greek at every point'. He had been studying Greek intensively ever since.[22] It was while he was working in the library of the Abbey of Parc in the same year that Erasmus discovered Lorenzo Valla's *Adnotationes* of 1444 to the New Testament. He was excited to find a grammarian (*grammaticus*) using his knowledge of Greek in the critical study of Scripture. For Erasmus himself and for others in the field, the work on the checking of the Vulgate became in practice inseparable from the attempt to establish a Greek and Hebrew text which could be regarded as authoritative. A team was working at Alcalá from 1512 to produce an Old Testament in Latin, Greek and Hebrew and a New Testament in Greek and Hebrew, and its Greek New Testament of 1514 antedated that of Erasmus by two years, although the whole Complutensian Polyglot was not issued until 1522.

The thrust of the endeavour for a number of scholars was to get back to origins, the *hebraica veritas* and the *graeca veritas* as preserved in the *fontes* of the manuscripts. Here again the Church's stewardship was called into question. Wyclif's position had been that the Christian must treat the manuscripts with the kind of respect he would accord to the text of his father's will. That is to say, he must not alter it, any more than he may go against it, or impose a different meaning on what it says from that which the author intended. Scripture is the unalterable will or testament (*incorrigibile testamentum*) of God his Father, and change to the manuscripts comes under the same heading as alteration of the *sententia*.[23] Wyclif was of course speaking of manuscripts of the Latin Vulgate, and did not rule out correction in the case of obvious copyist's errors which had made a single copy different from others. The assumptions from which Valla begins include an element of this respect for the integrity of the document as written, together with a tendency to equate 'older' with 'more reliable' and

21   On Colet's views, see Schwarz, *Principles*, pp. 113–14.
22   Erasmus, *Letters*, Letter 181, 2.86–7.
23   *VSS* I.ix, Vol. I.190.7–12.

Greek and Hebrew with 'original'. But at the same time he is willing to weigh one manuscript's written evidence against that of another and one language against another. He does so, however, in a manner which is not always consistent methodologically; his overall purpose is to produce a smooth and convincing reading in order to preserve a perhaps rather idiosyncratically conceived 'integrity' of the text. (He saw nothing wrong in making good a gap by translating from the Vulgate into Greek, or even in altering the Greek without warrant from manuscript.)

The 'authority of the oldest' was widely held to be important in the case of manuscripts. Erasmus (erroneously) thought his manuscripts *vetustissimi*. William Fulke (1538–89), much later in the century, describes 'an ancient copy of the Gospels and Acts in Greek and Latin' which 'Beza himself has recently sent to the University of Cambridge to be kept in the common library'. It is, says Fulke with respect, 'of as great antiquity by all likelihood as any copy this day extant in Christendom'. It is of particular interest because it omits the name of Canaan, as Beza himself has omitted it in his translation (Luke 3.36). Beza has authority for his omission, Fulke argues, not only from Moses, 'which of itself is sufficient', but also from 'the testimony of this most ancient book, both for the Greek and for the Latin, to approve his fact in putting out *qui fuit Canaan*'.[24]

Valla saw the manuscripts as streams flowing from the source, some clear, some muddy.[25] He blames the Fathers for not doing what they could, great luminaries of the faith as they were, to save the Scriptures from corruption.[26] Anything which could be done in his own time could certainly have been done in earlier generations, he points out. As it is, modern scholars are faced with a more difficult task than they need have been. If in the time of Augustine and Hilary, after only four hundred years, so muddy a stream flowed from the source, is it surprising, he asks, that after a further thousand years the stream should have become scummy and squalid?[27] There is a frank admission here that the Church has not been perfectly successful as witness and keeper. It has failed to transmit the text of Scripture, at least as a physical entity, a written record preserved in manuscript.

The Byzantine manuscripts used by the first Western scholars of our

24   *Defence*, pp. 41ff.
25   *Collatio*, p. 188.25–6.
26   *Ibid.*, p. 9.10–16.
27   Cf. J. H. Bentley, *Humanists and Holy Writ* (Princeton, N.J., 1983), p. 35.

period to try their hand at emendation were not always better than the text
rendered by the Vulgate (indeed the Vulgate is closer to what the apostles
wrote than the late Byzantine manuscripts), and early work was relatively
uncritical. Valla's first version of the notes on the New Testament does
not discuss the manuscripts or cite variant readings. In the later version
he provides fuller information and a number of alternative readings, but
although he seems to have collated at least seven Greek and four Latin
manuscripts, he makes no systematic comparisons between them and
does not attempt to evaluate them. Critical faculties about priority of one
reading over another were sharpened by the battle over the Vulgate.
Stunica, one of the Complutensian team who produced the Polyglot Bible,
pointed out one manuscript, the Codex Rhodiensis, which supported Vulgate
readings again and again. Erasmus suggested to him the likelihood that that
manuscript had itself been corrected against the Vulgate.[28]

If it was by no means obvious to everyone that the alternative readings
found in the Greek and Hebrew manuscripts carried weight against the
Latin, that was partly on the grounds of what might be called a 'Whig
theory' of Scripture's progress to perfection which might weigh against
the authoritativeness of what was oldest. If scholars were obliged always
to prefer these readings, it was suggested in the debates of the Council of
Trent, the authority of Scripture would be derived from the Jews (*Sacrae
Scripturae auctoritas ab Hebrais dependeret*), 'and on the whole they
have been our enemies'.[29] Something of the same line of thought in
defence of the superiority of the Latin can be seen in Maarten Dorp's
argument in a letter to Erasmus in 1515. He suggests that the Greek and
Hebrew texts could be regarded as in some sense preliminary or preparatory,
leading on as 'channels' to the making of the Latin text the Church has
used for a thousand years. That would make the Vulgate the culmination
of God's revelation of the Holy Scriptures to his people.[30] It was easy to
show that at the very least Latin had the status of being one of the sacred
languages because the *titulus* put up over Jesus' head on the Cross was
in Latin, Greek and Hebrew.[31] This 'argument from progress' for the
superiority of the Latin text had become a commonplace as the result of
what Erasmus calls 'the extremely foolish gloss by someone or other who

---

28   *Erasmus against Stunica*, and Bentley, *Humanists*, p. 201 n.19.
29   *Acta CT* 12.510.
30   Erasmus, *Letters*, Letter 347, 3.157 and 161.
31   See, for example, *Acta CT* 12.511.

fancied Jerome had stated in his letter to Desiderius that the Latin texts were more correct than the Greek and the Greek than the Hebrew. He failed to see what Jerome was doing [in the Prologue to the Pentateuch] which was to prove his statement [in a standard rhetorical manner] by drawing a manifestly absurd inference from its contrary.'[32] And the disqualifications attendant upon the Jewish origins of the Hebrew manuscripts could be matched in the case of the Greek by the claim that the presence of 'so many heresies in Greece and that long schism' must throw doubt upon the reliability of Greek copies.[33]

If the Latin is in this sense the authoritative and primary text of Scripture, it follows that textual criticism should be working the other way; the Greek manuscripts ought to be corrected against the Vulgate, not the other way round, suggests Dorp[34] in a letter of 1514 to Erasmus.[35] Here again we meet a complex of authority-problems which were imperfectly resolved in the course of the sixteenth-century debates.[36] We also encounter a group of critical difficulties to do with the proprieties of emendation and textual correction, which sixteenth-century scholarship was simply not yet technically equipped to deal with.

Greek, like Latin, had a literature of a rich and sophisticated sort surviving from the classical world. When the syllabus of authors to be 'read' by university students was drawn up, at Wittenberg and elsewhere, the New Testament could not have the almost exclusive prominence which the Old Testament had in Hebrew studies. And Greek, like Latin, had classical standards, not to say a snobbery of excellence. The critical study of the Greek New Testament made it plain that the problem Augustine had encountered in the intellectual climate of the late fourth and early fifth century was still real. The language of Scripture seemed stylistically rude and unworthy of its great subject-matter. How far should critical

---

32 Letter 182, 2.95, to Christopher Fisher, 1505.
33 Dorp, in Erasmus, *Letters*, Letter 347, 3.160. See A. Landgraf, 'Zur Methode der biblischen Textkritik im 12 Jahrhundert', *Biblica*, 10 (1929), especially 445–56.
34 On Dorp's eventual position, see J. H. Bentley, 'New Testament Scholarship at Louvain in the Early Sixteenth Century', *Studies in Mediaeval and Renaissance History*, N.S. 2 (1979), 51–79, especially 53–60.
35 Letter 304, 3.21. See, too, Latomus, *De Trium Linguarum et Studii Theologici Ratione Dialogus, Opera*, ed. J. Latomus jr (Louvain, 1550), fo. 160ʳᵛ.
36 See Hudson, *The Premature Reformation* for the *status quaestionis* on Lollard Biblical scholarship.

emendation go to improve the Bible's Greek? How far should the criteria of classical studies be applied in judging what the text meant and in analysing the behaviour of particular words and phrases?

Even those scholars of the sixteenth century who devoted massive effort to the study of Greek or Hebrew remained first and foremost Latinists; that is to say, they knew much more about the working of Latin than of any other language. These scholars could attempt an ambitious and sophisticated style in Latin in imitation (if not always a successful imitation) of a classical ideal. The fashionable conception was of 'true' Latin as a *lingua romana* restored. 'Roman speech' was seen as properly the speech of classical Roman authors. Valla remarks that many prefer to speak of *lingua romana* rather than of 'Latin'.[37]

It was within this context that the new wave of grammarians argued that classical usage is the basis of grammatical correctness. In 1519, Juan Luis Vives, who had been studying at the Collège de Montaigu in Paris, wrote *Against the Pseudo-Dialecticians*. His theme was the absurdity of letting grammar dictate rules to be imposed on human speech. The grammarian does not decree what is Latin, he explains; he describes it as it is.[38] Heinrich Bebel took it as a central theme that usage is the only valid norm of language.[39] Valla contended that 'sometimes little girls understand the sense of words better' than the learned (who could identify the rules which govern them): *melius de intellectu verborum mulierculae nonnunquam sentiunt.*[40] Rules are of limited value. Hegius argued that nothing in philosophy or logic can explain why *amare* takes the accusative or *meminisse* the genitive.[41]

But Vives makes an assumption, in common with a number of humanists of the period, that what is good Latin had been decided once and for all; he does not allow for the possibility that by evolution, new usages and patterns of speech may become themselves good and true Latin. Vives says that the people who first used Latin decided by their own usage what is good Latin. They handed on certain figures and ways of putting things

---

37   *Elegantiae*, Peroratio, facs. repr., fo. 221.
38   Vives, *Adversus Pseudo-Dialecticos*, ed. Majans, *Opera Omnia* (Valencia, 1782–90), I.42 and tr. R. Guerlac, *Juan Vives against the Pseudo-Dialecticians: a Humanist Attack on Mediaeval Logic* (Reidel, 1979), p. 57.
39   T. H. Heath, 'Logical Grammar and Grammatical Logic and Humanism in Three German Universities', *Studies in the Renaissance*, 18 (1971), p. 24.
40   *Ibid.*
41   Hegius, *Invectiva in Modos Significandi*, ed. J. Ijsewijn, *Forum for Modern Language Studies*, 7 (1971), 299–314, especially p. 306.

which they recognised to be beautiful.[42] Melanchthon (following Quintilian) sees a word as something like a coin. It must be no forgery, but true to its value; it is to be used in exchange; it is passed from user to posterity, preserving the true 'value' it originally had.[43] These humanist grammarians were, then, substituting a new static grammatical criterion for the old. It was not rules but the way the Romans spoke which determined what was good Latin. Conrad Neobarius suggests that a number of problems may be solved by the application of criteria of 'received usage': *recepta loquendi consuetudo in consilium adhibenda est*. And he still finds useful some of the critical vocabulary of the mediaeval modists with their own fixed system: *vocabuli natura nominisque ratio a grammaticis et recepta Latini sermonis consuetudine petenda est.*[44]

This tension between the urge to get away from the formal approach to language of later mediaeval schools, and the tendency to substitute for it a new formality in the conception of a fixed classical ideal, can be seen in philological criticism of the Latin text of Scripture. Lorenzo Valla argues, for example, that nouns in *–itas* can be formed only from adjectives because they signify a quality. *Divinitas* is acceptable, but not *deitas*. That is an innovation *a barbaries quodam gurgustio prolata.*[45] He notices that in Colossians 2.9, and only there as far as he has been able to discover (though manuscripts may differ), Paul uses the word qeóthtoV. Whether that is the case *in omni editione*, and what influence the form has had, he does not know. Latin translators (*nostri interpretes*) render it not *deitas* but *divinitas.*[46] He finds he can take the debate further. He looks at *identitas* and tautóthV,[47] and seeks to draw a general conclusion on propriety of usage.[48]

As a result, Valla felt that he could claim to have something new to say, although so many fine scholars had written on the Sacred Text. He explains that he has gone back to the source (*fons*), found the *graeca veritas*, and looked to see whether the Vulgate text agrees with it, what details disagree (*repugnent*), give a false meaning (*falsum praebeant*

---

42 Vives, *Opera Omnia*, I.42.
43 Melanchthon, *Encomium Eloquentiae*, CR 11.51 and cf. Valla, *Repastinatio* II.x.3, pp. 214–17 on Quintilian's 'coin'.
44 Conrad Neobarius, *Compendiosa Facilisque Artis Dialecticae Ratio*, b³. For a convenient discussion of the modists, see *CHLMP*, chapter 13.
45 *Repastinatio* I.iv.5, p. 32; cf. I.iv.1, pp. 30ff., I.iv.8, p. 33.
46 *Ibid.*, I.iv.5 citing Augustine, *De Civitate Dei* VIII.1 and Aquinas on Romans 1.20.
47 *Ibid.*, I.iv.9, p. 33.22.
48 *Ibid.*, I.v.1, p. 37.4–5.

intellectum), are not clear (*parum aperte enuntiant quod traducant*), render in a way which is inappropriate for the context (*minus aperte respondent locis unde ducuntur*), are expressed without grace (*minus ineleganter latine efferantur*).[49]

To say that good Latin is classical Latin is also to say that it ought to be both free of 'Greekisms' and purged of borrowings from the vernacular. 'Many things are beautifully expressed in Greek which are not expressed beautifully in Latin', comments Valla.[50] This growing awareness of what was proper to the differing grammatical patterns of different languages enlarged perceptions to take in the vernaculars. Valla was able to compare German usage over the placing of the negative with that of Greek, for example. On this broad canvas of his grammatical knowledge, he could see many points of similarity and difference. The fifteenth-century Italian humanist Pomponius Leto bemoans the adoption of German habits of speech: *recepit hunc loquendi modum a Germania*, he notes with disapproval.[51] Jacob Wimpfeling, who studied at Freiburg, Erfurt and Heidelberg and had both a scholastic and a 'humanist' background, expressed anxiety that Latin would be perverted by contamination with German usage and pronunciation.[52]

Melanchthon considers how *feigen* in German may be derived from the Latin *ficus* and the Latin in its turn from the Hebrew *phagim*. Calvin was competent to pronounce on the way a particle is used in Hebrew as compared with Latin and Greek, or to conjecture what has happened to a Hebrew copula, or to recognise the peculiarities of Hebrew word order. This heightened consciousness of differing idioms and behaviours in different languages had no exact mediaeval parallel, because vernaculars were not treated in the Middle Ages as being on a par of grammatical sophistication with Latin, and the study of Greek and Hebrew was comparatively rare. Even now the vernaculars were brought in primarily for purposes of illustration and comparison in the teaching of Latin, and the first grammars of German, French and English were in Latin, and

49   *Collatio*, p. 8.27–32.
50   *Dialecticae Disputationes contra Aristotelicos* (1499), p. 4: *multa belle dicuntur graece, quae non belle dicuntur latine.*
51   J. Ruysschaert, 'Les manuels de grammaire latin composés par Pomponio Leto', *Scriptorium*, 8 (1954), p. 107.
52   J. H. Overfield, *Humanism and Scholasticism in Late Medieval Germany* (Princeton, N.J., 1984), p. 81.

designed – with an imposed grammatical framework derived from Latin – to make it possible for foreigners to learn these languages. That is not to say that there was no pride in vernaculars. German-speakers in particular had a high patriotic sense of their language's destiny as the chosen vehicle of the Holy Spirit in the mouths of the reformers.

Augustine says that if the reader finds any ambiguity in Scripture, he should compare translations, and if necessary go back to the original language, until he is sure which sense is correct.[53] His sixteenth-century successors faced difficulties made more complicated by the coming into existence of versions not only in Greek, Hebrew and Latin, but in a variety of contemporary vernaculars. The sensitivity to differences of usage we have noted began to include an awareness first that the classical and Biblical languages differ. William Latimer writes to Erasmus protesting that he cannot help him with the revision of his New Testament because his knowledge of classical Greek does not equip him for the task. The study of the New Testament requires a competence in 'words and forms different from those of the classical Greeks'; 'neither the forms of speech, on which alone the sense sometimes depends, nor the peculiar meanings of the words, are sufficiently familiar'.[54] Erasmus himself saw the contrast between the urbanity of classical Latin and the simplicity, even rudeness, of the Greek of the New Testament. To render it into a polished Latin would be to change its style. 'My rule has been,' he says, 'to try first of all to maintain as far as I could a pure Latin style, while retaining the simplicity of the Apostle's language.'[55] It followed that one must take account of the differences between ancient languages and modern vernaculars. Fulke's opponent Martin, later in the century, distinguished between the 'original property' of the language of Scripture, and modern common usage.[56] In the seventeenth century, Robert Boyle was still remarking on the difficulty of translating from a primitive language into one of greater sophistication.[57]

Underlying all this is the question with which we began: which is the true text of Scripture, and how far can it be said to subsist in a version in a

---

[53] *De Doctrina Christiana*, II.ii.2–iv.8.
[54] Erasmus, *Letters*, Letter 520, 4.199.
[55] Erasmus, *Letters*, Letter 860, to Antonio Pucci, 6.97, 1518.
[56] *Defence*, p. 217.
[57] *Cogitationes de Scripturae Stylo* (Oxford, 1665), pp. 4–5.

language different from the original. Where lies the authoritative version? Jerome had long ago distinguished between Scripture's *sententia* and the actual words, and Wyclif follows him in saying that the mind's understanding is more truly 'Scripture' than the lines on the page;[58] or perhaps it would be more exact to say that Scripture is made up of both meaning and words. The principle that the meaning could be conveyed by different words was clearly Scriptural. Martin Chemnitz pointed out that the majesty of heavenly doctrine was not violated on the day of Pentecost, when it was set forth in many languages. The English translator Miles Coverdale (d. 1568) thought that 'it was never better with the people of God than when every Church almost had the Bible of sundry translation'. 'Like as all nations in the diversity of speeches may know one God in the unity of faith ... even so may divers translations understand one another.' In the *Prolegomena* which were provided in the course of the century to the Polyglot Bible of 1522[59] the multiplication of versions in different languages is seen as an implementation of the command given to the apostles to preach the Gospel to every nation. Thus the dispersion of peoples and tongues which occurred as a result of the episode of the Tower of Babel is being reversed, and the people of God brought together.

Not every commentator of the sixteenth century thought it right that such proliferation of different versions should go unchecked. It was argued in 1546 during the debates of the Council of Trent, for example, that God's intention in causing the legend to be written above the head of the crucified Jesus in Latin, Greek and Hebrew[60] was to indicate that these were the only three languages in which Scripture was to be handed down.[61] But this conservative backlash did not touch the realities of the situation. Everywhere we see scholars confronted with multiplex problems of translation in their work. In 1507 one of the former pupils of Jacobus Faber Stapulensis, now abbot of Saint-Germain-des-Prés, invited him to be librarian in his house. He was prompted to attempt his Latin commentary on the Pauline Epistles (1512). By 1523 he was completing a French translation of the New Testament, followed by an Old Testament in 1528. Melanchthon in his early Postills frequently mixes in German words and phrases in his attempts to explain the meaning of a word. We find

58 *VSS* I.ix, Vol. I.189.8–15.
59 See, for example, the *Biblia Maxima*, Paris, 1660.
60 John 19.20.
61 *Acta CT* 12.511.

Luther struggling in 1522 to reconcile the names of Biblical birds and beasts in Hebrew with those familiar in German; they seem to him *confusissima*.[62] The lesson on every side was that one language will not go into another word for word, that Jerome was right and there was a *sententia* to be captured which was not indissolubly bonded to the Latin or even the Greek or Hebrew.[63]

One result of the new deeper insight into this principle was that it became possible to move on from the method followed by Boethius in the sixth century in making translations from Greek into Latin, and by most of his successors.[64] The style of the first version of the New Testament in the Wycliffite Bible is literal, often word for word, following the order in the Latin text and even using Latin idioms. A similar literalness and sometimes error characterises the Old Testament rendering for much of which the Wycliffite Nicholas of Hereford (d. 1420) is likely to have been responsible.[65] But Valla and Erasmus have different requirements of a translation. Valla says that the meaning should be correctly rendered (*recte traducta sententia*), with due attention given to nuances; the translation should be apt, and its fittingness considered in relation to the context. It should be consistent, yet consistency should not be a hard rule, because sometimes the context may make it necessary to be inconsistent for the sake of clarity.[66] These three principles have their application in deciding how to deal with differences in usage or syntactical structure.[67] Valla speaks of the 'Greek sense'[68] and notes that in Greek a word is always the same (*semper uniformis*) in a certain *genus dicendi*.[69] 'To say that in Latin', comments Erasmus, 'it would be necessary to alter the form of the Greek.'[70] In Greek there are many *modi*. Hebrew has its *loquendi modus* too, points out Jacobus Faber Stapulensis, describing the way the generation of Jesus Christ is handled by St Matthew.[71] Elsewhere we find reference to the *Hebraica linguae consuetudo* and the *Hebraica dicendi*

62 Letter to Spalatin, 1522, *WA* 2.630.
63 Cf. *PL* 28.1138C.
64 See the forthcoming paper by A. J. Minnis.
65 Hudson, *The Premature Reformation*, p. 389.
66 *Collatio*, pp. 268, 223, 184, 141, 235.
67 Cf. *Erasmus against Stunica*, p. 78.
68 *Collatio*, p. 185.
69 *Ibid.*, p. 22.
70 Erasmus, *Annotationes in Novum Testamentum*, on Luke 7 and 3.
71 Jacobus Faber Stapulensis, *Commentarii initiatorii in quattuor Evangelia* (Cologne, 1541), p. 2.

genera.[72] Real knowledge of another language obliges one to respect its natural behaviour in using it in translation. Cajetan saw that as he strove to translate the Psalms directly from the Hebrew, at first intending to do so word for word. He used not only the help Jerome could give him, but also four modern translations made directly from the Hebrew (*ex Hebraeo immediate*); he consulted two Hebrew speakers, one of them a Jew and master of the language, the other a Christian. He worked with them in his own house (*coram me*), asking them to tell him the meanings (*significationes*) which the Hebrew words could carry, and in each case he chose that which 'seemed to square best with the context' (*quae magis quadrare contextui visa est*). Despite all his efforts he found it impossible to be faithful to the grammatical construction (*servata congruitate grammaticae*) and to match the Hebrew word for word.[73]

Alongside this respect for the character of the languages involved went a sense of the intention of the human author of Scripture, and of Jerome as a translator. Cajetan noticed that Jerome was in the habit of changing an adverb into a pronoun in certain contexts.[74] Valla finds him sometimes retaining the Greek word, rather than attempting to turn it into Latin.[75] Valla went to some trouble to render Romans 12.3 in a way which he believed would get the balance Paul intended in: *id ipsum invicem sentientes, non alta sapientes, sed humilibus consentientes.*[76] Erasmus remarks on the problem presented by words 'which are so peculiar to the language of Paul that they cannot be expressed in more than one way'.[77]

In these and other ways the actual text of Scripture was being thrown into something of a melting-pot as far as the *verba* were concerned. Luther's practice was to search the German dialects for words, make a literal translation in the word-order of the original, and then take each word separately and think of a series of synonyms. Then he would try a free rendering to catch the spirit. Then he brought this and his literal

[72] Robertus Stephanus, *Phrases Hebraicae* (Geneva, 1557), Prefatory Letter to the Reader; cf. Calvin, *Harmony of the Gospels*, on Matthew 5.2.
[73] Cajetan, Preface on the Psalms. Cf. Erasmus' comments on the same difficulty in the *De Ratione Studii*.
[74] Cajetan, Commentary on Job, chapter 3, *Opera Omnia*, 3.408.
[75] *Collatio*, p. 188.
[76] *Ibid.*
[77] Erasmus, *Paraphrases in Epistolas Pauli Apostoli* (Basle, 1520), p. 14 and Letter 188, 2.108.

versions together, in the hope of thus turning the idiom of one language into the idiom of the other, so that the result was readable and alive. In a letter to Spalatin in January 1527 he notes the way that in German the future is implied where in Latin the present tense is more natural: 'Ich will dich haben, ich will dich nemen'; *ego volo te habere*, or *volo te habere*.[78] In an earlier letter in the same month he speaks of the use of contractions in Greek, Latin, Hebrew and German.[79] Everyone was aware that a given word or phrase may be rendered in many ways. Valla explains that *dux* can be translated as *presidens, magistratus, ductor, procurator*.[80] 'I do not know whether this is better translated *presbyteros* or *compresbyter*', he reflects.[81] Renderings involve choices between words with fine shades of difference in meaning.[82] Calvin notes that the Hebrew translators disagree among themselves.[83]

So far could *sententia* seem separable from the actual wording that in a later generation Richard Hooker thought paraphrase an excellent method of avoiding the difficulty that 'every little difference' can seem 'an intolerable blemish to be spunged out'. So long as there is no discord or contradiction 'between the words of translation and the mind of Scripture itself' he thinks it 'fittest for public audience' to follow 'a middle course between the rigour of literal translators and the liberty of paraphrasts'. That seems the best way to 'deliver the meaning of the Holy Ghost' with 'the greatest shortness and plainness'.[84] It was certainly the case that paraphrase circumvented many difficulties. More wrote to Erasmus to tell him of a comment of the Bishop of Winchester, that he had found Erasmus' version of the New Testament 'as good as ten commentaries'. It shed so much light,' he says, 'to have the same matter expressed in good Latin without the Greek habits of expression, even if there had been no other faults in the Vulgate that needed to be changed'. Erasmus was engaged on a projected translation, paraphrase and commentary during the period when he was preparing his New Testament.

---

78 Luther, Letter to Spalatin in Altenburg, 7 Jan. 1527, p. 152.4–21, *WA* 4.153.
79 Luther, Letter to Spalatin 1 Jan. 1527, pp. 148.26 – 149.9, *WA* 4.149–50.
80 *Collatio*, p. 264.
81 *Ibid.*, p. 265.
82 *Ibid.*, p. 22.
83 Calvin on Genesis 1.2–3, *CR* 50.16, on the many ways in which interpreters may handle a particular passage (cf. on Ps. 7.1 and Ps. 5.1).
84 *Laws* V.xix.2.

He argued that those who 'reject any change in the letter of Holy Writ' might regard his paraphrases as 'commentary', 'while he who is free of such superstition may hear the voice of Paul himself'. By paraphrase it was possible, he thought, to open up a little those 'mysteries' on which Paul 'touched instead of going into them', and passages where he 'provided indications rather than explanations' because he was writing for recent converts.[85] He has had to bridge gaps, smooth rough passages, bring order out of confusion, make the complicated simple, throw light on dark places, give Hebrew turns of speech a Roman character.[86]

When we have come thus far we have reached a point where the *interpres* is indeed not only a 'translator' but an 'interpreter', and the *sententia* is being expressed independently of the original *verba*. In making translations, as in their work on the Greek and Hebrew texts, sixteenth-century scholars and their immediate predecessors were caught in a profound paradox. They found themselves showing an acute sensitivity to the fine detail of the points their scholarly labour was throwing up, and which challenged not only the authority of the Vulgate but also the verbal authority of the text in any language. All this made the determining of the *sententia* an infinitely more complex matter than it had been for patristic and mediaeval commentators. At the same time, for reasons we shall come to in later chapters, they called for a return to 'Scripture alone' as the source of Christian truth. This implied that Scripture could be thought of as a relatively monolithic and verbally quite secure piece of evidence, and in practice that is how it was often treated in theological debate. It is of some importance here that the reformers, like their opponents, worked for the most part from the Vulgate in the sixteenth-century debates; and although comments are made on points of textual criticism, they are not on the whole the stuff of the discussion.

This, then, is the hornet's nest of questions about the authority of the text into which new work on Scripture threw the scholars of the sixteenth century. It is a supreme irony that it was at the time when *Scriptura sola* became a reforming slogan that it became unprecedentedly difficult to point unequivocally to the Sacred Page and say, 'That is Holy Scripture.'

---

[85]   Erasmus, *Letters*, Letter 503, 4.171.
[86]   Erasmus, *Paraphrases*, Dedicatory Epistle to paraphrase of Romans.

ii. THE REAL MEANING

The obscurities and apparent contradictions in the text of the Bible presented problems from the beginning, and they were by no means ironed out in Jerome's version. Here, the richest seam mined by scholars working on the Latin versions of the text since Augustine, and especially upon the Vulgate itself, had been the notion that problem passages are simply Scripture's special way of speaking (*modus loquendi*; *usus loquendi*; *consuetudo loquendi*, to borrow Augustine's phrases). Such departures from the ordinary or obvious way of putting things are seen as necessary in view of the profundity of the mysteries which the language of the Bible has to express, and also as a reflection of the power of the divine Word to break the bounds of ordinary grammar. The theologian will expect grammatical surprises and figurative devices. It could be taken that these were all there for a purpose, and were indeed a kind concession of the Holy Spirit to the frailty of human understanding, meeting us where we were in our sinful condition, and speaking to us in ways we could understand.

Thus Wyclif (*c.*1329–84), in writing *On the Truth of Holy Scripture*, treats the curious features of Biblical language for the most part not as errors but as the *consuetudo Scripturarum*. He explains that though in our study of grammar we begin by learning the rules and then adapt them to the requirements of Bible study, that is working the wrong way round. We ought not to lose sight of the fact that Scripture's language is the exemplar on which human language is modelled.[87] Its usages are primary. If you insist upon the rules of ordinary grammar which children learn, Wyclif warns, you will find the Bible's usages inconsistent.[88] You must learn that the Lord spoke according to a hidden grammar and logic of his own. We must learn the *grammatica scripture* so as to understand such usages as that which makes the word 'hand' equivocal, sometimes meaning the bodily organ, sometimes 'power' (an Augustinian example).[89]

It is important that this sort of thing persisted in sixteenth-century exegesis. Revolutionary new approaches to textual criticism did not rule it out, only a proportion of the grammatical oddities proved to be errors of transmission or translation. It could still be assumed that the main task of scholarship was to illuminate the meaning of a given and undisputed

[87] *VSS*, I.ii, Vol. I.24.17–18.
[88] *Ibid.*, I.ix, Vol. I.205.5.
[89] *Ibid.*, I.i, Vol. II.2–5.

text. Valla (d. 1475), a fifteenth-century pioneer of the new textual scholarship, was still aware of being confronted by Scripture and by the demands of theology at large with the need to make allowance for special usages. He concedes that sometimes Scripture uses a word in a way peculiarly its own. *Ipse est, tenete eum* and *tenuerunt* are, he says, used for certain purposes only in the Bible, in a context where *capite* and *ceperunt* would be more obvious choices. This particular instance seems to him to have something to do with the translation from the Greek, but elsewhere he realises that 'since we lack appropriate words for divine things' (*cum in rebus divinis deficient apta verba*) we adapt the words we have (*accomodamus*) so as to speak as well as we can of the divine.[90]

We can see the contrast between the two approaches in earlier and later remarks of Erasmus. In 1504 he places the emphasis on Scripture's special usages. 'The Spirit of God has a certain tongue or speech appropriate to himself. He has his figures, similitudes, parables, comparisons, proverbs and riddles, which you must observe and mark diligently if you want to understand them.'[91] He explains that the special *modus loquendi* in the Bible is for our benefit. 'The Wisdom of God stutters and lisps like a diligent mother fashioning her words according to our infancy and feebleness.' A dozen years later he replies to a criticism of Johann von Eck's in a quite different style:

> You lay on the rod because I express surprise that the Evangelist should be willing to use the word *therapeuein*, which means to cure by the remedies physicians use. To begin with, this is a point more against the translator than against Matthew, since he is held to have written in Hebrew. Secondly, the word 'misuse' need not always mean to use for a wrong purpose; for we also misuse things which we have taken for our own use from some other source, and when we use a word in a different sense, we misuse it, but to good effect. Finally, a man who expresses surprise is not necessarily critical: we are surprised at things we admire, at new things, at things the cause of which we do not know.[92]

Erasmus' original comment on the usage of *therapeuein* had been prompted by noticing an anomaly of usage; but he had here attributed this

---

[90]   *Repastinatio* I.ix.22, p. 67.4–8, Matthew 26.48, 50 and Mark 14.44, 51; I.viii.5, p. 52.1–3.
[91]   *Enchiridion Militis Christiani*, 2.
[92]   Letter 844, 6.30–1.

oddity not to God's wish to adapt his language to limited human understanding, but to human error or human design. He suggests that Matthew or his first Greek translator (he was familiar with the tradition that Matthew wrote in Hebrew) had perhaps adopted the word for effect. Here the special features of the language are not being seen as a challenge to the rules of grammar; instead an attempt is being made to accommodate them within those rules.

It was in this spirit that Erasmus contended that 'the authority of the whole of Scripture' would not 'be instantly imperilled ... if an evangelist by a slip of memory did put one name for another, Isaiah for instance instead of Jeremiah, for this is not a point on which anything turns'. A book does not 'forthwith lose all credence if it contains some blemish'.[93] There is no question of 'negligence' on the part of the Holy Spirit. If the human authors are allowed to be themselves, of course there will be some 'clumsiness of language, not to say barbarism'.[94] 'Perhaps it is not for us to dictate how' the Spirit 'shall tune the instrument he makes of his disciples ... he has done it in the way he knew to be most conducive to the salvation of the human race. He was present in them so far as pertained to the business of the Gospel, but with this limitation, that in other respects he allowed them to be human none the less.'[95] The kindness of God in meeting us where we are in his teaching and making allowances for our human fallibility is still being put forward as the fundamental reason for the anomalies of Scripture's usages, but there is now a proximate cause in the picture, the human author or translator, whose mistakes God permits to remain, while safeguarding the truth of Scripture in all its essentials.

A willingness to make special allowances for Scripture's language runs alongside a new critical rigour where corrections seem necessary, in both Luther and Calvin. Luther, for example, insists that unless the context manifestly compels it, 'the words of God ... are not to be under-stood apart from their grammatical ... sense'. He is prepared to criticise Moses for inconsistency and repetitiousness.[96] Some speculate vainly over the adverb in the command: *vade retro*. Luther thinks Christ was simply telling Satan to be off. But in Luther's early work on the Psalms a sensitivity to Scripture's special usages is apparent. Writing on Psalm 8.4, Luther points out that 'man' in the singular is often used in the Bible

93   Letter 844, 6.27–36.
94   *Ibid.*, p. 29.
95   *Ibid.*, p. 28.
96   On Deuteronomy, *WA* 14.644.

as a collective noun, 'when God speaks to many as to one individual'. Again, 'It is customary with Scripture frequently to put the word in an absolute and unqualified way. He does not say what he "enlarged" but gives the verb without modification.'[97] Calvin discusses the tense of 'Adam called' (Genesis 3.20). If it is pluperfect, 'the sense of Moses will be that Adam has been greatly deceived in promising life to himself and his posterity from a wife whom he afterwards found to be the introducer of death'. Calvin points out that Moses frequently adds later in the order of the narrative things which came earlier in time. Or the passage may be taken in the preterite tense, and then it will have other meanings.[98]

The nexus of sense and usage and rule was of perpetual live concern throughout the Middle Ages and the sixteenth century, but a new alertness to the range of behaviours possible in natural languages was fostered by the study of Greek and Hebrew and the attempts to translate the Bible into various vernaculars. Scripture's special usages began to be explored in ways increasingly sensitive to the fact that usage always stands in a somewhat uneasy relationship to the syntactical proprieties laid down in grammatical textbooks. A degree of extraordinariness is human as well as divine.

Origen had encouraged readers of the Bible to look for deeper truths in the text than those which were apparent on the surface.[99] Augustine and Gregory the Great made it a commonplace in the mediaeval West that the literal sense was only one of several possible interpretations of a given passage, and that the figurative meanings were especially rich in spiritual instruction. The respect for figurative interpretations always depended in this way on their claim to greater profundity, their ability to bring the reader closer to the mind of the divine Author. Origen saw it as the proper goal of those who are 'ambitious' in their reading to search the text for the wisdom of God, to the point where the literal meaning is sometimes set aside altogether.[100] This high doctrine of the spiritual sense is upheld in the 'rules' of the Donatist Tichonius (d. *c*.400), to which Augustine gave

---

[97]   Luther on Psalms 8.4, 4.1, *WA* 3.79 and 44–5.
[98]   Calvin on Genesis 3.20, *CR* 51.77.
[99]   Origen, *De Principiis* IV.9; on the Jewish tradition which lies behind, see *The Cambridge History of the Bible*, vol. I, ed. P. R. Ackroyd and C. F. Evans (Cambridge, 1970), chapter 8.
[100]   Origen, *De Principiis* IV, says that if no spiritual significance is apparent we should take the surface meaning to be symbolic.

lasting currency by discussing them in his *De Doctrina Christiana*.[101] Tichonius saw his rules as 'keys' to open up and 'lamps' to reveal the secrets hidden in the treasury of truth. They proved useful enough to be reproduced in the later Middle Ages by Nicholas of Lyre, Jean Gerson (1363–1429)[102] and many others.

But alongside this tradition ran reservations about the propriety of Scripture's using language in a way which was not plain and straightforward. The concern was expressed on a number of grounds, several of them brought together by Aquinas when he considered the question in the thirteenth century. Should Holy Scripture use metaphors, asks Aquinas? On the face of it, it seems that it should not, for figurative language is proper to poetry, and poetry is the lowest of the sciences. It is also likely that imagery will obscure the truth, and that cannot be right in the study of the divine. The creaturely things which provide the images are in any case unfit comparisons.[103] In answering this question and the related one which follows it (as to whether Scripture ought to have more than one sense), Aquinas addresses himself to matters of long-standing debate in exegetical tradition. He answers, as Augustine or Gregory the Great would have done, that it is fitting for Holy Scripture to teach spiritual things in corporeal guise. It is natural for man to learn from what his senses tell him. Scripture is simply using the best method of instruction for human capacities. Scripture differs from poetry in making use of figures not to give pleasure but out of necessity.[104] As to its truthfulness: 'the ray of divine revelation is not destroyed by the wrapping of corporeal figures which surrounds it'.[105]

The spiritual or figurative senses of Scripture were in principle unlimited in number, but in practice they were usually limited to three in the mediaeval West. Accordingly, a fourfold system of interpretation dominated mediaeval exegesis from the time of Gregory the Great, and gave shape to the search for meanings beyond the literal. Gregory drew

101 III.xxx.42ff. See, too, *The Book of Rules of Tichonius*, ed. J. Armitage Robinson (Cambridge, 1895), Preface; also the article by H. Chadwick, 'Augustine and Tyconius', in *Colloquy* 58 of the Centre for Hermeneutical Studies in Hellenistic and Modern Culture, Berkeley, California (Berkeley, 1989).
102 Jean Gerson, *De Sensu Litterali Sacrae Scripturae, Oeuvres complètes*, ed. P. Glorieux, vol. 3 (Paris, 1963), pp. 334–5.
103 *ST* I q.1.a.9.
104 As Bede explains in his *De Schematibus et Tropis*, 1.
105 *Ibid.*

it in part from Origen, and in part from other sources, including Augustine (although Augustine does not set it out in quite the same way). He distinguished a literal or historical meaning which is the straightforward sense of the words as they appear at first reading; an allegorical or spiritual meaning; a moral or tropological sense which looks to the practical application of the words of Scripture to the living of a good Christian life; and an anagogical sense, looking forward prophetically to future time in this world or to the life to come.[106] This fourfold pattern was not adhered to rigidly. For one thing, many passages lacked one or more applications. For another, 'allegorical' could be used as an umbrella term for all the spiritual senses. William Brito produced in the second half of the thirteenth century a handbook of expositions of Biblical terms which became a much-used basic reference book in the fourteenth century. He drew on earlier work in making his compilation, and he was anxious to be methodical and thorough. In his account of allegory in this broader sense, he defines it as 'the trope by which something is signified other than what is said': *tropus quo aliud significatur quam dicitur*.[107] He sees this transference of signification as taking place in various ways. Isaac may signify Christ. Something which is not a person may also have a transferred signification, as the sacrificed Lamb signifies the flesh of Christ crucified. The place may be significant. (In the Sermon on the Mount, the eminence of the place signifies Christ's wisdom and eloquence.) Or the allegory may involve numbers or times.

The abbot Trithemius (1462–1516), writing in the context of a late mediaeval German monastic humanism, speaks of the ways in which the rhetorician may reveal 'the figures of Scripture, elucidate its tropes, display its complexions, resolve its doubts and clarify the shades of the words'. He sees these skills as means of overcoming the objections of heretics. 'O, if only the theologians of our time would cultivate oratory,' he exclaims, 'how much fruit in the Church of God would they not be able to produce by their exhortations!' Like Augustine, he sees the orator as holding the souls of his listeners in his hands as he moves them to holiness of life,[108] and he describes the uses of rhetoric in drawing comparisons

---

[106]   See H. de Lubac, *Exégèse médiévale* (Paris, 1959), 2 vols., for a comprehensive survey of the development of a fourfold interpretation.

[107]   *Summa, Britonis sive Guillelmi Britonis Expositiones*, ed. L. W. Daly and B. A. Daly (Padua, 1975), p. 25.

[108]   Trithemius to Morderer, Sponheim, 2 April 1492, in *Opera Historica*, ed. M.

with ordinary experience, so that people may see more clearly what Scripture has to say to them.[109] Such means, formally or informally, are fully exploited in the preaching of the reformers, and in different ways, in the stirring tirades of polemic.

When Luther declared that the Christian reader should make it his first task to seek out the literal sense, 'for it alone is the whole substance of faith and Christian theology', he was apparently throwing down a challenge to the long-standing assumptions of this approach to exegesis. Far from leading us to a more profound understanding of Scripture's teaching, he says, Jerome, Origen and other Fathers like them must be read with a mind critically alert, for they 'constructed and taught arbitrarily from Scripture according to their whim'. The spiritual interpretation is a licence for fancy. Nevertheless, he was aware that sometimes in Scripture 'every sense of the flesh has been put away', so that there is no literal meaning but only a 'spiritual'.[110] The remark comes from one of his earliest commentaries, but in his mature work we find him still making a place for figurative interpretation. He looks to what he calls 'the rule of St Paul'. The function of allegorical interpretation is seen as 'the strengthening, adorning and enriching of the doctrine of faith'. The exegete's task is to 'explain according to the literal sense, and then at the end connect this to an allegorical meaning which says the same thing'. Then there will be no flights of fancy, and it will be clear that the allegorical meaning rests upon the literal, 'just as a house does not hold up the foundation, but is held up by the foundation', he says, using a traditional 'architectural' image of exegesis.[111] The figurative sense may be higher, but only because it is erected on the basis of the literal; and airy constructions will fall down if they do not stand on a firm base.

Calvin seeks to establish the same legitimate use of figurative interpretation. He accuses Augustine of triviality and Origen of playing games.[112] He calls the allegories of Origen and others a device of the Devil to make the Bible's teaching ambiguous and its interpretation

Freher (Frankfurt-am-Main, 1601, facs. London, 1966), I.187, and see N. L. Brann, *The Abbot Trithemius (1462–1516): The Renaissance of Monastic Humanism* (Leiden, 1981), p. 226.

109   Brann, *Trithemius*, p. 227 (*Opera Historica* II.476).
110   *WA* 3.262.
111   *WA* 14.560–1 and 500.
112   On Genesis 6.14, *CR* 51.123.

uncertain,[113] and argues that the Papists have 'come to an arrangement with Satan' to obscure the meaning of Scripture.[114] Yet he sometimes concedes that the allegory proposed by one of the Fathers is not 'displeasing',[115] and he is able to point to at least one blunder when Lactantius and others take what is clearly meant to be a figure as a literal statement.[116] Bede had set out clearly in his *De Schematibus et Tropis* the principle that figures may be used to give beauty and excitement or because there is no other way in which a spiritual truth can be expressed. Luther and Calvin point to abuses of both the law of 'beauty' and the law of 'necessity'. The law of beauty is broken when allegorising is carried to absurd and misleading lengths, so that the soul is not uplifted but misled. The law of necessity is broken when the sense is distorted by being made to seem figurative when it is really literal, or literal when really figurative.

So Luther's challenge, like Calvin's, is not to the use of figurative interpretation as such, but to its misuse, what Calvin calls 'playing games with the sacred Word of God', like tossing a ball back and forth.[117] Both accept the power a figure may have to elevate the understanding, and both perceive the need for figurative expression in certain contexts.

It is of the first importance in understanding the reformers' approach to the study of the Bible to recognise the continuity of tradition which underlies their questioning of accepted methods, and their recognition of the subtlety and complexity of the problems they seek to resolve. Luther's blunt bombast is a front for a refined discrimination; Calvin's anger with those who get it wrong does not blind him to what is of value in the established procedures.

The moral (or tropological) interpretation is pressed by the reformers as enthusiastically as by any of their mediaeval predecessors. 'Whenever we are endeavouring to turn men towards piety or from wickedness, we shall find very useful anecdotes drawn from the Old or New Testament, that is, from the Gospels.' 'The hidden meaning of these can be variously handled; it can be explained in terms of human life, or of the body of Christ joined and connected to Christ the Head, or of the fellowship of

[113] On Genesis 2.8, *CR* 51.37.
[114] *Harmony of the Gospels*, Luke 4.4.
[115] On Genesis 27.20, *CR* 51.378.
[116] On Genesis 6.3, *CR* 51.114.
[117] Comm. on 2 Cor. 3.6–7.

heaven, or of those early days when the faith was new-born, or of our own times.' Calvin insists that exhortation and practical application are essential parts of pulpit teaching and ought to have a place in every sermon.[118] We must be Christians 'in deed'.[119] The Puritans came to divide their sermons into 'Doctrine, Reason and Use',[120] with the same consciousness of the importance of the practical application of teaching to the living of the Christian life.

John Cosin (1594–1671/2), Master of Peterhouse, Cambridge, Chaplain to the Protestants in Henrietta Maria's household in Paris, and later bishop of Durham, preached a sermon in Paris in 1651 much of which could have been delivered centuries earlier without seeming out of its time. Cosin took as his text John 20.9 and explored the ways in which Abraham's readiness to sacrifice Isaac could be seen as a type of the Passion and resurrection of Christ. He points out that Isaac and Christ were both only sons, and beloved. Both were obedient; both were bound ready to be sacrificed; both carried on their shoulders the wood on which they were to be sacrificed. Both were led to a mountain. The thorn bush which held the ram Abraham eventually sacrificed in place of Isaac is the crown of thorns. Both Isaac's deliverance from death and Christ's resurrection took place on the third day.[121] This use of 'types' was still familiar in the seventeenth century, among protestant as well as Roman Catholic interpreters.[122]

In the early seventeenth century, John Donne considers the spiritual senses 'usefull, for the raising and exaltation of our devotion', and he is sure that 'the Scriptures doe admit ... divers senses', although he thinks it is important to keep a rein on interpretation and always keep the literal sense in mind.[123] He was familiar with Augustine, Gregory and a wide range of mediaeval authors[124] and he certainly understood the possibilities of the standard fourfold scheme. In his plan of exposition for a series of six sermons preached at Lincoln's Inn, he includes literal, moral and

---

[118] Comm. on John 20.21.
[119] *Ibid.*, Preface to the Reader.
[120] H. Davies, *The Worship of the English Puritans* (London, 1948), pp. 328ff.
[121] Davies, *Angels from a Cloud*, pp. 469–70, and cf. Calvin, *Psychopannia*, p. 428, on this stock typology.
[122] Davies, *Angels from a Cloud*, pp. 469ff.
[123] *Sermons* III.353.
[124] On Donne's sources, see *Sermons* X.345ff.

anagogical senses.[125] But elsewhere he adopts other schemes. In a
sermon on Psalm 38.3, for example, he takes the words of his text 'first
... as they are historically and literally to be understood of David; and
secondly, in their retrospect, as they look back upon the first Adam, and
so concern mankind collectively, and so you, and I, and all have our
portion in these calamities; and thirdly, we shall consider them in their
prospect, and their future relation to the second Adam, in Christ Jesus'.[126]
In a subsequent sermon we find, 'First ... all these things are literally
spoken of David: By application, of us; and by figure, of Christ.
Historically, David; Morally, we; Typically, Christ is the subject of this
text.'[127] We find, then, in the seventeenth century, a sense of freedom to
experiment with the fourfold pattern and a new stylishness in handling it.
One might compare the way Staupitz handled a text in his preaching in
the early days of the University of Tübingen: 'Ahasuerus held a great
feast for all his princes and sons. The purity of innocence is correctly
signified by the sons',[128] with the seventeenth century, 'Peace is a faire
Virgin, every ones Love, the praise of all tongues.'[129]

Two further views of the reasons why figures must be allowed for in
Scripture had been current throughout the Middle Ages. Bede explains
in his *De Schematibus et Tropis* that human language lacks an adequate
vocabulary and power of expression, so that it is sometimes necessary for
the Word of God to speak in figures to make itself clear. And sometimes
it uses figures because they are beautiful. We have seen something of the
results of reflection upon the first reason in the chapters on grammar.
Wyclif speaks in this tradition of the *scripturae penuria* which sometimes
makes equivocation unavoidable.[130] Zwingli points out the 'narrowness' of
the Hebrew language, whose 'poverty' forces it to use figures.[131] He was able
to identify a comprehensive list of figures by their technical terms.[132]

The second falls into the province of rhetoric, and it became of fresh
live concern with the revival of the study of classical rhetoric. Augustine

125   *Sermons* X.362.
126   *Sermons* II.75.
127   *Sermons* II.97.
128   *Sermons* IX.65.
129   Davies, *Angels from a Cloud*, pp. 469–70, and cf. Calvin, *Psychopannia*, p. 428, on this stock typology.
130   *VSS* I.ii, Vol. I.27.
131   Zwingli, *De Peccato Originali* (1526), *Werke* V.386.22–3.
132   Zwingli, *Werke* XIII contains a good sample.

had defended Scripture's use of identifiable rhetorical figures in Book IV of the *De Doctrina Christiana*, with the purpose of demonstrating to a readership whose education had made them stylistic snobs that, despite its apparent simplicity, the Bible's expression easily stood comparison with the best work of secular stylists. The need now was rather different. Melanchthon discusses the way 'philosophers' debate among themselves about figures of speech[133] and asks whether there is a place for such discussions in the interpretation of Holy Scripture.[134] Where Augustine was defending the text of Scripture Melanchthon is defending oratory. 'Sheer necessity breeds elegance,' he claims, 'because what is put crudely is unclear and what is illuminated with ornaments of rhetoric is seen more clearly.'[135]

Luther recognised and strongly approved the signifying power of 'things', the vivid images Scripture introduces and which greatly add in his view to the power and brilliance of its teaching. 'Holy Scripture … points to things to show their properties and powers; for example in the Psalm (103.5), "Your youth is renewed like the eagle's", or Deuteronomy 32.11, "As an eagle provokes its young to fly" … The Scriptures are all so full of such metaphors and parables taken from the nature of things that if someone were to remove these things from the Holy Scriptures, he would also remove a great light.'[136] But he is sometimes afraid that to identify a *schema* of rhetoric in such an image is to obscure the sense.[137]

In Calvin, too, there is a recognition that the beauty and *decorum* added by rhetorical figures has a place. 'Although a figurative expression is less precise, it expresses with greater significance and elegance what, said simply and without figure, would have less force and point. That is why figures are called the eyes of speech, not because they explain things more correctly than simple, proper usages, but because they capture the attention … arouse the mind by their brilliance and represent what is said by a striking likeness so that it is remembered.'[138]

Both Luther and Calvin display a grasp of the technical names of a good range of at least the more common rhetorical figures. Luther comments

133 Melanchthon, *Encomium Eloquentiae, Werke*, ed. H. Engelland *et al.* (Gütersloh, 1951–), vol. 1, pp. 48.38 – 49.1.
134 *Ibid.*, p. 48.12–15.
135 *Ibid.*, p. 48.7–10.
136 Luther on Ecclesiastes, *WA* 20.12; cf. Davies, *Angels from a Cloud*, p. 431.
137 Luther, *De Servo Arbitrio, Works*, vol. 33, pp. 222–3; *WA* 18.551ff.
138 *De Vera Participatione Carnis et Sanguinis Christi in Sacra Coena, Calvini Opera* 9.514.

that 'it is the custom of Scripture to refer to the whole through synecdoche when it intends only a part ... in the verb "to call upon" there is a synecdoche, for it embraces generally the whole worship of God'.[139] Calvin points to an *eliptica oratio*[140] and *hyperbolicae locutiones*.[141] He is careful to emphasise that the latter is not an ordinary poetical hyperbole, but the best way of stating plainly the depth of David's sorrow.[142] In a similar way, Luther explains a hyperbole in the same Psalm by showing that it is the best way of relating what is meant to something which human beings can understand. To show how love makes every delay seem too long, the Psalmist uses the word 'old'. Luther reminds the reader of the way 'we say in everyday language', 'My hair all but turned grey because of this.'[143] Calvin identifies an instance of a figure used to illustrate the judgements of God as clearly as possible in the vivid story of the Tower of Babel.[144] 'Generations' (Genesis 6.9) is emphatic, says Calvin, 'so as to stress the corruption of the age'.[145] There is amplification.[146] There is progression.[147] Luther describes a climax in terms which cover a number of examples of figures:

> This verse and many others are beautifully woven into a cord, the following one proceeds always from the one before, and the expression or utterance always seems to be the reason for what follows, and what precedes it, as it were the fountain and source of all that follows. It is as if you were fashioning a chain or a necklace or a garland.[148]

Calvin finds irony in Genesis,[149] Melanchthon antithesis in 1 Corinthians 1.21,[150] Calvin similitude in Jacob's ladder,[151] and in Jeremiah's figure of

139   Luther on Deuteronomy 21.1, *Works*, vol. 9, p. 214, *WA* 14.698–9.
140   *Calvin on the Psalms*, ed. A. Tholuck (Berlin, 1836), 2 vols., vol. 1, p. 33, on Psalm 6.4.
141   Genesis 11.4, *CR* 51.165.
142   Calvin on Psalm 6.8 (ed. Tholuck), p. 35.
143   Luther on Psalm 6.7, *Works*, vol. 10, p. 78, *WA* 3.70–1.
144   Calvin on Genesis 11.7, *CR* 51.166–7.
145   Calvin on Genesis 6.9, *CR* 51.120.
146   Calvin on Genesis 9.6, *CR* 51.146.
147   Luther on Psalm 1.1, *Works*, vol. 10, p. 11, *WA* 3.15.
148   Luther on Psalm 4.1, *Works*, vol. 10, pp. 51–2, *WA* 3.46.
149   Calvin on Genesis 3.22, *CR* 51.78.
150   Melanchthon's Early Exegesis, *Werke*, vol. 4, p. 21.24, on 1 Corinthians 1.21.
151   Calvin on Genesis 28.12, *CR* 51.391, cf. Calvin on Psalm 1.3 (ed. Tholuck), p. 3; Calvin on Genesis 15.3; Calvin on Psalm 1.2, p. 2.

Rachel grieving for her children a vivid way of referring to the future desolation of the land. He notes on this passage that 'rhetoricians set a high value on personification'. When Cicero wants to describe the greatest glory of oratory he says that nothing moves an audience more than to raise the dead from below. Although Jeremiah did not go to school with rhetoricians, he was taught this device by the Holy Spirit so that he might bring the point home harder to people's hearts.[152]

---

152 Calvin on Jer. 31.15–16; cf. on Matt. 2.18.

2. Authoritative testimony

i. THE WITNESS AND THE JUDGE

In the earliest days Jesus' followers proclaimed his message and recorded what eye-witnesses remembered of his life and teachings. The missionary work of the young Church consciously depended upon the witness of those who had known Jesus. There followed a period during which the New Testament books were written, making use of the testimony of the existing Jewish Scriptures, and the Canon came to be accepted as itself authentic witness within the community of the Church. Once the Canon was settled, Scripture's relationship to the Church was set on a new footing. The Church's task of witnessing now became one of stewardship of an existing Scripture. It is with the nature of that stewardship that the sixteenth-century debates in that area were primarily concerned.

It would be historically inaccurate to speak of *sola Scriptura* in any sense which implies that Scripture came into being independently of the Church. It is a product of the life of the early community,[1] and an act of witness by that community; its preservation and transmission continued to depend on that community after the Canon was fixed. This historical process was not yet clear to sixteenth-century scholars. We can see the *Liber Ratisbonensis* of 1541 trying to reconstruct in a historical way the process by which Scripture came to be written. First, it says, there was oral tradition, because God wanted the Gospel to be transmitted 'as it were from hand to hand' (*quasi per manus*). It is the inner action of the Word which opens hearts; 'God uses the external Word only as an instrument'. Later, God added a written text as a kindness (*beneficium*) and a help to human frailty and foolishness. This was so that there might be a fixed point of reference to prevent any sliding into error as a result of the Devil's deceits. For God knew that in time to come there would be

---

[1] That is to say, Scripture was the text which the Church, 'from within its own experience in the Holy Spirit of the apostolic, Gospel tradition, acknowledged as primary and authoritative' witness to the truth in 'the things concerning Jesus', The House of Bishops of the Church of England, *The Nature of Christian Belief* (London, 1986), pp. 5–6.

Satanic endeavours both to corrupt Scripture and to arrogate to Satan 'divine and apostolic authority'. Therefore God arranged for there to be a twofold authority (*duplex auctoritas*) in the Church. The first is the authority to discern canonical from non-canonical writings.[2] The second is the authority to interpret Scripture.[3] The loudest contentions of the sixteenth century arose here, over the question of the continuing task of the community once the written text of Scripture had come into being. There was an awareness that the Church had a responsibility as 'witness and keeper' (*testis et conservatrix*).[4]

The events described in Acts 15 show the young Church dealing, with common sense and charity, with the problem of disagreement about the application of Old Testament teaching about circumcision and about the relevance of other points of Jewish Law to the life of the new community. Again and again the problem of difference of opinion arose, making it apparent that private enterprise in the interpretation of Scripture by those who were unschooled, or willing to set their views over against the community, could lead to error; and that error persisted in heresies, obstinately held opinions which went against the judgement of the community. The Council of Ephesus in 431 gave a warning of the danger, and Leo the Great made the same point in a letter to Flavianus about the error of Eutyches in 449. It did not always prove possible to win in the short term the co-operative and receptive response described in Acts 15.31–2. It became necessary to try to legislate 'officially' on contested points of doctrine, as a means of achieving, in an emergency, at least a working settlement. We shall come in later chapters to what that meant in terms of conciliar and papal pronouncements. Our immediate concern is with its implications for the interpretation of Scripture 'authoritatively' by the Church.

At first the thrust of such endeavours, for practical reasons, was to deal *ad hoc* with problems as they arose, rather than to attempt to formulate the principles of an 'authorised' system of interpretation of Scripture. In the event, the study of the Bible in the Middle Ages developed along two main lines: the *lectio divina* of monastic life in the earlier Middle Ages, with the emphasis upon reflective readings of Scripture and of the

---

2   The question of the Apocrypha was first seriously tackled in our period when negotiations over the Coptic Christians made it necessary for the Council of Florence to attempt a ruling (1431–5).
3   *CR* 4.108–9.
4   Church of England, Thirty-Nine Articles, 20.

commentaries of the Fathers; and, in the schools which grew up from the late eleventh century, the more briskly paced glossing of the text by a Master in a series of lectures. By the end of the twelfth century there was a standard gloss, the *glossa ordinaria*, which brought together key passages from patristic commentators, supplemented where there were gaps by the work of more recent Masters of the Sacred Page. This provided a secure and orthodox basis for routine Bible study, which there was at first no need to make 'official'. The burgeoning academic world of the twelfth century and after threw up a few cases where individuals were 'tried' for their teaching (Peter Abelard; Gilbert of Poitiers; the condemnations of 1277, for example); but broadly speaking the *studium sacrae Scripturae* proceeded peaceably in the schools along lines already laid down by the Fathers, with nothing worse than scholarly squabbles.

The first serious disturbances of this pattern in the mediaeval period occurred as early as the late twelfth century, when Waldensian heretics, and also the Albigensian dualists, proved able to quote the Bible back smartly in answer to preachers sent by the Church authorities to win them to orthodoxy. The same articulate use of Scripture by dissenting lay-people was evident in the Lollard upheaval of the years before and after 1400.[5] The Council of Constance at the beginning of the fifteenth century, and the Fifth Lateran Council of 1512–17, found it necessary to speak of the right of the Church to settle matters of interpretation and to instruct preachers to be careful not to depart from the teaching of Scripture's actual words, or from the interpretations of the Fathers (Session XI). The Council of Trent puts it more strongly. No-one is to trust his own wisdom, or 'twist' Scripture to make it mean what he likes, against the interpretation placed on it by Holy Mother Church, to whom it belongs to judge (*cuius est iudicare*) the true sense and interpretation of Holy Scripture.[6]

The reformers of the sixteenth century, like their opponents, inherited the mediaeval understanding of Christian faith as an *obiectum* or *depositum*,[7] a fixed quantity. Wyclif assumes with the majority of

---

[5]   On Lollard Biblical scholarship, see Hudson, *The Premature Reformation*, pp. 228–76.

[6]   Trent IV, 1546, Decretum Secundum.

[7]   Denzinger 1507 (Trent), 3018, 3070 (1870), in H. Denzinger and A. Schönmetzer, *Enchiridion Symbolorum*, 23rd ed. (Rome/New York, 1965). But cf. Anselm of Canterbury, *Cur Deus Homo*, Prefatory letter to Pope Urban II, 'the rational basis of truth is so deep and so wide that it cannot be exhausted by mortals. The Lord does not cease to impart the gifts of his grace within his Church' (*Opera Omnia*, ed. F. S. Schmitt (Rome/Edinburgh, 1938–68), II.40).

mediaeval scholars that one and the same truth is taught by Christ and the apostles, by the Fathers and by General Councils, and that it is not only *recta* and *eadem* but also complete.[8] It still seemed to Nowell in his *Catechism* of 1570 that 'it were a point of untolerable ungodliness and madness to think, either that God had left an imperfect doctrine, or that men were able to make that perfect, which God left imperfect',[9] and to Whitgift that 'there is but one Truth, and that is certain'.[10] This identity and permanence and fullness of the faith in all ages is constitutive for the unity of the Church, it is argued in the correspondence surrounding the abortive Colloquy of Ratisbon in 1541. 'The unity of the Church consists in this association (*consociatio*) under one Head through the same Gospel and the same ministry ... So that there should be one consenting Church, God has always passed on the same Gospel through the fathers and prophets and afterwards through Christ and the apostles, and Christ instituted its ministry to endure until the end of the world.'[11]

We find a similar reaching after what is solid and fixed, in the Lutheran Formula of Concord of 1577:

> The primary requirement for basic and permanent concord within the Church is a summary formula and pattern, unanimously approved, in which the summarized doctrine commonly confessed by the churches of the pure Christian religion is drawn together out of the Word of God. For this same purpose the ancient Church always had its dependable symbols. It based these not on mere private writings, but on such books, as had been written, approved and accepted in the name of those churches which confessed the same doctrine and religion. In the same way we have from our hearts and with our mouths declared in mutual agreement that we shall neither prepare nor accept a different or new confession of our faith. Rather, we pledge ourselves again to those public and well-known symbols or common confessions which have at all times and in all places been accepted in all the churches of the Augsburg Confession before the outbreak of the several con-

---

8 *De Ecclesia*, p. 112.
9 *Catechism*, p. 115.
10 John Whitgift, *The Defence of theAnswer to the Admonition against the Reply of Thomas Cartwright*, ed. J. Ayre (Parker Society, Cambridge, 1851), p. 44.
11 *CR* 4.367–8, cf. S. Sykes (ed.), *Authority in the Anglican Communion* (Toronto, 1987), p. 72.

which were kept and used during that period when people were
everywhere and unanimously faithful to the pure doctrine of the Word
of God as Dr Luther of blessed memory had explained it.[12]

There is a great deal here beside a concern to hold fast to a truth given once
and for all, but the central idea is of a 'maintaining' in this comparatively
limited sense of preserving a fixed quantity. Over against this must be set
the contention that the apostles 'clearly wanted to leave something to
their successors, so as not to clip their wings', as the Paris theologians put
it in 1544.[13] Scripture says that the disciples were promised that the Holy
Spirit would lead them into all truth, that there was more to be revealed.[14]

When the protestant reformers called for *sola Scriptura*, a return to
primitive truth, Gospel simplicity and the early vision of the apostolic
community, they were in large part expressing disenchantment with
the Christian scholarship of recent mediaeval centuries. They shared a
conviction that the official pronouncements of the Church had gone too
far, in adding to Scripture, in imposing unnecessary rituals upon the
faithful, and above all in claiming that these were necessary for salvation.
But the call for 'Scripture alone' did not seem to all the reformers to
necessitate refusing help from earlier Christian scholars. Many of them
found a place for patristic researches, especially the reading of Greek
Fathers who, with the exceptions of Origen and Chrysostom, had been
comparatively unfamiliar or inaccessible during the later Middle Ages in the
Latin West. Nor did 'Scripture alone' mean that the preacher simply read the
Scriptures to his hearers. He expounded the text, and thus the 'preaching of
the Gospel' necessarily contained an element of interpretation.

The debate as to whether Scripture alone contains all that is necessary
to salvation had a long mediaeval pedigree, but with a rather different
emphasis. Aquinas' first and central question in the *Summa Theologiae*
is whether the study of *sacra doctrina* through Scripture is 'necessary
to salvation'.[15] He answers in terms influenced by his knowledge of
Aristotelian teleology and by mediaeval ideas of order, but which can be
translated readily enough into notions which can be found in every
Christian century. Man is made for God, in the order of things (*ordinatur*

---

12   Formula of Concord, Solid Declaration, Summary Formulation, Tappert, p. 503.
13   Paris Articles, *CR* 35.32–3.
14   E.g. John 14.25; 20.30; cf. *Acta CT* 5.14ff.
15   *ST* I q.1.a.1.

ad Deum, sicut ad quemdam finem).[16] But God exceeds the grasp of reason. Therefore it is necessary, if man is to fulfil the purpose for which he was made, that God should make certain things known to him by revelation, which his reason would not otherwise be able to discover:

> *unde necessarium fuit homini ad salutem quo ei nota fierent quaedam per revelationem divinam, quae rationem humanam excedunt.*[17]

Aquinas does not spell out the connection between being saved and realising the purpose of one's creation; it is built into the assumptions on which he proceeds. But he does underline for us an emphasis upon the saving power of the Word which has a particular thrust. The Word saves by making known to the mind of man the end for which he was created; it brings man to God through the knowledge of the truth. *Tota hominis salus,* he says, depends (*dependet*) on the knowledge of the truth (*a veritatis cognitione*).[18]

Aquinas' concern is not primarily with the Church's role in the Word's ministry. He takes that for granted. But sixteenth-century preoccupations are specifically with this aspect of the idea that Scripture contains all that is necessary for salvation. Calvin says plainly that nothing is necessary to salvation which is not in Scripture.[19] The 1552/3 version of the Church of England's Articles, like those of 1571, says that the Church may add nothing to Scripture as 'necessary to salvation'. On the other side, the theologians of Paris in 1544 insist that 'it is certain that many things must be believed which are not expressly and individually handed down (*tradita*) in the Holy Scriptures. We must accept as certain what is drawn out (*elicitum*) by the finely tuned reasoning of learned men from the text of Scripture.'[20] Taking a balanced position between the two extremes, the Church of England's Thirty-Nine Articles say that what is implicit in Scripture carries the same authority as what is explicitly stated there.[21]

Two anxieties were consistently expressed by protestant reformers: that the Church might abuse its authority by seeking to override or manipulate the

---

16 *Ibid.*
17 *Ibid.*
18 *Ibid.*
19 Paris Articles 20, 1544; *Antidote, CR* 35.32–3.
20 *Antidote* to Art. 20, *ibid.*
21 Article 6: 'Whatever is read there, or can be proved from Scripture' (cf. E. Cardwell (ed.), *Synodalia* (Oxford, 1842), I, pp. 3–4 on the version of 1552).

teaching of Scripture; and that it might attempt to limit the freedom of the individual Christian to make his or her own direct response to the text.

There was some warrant for the first anxiety. The Paris theologians of 1544 state baldly, 'Whatever our Masters lack by way of Scriptural witness, they compensate for by other authority which they have ... which is equal to that of Scripture, or even, according to learned men, exceeds it in certainty'.[22] They were willing to describe Scripture as 'a nose of wax', mere raw material (*rudis materia*) to be shaped by theologians in formulating statements of doctrine. Calvin comments that this is a 'saying common among them'.[23] This concept of a relationship of master and servant between Church and Scripture[24] was so entrenched in the sixteenth century that it naturally presented itself as the leading idea when Melanchthon discussed the Church's teaching authority in the preface he wrote to the *Acta* of the Colloquy of Ratisbon in 1541. The Ratisbon article on the *potestas* of interpreting Scripture has, he explains, three prongs. It places in the Church a 'power of interpreting' envisaged on a human model (*humano more*), that is, on an analogy with a magistrate's authority to interpret the law. It does not allow that individuals or a minority can correct the judgement of the majority, nor dissent from their view. It asserts that the decrees of Councils must be obeyed.[25] Melanchthon makes a similar point in Article 28 of the Augsburg Confession, where his objection is to the transference of a political frame of reference to the Church; he speaks of 'profane men, who dream that Christian righteousness is nothing else than civil or political righteousness'.[26] In a kingdom there is power to interpret law, kingly or residing in a magistrate. That authority must be obeyed. A magistrate's rules and opinions are valid as reasonable judgements of one to whom God has entrusted an office.[27] In the Church things are very different. 'Let us set aside that image of a human polity.' There is a huge gap (*ingens intervallum*) between the magistrate's power and the gift of

---

[22] *CR* 35.5, and cf. 31–2, Article 19.
[23] *CR* 35.31–2, *Antidote* to Paris Articles, and see Luther, *On the Papacy in Rome*, 1520, *WA* 6.280ff. The 'nose of wax' conceit goes back at least to the late twelfth century.
[24] Firmly reversed in recent ecumenical texts, e.g. L–RC Malta (21), *Growth*, p. 173.
[25] *CR* 4.670.
[26] Article 28.18.
[27] *CR* 4.640.

divine light by which Christian people see the truth.[28] It is of some importance that Melanchthon identifies the authority of the ministry of oversight here with this falsely conceived 'magistrate's power' and opposes it to the active involvement of all the faithful in interpretation of Scripture and *a fortiori*, in decision-making about doctrine; the point is covered in much the same terms in a disputation of 1539.[29]

In response, the Roman Catholic authorities accused the reformers of granting licence to every individual to use his private judgement independently of that of the community, and to make his personal interpretation of Scripture his warrant for any opinion he cared to hold. Each side saw the other as misrepresenting the relationship between the revealed Word of God and human judgement. In *The Protestants Theologie*, published at the beginning of the seventeenth century, the English recusant William Paterson sees the problem in exactly these terms. Using the format of a disputation, he argues against the 'objection' that Scripture itself tells us to search the Scriptures. The Protestants say, he explains, that this means 'the certaine way to compose controversies of religion, is by the searching of the Scriptures, not by decision, and sentence of counsell'. But his own view is that 'the Scripture beareth the place of a witness and not of a judge'.[30] 'It is not the office of a witness to give sentence: but only to give testimony.' 'It is the judge's part to hear, search and examine the witness, and so all things heard and pondered, he giveth sentence.'

The concept of a 'witness' is limited here by the forensic context in which Paterson envisages the process; but with a rather broader metaphorical signification, *testimonium* had been used in the Latin West from classical and patristic times, in connection with *auctoritas*, to signify a text which constituted proof. The forensic context so congenial to the late Roman world is a major reason why it continued to be natural to make use of 'testimonies' after the period when there were still eye-witnesses, and when the Canon was complete. Their character changed; they could no longer be evidence in the same ways, because they rested neither on the case from 'prophecy fulfilled', nor on the direct experience of persons who had seen for themselves. They could, however, be held to have a certain reliability for other reasons. Although the distinction is not always perfectly clear, these were principally two: that they came

28 *CR* 4.670.
29 *WA* 39[ii].52ff.
30 Cf. the *testis* of the Anglican Thirty-Nine Articles.

from a respected individual; or that they had been given some official sanction by the Church. Into the first category fall the writings of the Fathers, for example; into the second the decrees of Councils, or enactments of canon law. In sixteenth-century citation of, say, Gregory the Great or Innocent III, some personal authoritativeness seems to be attributed, as well as the 'institutional' authoritativeness of a papal pronouncement.

In the Ratisbon discussion of 1541 it was suggested that among the authorities given by God to the Church is the *auctoritas constituendi judicia de doctrina*, the authority of establishing judgement in matters of doctrine.[31] In 1546 in the course of the Trent debates on justification, one speaker suggested that traditions are mutable precisely in that they may be deleted by the Church or altered according to its judgement, *pro eius arbitrio*.[32] Luther states in one of his theses of 1542[33] that judgement in the interpretation of Scripture is a gift to the Church. There seems to be no doubt that Paterson was right in drawing attention to the idea of 'judgement' as of central importance to both sides.

Like Paterson, other thinkers naturally associated 'judgement' with the legal world. The longstanding linking of the notion of *iudicium* with a legally constituted higher authority is noted by Wyclif. It is, he says, unacceptable to most people that ordinary people should judge (*populus iudicare*), and especially that they should be judges of their clergy.[34] There is a further association here which it is important to be aware of: an assumption that judgement is properly exercised over legal subordinates. By implication, if Scripture is judged by the Church, Scripture is a subordinate of the Church in authority. This was one of the habits of thought Luther and others sought to change. The power of interpreting Scripture (*potestas interpretandae Scripturae*) is not, he argues, a royal or praetorian power (*potestas ... regia aut praetoria*).[35] What Thomas More calls the *Ecclesiae iudicium in fidei causa*, the judgement of the Church in the *causa* or 'court-case' about faith,[36] involves for Luther judgement by the congregation. He argues from 1 Thessalonians 5.21

31   Martin Bucer, *Acta Ratisbonensis* (Strasbourg, 1541), p. 29ᵛ.
32   *Acta CT* 5.39, 27 March 1546.
33   *WA* 39ⁱⁱ.147, Thesis 8.
34   *Opera Minora*, p. 314.12–13.
35   *WA* 39ⁱⁱ.147, Thesis 8.
36   More, *Responsio ad Lutherum*, ed. J. M. Headley, *Complete Works*, vol. 5 (London/Yale, 1969), p. 216.17–19.

that Paul did not want to see any teaching or decree obeyed unless it is examined and recognised as good by the congregation which hears it. 'Test everything but hold fast to that which is good.' This testing is not the teacher's task; the teacher may only state what is to be examined. Judgement is given to the Christian people.[37] He sees Christ as positively taking the right and power to judge teaching from bishops, scholars and Councils, and giving it to all Christians equally (John 10.4: 'My sheep know my voice').[38] The same linking of judgement and 'imposition' is noticeable in Thomas Rogers' account. He argues that the 'Papists' maintain that 'the pope of Rome hath the power to judge all men and matters, but may be judged of no man',[39] that judgement goes with orders, 'the power to judge of religion and points of doctrine is either in bishops only ... or in their clergy only ...'.[40] He himself contends, as Luther does, that 'authority is given to the Church, and to every member of sound judgement in the same, to judge in controversies of faith'.[41]

It will be clear that two senses of the word 'judgement' are being used here, one having forensic connotations and implying imposition by a higher and legally constituted authority; and the other closer to *sensus* or *opinio*: a testing and deciding where the truth lies, settling upon a viewpoint which seems good and embracing it. It is in this latter sense of the term 'judgement' that Luther interprets Paul's words in 1 Thessalonians. This latter sense is not far from what we should now call 'reception'. It is both judgement and response, an active welcoming and not mere acquiescence to orders.

It will also be clear that this distinction corresponds loosely with a division in mediaeval practice which took it that the authority to make judgements in matters of faith lay with the academic community (who did the spadework), and the bishops and Pope (who made authoritative pronouncements), and consisted in the formulation of doctrinal statements on points needing elucidation or a ruling. The communication of the finer points of doctrine to the mass of the faithful was not attempted.[42] Such

37 Luther, *That a Christian Assembly or Congregation has the right and power to judge all teaching*, WA 11.408ff.
38 *Ibid.*
39 Thomas Rogers, *An Exposition of the Thirty-Nine Articles*, ed. J. J. S. Perowne (Parker Society, Cambridge, 1844) p. 191.
40 *Ibid.*, p. 192.
41 *Ibid.*, p. 190.
42 But on Wycliffite education, see Hudson, *The Premature Reformation*, pp. 174–226.

sermons as came their way were predominantly concerned with right Christian living, questions of morals rather than faith, and with the implementation of the system of selling indulgences – with the result that popular piety was perhaps characteristically affective rather than intellectual. The reformers set out to reach the faithful directly, and to communicate to them forcefully and simply the good news of their salvation. They understood their teaching responsibilities as ministers of the Word to lie in bringing Scripture to ordinary people, rather as Margery Kemp's local priest in fifteenth-century Norfolk used to read the Bible with her. But in so doing they were also countenancing judgement by the *consensus* of all the faithful.

This direct appeal to common judgement remained controversial in conservative circles. There was a longstanding notion that it was unsafe to let uneducated people have direct access to the Scriptures in a language they could understand.[43] Elsewhere in the Trent debates it was argued that such free access, without guidance from a responsible, trained and licensed person, was precisely what had led to such heresies as those of the Waldensians and Albigensians in the past.[44]

The problems of reaching agreement on all this in the sixteenth century were compounded by the growing combativeness of the situation. In any case there could be in the divided Church no universally agreed procedure for reconciling contradictory interpretations. The particular difficulties thus added to what was already a profoundly complex question must wait for our concluding chapters. But we can find a place here to look at the 'personal' authoritativeness of individual authors as sixteenth-century perceptions shifted.

ii. 'STILL HE WAS ONLY A MAN': ATTITUDES TO AUTHORITIES

Erasmus wrote to a friend at Court, Johan Poppenruyter, in 1501, to give him advice on the practices he should cultivate if he wanted to take the Christian life seriously. 'Read Scripture', he says, and take the holy

---

[43] Although one of the Trent theologians points out that Greek and Hebrew and Latin were vernaculars when they were used as vehicles for Scripture, and that a case can certainly be made for translating the Bible into contemporary vernaculars on that ground, *Acta CT* 12.534.

[44] *Acta CT* 12.511, Spring 1546.

prophets and Christ himself for your companions. In your daily life associate with those who seem like him. Otherwise withdraw from human intercourse as far as you can. 'Above all, make Paul your special friend; him you should keep always in your pocket.' His words should be referred to constantly and eventually learned by heart.[45] Erasmus' strong sense of Paul as an individual was shared by others. Calvin can be found discussing Paul's purpose in putting a point in a particular way.[46] Theodore Beza later in the century made notes on Galatians designed to elucidate the views of the Apostle and to bring the reader to an understanding of the real Paul.[47] It is hard to point to anything quite like this in earlier Bible study, anything so immediate and unaffected and personal. Erasmus already felt that he could talk to Paul man to man.

This fresh view of what we may call the human face of Scripture[48] is part of a movement which challenged a number of old assumptions about authors and *auctoritas* and encouraged readers to assess the words of those they read with a new boldness and, in the case of secular authors and the Fathers, even with confidence in their own potential equality as authors. We need to glance at this context here, as a setting in which to look at the wider question of the place of the Church as Scripture's 'witness and judge'.

In a thirteenth-century treatise on grammatical theory Simon of Dacia ventures a criticism of Priscian. Priscian agrees with the Stoics that 'voice' (*vox*, a sound capable of signifying) is 'air'. 'But voice is not air, with all due respect to Priscian.' 'If we want to excuse Priscian' we must understand him to say that voice is uttered or comes into being in the air.[49] Simon disagrees with this standard authority politely and reluctantly and is anxious if possible to save his face. In the fifteenth century a few influential individuals began to be more robust in their criticism. 'These Greeks whom Priscian is following are wrong', says Lorenzo Valla roundly.[50] He faults Porphyry for giving only half a definition.[51]

---

45 Erasmus, *Letters*, Letter 165, 1.53–4.
46 Calvin on Genesis 21.12, *CR* 51.302.
47 *Epistolam D. Pauli Apostoli ad Galatas notae ... a Theodoro Beza editae* (Geneva, 1578), pp. 12, 70.
48 *Language and Logic* II, pp. 15ff. on the human authors of Scripture.
49 Simon of Dacia, *Opera*, ed. A. Otto, *Corpus Philosophicorum Danicorum Medii Aevi*, 3 (Copenhagen, 1963), p. 5.18–28.
50 Valla, *Dialecticae Disputationes* (Cologne, 1531), p. 26.
51 *Repastinatio* I.xx.4, p. 164.16–26.

This sort of talk represents a departure from the tradition that we men of later days are but dwarfs sitting on the shoulders of the intellectual giants of old.[52] Mediaeval masters were ready enough to disagree with their contemporaries,[53] but it is comparatively rare for anyone to call an ancient author a fool. Valla's comments on the Greeks, and on Priscian and Porphyry, are made as upon his equals, or at any rate, as upon fellow mortals capable of human error and inadequacy exactly as more recent scholars were. Rudolph Agricola argues along similar lines that 'Aristotle was a man of supreme intelligence, learning, eloquence, knowledge and wisdom, but still he was only a man.'[54] Erasmus felt free to note that 'in some places slips have been made by Hilary, by Augustine, by Thomas [Aquinas]'. He sees them as 'very great men, but only men after all'.[55] He points to mistakes in Nicholas of Lyre or Hugh of St Cher just as impartially, 'to encourage caution in those who read such writers with complete confidence and no critical sense'.[56] This new readiness to consider authorities on their merits extended not only to ancient authors, but also to standard works of the mediaeval universities such as these; and not only to secular but to Christian authors,[57] and even to the human authors of Scripture. It was nothing new to make use of the same methods of study for the Bible and secular authors. The staple method of instruction in the schools of the Middle Ages and the sixteenth century alike was the reading ('lecture') of a text with a running commentary. The lecturer might point out features of the style ('This smacks of irony'; 'note the figure of speech'),[58] or explain the argument or deal with an anomaly in the grammar. Or he might discuss the content, bringing in a considerable baggage of opinions from other commentators. Each text was approached with an *accessus* to set it in context in its field of study, to explain who the author was and why he wrote it.[59] Such text-based teaching included

---

52   On dwarfs and giants, see my *Old Arts and New Theology* (Oxford, 1980), p. v.
53   On mutual criticism by contemporary masters, see *ibid.*, pp. 8ff.
54   Agricola, *De Inventione Dialectica Lucubrationes*, I.iii, p. 15.
55   Erasmus, *Letters*, Letter 456 to Henry Bullock, 4.48, 1516.
56   *Ibid.*
57   On Nicholas of Lyre and Hugh of St Cher, see H. A. Oberman, *Forerunners of the Reformation* (London, 1967), p. 286, and B. Smalley, 'The Gospels in the Paris Schools in the late Twelfth and early Thirteenth Centuries', *Franciscan Studies*, 28, 29 (1979, 1980), 230–55 and 298–369.
58   Latomus' commentary on Cicero, *Orationes*.
59   The most recent study is A. J. Minnis' excellent *Mediaeval Theory of*

impartially both the textbooks of the liberal arts and the text of Scripture – impartially, that is, in the assumption that all alike could be taught by similar means. We find Luther discussing Paul's *intentio* in writing to the Galatians,[60] Calvin explaining who the Galatians were, where they lived and how it came about that Paul had to write to them as he did,[61] in *accessus* or prefaces, just as any lecturer would have done for any text. Fisher, Bishop of Rochester, wrote a Psalm commentary for Margaret, Countess of Richmond and Derby and mother of Henry VII of England: 'But or we go to the declaracyon of this psalme, it shall be profitable and convenyent to shewe who ddyde wryte this psalme, for what occasion he wrote it, and what fruyte, profyte and helpe he obteyned by the same.'[62]

But now, like Scripture, both Fathers and secular authors were being approached afresh. Praise or blame are apportioned in ways which show that the commentator thinks his own judgement worthy to stand comparison with that of his cited authority. 'The exposition of Augustine is forced', comments Calvin on one passage; in another passage, 'the subtle reasoning of Augustine ... is too constrained'.[63] Luther can be rude and arrogant: 'Jerome exerts himself mightily here';[64] 'Here Jerome plays around with the mystery of the fifteen days.'[65]

One of the factors in bringing about this gradual change in the old patterns of respect for authority seems to have been wider reading. Aristotle had come to be called 'The Philosopher' *tout court* in the thirteenth century. But Valla gives a catalogue of philosophers and schools of philosophy with the intention of putting Aristotle in his place. He makes a good deal of the limitations of Aristotle.[66] We see in the case of the study of grammar, logic and rhetoric how the rediscovery of lost works of classical and post-classical authors altered the balance of the syllabus and encouraged teachers and scholars to think afresh about the

---

Authorship (London, 1984). See pp. 15–39 on the types of academic prologue and pp. 40ff. on how these were adapted for Scriptural *auctores*.
60 Luther on Galatians, *Works*, vol. 27, pp. 327-8; *WA* 2.561.
61 Calvin on Galatians, T. H. L. Parker, *Calvin* (London, 1975), p. 4.
62 *The English Works of John Fisher*, ed. J. E. B. Mayor (London, 1876), pp. 2.32 – 3.2.
63 *CR* 51.317.
64 Luther on Galatians 1.15–18, *WA* 40.135–6.
65 *Ibid.*, *WA* 40.148.
66 Valla, *Dialecticae Disputationes*, pp. 2–3. Aquinas normally refers to Aristotle as Philosophus.

content and purpose of their teaching and to reassess the doctrine of the standard authors of the mediaeval universities.

A deeper and more elusive reason was the new radicalism which sought to cut through irrelevant complications to essentials. It is the great fault of scholastic method that it makes it difficult to see the wood for the trees. The technique of *divisio* which listed all possible aspects of a problem failed to provide machinery for subordinating the less important and bringing out what really matters. In *summa* and *quodlibet* and *disputatio* the views of the authorities are imported piecemeal in support, often, of contradictory positions, and almost always with the assumption that they can be satisfactorily deployed like this without reference to the context from which they came. All this began to seem unsatisfactory. Wolfgang Capito writes to Erasmus in 1516 that he has 'grown tired of Lyra and Hugh of St Cher and other commentators of that kidney', thanks to Erasmus, 'having been encouraged' by his work 'to expect more wholesome fare'.[67] Luther, considering Nicholas of Lyre's discussion of the views which have been variously advanced about the rib taken from Adam to make Eve, dismisses the debate with impatience. There is much concern about the source of the remaining substance of Eve, since one rib could not make a woman. 'Why is it necessary to discuss where God found the remaining material?' asks Luther. God is able to do anything by a single word and he creates all things.[68] 'Let's blow up the tropes and glosses of men and simply accept the words of God!' he exclaims elsewhere.[69]

One response was to explore beyond the scissors-and-paste method of using authorities, with its attendant risk of being led into preoccupation with irrelevant or absurd minutiae, and to read the books of standard authors as a whole, as we have seen Chemnitz and Cranmer doing. That was in itself a major new departure. As early as Carolingian times it had been customary to work with an *Expositor*,[70] a ready-made collection of extracts, and the tradition was greatly strengthened from the twelfth century by the development of the *Glossa Ordinaria* and the publication of Peter Lombard's *Sentences*. The Gloss gave extracts keyed to the text of the Bible bit by bit. The *Sentences* arranged extracts under the topic

---

[67]   Erasmus, *Letters*, Letter 459, 4.61, September 1516.
[68]   Luther on Genesis 2. 21, *WA* 42.97–8.
[69]   Luther, *De Servo Arbitrio*, p. 207.3; *WA* 18.712.
[70]   On the *Expositor*, see B. Smalley, *The Study of the Bible in the Middle Ages* (3rd ed., Oxford, 1983), p. 63.

headings of systematic theology. Melanchthon seems to have been sent back to the Fathers by the demands of contemporary controversy.[71] He proceeded as his predecessors for centuries had done by collecting extracts, for example on *Hoc est corpus meum*.[72] In a similar way, Thomas Cranmer collected quotations from his reading to help him in writing on topics of current controversy.[73] The difference was that both worked at least some of the time from complete texts and that they were able to read their authorities' opinions in context and as a whole.

Standing back and considering what the authors were saying as a whole and in its larger context, using common sense and a sense of proportion to determine what mattered and what was less important and above all, reading earlier work as one might read the work of one's colleagues, the new generation of scholars were ready to be selective and innovative. But they retained a sense that there had, for classical authors as for the early Church, been a special period when definitive standards of language and teaching were established.

---

[71] P. Fraenkel, *'Testimonia Patrum*: the function of the patristic argument in the theology of Philip Melanchthon', *Travaux d'humanisme et renaissance*, 46 (Geneva, 1961), pp. 46–8.

[72] *Ibid.*, pp. 22–3.

[73] Cf. Cranmer, *A Confutation of Unwritten Verities* and *A Collection of Tenets from Canon Law*, both in *Miscellaneous Writings*.

3. Authoritative proof

i. FORMAL REASONING

Testimony from 'authorities' other than Scripture was used by Protestants in the sixteenth century with restraint, by Roman Catholics much as it had been throughout the Middle Ages. Protestants who employed it at all drew principally on the Fathers, especially Augustine, in a deliberate attempt to cut out what they deemed a millennium or so of corruption in the Church's life. But both alike found themselves needing to use authorities in a context of more or less formal argumentation as a means of proving theological truths, because 'authorities' and 'reasons' had always gone hand in hand here.

It seemed to Luther and others that formal logic had in recent generations created a scholastic obfuscation of plain Scriptural teaching, so that 'reason' could be seen as confronting Scripture not harmonising with it; and furthermore, the institutional Church was seen as supporting a professional class of academic theologians in their claim to an authority which overrode that of Scripture.[1] As early as 1516 Luther was mocking 'the subtlety of the philosophers' who entertain themselves with proving that what is true is also false.[2] In a similar spirit Melanchthon laughs at attempts to make a difference between *Papam vidi* and *vidi Papam*, and the seriousness about these logical squabbles which calls anyone who disputes that *ego currit* is bad Latin not a poor grammarian but a 'heretic'.[3] 'Scholastic', 'school' and their cognates are frequently a term of abuse among humanists and reformers. 'Their definition contains nothing but some trite dogma of the schools', says Calvin dismissively.[4]

Two points of importance need to be borne in mind in reading these and a host of other comments of a similar sort, if they are not to give a false impression of Luther's and others' attitude to the use of formal reasoning in drawing out the implications of the words of Scripture. First, these

---

[1] Cf. the Paris theologians of 1544, *CR* 35.5.
[2] On the *Sentences* I Dist. 23.4, *WA* 9.47.
[3] *Encomium Eloquentiae, CR* 11.63.
[4] *Antidote* to Trent, *CR* 35.442.

reformers make them as critics who understand very well that there are deep and serious linguistic and philosophical principles at issue in such games-playing with language and truth. Luther and Melanchthon could follow the ramifications of the argument which proves truth false, and they were familiar with *Papam vidi* and *ego currit* and a multitude of other standard examples and debating-points. Secondly, we find references to instances of this sort of thing at the end of Luther's life as well as at the beginning of his career. These are evidences of the durability of the detailed texture of mediaeval logic teaching. The continuing familiarity with a substantially continuous tradition needs to be emphasised because educationalists were loud in their discussions of the need for change, and it is easy to come away with the impression that there was a thoroughgoing revolution in the study of logic in the first half of the sixteenth century. Change there certainly was, but its effects were slower to spread than at first appears.

The objection Luther and Melanchthon, and to a lesser extent Calvin, were making was primarily to the misuse and especially the trivialisation of the arts of argument. Their value when properly used is not really in question. As we shall see, Luther pressed hard in his middle years for the reintroduction of regular disputations in his own university, when they had begun to be neglected in the excitement of syllabus revision and reform.

There were two main areas of reforming disquiet about wrong use of skills of argumentation. The first is a point of substance, methodologically speaking. Luther stresses the limitations logic must always have in the service of theology. Logic does not hold for divine truths in exactly the way it does for things in the created world, any more than the rules of grammar can always be applied straightforwardly to the analysis of theological language. No syllogistic form holds for talking about God, unless allowance is made for the uniqueness of the subject-matter.[5] It is for reasons of this sort, Luther suggests, that uncritical study of Aristotle does not make for good theology.[6]

Secondly, Luther calls for the application of common sense, seriousness and a sense of proportion in the framing of questions. He says in the Heidelberg Disputation of 1518 that he has set out his *conclusiones* so as to show how far the scholastics have strayed, and how they have fallen into the habit of asking certain questions without considering how unhelpful they may be. What use is it always to ask (in imitation of

5   Luther, *Contra Scholasticam Theologiam*, Thesis 47, WA 1.226.
6   *Ibid.*, 46–9; 41–5; 50–3. Cf. WA 39ii.7–10 (1539) for one of many later examples.

Aristotle) about matter, form, movement and purpose, he enquires? These questions are not always relevant, yet we find scholastics constantly asking them.[7] He points in the *Contra Scholasticam Theologiam* to particularly 'vain' conclusions drawn by contemporary scholastics as a result of approaching problems in this way.[8] At the time of the Ratisbon Colloquy in 1541, Melanchthon is making the same sort of complaint about triviality. Writing on transubstantiation, he remarks on the way in which 'an infinity of useless questions' are generated, 'about mice gnawing the consecrated bread and suchlike, which are unworthy of the gravity of the Church'. Here, he was certainly aware of the long mediaeval history of the mouse question.[9] Similar criticisms were made by others. Martin Bucer talks about 'obsolete' procedures, sophistries and 'Aristotelian trivialities' (*Aristotelicae nugae*) in 1518; Thomas More talks of *questiunculae*; Melanchthon (in 1544) of the importance of keeping to what is clear, necessary and explicit in argument; the problem of trivialisation is still irking Gisbert Voetius (1589–1676) in the seventeenth century.[10]

What was being asked for, then (and it clearly needed to be fought for continuously as time went on), was a radical rethinking of the application and relevance of the late mediaeval logical tradition, not a wholesale rejection of all it had to offer. 'Scholastic' was not universally a term of abuse in the sixteenth century. It could be used quite neutrally to describe a particular approach and method. The phrase *more scholastico* occurs in this way in the debates of the Council of Trent. 'In the discussion of the question, to conduct it in a scholastic manner (*ut more scholastico agamus*), we offer five propositions.'[11] 'I shall frame certain arguments first in the scholastic way.'[12] Here the reference is simply to a formal method of disputation. Syllogisms certainly still came naturally.

---

7   Luther, Heidelberg Disputation, *WA* 1.355.
8   *Contra Scholasticam Theologiam*, Theses 31, 32, *WA* 1.225.
9   *CR* 4.276.
10   *Correspondance de M. Bucer*, p. 60, to Rhenanus, May 1518; Gisbert Voetius, in Beardslee, *Reformed Dogmatics*, pp. 276ff. See *WA* 39ii.318, for Melanchthon's contribution to the degree disputation of Major and Faber, 1544; B. Gogan, *The Common Corps of Christendom* (Leiden, 1982), p. 65. On the question of early manifestations of 'anti-scholasticism', it is interesting to compare Wycliffite contrasting of 'our English bookys' and 'their doctouris'. See Hudson, *The Premature Reformation*, p. 275.
11   *Acta CT* 12.473, Johannes Calvus, Feb., Mar. 1546.
12   *Acta CT* 13.392.

Everywhere debates proceed by putting the arguments into syllogisms and examining the syllogisms for flaws. Luther easily spots a deficiency in the construction of one of Melanchthon's syllogisms. Melanchthon had argued that 'whatever is against Gospel freedom is eternally accursed. Taking religious vows comes under that heading. Therefore ...'. That will not do, says Luther. Many are free in the service of a vow.[13] Much more than competence in syllogistic proved to be of continuing relevance[14] in theological argument and the heritage of argumentational skills which survived from late mediaeval scholasticism probably outweighed what was discarded.

The interplay of reasoning and authority became very complex in actual use in the academic disputations which formed the backbone of the Reformation controversies. In debate a premiss is proposed, and if it is not itself a quotation from an authoritative text or self-evidently true, it will be supported either by a further argument (reasoning) or by a quoted text (authority). Two premisses thus guaranteed and put together in a syllogism of valid form should produce a conclusion whose truth can be relied upon. But again and again we see the respondent pointing out a flaw in the way a supporting text is being understood, a misreading of the signification of a word or of the whole. The simple scheme breaks down at this point because in practice it proved impossible to use the quoted text as though it were merely an object of the right thickness to prop up one of the legs of a table so as to achieve a level surface. Sometimes it gave way at the point where weight was being placed upon it in the argument in question. Reasoning necessarily infiltrates the process of reading the authority; judgement is exercised upon the witness before it is allowed to speak in the argument at all. So an intimate interdependence of reasoning and authority, judgement and witness was a reality familiar to both sides.

Between Peter of Spain (d. 1277) and Paul of Venice (d. 1429), mediaeval logic reached a peak of refinement and systematisation, as well as of sophistication. In a number of areas not covered, or incompletely covered by Aristotle, there was original work: notably in the analysis of meaning and reference in connection with supposition theory; in the exploration of forms of inference in the theory of 'consequences', and in

13 Letter of Luther to Melanchthon, p. 65.15–17, and 35–8, *WA* 2.382. Cf. Coverdale, *Remains*, pp. 369ff.
14 Into that complex of ideas about laws of thought and the mind's openness to reason, Hooker later draws other contemporary preoccupations: the notions of 'judgement' and 'knowledge' and 'discretion' (*Laws*, Preface III).

the allied field of *insolubilia* or logical paradoxes. In this work William of Ockham (*c*.1280–1349), John Buridan (d. after 1358), Walter Burley (d. 1344–5) and their followers and pupils (Albert of Saxony, d. 1390; Marsilius of Inghen, d. 1396) were particularly important. Peter of Spain's *Summulae* remained the standard introductory textbook in most university courses throughout this period and beyond.[15] But by the end of the fifteenth century, in some of the schools at least, in the teaching of logic – though not its use in formal disputations – the sophistication of the later Middle Ages was beginning to give way to a readiness to take short cuts, and claims that the old courses contained a good deal of dead wood.

[15] The corpus of study of the Old Logic (Aristotle's *Categories* and *De Interpretatione* with Cicero's *Topics* and Boethius' commentaries and monographs, and sometimes Marius Victorinus and Apuleius' *Perihermeneias*), which formed the staple of teaching in the earlier Middle Ages, was enlarged in the twelfth century by the arrival of the remainder of Aristotle's logical works in the West. To this New Logic (the *Prior* and *Posterior Analytics*, the *Topics* and the *Sophistici Elenchi*) was added fresh commentary and a series of manuals of 'Modern Logic', dealing with subjects omitted or not fully covered by Aristotle: consequences, obligations, *insolubilia*, the properties of terms, suppositions and so on. The corpus of textbooks thus became very large indeed. It was not universally the same, because of local variation in the mediaeval commentaries and monographs studied, but from the mid-thirteenth century the *Summulae* of Peter of Spain, written in Paris probably during the 1230s, began to establish itself as the most widely used outline for students. Most universities based their first- and second-year logic courses on Peter of Spain. He covered the volumes of the Organon and also the *parva logicalia* and the topics of Modern Logic (Tract VII). Paul of Venice composed a *Logica Magna*, much used in Italy, which laid a greater emphasis on the material of Modern Logic, condensing much of the Aristotelian material. See Ashworth, *Language and Logic*, p. 1 for a summary. See *CHLMP*, pp. 74–9 for a table of mediaeval translations of Aristotle's works and of Greek and Arabic commentaries. J. Hillgarth's forthcoming study makes a most important contribution on the resources available in Spain. Peter of Spain's *Tractatus (Summulae Logicales)* is edited by L. M. de Rijk (Assen, 1972). On the use of the *Summulae* in universities, see T. H. Heath, 'Logical Grammar', pp. 41–3. At Freiburg, Ingolstadt and Tübingen at the end of the mediaeval period as elsewhere, the method of approach was to lecture on Peter's *Summulae* in the first year, and then to study the Aristotelian texts in the second year. See, too, J. Buridan, *Perutile Compendium Totius Logicae* with John Dorp's commentary (Venice, 1499, repr. Frankfurt, 1965); Paul of Venice, *Logica Magna*, ed. N. Kretzmann et al. (London, 1979), I. See *CHLMP*, pp. 792–5 on areas of the *logica parva* in which new work was done in the sixteenth century and E. J. Ashworth, 'Andreas Kesler and the Later Theory of Consequences', *Notre Dame Journal of Formal Logic*, 14.2 (1973), 205–14, and *CHLMP*, p. 791.

Erasmus and Calvin both studied at Paris, a generation apart. In 1495 Erasmus was at the Collège de Montaigu while the Scotsman John Major (Mair) taught logic.[16] Major was a prolific author of commentaries and monographs in many branches of the logic course of the Middle Ages, and he pressed energetically upon his pupils the need to preserve exactness in an age too fond of getting its effects with fine language. The need to defend a valued tradition seems to have been felt by a number of the logicians at Paris in the early sixteenth century; there they forced what proved to be a final flowering of the great bush of mediaeval logic in its unpruned state. A factor perhaps as compellingly counter-suggestive as the criticisms of humanists in bringing this about, was a royal decree of 1474 forbidding the study of nominalism at Paris; that revived interest in the banned work of Ockham, Buridan, Albert of Saxony, Marsilius of Inghen, Peter d'Ailly (1350–1420), John Dorp, and a new enthusiasm for late mediaeval logic in general; and it led to some original work in the old tradition. Nevertheless, the old guard retreated from Paris in the end, many of them to Spain, for Paris had had not only teachers from Scotland (George Lokert, d. 1547; David Cranston, d. 1512; Robert Caubraith) and logicians from the Low Countries (Pierre Crockaert, John Dullaert, *c.*1470–1513), but also Spaniards: Antonio and Luis Corel (brothers), Juan de Celaya, Domingo de Soto, Hieronymus Pardo, Juan Dolz, Fernando de Encinas.

When Calvin registered at the Collège de la Marche[17] in Paris in 1523 and then transferred to the Collège de Montaigu, John Major was back in Paris after a period of teaching in his native Scotland. There is every likelihood that he taught Calvin, and that Calvin was, in the intellectually formative years between fourteen and eighteen, imbued with methods and assumptions of scholastic logic, though perhaps less thoroughly than Luther. Natalia Beda (d. 1537), who was probably Calvin's principal teacher of logic at Montaigu, was a traditionalist.

Meanwhile, the humanists were addressing themselves to the old methods with a new broom. Valla's *Repastinatio dialecticae et philosophiae* had questioned their very foundation-principles. Others were pressing for plain simplification. Thomas Bricot wrote an introductory manual in the form of an abbreviation of standard texts. He has, he assures his readers, kept away from deeper questions and concentrated on

---

16   See T. F. Torrance, *The Hermeneutics of John Calvin* (Edinburgh, 1988), pp. 23–57 on Major.
17   On the 'shaping of Calvin's mind', see *ibid.*, Part II.

those which are *simpliciores*. In the 1534 edition of Rudolph Agricola's *De Inventione Dialectica*, first printed in 1515, we find the recommendation that this is clearer and more succinct and certainly easier to grasp than anything to be found in Peter of Spain's *Summulae*. Agricola, who was educated at Erfurt, Louvain and Cologne, began his book in Italy. It placed a Ciceronian emphasis on the techniques useful for hitting upon an appropriate argument ('invention'), rather than upon the syllogistic and other aspects of 'judging' arguments. Agricola's work circulated in manuscript for many years before it was printed in 1515, and although its thrust was primarily rhetorical, it exercised a considerable influence on Melanchthon in his reforms at Wittenberg, and upon teaching in Paris, where it was printed in 1529. Johan Sturm, Caesarius, Latomus, all taught Agricola there. Melanchthon approved of Agricola's revision of the logic course and wrote his own textbook on similar principles, emphasising the importance of 'invention' and 'topics'. His *Compendiaria Dialectices Ratio* of 1520[18] was revised twice and became an important textbook, much reprinted in the sixteenth century. Part of the work was enlarged into a treatise on dialectical method.[19] He produced a number of further teaching texts on dialectic,[20] and along with Caesarius' *Dialectica*, also modelled on Agricola, his *Dialecticae* provided manuals of instruction in logic in Wittenberg in the 1530s.[21]

During the late 1520s Peter Ramus studied logic in Paris; he has perhaps a claim to be the last of the leaders of this movement to revise the teaching of logic, who had himself been educated in both the old and the new methods. Ramus' logic leaves something to be desired technically and in clarity of exposition, but his intention was laudable, given his priorities. He thought he saw in Aristotle's *Posterior Analytics* a view of the matter and form of each art which could be applied in greatly simplifying the study of logic. He believed such simplification was desirable not only for negative reasons (logic had become too complicated), but for positive ones. A training in the arts ought to fit students for a life in which they would be able to apply their learning practically, in ethics,

---

[18]   *CR* 20.573–8.
[19]   *Ibid.*
[20]   On the chronology of Melanchthon's texts on dialectic, see C. Vasoli, *La dialettica e la retorica dell' umanesmo* (Milan, 1968).
[21]   Cf. Caesarius' comment in the 1532 Preface to his *Dialectica* (Cologne, 1559), associating his work with that of Melanchthon at Wittenberg.

civics, politics. Educators ought to be seeking to produce not just more teachers, but a literate population. He tried to include nothing in his course which would be too difficult for the average or below-average student. In practice his method was to introduce no more than a shortened list, of topics and aspects of syllogistic method, and to leave out of account altogether the kinds of problems not covered by Aristotle, which had formed the subject-matter of the *logica moderna* in recent centuries. This was to sacrifice a good deal which is of serious philosophical interest.

Again, the universities' statutory curricula were slow to change. The *Summulae* of Peter of Spain and others continued to be printed, and Eck, leading humanist, but always a conservative when he saw fit, published a *Bursa* of exercises on the *parva logicalia* at Strasbourg in 1507. He was commissioned to write a new commentary on Peter of Spain for the university of Ingolstadt (1516–17). But there was change. Leipzig, anxious to follow Wittenberg's lead, did not abandon Peter of Spain all at once, but from 1519, the 'complex questions' were left out, and there was steady continuing change throughout the 1520s.[22] At Freiburg in 1523 Peter of Spain had 'disappeared' in favour of Agricola and 'Melanchthon's little books'. A visitation at Tübingen in 1531 noted that the *moderni* had replaced Peter of Spain with Agricola.

During this period of experiment, and despite his exposure to old-fashioned influences, Calvin seems to have leaned towards the humanists. He went from Paris to Orleans at nineteen to study law. There he was to encounter Melchior Wolmar, a German, himself touched by Luther's influence, and the author of a book on Homer. Wolmar encouraged Calvin to learn Greek. When Calvin returned to Paris in 1531, after his father's death, he concentrated on the study of the humanities, and his first book, published in 1532, was a commentary on Seneca's *De Clementia*. The urge, which a number of logicians shared, was to get back to the textbooks and traditions of what was seen as a classical golden age. Rudolph Agricola describes the 'corrupt' state of today's practices by comparison. There was a return to Aristotle's texts in preference to those of mediaeval commentators and to mediaeval monographs. Some of the Greek commentators on Aristotle's logical works began to be published: Alexander of Aphrodisias, Themistius, Ammonius, Philoponus, Simplicius. New modern commentaries on Aristotle were composed

---

[22] Overfield, *Humanism*, pp. 304ff.

(Agostino Nifo, 1473–1546; Jacopo Zabarelli, 1533–89); there were new editions and translations. Bucer had a complete *Organon* with Faber's paraphrases and notes, which he lists under 'philosophy'. There was a sufficient bulk of new work to justify the production of a commentary synthesising recent studies by the Jesuits of Coimbra in 1606.[23] Alongside the call to simplify, then, there continued a serious scholarship, but increasingly directed towards classical revival and purification, rather than to pursuing the particular themes which had engaged late mediaeval attention.

ii. FALLACIES, PARADOXES

'It is one thing to make law, another to keep it, another to make it perfect', says Seripando; 'it is one thing for a man to be just, another for him to be justified', comments another of the Trent theologians.[24] There was much mutual suspicion over the matter of playing fair in the use of words. It had been recognised for several centuries that the detection of fallacies depended heavily upon the interpretation of terms, as well as upon the ability to recognise flawed construction in an argument. In an atmosphere of mutual hostility it was tempting not to trust what the other side said, on the grounds that it might be a trick. Eck was thought by the Protestants at Ratisbon to be conjuring with words like a magician and playing games with sophistries and vocabulary alike.[25] Both sides in the debates of the sixteenth century were alert to attempts by the other to fob them off with fallacious arguments. In the discussions of the Council of Trent, as by Luther, grief was expressed at the extent to which the influence of fallacious arguments had been responsible for troubling and damaging the Church of Christ and causing many of the faithful to fall away.[26] Calvin complains to Melanchthon in the Preface to his *Defence of sane and orthodox teaching about the servitude and freedom of the human will* in 1543 about the importance of avoiding sophistries and keeping to a 'naked plainness' (*nuda perspicuitas*) in argument, so that the matter may

23   J. M. McConica, 'Humanism and Aristotle in Tudor Oxford', *English Historical Review*, 94 (1979), 291–317. See, too, Ashworth, *Language and Logic*, p. 3, and Robert Sanderson (ed.), *Logicae Artis Compendium* (Bologna, 1984), p. xviii; *CHLMP*, p. 801; C. B. Schmitt, 'Towards a Reassessment of Renaissance Aristotelianism', *History of Science*, 11 (1973), p. 170.
24   *Acta CT* 12.272, 670.
25   *CR* 4.725.
26   *Acta CT* 5.95, 8 April 1546.

stand clearly without any complications.[27]

Much of such talk was rhetoric. But technically identifiable fallacies crop up everywhere in the debates, and most notably in the formal disputations of theses. They are not always intended to deceive. The skill of the respondent lay partly in pointing out technical faults in the arguments which were advanced, so that it could be seen by all present precisely why they were flawed and therefore not to be accepted. An example from the degree disputation of Major and Faber in 1544 illustrates the way this might happen. 'The Son is God. The Son is other than the Father. Therefore the Son is another God.' This is quickly identified as a *fallacia accidentis*. The Son is other than the Father as a Person, *quoad personam*, but in his nature (*quoad naturam*) he is one and the same God with the Father and the Holy Spirit.[28] A fallacy of division is identified in a 1535 disputation. In another disputation there occurs an example of a common error. The syllogism really has four terms, not three, and so there is no connection through a middle term between major and minor premisses. 'Articles of faith are not visible. "I believe in the Church" is an article of faith. Therefore the Church is not visible.' We do not 'see' 'articles of faith' in the sense of propositions, it is pointed out, but we may 'see' that to which the proposition refers. We can recognise the absurdity of the argument if we substitute the proposition 'I believe that God created Heaven and earth'. We do not see that proposition, but we see Heaven and earth. Again the fault is identified by means of a technical explanation. ('There are four terms.') There are examples everywhere, a proliferation of fallacies. 'Whatever the Scriptures approve must not be rejected. The Scriptures approve of doubt. Therefore doubt must not be rejected.' 'God justifies on account of faith. God is love. Therefore love justifies.'[29]

It was already apparent to mediaeval disputants that the fallacy theory of the logicians was especially stretched to accommodate theological arguments. Luther was saying nothing new here when he points out in the disputation of 1539 on John 1.14 that what follows beautifully (*pulchre*) from the theory of predicables may not be good theology. In

27   *CR* 34.230.
28   *WA* 39ii.329–30, Examination of Major and Faber, 1544, Argument on Thesis 11. On the *fallacia accidentis* see *Logica Modernorum*, ed. L. M. de Rijk (Assen, 1967), I.33, 96–7. It is one of seven *extra locutionem* identified in the *Sophistici Elenchi*. See below Chapter 5 on justification for further examples of fallacies of this sort.
29   *WA* 39i.69 (1535).

Thesis 10 we find the following: 'God is man. Therefore he is a rational animal, sensitive, a body, a created substance', and so on. It is not a flaw (*vitium*) in syllogistic form which is responsible for the error here, but the majesty of the subject-matter, which cannot be confined within the narrow bounds of reason. In treating of articles of faith we must look to another dialectic and philosophy.[30] Gisbert Voetius, Dutch Reformed theologian and author of a series of *Disputationes Theologicae*, preferred to use a rhetorician's approach. There are Ciceronian echoes in his account of the way fallacies may be avoided. He explains how the facts presented should be examined to see whether they are true, to ensure that they are not being applied to a case other than that which is ostensibly under discussion, to check whether it really is the facts which are at issue and not some point of interpretation or application. We must, he says, be ready to notice attempts to beg the question, change the subject, pretend that a decision has been reached when it has not. But in the mid-sixteenth century logical fallacy-theory was still actively in use, in the tradition which goes back before the advent of the translation of Aristotle's *Sophistici Elenchi* in the West in the twelfth century and which had been comprehensively developed since then.[31]

Not only do we find traces of a thorough technical understanding of the different types of fallacy Aristotle and his successors had identified, but also indications of the continuing familiarity of our disputants with the mediaeval game of 'obligations'. The roots of this game, probably played as a method of training students in flexibility, quick-wittedness and an ability to think several moves ahead in a dialectical game of chess, may lie in the rules Aristotle lays down in his *Topics* for the responses which may be made in a disputation.[32] Its mediaeval rules, found from at least the thirteenth century, set two players against one another. The first is to maintain a thesis and his opponent is to argue against it. The trick is to get one's opponent to concede or deny a premiss which will lead him into ultimate contradiction of his own position, and so to absurdity or denial of the rules of inference; and thus to defeat. Once he has conceded a premiss he may not thereafter deny it, and so it is essential for him to see ahead and realise where his concession may lead him. We find the

---

[30] *WA* 39ii.4.
[31] See my *Language and Logic* I and II for a brief account, and *CHLMP*, chapter 12 for the *status quaestionis*. For texts, see Rijk (ed.), *Logica Modernorum*.
[32] *Topics* VIII.3 (159a15-24).

formal terms of the game (*concedo, nego, distinguo*) being used in the disputations over which Luther presided, together with procedures highly reminiscent of those of 'obligations', as the combatants strive to trap one another into nonsense.[33]

The infection of a real debate with the techniques of a logical game was not in itself offensive. The game of 'obligations' always had a serious purpose of training. More importantly, it was a testing-ground for the learning of skills in handling paradoxes, for paradoxes were frequently generated as one of the participants was 'obliged' by the rules of the game to grant a nonsense to be true or a contradiction acceptable. Among the knots thus traditionally tied in playing the game were some of the classic *insolubilia*. Both *insolubilia*-treatises and obligations-treatises were being produced in the early sixteenth century and there is evidence that they were in some demand.[34] Among the stock examples used by logicians were many theological ones.[35]

It is because of the underlying seriousness of the issues they raise, both philosophically and theologically, that we hear so much talk of sophists and sophistry in the sixteenth-century debates. Luther speaks of 'disseminating heresies' by using 'fallacies, that is sophistries'. We find Calvin identifying 'a vulgar dogma of the sophists', or promising that his teaching will 'turn aside that comment of the sophists', frequently referring to his opponents simply as 'sophists'. 'Now it is not amiss to close and buckle and to hand with these disputers, that in this little ye may perceive that they be mere shifts of sophistry, which they set to sale [*sic*] under the name and colour of very sound arguments', advises Bullinger.[36] There was a concern in all this with the importance of approaching the true paradoxes of the faith with reverence for their mystery, of knowing a trick from something too deep for human comprehension. Theologians needed a logician's training, it was argued in the late mediaeval centuries,

---

[33] On the present state of knowledge about obligations, see *CHLMP*, pp. 315–40.

[34] The *Tractatus Insolubilium* of Thomas Bricot went through nine editions between 1489 and 1511. On the general position, see the introduction of E.J. Ashworth to her edition of this text, *Artistarium*, 6 (Nijmegen, 1986). Semantic paradoxes are discussed in the Middle Ages as a rule under the heading of *insolubilia*. See E. J. Ashworth, 'The Treatment of Semantical Paradoxes from 1400–1700', *Notre Dame Journal of Formal Logic*, 13.1 (1972), 34–52.

[35] Bricot, *Tractatus Insolubilium*, pp. 59, 101, 102, 104–5, 69, 70.

[36] Luther, *WA* 39[ii].209.23 (1543); Calvin, *Antidote* to Trent VII, Canon 2 and *CR* 35.719; Bullinger, *Decades* III, ix.329.

so that they might tell the difference.

Paradox served two purposes in patristic and mediaeval theology, one logical and the other rhetorical.[37] Luther had the rhetorical purpose in mind in his Heidelberg Disputation of 1518; he formulated his twenty-eight 'theological' theses and twelve 'philosophical' theses as *paradoxae* in order to make them more challenging and stimulating. 'The law of God ... cannot help man progress in righteousness, but rather hinders him' (1). 'Works of men which appear to be good are probably sins' (3). 'Sins are truly venial in the sight of God when men fear that they are mortal' (12). He succeeded in his purpose, and Martin Bucer notes more than once that these are 'paradoxes'.[38]

But they are more than a striking stylistic device, a figure of thought. Luther wanted to force those who heard his theses to rethink fundamentals. In a sense, paradoxes are the obverse of fallacies. A fallacious argument looks acceptable on the surface, but it deceives. A theological paradox looks unacceptable on the surface because it seems to contradict itself, but it points to a divine truth which stretches human understanding to the limit; that is the deeper purpose of Luther's Heidelberg paradoxes. As he explains in the *De Servo Arbitrio*, the question of the relationship of human free will to divine foreknowledge and predestination and to grace has been tackled in every age and never resolved. But he thinks that what is 'insoluble' (*insolubilis*) paradox in the light of natural human understanding may be easily resolved in the light of the grace and glory of God. By the light of nature we cannot explain why the good should suffer and the wicked prosper. We understand it by the light of grace. Even in the light of grace, however, we cannot see how God can justly condemn someone who cannot of himself help but sin. But in the light of the glory of God all appears shining and perfect justice.[39]

iii. AUTHORITY IN DEBATE

Aquinas says that *sacra doctrina* differs from other sciences in its use of argument, in that when the principles of other sciences are challenged, they rely upon a higher science to support them. *Sacra doctrina* is itself the supreme science, so it must contain within itself the resources to stand

---

[37]   See my article, 'The "Secure Technician": Varieties of paradox in the writings of St Anselm', *Vivarium*, 13 (1975), 1–21.

[38]   *Correspondance de M. Bucer*, May 1518, Letter to Rhenanus, pp. 62, 98.

[39]   Conclusion of the *De Servo Arbitrio*, WA 18.785.

up successfully against those who deny its fundamental principles, the articles of faith. We may be confident, says Aquinas, that no arguments brought against these can be demonstrative; they must all be *solubilia*.[40] His own endeavour in the highly formalised disputations of the *Summa Theologiae* is to prove by applying reasoning or authorities that all arguments against the truth can indeed be disposed of.

One of the most useful survivals of mediaeval logical method in the sixteenth- and seventeenth-century universities was the mediaeval type of formal academic disputation. Disputations were still being held as a matter of course in protestant Europe,[41] despite revolutionary change in the textbooks and syllabus of the logic course, and the participants continue to show a high degree of competence in the old methods. It is perhaps from this evidence of the practical use of logic rather than from talk of innovation that we should begin to assess the extent of the changes which had really been brought about.

The disputation clearly continued to meet the educational needs which it had evolved to supply. Its origin probably lies in an attempt to resolve a practical difficulty which arose in the course of the lecturing on set texts which formed the staple of all teaching from the beginning to the end of the Middle Ages and beyond. Sometimes a lecturer had to deal with a passage which required more than a brief comment. Where it raised a point which had been the subject of long controversy, there might be a great deal to say. Calvin deals with such a text in his remarks on Genesis 1.26 ('Let us make man'). He keeps his comment as brief as he can, noting that 'Christians properly contend, from this testimony, that there exists a plurality of Persons in the Godhead. God summons no counsellor except himself. So we infer that he finds within himself something distinct.' He refers to the longstanding debate on the relationship of the divine wisdom and power to the Persons of the Trinity. (Is the Father Power, the Son Wisdom? Or are wisdom and power attributes of the Godhead as one?[42]) He summarises here a vast corpus of debate, patristic and mediaeval. Where such an exposition ran to some length, it might interrupt the flow

---

40 *ST* I q.1.a.8.
41 Cf. P. Fraenkel, *De l'écriture à la dispute* (Lausanne, 1977), p. 5. See, too, H. Bornkamm, *Luther's World of Thought*, tr. M. H. Bertram (Missouri, 1958), pp. 36–7 and cf. Melanchthon's Preface to vol. II of Luther's Latin Writings (Wittenberg, 1546), *CR* 6.157–9.
42 Cf. the trial of Peter Abelard in J. G. Sikes, *Peter Abailard* (Cambridge, 1932).

of the lecture in a way which was confusing to the student, especially if he did not have the text in front of him so that he could follow.[43] From the middle of the twelfth century it became usual to hold such topics over as *quaestiones* to be dealt with in a separate session, so that they could be discussed and settled or 'determined' by the master.[44]

The term *quaestio* is significant. Gilbert of Poitiers, commenting on Boethius in the middle of the twelfth century, emphasises with Boethius that a *quaestio* must involve at least one argument for and against. Not every contradiction is a *quaestio*, however; there must be a *prima facie* case for both sides, a real question at issue.[45] Informal *disputationes* which begin to show this adversarial pattern survive in the work of Simon of Tournai in the mid-twelfth century.[46] Something much more organised underlies the structure of Aquinas' *Summa Theologiae* a century later. Here the procedure is brought to a high pitch of refinement. Aristotle describes the method for problem-solving in the Nichomachean *Ethics* (I.1145^{b2-7}). The problem should be presented, the conflicting views set down, then the difficulties resolved. Finally, the conflicting views should be restated so as to show how the difficulties have been disposed of. This is not far from the standard procedure adopted in mediaeval disputations. Arguments are marshalled in support of the view to be proved erroneous, with the reasoning or evidence which supports them; and then the matter is 'determined', and the proceedings are concluded by demolishing all the *objectiones* already given.

This method, which came to be used in the teaching and also the examination of students, was an efficient means of determining how clear a grasp had been achieved of the *status quaestionis*, as well as of the literature, Biblical, patristic and modern. Formal *disputationes* of various sorts became a standard feature of university teaching, developing into *quodlibets* and *quaestiones disputatae*, as well as providing a framework for the *summa*.

In the thirteenth century the pattern in theology faculties was already more or less settled. The time and topics of a disputation were announced

---

[43] Some lecturers took the trouble to include every word of the text in the lemmata they discussed (Gilbert of Poitiers); others seem to have given merely the opening words of a passage (Peter Abelard).

[44] For (alternative) theories about the origin of the *disputatio*, see *CHLMP*, p. 25.

[45] Cf. Gilbert of Poitiers, *De Trinitate, Commentaries on Boethius*, ed. N. M. Häring (Toronto, 1966), p. 37: *ex affirmatione et eius contradictoria negatione quaestio constat*, and H. C. van Elswijk, *Gilbert Porreta* (Louvain, 1966), p. 271.

[46] *Les questions disputées, Typologie des sources du moyen âge occidental*, ed. B. C. Bazan *et al.* (Turnhout, 1985), p. 27.

in advance. All bachelors were required to attend, but Masters and their students were free to come too. On the first day of the disputation the Master would give an introduction. Then one of his bachelors would listen and reply to arguments presented by those in the audience. The order of disputation was decided by the sequence of the topics published in advance. With the Master's help if he needed it, the bachelor answered the objections made to each of these theses. The whole process was recorded by a secretary in the form of a *reportatio*. On a second day, the company reassembled and the Master summarised the arguments which had been advanced and gave his own solution (*determinatio*). The record was normally published, either as a *reportatio* or in a polished form rewritten by the Master which was known as an *ordinatio*. The disputations held regularly throughout the year followed a co-ordinated plan in their subject-matter. In addition to these 'ordinary' disputations, there were special occasions, in Advent and Lent, when a wider public was invited and the disputation might be on any topic (*de quolibet*) raised by anyone present (*a quolibet*). These involved real display of skills by a bachelor who had to answer off the cuff; and by the Master, who had to determine on the spot.[47]

Meanwhile the detailed handling of the *quaestio* evolved into structurally quite complex forms. Peter Aureoli (d. 1322), for example, takes a question arising out of Peter Lombard's *Sentences* (I Dist. 8.23), whether there is a contradiction between plurality of attributes in the Godhead and divine simplicity. He first gives a series of propositions, each followed by the formula, 'It would seem that ...' and a list of supporting arguments. Then he gives a Response to the question, and explains the order he will follow in dealing with the questions thus raised. He gives a list of the views of the *doctores*, and explains where each falls short or is in error. Then he summarises what he has been saying, and gives an answer to the whole question. Finally, he lists the replies to the points he outlined at the outset.[48]

Gabriel Biel (*c.*1420–95) approaches the discussion of the same distinction of Book I of the *Sentences* rather differently. His task is complicated by the still larger and still growing body of opinions of former and contemporary doctors which he has to accommodate in his structure. He takes care to show exactly how Ockham makes his case and

47 *Typologie*, p. 31; pp. 40ff., cf. *CHLMP*, pp. 21–2.
48 Peter Aureoli, *Super Primum Sententiarum*, ed. E. M. Buytaert (New York, 1956), vol. II, I Dist.8.23, pp. 968ff.

how it is to be balanced against that of Gregory of Rimini.[49] The significant difference in his arrangement is that he begins with a *summarium textus*, in which he digests the whole *distinctio* into three *conclusiones*. He thus offers as an opening not a *quaestio* but a *conclusio*, although he goes on to present the evidence under the headings of a series of *quaestiones*. This shift from *quaestio* to *conclusio* (or *thesis* or *propositio* as it is often called) is noticeable in later mediaeval disputations. It did not take away the adversarial character of the disputation. But it altered the emphasis. Instead of arguing for and against what is presented as an open question (*utrum*), the disputants now attack and defend what is presented or proposed as a statement of the truth. (A proposition is, of course, different from a conclusion in inferential status, but not in the truth-claim it makes.)

The normal pattern in the disputations in which Luther was involved was still for the examiner or challenger to make public a series of theses in advance. These were then debated when the disputation took place. The change did not alter the fundamental pattern of confronting *objectio* with *responsio* in the course of discussion; that remained the very stuff of disputation. *Contendunt autem aliqui ...* We find the theologians of Trent making a *reportatio* of their own discussions of the 'Lutheran articles' in February 1547. The Decrees and Canons of the Council were referred to by Cochlaeus as a *determinatio*.[50] All the old apparatus is still in evidence. But the flexibility of structure of the disputation seems to have been greater in sixteenth-century disputations, and it was matched by a growing flexibility in the range of uses to which the disputation could be put. The university context remained central, and the disputation was regularly held (*circulariter*). It was still a standard method of instruction and the normal method of conducting examinations. Public disputations also proved popular. The Statutes of Wittenberg in 1508 mention the routine weekly disputation, the degree disputation and quarterly disputations (also held on feast-days).[51]

Through the invention of printing the 'invitation to debate' could be addressed to a much wider audience and readership, and we find interested

49   Gabriel Biel, *Collectorium circa quattuor libros Sententiarum*, ed. W. Werbeck and U. Hofmann (Tübingen, 1973), pp. 303–5.

50   J. Cochlaeus, Letter to J. Pflug, 17 March 1547, Pollet II.725, Letter 347; cf. *Acta CT* 6[iii], prolegomena, p. xxxi on recording discussions, *Acta CT* 5.307 and 319, July 1546.

51   Cf. the account in Luther, *Works*, vol. 34, pp. xiii–xiv and WA 39[i].14 and WA 39[ii].52.14–15 on the use of the term *circulariter*.

enquirers trying to get hold of copies of published theses.[52] Such public displays might be used to 'try' a theologian accused of heresy, or to give him a chance to defend himself, as we see happening in the case of Luther. Although from the mid-1520s the degree disputation fell somewhat into disuse at Wittenberg, Luther himself did a good deal to revive it; in 1533 new statutes brought it back into play and several examples survive from the next decade or so. 'We theologians, more even than the lawyers and doctors, are bound to labour in the Lord's vineyard', says Luther. 'We are a *spectaculum* to all the world and we are accused of heresy and of being authors of new doctrine. So we must defend ourselves in public disputation. Indeed, the civil authorities require us to do so.'[53] In the middle years of the century the disputation came to be employed in a series of colloquies, in an attempt to heal the breaches between reformers and conservatives in the Church. At Ratisbon in 1541 each side put forward theses and counter-theses and the colloquy proceeded by formal debate.[54]

Luther's career as a reformer began with a series of more or less formal disputations. The *Disputation against Scholastic Theology* of 1517[55] was written as a set of theses for the degree examination of Franz Günther, at which Luther presided as Dean of the Faculty of Theology. Luther did not compose these theses in the spirit of one setting a routine examination paper. He put into them ideas which were actively concerning him at the time. (The theses were all that Luther seems to have rescued from the commentary he was then engaged in, on Book I of Aristotle's *Physics*, in which it appears that he intended to review the value of Aristotle to Christian scholars, as it was then fashionable to do, and in particular to look critically at the uses to which recent scholastic thinkers had been putting Aristotle.) He took his theses seriously enough, as a statement of his ideas, to send a copy to a friend in Nürnberg, Christopher Scheurl. Scheurl was impressed and thought they would make a useful contribution to the campaign to put Aristotle in his proper place in a Christian syllabus. Eck, the staunchest of Catholics in the long term, was engaged in similar disputation on such lines in 1517, discussing divine essence and angelic substance and the nature of blessedness with references to the errors of

---

52   E. L. Eisenstein, *The Printing Press as an Agent of Change* (Cambridge, 1979), and see Bucer, *Correspondance*, passim.
53   Published in *WA* 39[i-ii]; see, too, *WA* 39[ii].6.
54   *Acta Ratisbonensis*, as published by Martin Bucer (Strasbourg, 1541).
55   *WA* 1.224ff.

Ockham and Biel in a manner not wholly unreminiscent of Luther's. Such disputations were the equivalent of academic conferences.[56]

From the outset, then, we can see the disputation as providing a challenge to Luther to take stock of his position and to make a statement. Sometimes, as we shall see, the challenge was explicit and came from outside. But even where Luther was acting in his academic capacity as Dean or chief examiner, the requirement to frame his ideas in the format of a set of theses seems to have helped him to clear his mind. Few things concentrate the mind so well as writing propositions, especially when they are to be thoroughly challenged in open discussion. The theses in the *Disputation against Scholastic Theology* form loose groups. The first group deals with free will, the second group with actions, the third with nature and grace, and so on; there is a good deal of overlap, and there are digressions. In Thesis 40 Luther contends that righteous deeds proceed from righteousness rather than making a man righteous. This, he says, is in opposition to what the philosophers teach. This leads him to state in the next thesis that almost the whole of Aristotle's *Ethics* is incompatible with a Christian doctrine of grace. Thesis 42 follows: it is an error to hold that Aristotle does not contradict Christian doctrine on the subject of happiness. Thesis 43 tells us that it is wrong to say that no-one can become a theologian without Aristotle; the contrary is true (Thesis 44); no-one can become a theologian unless he does so independently of Aristotle.

In defending these theses the examination candidate was expected to take a position on what, in the case of most of them, was a well-worn topic of debate. It was reasonable to expect him to show a knowledge of the *status quaestionis* and the views of a range of authorities. In the by now multitudinous commentaries on Lombard's *Sentences*, to which every scholar had contributed for three centuries, are to be found discussions of these and similar points, and the candidate would marshal arguments – as Luther himself does from time to time in a reference.[57] It is of some significance that Luther's own specific references are confined to Ockham, Biel, Duns Scotus (*c*.1264–1308) and Peter d'Ailly, with a few general stabs at 'the scholastics'. It seems likely that in practice students would be most familiar with more recent scholarship, and with those key ideas of earlier generations which were still being actively discussed. On the freedom or

---

[56]   Eck, *Disputatio Viennae Pannoniae Habita* (1517), ed. T. Virnich, *C. Cath.* 6 (Münster, 1923).
[57]   Theses 56, 57, 61, for example.

servitude of the will (Thesis 5) Luther has in mind *Sentences* II Dist. 24, c.5, and here and in the following theses he borrows perhaps from Biel's Commentary on the *Sentences* (III Dist. 27) and that of Scotus (*In Sent.* III Dist. 27). In Thesis 35 ('It is not true that invincible ignorance excuses everything'), he depends on *Sentences* II Dist. 22, c.9. The technicalities in Theses 46–9 seem to owe much to Biel on the *Sentences* (I Dist. 12, q.1). This wholesale derivativeness in the formulation of these early theses does not detract from their importance in helping to form Luther's own thought, but it is nonetheless true that he is simply proceeding in the manner proper to disputation.

It is clear that Luther was already, in framing these 1517 Theses, anxious to make certain points himself. He did so with still greater forcefulness in the Ninety-Five Theses which he published in October of 1517, challenging to a debate those who found his view unacceptable. The disputation did not take place, but the Theses were disseminated sufficiently widely to cause a furore, and Luther prepared a series of *Resolutiones* which constitute a written defence. In the meantime, he was invited to Heidelberg in April 1518, to take part in a disputation at the Augustinian house there. The occasion was the three-yearly meeting of the General Chapter of the German Augustinians. The Vicar of the German Congregation, Staupitz, asked Luther to confine himself to familiar topics (sin, free will, grace), and not to make the occasion a vehicle for disseminating his newer and more controversial ideas. Among those who heard him and were impressed were Martin Bucer, Johann Brent and Billichanus. At Heidelberg Luther was using the *disputatio* for what had been its first purpose in the Middle Ages: discussion of problems among scholars in a public forum where students could come to listen and learn.

He prepared in advance twenty-eight 'theological' theses and twelve 'philosophical' ones.[58] Although he duly kept to the desired topics, there proved to be plenty of scope to develop concerns voiced in the Ninety-Five Theses, and there is every indication that his mind was working on the whole complex of debate. He develops substantially the case he made in the Ninety-Five Theses for justification by faith and his arguments against the efficacy of works. The method is to argue on the basis of Scriptural evidence, and to tie the whole together wherever possible by cross-reference from one thesis to another. The intention is apparently to make a

---

58 *WA* 1.353–74. The surviving defences suggest that the theological theses attracted the bulk of the attention.

Euclidean nexus of theoremata which will stand as a coherent system; the impression given by the surviving explanatory material is that this was not primarily an adversarial disputation, in which objections and responses are systematically marshalled, but rather something of a display piece.

(It is worth noting, even stressing, here, that there was no disjunction between the continuing use of the disputation and the reformers' focus on the study of the Bible. More than one of Luther's disputations is upon a Biblical text, where all the theses concern points of interpretation of a single text, as in the disputations of 1539 on John 1.14 and Matthew 19.21.)

The inherent flexibility of the disputation is clearer still in the *Resolutiones* of the Ninety-Five Theses (*WA* 1.525–628). Some of the theses Luther 'asserts' at the beginning of his proof (4), some he 'discusses' (5), some he 'maintains' (7), some he 'examines' (8), some he derives by deduction from others (10 from 8). Everywhere he proceeds by reasoning (usually syllogistically), and supports his premises (predominantly from Scripture). He is able to advance closely reasoned theological arguments and at the same time to mix in polemic and irony. 'Christians are to be taught that the Pope, in granting indulgences, needs and thus desires their devout prayer more than their money' (48). The Pope, says Luther, badly needs his people's prayers if he is to be saved from the seductions of those who tell him 'it is not presumed that one of such distinguished prominence should err'. Thesis 50 states that if the Pope knew how preachers of indulgences are behaving, he would rather that the basilica of St Peter were burned to the ground than see it built with the skin, flesh and bones of his sheep, and 51 that he would and should wish to pay money of his own to those who are being fleeced by the sellers of indulgences. In discussing both Luther falls into the mocking rhetoric of the polemicist.

The Leipzig debate of 1519 was not of Luther's seeking, but it proved to be of huge importance in opening up the subject-matter of debate and bringing Luther's attention, which had been chiefly engaged with the complex of questions on justification (faith, free will, grace, predestination, works) to a more clear-cut concern with authority in the Church. Johann Eck was corresponding with Luther in a friendly way until 1517. Then he published the *Obelisks*, an abusive attack on thirty-one of the Ninety-Five Theses. Luther responded in a similar vein with his *Asterisks* (March 1518).[59] Eck did not reply, but the then Dean of the Wittenberg Theology

---

[59] Both published in vol. 1 of Luther's *Opera* (Wittenberg, 1545), and see *WA* 1.278–314.

Faculty, Karlstadt, did not want to let the matter drop. He published 370 theses of his own. Eck responded to these with more theses and challenged Karlstadt to meet him in a public disputation. It was agreed, not without some reluctance on the part of the Theology Faculty at Leipzig, that the disputation should be held there. Eck published twelve theses which he would defend. One of these attacked Luther's defence of Thesis 22 of the Ninety-Five in his *Responsiones* and helped to bring openly into the arena the subject of papal supremacy. It was now clear that it was Luther and not Karlstadt whom Eck was challenging, and Luther himself responded by publishing counter-theses and once more Eck responded with revised theses of his own.

Something of the scope for theatre the disputation could give is apparent in Luther's account of Eck's performance in the debate itself. 'Eck stamped about with as much ado as though he were in an arena, holding up the Bohemians before me and publicly accusing me of the heresy ... of the Bohemian heretics' ... 'At this point the adder swelled up, exaggerated my crime, and nearly went insane in his adulation of the Leipzig audience.'[60] This sort of playing to the gallery was common practice with Eck, as other accounts of his performances show, but it brings vividly before us the importance of the presence of an audience in public disputations of this polemical sort. The audience was not confined to members of the university. Luther charges the people of Leipzig who joined the audience with stupidity and prejudice. 'Eck ... they followed around town, clung to, banqueted, entertained, and finally presented with a robe and added a chamois-hair gown.' Mediaeval university statutes had sometimes been directed against enjoyment of the theatrical possibilities of a disputation, excluding those who shouted, hissed, made a noise or threw stones from the audience.[61] How far popular understanding of the theological implications went, it is hard to say, though the records of disputations in German and other vernaculars[62] suggest that we should not underestimate serious interest among non-academics. As a spectacle and as a forum for serious debate, disputations could play a part in the popular spread of support for factions among theologians, and the authorities sometimes used them to try to curb such support. Zwingli was

60 Translation in Luther, *Works*, vol. 31, pp. 321–2.
61 *Ibid.*, p. 323. On such statutes, see L. Thorndike, *University Records and Life in the Middle Ages* (Columbia, New York, 1944), p. 237.
62 A number of examples survive from Zwingli's circle, *Werke* VI.

called to a public disputation before the City Council of Zurich and representatives of the Bishop of Constance in 1523 in the hope that it could thus be determined whether the city could stay loyal to Catholicism, or accept Zwingli's understanding of the Reformation.[63]

Disputations were held in various parts of northern Europe as a means of airing, resolving or silencing contentions put forward by reforming groups. From his disputations at Leipzig in 1519, Baden in 1526 and Berne in 1528, Eck drew 404 Articles, which he published in 1530 as a challenge to further debate. ('The day and time of the disputation Eck will publish *ad divi Caesaris arbitrium.*'[64]) In the same year he addressed himself to the Zwinglian Articles in a *Repulsio Articulorum Zwingli*, which constitutes a reply to the 'challenge' of these Articles. Eck certainly saw himself as a champion of the truth in combat. 'I was the first whom God put into this field', he boasts. 'If I had wanted to make a charge I could have brought great bloodshed to Germany. I could well have begun the game at Worms.'[65] A disputation at Lausanne in 1536 was closely modelled on that of Berne.

In 1535 there took place the first doctoral examination in the Theology Faculty at Wittenberg since the new statutes had been introduced.[66] Two friends of Luther were to graduate, Hieronymus Weller and Nikolaus Medler, and many of Luther's supporters among the reformers were present: Melanchthon, Cruciger, Amsdorf, Hieronymus among them. The examiners raised formal objections to the theses in the usual way, and the candidates defended them. A few fragments of *reportatio* survive. Melanchthon, for example, raised the following difficulty about Theses 81, 84 and 65 on Law:

> If justification is only forgiveness of sins, Paul is righteous by the same obedience as before justification. So I ask what is obedience?

The candidate responded that obedience is inseparable from the remission of sins in justification. Paul does not become righteous by obedience but by forgiveness of sins, and the obedience follows. An objection was raised. 'Why, then, is obedience necessary if we are justified without it?' Is it not another kind of righteousness? There is certainly a difference between one who obeys and one who does not. The candidate responded by identifying

---

[63] Zwingli, *Writings*, tr. E. J. Furcha (Pennsylvania, 1984), *The Defense of the Reformed Faith*, 1523.
[64] Published Strasbourg, 1530.
[65] Note after the 404th thesis.
[66] *WA* 39i.44–62.

obedience as only a partial righteousness. Partial righteousness does not justify because God demands that we fulfil his law perfectly.[67] The tone is quite different from the rhetorical bombast of Luther's earlier encounter with Eck, but the structure of the exchange is closely similar. The pattern of thesis, objection and response is still the staple of the disputation.

'Teaching' disputations were still going on in the 1530s. Luther himself gave one in January 1536, on Man.[68] Such an occasion provided opportunities for games-playing, as it had in the Middle Ages. One objection raised attempted to prove that free will is not in control of civil affairs:

> To commit murder is not an act of free will.
> To commit murder is a public matter.
> Therefore public matters are not under the control of free will.

The major premiss is proved from John 8.44: the Devil is the father of deceit and murder. And so, by implication, murder is not an act of human free will. It is to be supposed that this sophistry provoked amusement. Luther does not bother to point out the trickery which is involved in deriving the conclusion from the two premises, or to challenge the proof of the major premiss. His comment is that this shows that philosophy must be distinguished from theology. Aristotle and other philosophers do not have the evidence to help them define 'the theological man'. Christians alone can do it, because they have the Bible.[69]

In another disputation, the examination of Heinrich Schmedenstede (1542), we get in the surviving fragments of *reportatio* a fuller than usual picture of the ways in which the participating examiners could help to make the debate a real pooling of ideas. Luther himself, in his prefatory remarks, sees the adversarial contest as now lying not within the examination room but between the reformers and those who constantly attack their teaching. 'These adversaries make it necessary for us to be energetic and lively so that we may defend the wisdom of God against them to his glory and for the salvation of mankind.'[70] Johann Bugenhagen from Pomerania quarrelled with the contention that dead faith produces miracles. The effect is a living thing, and so its cause must also be living. It was Luther, not the candidate, who responded with the argument that the cause is the power of the Holy Spirit, who may work miraculously

67 *WA* 39[i].58–9.
68 *WA* 39[i].175–80.
69 *WA* 39[i].178–9.
70 *WA* 39[i].191.

even in the unworthy, as he does in the sacraments when they are administered by unworthy ministers. Bernard Ziegler, a friend of Melanchthon, and a lecturer in Hebrew at Leipzig, took up another classic difficulty. It is impossible for anyone to be righteous without love. But if we say that faith alone justifies, it seems that we are righteous without love, and that appears to be false, on the basis of 1 John 3.14. Luther explains that love follows on faith, with a reference to the old debate on premiss and precept.[71]

Interventions such as these show that, despite the scope for popular entertainment the disputation could hold, we are in an academic world, where it is still the case that stock topics of the later Middle Ages can be recalled by a word, in the expectation that everyone present will understand the context. Two series of theses produced by the Faculty of Theology at Louvain in 1544, at the request of the Emperor, seem to have been designed to meet the needs, respectively, of a more popular and a specialist readership. The Dean of the Faculty prefaced the Articles published for 'all the faithful in Christ' by explaining that they were framed 'for the people's sake', and 'as simply as possible, so that the most inexperienced could understand them'.[72] The emphasis here is on setting out what is and what is not necessary to salvation, beginning with the sacraments, as the point at which most ordinary Christians are brought up against theology in a practical way. 'Baptism is necessary to salvation for all, including infants' (2). 'The sacrament of penance ... is necessary after baptism for salvation for all the lapsed' (3). 'One who wants to confess must show real effort to reveal to the priest, his judge, all his mortal sins and also the hidden sins of the heart, so that he may be absolved of them by the priest' (5). Simply and clearly though these and all the other points are put, it is apparent that they rest upon a vast substructure of assumptions about the way topics are to be identified and the way propositions are to be expressed, and also about the nature of the questions at issue. These are not spelt out, but like the iceberg under its tip, they are nine-tenths of the matter in hand.

We go on, on these assumptions, through the Decrees and Canons of Trent, themselves Theses in format, through Calvin's responses as adversary in disputation in the *Antidote*. (He found such an *Antidote* as appropriate for Trent as he had for the Articles of the Paris Theologians of 1544.) The genre is everywhere. It suggested itself as a literary form

---

[71] *WA* 39ii.201. For Melanchthon's disputation theses, many of them used at Wittenberg, see *CR* 12.399–704.

[72] *WA* 54.416–22.

to Seripando, when he sketched his plan for a book on *Righteousness and Christian Liberty*. He wrote to Cocciano in February 1553 about a previous attempt to draft it (*schizzai*) at Bologna between 1547 and 1548. He thought of arranging his material in three 'controversies' set at different periods of the Church's history, the first at the time of the apostles, the second in Augustine's day and the third 'as it stands today'. These three fictional *congressus* were to take place as imaginary disputations between an *oppugnator* and a *propugnator*.[73]

The disputation is still the natural arena in England in the second half of the sixteenth century. In the reign of Mary Tudor Cranmer was tried for his opinions on transubstantiation by the assembled doctors of Oxford and Cambridge in the Divinity School at Oxford. He was examined by disputation, as was Ridley. The form of the disputation here too was the traditional one of late mediaeval universities. Notice was given of the questions at issue:

> Whether the natural body of Christ be really in the sacrament after the words spoken by the priests or no?
> Whether in the sacrament, after the words of consecration, any other substance do remain, than the substance of the body and blood of Christ?
> Whether in the mass be a sacrifice propitiatory for the sins of the quick and the dead?[74]

Cranmer was 'set in the answerer's place'[75] (as a candidate for a degree would have been when he disputed *viva voce* before his examiners). The prolocutor, Dr Weston, opened the debate with an oration in Latin and the first opponent, Chedsey, began by stating the 'conclusions' or answers to the questions to which Cranmer was asked to assent.

England saw a considerable number of disputations and conferences before and after the trials of Cranmer and Ridley at Oxford: at Westminster in 1559; between Grindal and Glin in Cambridge in 1549, Campion and Nowell and Fulke at the Tower in 1581; between Rainolds and Hart again at the Tower in 1583, FitzSimon and Ussher at Dublin Castle in 1599, Walshingham and Covel in 1604 and numerous others. Robert Parsons (writing as N.D.) was able to assemble a *Review of Ten Public Disputations or Conferences, held within the Compass of Four Years, under King Edward and Queen Mary* (St Omer, 1604). In May 1622, at royal request,

---

73   *De Iustitia et Libertate Christiana*, p. xiii.
74   Cranmer, *Remains*, ed. H. Jenkyns (Oxford, 1833), p. 391.
75   *Ibid.*, p. 393.

the combatants met to try to satisfy the Duchess of Buckingham on the question of the existence of a 'continual, infallible, visible Church'.[76] The structure is notably more informal than that of the academic disputations of the mid-sixteenth century, and we are visibly progressing towards a freer and more flexible pattern of debate. But as the parade of technicalities becomes less overt much remains. There is a consistent concern with exactness in the interpretation of words. What does *perfidia* mean?[77] There is a concern for fundamentals.[78] There is an echo again and again of the old rigidity of question and answer.[79] A hard look at modes of proving[80] runs hand in hand with a concern about definitions and questions of language as strongly as it had done in the late mediaeval centuries.

Methodologically and epistemologically, the authority-questions which arose in these areas of text, testimony, formal reasoning, underlay all the other debates with which we shall be concerned. These are the prior and primary issues because they concern the authority of the very evidence and grounds on which other kinds of claims to authority are to be judged. The reformers' appeal to 'Scripture alone' asserted that only the Word of God constituted authoritative evidence for truths of faith. But that evidence itself was proving more and more elusive in the light of contemporary scholarship, and the breakdown of the certainties afforded by mediaeval reliance on the Vulgate text. The use of supportive testimony for the Church's tradition became an extremely vexed matter, with the Fathers set against most recent witnesses, and suspicion of anything which could be construed as addition to Scripture. Human reason had always been an indispensable, but often a suspect addition to Christian scholarship. It is the great paradox – and irony – of the sixteenth century that, at a time when the subtlety of the question of evidence was becoming more apparent than ever before, both sides in the debates should need, for polemical reasons, to oversimplify, to assert sometimes rather crude dogmatic statements about the grounds on which they were prepared to consider a truth authoritative. There is, as a result, an almost unbearable tension straining the very foundations of the discussions about authority in the Church to which we must now turn.

[76]   W. Laud, *The Conference between William Laud and Mr Fisher the Jesuit, Works*, vol. 2 (Oxford, 1849), p. 2.
[77]   *Ibid.*, p. 6.
[78]   Parsons, *Review of Ten Public Disputations*, p. 30.
[79]   Laud, *Conference*, p. 75.
[80]   *Ibid.*, pp. 81–3.

PART II

Saving authority

4. *Powerlessness before sin*

Everywhere in the background to Luther's thinking, and that of other reformers, was the habit of looking for what 'counts' in the forgiveness of sins, what 'causes' salvation, what has 'power to save'. This is the area of authority with which the Reformation was first and most consistently concerned.

Luther's agenda began with the crisis created in human lives by sin. All that he came to hold in later years about the order and constitution of the Church, and the erection of the many planks of his polemical platform, depended upon the position he took on the remission of sins in the first years of his prominence as a controversial figure. Melanchthon, too, put first, of what he saw as the two great areas of contemporary dispute, 'I believe in the remission of sins'; the debate over the clause, 'I believe in the Holy Catholic Church', he put second as depending in large measure upon it.[1] The problem, as both perceived it, was that human beings stand in absolute need of saving from the consequences of their sinful condition, and are desperately vulnerable to false promises of rescue, easily led into parting with their money and their trust. Luther was moved in the first instance by pastoral concern for the spiritual welfare of the people he saw becoming the victims of indulgence-sellers. The theology came later. It proved immensely subtle and complex, and far from the clear-cut matter Luther had first thought it when he framed his notion of a salvation which required only simple faith.

Today's tendency is to see the horror of human wrongdoing in terms of its destructive effects upon the world and man's inhumanity to man. For patristic and mediaeval thinkers, and for Luther's generation, its ultimate horror lay not so much in these practical this-worldly consequences as in the obscenity of man's alienation from God and the death and eternal condemnation which must result. It was not in dispute in the sixteenth century that sin is the cause of the ills of the human condition, although among the proliferating dissenting groups sufficiently vociferous to be mentioned in the Augsburg Confession,[2] the Anabaptists[3] and neo-

---

1   *Confessio Saxonica*, especially *CR* 28.377.
2   2.9; cf. *Apologia*, Art. 2.
3   See R. Heath, *Anabaptism from its rise at Zwickau to its fall at Münster, 1521–36* (London, 1895), on this period.

Pelagians discounted 'original sin'. There is no discrepancy here between the ingredients of the decree of the Council of Trent on original sin and those of Luther's definition given in a disputation of 1536 on justification. 'Original sin is an inborn and perpetual evil in us, making us guilty and subject to death, ... and which may be described as a "congenital habit".'[4] The Trent text says that Adam lost both holiness and righteousness by his sin, and that loss is transmitted to all his posterity, who have it not by imitation but by inheritance. There was, however, a most important difference of emphasis (though not one which Calvin saw as having constituted an obstacle to agreement at Ratisbon in 1541).[5] Luther wanted to stress, more strongly than he thought scholastic tradition had been ready to do, the terrible energy of sin in men and women, in 'inclinations, provocations, stirrings, stingings, buds, branches, dregs, infections', as the Anglican Homily on the Misery of Man graphically puts it.[6]

Two definitions of Aquinas' are mentioned in Luther's 1536 disputation, or, more exactly, a double definition. Aquinas describes the 'habit' of original sin as being in substance (*materialiter*) 'desire' (*concupiscentia*) and in form (*formaliter*) a *defectus iustitiae*, a lack of the righteousness which was in Adam when he was created and which ought to be in man.[7] To call it 'desire', says Luther, is an insufficient definition. Even if we add that it derives from a lack of the original righteousness which ought to be present, we are still left with only a vague (*tenuis*) definition. Original sin is not 'merely' (*tantum*) a lack of righteousness, but an inbred and forceful evil which makes us guilty of sin, liable to eternal death, deserving of divine anger, and which remains in us even after baptism, denying the law of God and resisting the Holy Spirit. These are the *differentiae* of this definition.[8] But they are unknown to the 'Papists', says Luther, and he who does not know the full definition does not know what sin is. He sees

4   *WA* 39[i].95.10–12, cf. Trent V, *Decretum super Peccatum Originale*, 1546.
5   Letter to Farel, *CR* 39.251.
6   *The Anglican Homilies* (London, 1833, repr. Sussex, 1986), p. 9.
7   Cf. Aquinas, *ST* I[a]II[ae]q.82[a]3; *peccatum originale materialiter, quidem est concupiscentia, formaliter vero defectus originalis iustitiae.* Duns Scotus, *Opus Oxoniense*, II.d.30; d.32, q.un.7.8.11–12, d.37, q.1, in *Commentaria Oxoniensia ad IV Libros Magistri Sententiarum*, ed. P. M. F. Garcia (Florence, 1912); Ockham, *In Sent.* II.d.26; Gabriel Biel, *In Sent.* II.d.30, q.2, a.1.
8   The reference here is to the method of definition with which all mediaeval students of logic would be familiar. It is outlined by Porphyry in the *Isagoge*, which was studied as a beginner's textbook. One began from the genus and narrowed the description down to the species, and then to the special characteristics (*differentiae*) which marked the individual, and made it impossible to confuse it with anything else.

Paul as having the right definition. The whole of the Epistle to the Romans and the Epistle to the Galatians is a definition of original sin as a corruption of nature which 'impels' us to deny the Spirit.[9] If I claim to 'know my iniquity',[10] Luther replies that the whole world fails to understand the magnitude of sin, and even punishes those who try to point it out.[11]

Luther's emphasis upon the positivity of evil in man (for that is the paradox which underlies all that Augustine says about its negativity) is sustained elsewhere, so as to make a further point. Sin makes us powerless. Sin is slavery. In another disputation of 1536, on Man, Thesis 22 proposes that 'after the Fall of Adam' humanity became 'subject to the power of the Devil, to sin and to death', and that these are evils 'everlasting and unconquerable by human effort'.[12] This was a line of thought which Luther explored at length in his *De Servo Arbitrio* of 1525, and on which not all the reformers were in agreement with him. There was a debate with Erasmus, and Zwingli seemed to Luther too ready to let in free will. But much hung upon it in Luther's system: the powerlessness of sinful man to help himself, the lack of any merit in human effort, the sinner's dependence on God's grace and mercy for all his help. Luther was always acutely sensitive to any implication which would diminish the power and glory of God and the completeness of the work of Christ in the salvation of mankind. To avoid any hint of such consequences, he underlines in definition and argument those elements of the doctrine of original sin which make fallen man appear utterly abject and worthless, paralysed by his own enslavement to sin, and thus in some measure unavoidably devalues the dignity of the humanity Christ came to save.[13] The problem of sin, then, appeared to Luther in the light of a power-struggle within the soul, in which the individual, unaided, must always lose.

Luther's was not the only reforming voice raised on the subject of original sin in the first quarter of the sixteenth century. Zwingli, rather less preoccupied than Luther with the abuses of the penitential system,

9   *WA* 39ⁱ.117.
10 Psalm 50/51.5.
11 *WA* 39ⁱ.107.2ff. The definition of the 1548 Interim links want of righteousness with a vicious active concupiscence in fallen man (II.1). Something of Luther's idea of the sheer forcefulness of evil is here, but for Luther, now dead, it would still perhaps have seemed a *tenuis definitio*, because that is not the key element.
12 *WA* 39ⁱ.176.
13 On the question of human dignity, see Vatican II, *De Ecclesia in Mundo huius Temporis* (*Gaudium et spes*), 41.

was ready to assert against his accusers among the reformers that he did indeed see the terrible power of sin and that he had never said that original sin cannot damn us. But he was inclined to understand the term *culpa originalis* as a 'transferred usage' (*metonymice*),[14] so that although we certainly and inevitably derive our tendency to sin from our first parents, we need not be seen as doing so by an inheritance, strictly speaking. He says this not in order to sustain a debate about words. 'You see ... clearly that we are not contending about what to call it (*de nomine*) but we wanted to bring out more clearly and in its fuller meaning (*significantius*) the thing itself.' His own emphasis is upon the conception of original sin as a sickness (*morbum*) disposing us to the sins which are blameworthy (for sin is linked with *culpa*).[15]

Here Zwingli echoes a longstanding theme of penitential literature, the notion that the priest is a physician to the soul when he hears confessions. But, like Luther, he rejects the view that there can be any 'priestly power' to mend the damaged soul, because (as Luther would put it) that would be to impute power to the powerless, to mere human beings themselves helpless in the grip of sin. Questions of power and authority to forgive are, then, at the heart of the problem posed for Luther and others by sin.

[14]   On transferred usages, see *Language and Logic* I, chapter 7.
[15]   *De Peccato Originali* (1526), *Werke* V.381.21ff.

5. Justification

i. ACCEPTANCE, LOVE AND FAITH

The Trent theologians remarked early in their discussion of justification[1] that there was a sense here of treading new ground of vocabulary. In discussing original sin they had a conscious and comforting sense of familiarity, a mass of patristic literature and precedent to turn to,[2] and above all, a sense of connection with the many-layered patristic and mediaeval understanding of right order. In the part of the controversy which deals with 'faith' and 'love' everyone was on this 'home ground'; we frequently see a reaching down into tradition for a term, a reference or a concept as the adversaries struggle to express their positions clearly.

The focus of the late mediaeval debate over what Luther calls 'justification' had not been upon the problem of what makes an individual righteous in the sight of God, but upon what makes him acceptable; and not upon faith, so much as upon love. There was a preoccupation with the salvific work of the Holy Spirit within the soul rather than with the work of Christ. These concerns formed a bridge, historically as well as theologically, between the fourteenth-century revival[3] of old controversies over grace, free will and predestination[4] and Luther's ideas about 'justification'. Luther knew of the late mediaeval work on 'acceptance', and he echoes it in both his early and his later writings on justification. It is worth giving a little space to the issues here, because they touch on the question of 'power to save' by raising the possibility that the work of the Holy Spirit does by love what is necessary to make the soul acceptable to God in a manner which is in some way complementary to the work of 'justifying' accomplished through faith in Christ.

The most important text in drawing mediaeval scholars' attention to the

---

1   A. McGrath's invaluable recent two-volume study, *Iustitia Dei* (Cambridge, 1986), contains full and up-to-date bibliographical references on this still-vexed question.
2   *Acta CT* 5.257.
3   G. Leff, *Bradwardine and the Pelagians* (Cambridge, 1957).
4   Cf. Formula of Concord, XI, Tappert, pp. 494–6.

question of 'acceptance' was Distinctio 17 of the first book of Peter Lombard's *Sentences*. It is asked whether anything more than the gift of the Holy Spirit, who is himself the *habitus* of charity, is needed to make the soul acceptable to God. Duns Scotus emphasised the importance of the *habitus* of charity in the accepted soul.[5] Peter Aureoli argued that this *habitus* could not be the Holy Spirit, love himself, dwelling in the soul, or God would himself be that in the soul for which he loves and accepts it. Almost every commentator after Aureoli discussed the solution he proposed. He sought to separate the divine acceptance from that in the soul which made it possible, by postulating that God creates in the soul a 'form' which is by its nature agreeable to him, and which makes acceptable to him the soul which possesses it.[6] This 'form' cannot, however, come from the nature of the creature, or God's acceptance would be merely a recognition of merit and not an act of merciful generosity; it is a disposition to love God which has to be separately and additionally bestowed on the creature. Every commentator after Aureoli gave a major place to his ideas, some to criticise them, others to approve them at least in part. The debate came to focus not on whether it is love which is the indispensable thing, but on what happens to transform the soul and make it acceptable to God.

Gabriel Biel summarises Peter Lombard's account thus: the Holy Spirit is 'given' or 'sent' to us, when he makes us love God and our neighbour. He himself is that love by which we love God, the love which is indispensable to salvation.[7] This love grows in us, but that does not imply that the Holy Spirit himself is subject to increase or decrease. The essential points which Biel picks out here are (1) the need for love to be added by God to the soul to make it acceptable to him; (2) the indispensability of this acceptance for salvation; and (3) the unsatisfactoriness of saying that this *habitualis dilectio* is simply the Holy Spirit.

The shift of emphasis in Luther's generation from the discussion of 'acceptance' to the discussion of 'justification', from talk of love to talk of faith, involves a change in this understanding of what it is which makes a person pleasing to God.[8] There was considerable concern among the mediaevals to show that something is there in the individual who is

5   Duns Scotus, *Commentaria Oxoniensia*, I.875ff.
6   Peter Aureoli, *In I Sent.* xvii, p. 1, a.2. 508D.
7   G. Biel, *Collectorium*, p. 413.
8   *Ibid.*

accepted which makes him or her pleasing to God. Otherwise, it would seem that God is an 'accepter of persons', able to be bribed or persuaded by high position or influence. The preoccupation with the difference between *acceptatio personarum* and the just preference of God for one individual rather than another is already widespread in Aquinas' writings.[9] 'The acceptance of persons is opposed to distributive justice, by which someone gives another what he is worthy of (*secundum dignitatem personarum*); acceptance is when someone is given more than he deserves.'[10] So 'acceptance' is understood as an act of justice recognising the state of the individual as actually pleasing to God, not a mere pronouncing righteous. William of Ockham looks at the problem in one of his *Quaestiones Variae*, in a way which links it directly with the debate about predestination. If two persons are equal in all except that God has prepared one for eternal life and the other not, so that one is *carus* and *acceptus* to God, is not God preferring one to another; is God not behaving as an *acceptor personarum*? No, says Ockham, not unless God's acceptance is subject to improper influences which would make it not consonant with justice.[11]

There seems, then, to have been a conscious late mediaeval effort to underline the difference between *acceptio personarum* (normally a pejorative expression in Scripture) and *acceptatio*, that acceptance without which no-one can enter the Kingdom of Heaven.[12] *Acceptatio* does not occur in the Vulgate, and is a late Latin coining. (Tertullian has it as a synonym for *acceptio* with *personarum*.[13]) The preference for *acceptio* in the discussions of God's acceptance of those he saves helps to set it apart from the dubious 'acceptance of persons' from which our authors are anxious to distinguish it. Aquinas sets out perhaps most clearly of them all the fine distinction of signification which needed to be made between *acceptio* and *acceptatio*. If God accepts a person justly, then he must be giving that person what it is proper for him to have, finding him pleasing for what he is. On the other hand, no-one can be pleasing in the

9   Aquinas discusses the topic in his Sermons and Quodlibets as well as in Scriptural commentary and the *Summa Theologiae*.
10 Aquinas on Romans 2.11, para. 20, cf. *Quaestiones Quodlibetales*, ed. R. Spiazzi (Turin, 1956), Quodlibet IV, q.9. a.4, para. 84.
11 Ockham, *Quaestiones Variae*, ed. G. I. Etzkern *et al.* (New York, 1984). *Opera Theologica*, ed. G. Gal, S. Brown *et al.* (New York, 1967–), VIII.14; cf. p. 22, q.1.
12 Cf. Aquinas on Romans 5.17, para. 441; see, too, B. Hamm, *Frömmigkeitstheologie am Anfang des 16 Jahrhunderts* (Tübingen, 1982), pp. 210ff.
13 Tertullian, *De Pudicitia*, 5.

sight of God as a sinner, and all men are sinners. So God's acceptance (*acceptatio*) is understood in a twofold way, suggests Aquinas (*dupliciter accipitur*). It signifies both the divine acceptance which is God's free will (*gratuita dei voluntas*) (and thus no reward for merit); and also that which stands for a certain created gift which formally perfects man. These two *significationes* are ordered in relation to one another (*ordinem habent ad invicem*); in such a way that they are in fact inseparable. Acceptance is not freely given; he to whom it is given is in some way 'accepted'.[14] God has, then, given the individual that for which he accepts him, and yet his acceptance is free and in no way a favouritism. He both accepts the individual, pronouncing him righteous, and actually makes him so. This of course is one of the paradoxes with which Peter Aureoli was subsequently trying to deal in formulating his three much-contested principles.

Yet Aquinas' device saves the divine acceptance not only from the imputation of favouritism, but also from the implication that there is changeableness in God. Biel sets out this particular difficulty neatly in his *Questions on Justification*, with reference to views of earlier authors. Since there can be no *transitus* from one state (unacceptability) to another contradictory one (acceptability) without a change taking place, either he who is now accepted must have changed, or God must have changed, which is impossible.[15] So it seems that the change must be objectively present in the person accepted and not merely *quoad Deum*.[16] Again, Peter Aureoli's principles had sought to meet the difficulty, by explaining how something is indeed bestowed on the accepted soul, objectively speaking, which makes it possible for God to find it pleasing. But whereas Aquinas indicates that both the giving of that which makes a person acceptable and the acceptance itself are included in *acceptatio*, Aureoli wanted to separate the two for the sake of the objective reality of the soul's acceptability. It is as heir to this debate that Luther says that 'God cannot accept a man without justifying grace'.[17] There is an echo of the assumption of the same rule in the Heidelberg Disputation where Luther claims that the love of God does not find but creates that which is pleasing to

[14]   Aquinas, Quaestiones de Veritate, 27.5. In *Quaestiones Disputatae*, ed. R. Spiazzi (Turin, 1964).
[15]   G. Biel, *Questions on Justification*, ed. C. Feckes (Aschendorff, 1929), Q.1. a.3, dub.1, p. 12.
[16]   For the phrase *quoad Deum*, cf. Wyclif, *VSS* I.x, Vol. I. 219.
[17]   Luther, *Contra Scholasticam Theologiam*, Thesis 56.

it,[18] and again in *Two Kinds of Righteousness*, where he emphasises that righteousness is something which comes to us from outside ourselves, and also in the *Disputation on Justification* of 1536 where again he stresses that righteousness is alien to us and comes to us from outside.[19]

Peter Lombard notes that some say that the Holy Spirit is not himself the love by which we love God and our neighbour. He thus encouraged generations of his commentators to ask whether this 'gift from outside us of that which makes us acceptable to God' is anything more than the gift of the Holy Spirit himself. Is that grace without which (Luther reminds us) we cannot be acceptable to God, the Holy Spirit, or a something other than the Holy Spirit put into the soul; or is it itself the act of acceptance? Again Aureoli's three principles are central to the debate. But before him we can see Aquinas grappling with the question. He reviews various opinions. 'It seems that grace puts nothing created into the soul' (*in anima ponat*). 'Yet grace puts a certain *acceptatio* into him who is said to have grace, so that he is *acceptus* to him whose grace he has.' 'When someone is said to "have" the grace of God, that does not mean that something is "put into" his soul (*ponitur in anima*). It signifies only divine acceptance.' Aquinas himself argues that talk of 'having the grace of God' must imply actually having something in one which makes one pleasing and acceptable to God.[20] Duns Scotus again asks whether we must postulate that a created love (that is, not simply the Holy Spirit) is made to inhere in the nature which is capable of bliss.[21] Ockham puts a similar question: Whether apart from the Holy Spirit it is necessary to postulate that love informs the soul to make it dear and acceptable to

18   Heidelberg Disputation (*WA* 1.353–74), Thesis 28.
19   Thesis III.27 of the 1536 *Disputation on Justification* states that 'Christ, or Christ's righteousness cannot be embraced (*comprehendi*) by our works, since it is outside us and alien to us' (*aliena a nobis*). The argument in reply proposes that the righteousness of Christ justifies us as something internal to us (*interna*) and our very own (*propria*). So it is not alien to us or external to us. This turns, it is suggested, on a grammatical point (*phrasis grammatica*). To be external to us is not to derive from our efforts. But Christ's righteousness is still our possession (*possessio nostra*), because it is given to us in mercy; at the same time, it is *aliena a nobis* because we do not deserve it. Luther, *Two Kinds of Righteousness* (*WA* 2.145–52), *Disputation on Justification*, Argument 17, against Thesis III.27 and cf. 28.35; *WA* 39^i.83 and 108–9.
20   Lombard, *Sententiae* I. xvii (Florence, 1971); Aquinas, *In Sent.* II. 26. 1. 1; *ST* I^a II^a. q.110. a.1, obj.1 and reply.
21   Scotus, *In Sent.* I. xvii.

God.[22] We meet the question again in Biel. Is it necessary to postulate a created absolute love (*caritas absoluta creata*) formally informing those souls God finds dear and acceptable?[23] Biel thought Ockham right in holding that God can, in principle, accept a person by his absolute power (*potentia absoluta*) without any *habitus* of charity informing his soul, although, obeying his own laws, he would refrain from doing so. (This voluntarily limited power is his ordered power (*potentia ordinata*).[24]) Biel argues that God blesses in mercy out of pure grace, and not because of some imposed form or gift.[25] Luther quarrels with this view in his *Contra Scholasticam Theologiam* (identifying it as Biel's). The grace of God cannot so act, he says, even through its absolute power, that an act of love may be present without the presence of the grace of God.[26] The notion of the independent, if created, existence of something in the soul which makes it acceptable to God, something over and above the presence of the Holy Spirit, was, then, uncongenial to Luther even at this early stage in the development of his thinking.

This debate brought about a shift of emphasis in Luther's mind from the mediaeval discussion of the work of the Holy Spirit in making an individual acceptable to God, to a consideration of the work of Christ. God forgives us and is merciful to us, says Luther, because Christ our great High Priest intercedes and sanctifies our beginning in righteousness. The faith which is poured into us as we hear about Christ 'comprehends' him and makes us one with him.[27] And, in accordance with the vocabulary of Romans 4, the terminology of the debate changes too. Instead of *acceptatio*, the discussion now turns for Luther on 'justification'. It seemed to Luther as he read St Paul that he was being shown something quite new, and in certain respects that is undoubtedly the case. But a complex of influences, both positive and the ones against which he reacted, are demonstrably interfused in the process of arriving at that perception, and in his subsequent working out of what it meant for him, especially in singling out certain elements of the 'power-struggle' against sin.

'Love' did not cease to be a subject of dispute. One of the Wittenberg

22   Ockham, *Quaest. Var.*, q.1, citing Peter Aureoli, *In I Sent.* xvii a.2.
23   Biel, *Questions on Justification*, Q.1.
24   Ockham, *Quaest. Var.*, q.1, p. 9.
25   Biel, *Questions on Justification*, Q.1.
26   Luther, *Contra Scholasticam Theologiam*, Thesis 55.
27   *Disputation on Justification*, Theses III.25–8.

debates took as its theme the text, 'Much is forgiven her, for she loved much' (Luke 7.47). There is, argues Luther, the later passage where Jesus says, 'Your faith has saved you' (Luke 7.50). If he had wanted to include love as necessary to salvation, he could have said, 'Your faith and love have saved you.'[28] It is argued that love deserves the remission of sins. Luther explains that Christ was speaking of the love which proceeds from faith, and is an indication of the presence of justifying faith but not a constitutive part of its justifying.[29] He goes on to develop a distinction between that justification which is spiritual, between God and man, and which proceeds from an efficient cause; and a justification between one human being and another, which derives as an effect from that cause (*est ex effectu*). What is needed before God is faith, not works. What is needed before men is good works and love, which declare us righteous before one another and before the world.[30] If the woman had not had trust (*fiducia*) in God, she would not have poured out the tears which showed her love to all observers. The love is effect of faith not part of it. Melanchthon elaborates elsewhere on this point. There is a familiar figure of speech, called *synecdoche*, he explains, by which we sometimes combine cause and effect in the same phrase. Christ says in Luke 7.47, 'Her sins, which are many, are forgiven, because she loved much …' Now Christ did not want to say that by her works of love the woman had merited the forgiveness of sins. Therefore he clearly says, 'Your faith has saved you'.[31]

It is against this elimination of love as a causative element in justification that Trent speaks in one of its canons. 'We are justified not solely by the imputation of the righteousness of Christ, and not solely by the remission of sins, but also by grace and love shed abroad in our hearts by the Holy Spirit.'[32] Eck contends that in fact love is better than faith.[33] But love has its place for the reformers, as an inevitable consequence or effect of justification. 'Who is there whose heart … will not rejoice and grow tender, so that he will love Christ, as he never could by keeping the law or doing good works?' asks Luther of the justified.[34]

28 *WA* 39i.129, Thesis 3.
29 *Disputation on Justification*, Argument 22 and Argument against Thesis III.29. *WA* 39i.91 and 115.
30 *WA* 39i.91; cf. p. 132.
31 *Apologia* for Augsburg Confession, Art. 4.152, Tappert, p. 127.
32 Trent VI, Canon 11.
33 Eck, *Loci*, p. 96.
34 *The Freedom of a Christian*, 1520, *WA* 7.49f.

In all this it is striking that more attention was not given to those key passages in which reference is made to the *fides Iesu Christi* (Romans 3.22 and 26; Galatians 2.16 and 20; Galatians 3.22; Philippians 3.9), and where the genitive is ambiguous. The reformers tend to take it to refer not to Christ's own faith, but to faith in Christ. *Per fidem Iesu Christi, qua creditur in Ihesum Christum*, says Luther;[35] Calvin, on the same passage, comments:

> *paucis verbis ostendit qualis sit haec iustificatio, nempe quod in Christo resideat, per fidem apprehendatur.*[36]

There is an instance here of the persistence of Vulgate readings and assumptions even where work on the Greek would prompt discussion.[37]

Bullinger comments that the word 'faith' has many significations 'in the common talk of men'.[38] That was equally apparent to the Roman Catholics. Contarini lists the most important of them during the Trent debates. In the Creeds it refers to the content of belief (*quod creditur*); for example in the Athanasian Creed we have: *hec est fides catholica*. Or it may refer to the disposition to believe or to the act of believing, *habitus* or *actus*. Faith is also sometimes called assurance (*quandoque appellatur fiducia*); by this faith we trust in the promise made to us. This faith (*fiducia*) is intimately related to hope, although properly speaking hope refers to the future and faith to the present and the past, he says.[39]

The first of these meanings of the word 'faith' was generally and uncontroversially separated from the rest in the disputes. Assent to the truth of the Gospel is found even in devils, who know the facts of the faith, and of whom it is said, 'They believe and tremble' (James 2.19), as both Luther and Melanchthon point out more than once.[40] Faith which embraces with commitment is something different, giving no merely intellectual assent to the articles of faith, and especially that which states, 'I believe in the remission of sins.' It is a commitment of the will to God in repentance and obedience to his call. Faith here, Melanchthon says, signifies belief in the 'effect' of the content (the *historia*) of what is believed, 'namely, this article of the forgiveness of sins, that is, that we

---

35 On Romans 3.22, *WA* 57.39.
36 *CR* 49.59–60.
37 See M. Hooker, 'ΠΙΣΤΙΣ ΧΡΙΣΤΟΥ', *New Testament Studies*, 35 (1989), 321–42.
38 *Decades* I.81.
39 *Acta CT* 12.317.
40 For example, *WA* 39ii.206, cf. 318–19 and Augsburg Confession 20.23.

have grace, righteousness and forgiveness of sins through Christ'.[41] Those who interpret Paul's words, 'we are justified by faith', in terms of the more limited definition, perpetrate a synecdoche, taking the part for the whole.[42]

There is an intervention on the same point by Melanchthon in the degree disputation of Major and Faber in 1544. Melanchthon throws down this syllogism as a challenge:

It is impossible for a person to be just by knowledge [of the faith] alone.
You say that man is just by faith alone.
If faith is *notitia* you posit something impossible.

'Or are you proving that faith signifies something other than knowledge?' he asks. Faber offers a passage from Romans 4. Melanchthon gives a warning. 'If you want to say that faith does not signify knowledge (*notitia*) alone, but also embraces many other virtues, you do as the scholastics do, and make justifying faith a "formed" faith (*fides formata*), and that will produce an equivocation in the use of the word "faith".' That gives Faber his cue. 'It does not signify knowledge in this context, but firm assurance (*fiducia*) and assent to God's promises.'[43] The faith which saves, then, is seen here as a laying hold on the divine promise of mercy.

The emphasis on 'assurance' was not without its negative implications. Some Protestants pointed to a danger that lack of confidence in the sufficiency of Christ's work led to too much reliance on human efforts. Catholic apologists argued that if assurance was overemphasised and linked with a doctrine of predestination it was difficult for Christians to understand the importance of holiness of life.[44] The Interim of 1548 warns, 'Care must be taken that we do not either make men too secure and confident in themselves, or drive them by anxious doubting to despair.'[45] Adrianus Saravia offered a crisp distinction in his *Memorandum* of 1595. 'There is a great *discrimen* between certainty of salvation and security. Certainty begets faith, security presumption and arrogance.' To use the word *securitas* for *certitudo* is a catachresis or hyperbole. The Word of God everywhere discourages us from security; certitude arms Christians

---

41 Augsburg Confession 20.23, Tappert, p. 44.
42 *Synecdoche* is of course one of the most frequently referred to of the classical *topoi* in mediaeval debate; see above, p. 68.
43 *WA* 39ii.318.
44 Trent VI, Canon 2.
45 VIII.1.

against all temptations; security betrays them to the enemy. The faith which brings certitude of salvation renders us anxious to keep it, not secure. True *fiducia* is knowing that provision for my salvation is infallibly there.[46]

ii. THE SOFTENING OF GOD'S WRATH

It had long been recognised that Scripture's use of words such as 'anger' can be only metaphorical in connection with God.[47] The appeasing of divine 'wrath' and 'indignation' is not a soothing of displeasure or outrage in an offended deity, but the restoration of right order.[48] As Anselm of Canterbury described it, *iustitia* is inseparable from *rectus ordo*. Contarini, who was to be one of the Trent theologians, wrote in his own confutation of the 'Lutheran articles' of Augsburg that to be forgiven is to be no longer at odds with God's law, but at one with it. That is what being 'just' means. 'Christians understand justification to be nothing other than to be made a participator in divine righteousness' (*fieri participem divinae iustitiae*). He sees this as something which is not proper to human nature, even in its unfallen state (*non convenit*), but a gift of divine liberality and goodness. By that righteousness man is lifted above his human condition (*hominis status*).[49] In his *Apologia* for the Augsburg Confession, Melanchthon also stresses the connection between justification and forgiveness. Forgiveness is not only 'supremely necessary in justification'; according to Psalm 32.1, it can be identified with it, says Melanchthon. 'Blessed is he whose transgression is forgiven.' But he draws another inference, which makes all the difference to the reformers' conception of the nature of justification. The major premiss that justification is forgiveness of sins is followed by a minor premiss (with which his opponents would agree), that 'We obtain the forgiveness of sins only by faith in Christ.' The conclusion which follows for Melanchthon is that 'We are justified by faith alone.' Melanchthon reads this faith as a trust which is placed in the mercy promised for Christ's sake. The law shows us God's anger against sin, and so we are afraid while we remain

[46]   Thesis 20, and ARCIC II, *Salvation and the Church*, cf. Louvain, Theses 9, 10, and *WA* 39[ii].148.
[47]   See my *The Thought of Gregory the Great* (Cambridge, 1986), p. 39.
[48]   See my *Anselm* (London/New York, 1989), pp. 71ff.
[49]   *Confutatio Articulorum seu Quaestionum Lutheranorum*, ed. F. Hünermann, C. *Cath.* 7 (Münster, 1923), p. 1.

in our sins. When we are reassured that they are forgiven our 'terrified consciences' are comforted.[50] Forgiveness is thus freedom from fear.

This differentiation of emphasis in the framing of the definition of 'justification' was important in the debates about justification which followed on Luther's first assertions of the principle of justification by faith. The definition which stresses 'freedom from fear' puts the emphasis on our deserts and the real and terrible cause we have to be afraid; and promises that if we have faith God will not count our sins against us (imputed righteousness). The definition which emphasises 'rectification', a real 'putting right', the restoration of 'right order', sees an actual not an imputed change resulting from the application of Christ's merits (inherent righteousness). To put it crudely, the difference at its most extreme was between a helpless trust that one will not receive one's deserts as a sinner because God in his mercy chooses to see only Christ's merits; and the view that the union of the soul with Christ in faith makes us in some understanding of the term 'really' participators in Christ's merits. The contrast is between a system which diminishes human dignity in the interests of defending God's sovereignty, and a system which elevates it for the same reason: arguing this time that our human nature must be unimaginably elevated by our union with Christ, so that we become 'consorts' of his divine nature in sharing the perfection of his humanity.[51] It is also a contrast between a system in which right action and conformity with divine law and right-heartedness are important as constitutive parts of the process of justification, and an account of things in which these, though important (and the mainstream reformers insisted that they were important), do not ultimately 'count' in the salvation of the individual.

Bullinger's point about law needs to be read here with a gloss. It was a commonplace among reformers that Christ came to make an old obligation unnecessary, so that Gospel freedom replaced the petty legalism of trying to please God by keeping his law. Their immediate concern was with the legalistic requirements of the penitential system, and all the apparatus of 'doing good works' which we shall come to in due course. But mediaeval scholars – Anselm conspicuously among them – had a rather different understanding of the meaning of conformity with God's

---

50 Article 4, Tappert, pp. 117–18.
51 The theme of the elevation of humanity to the divinity of Christ is explored by Anselm in the *Cur Deus Homo, Opera Omnia*, vol. II.

law, a perception of the importance of order to the well-being of human nature, and of 'being what one ought'. This underlay the penitential procedures at the profoundest level.

iii. THE LANGUAGE AND LOGIC OF JUSTIFICATION

Formal skills drawn from the study of the arts of language were particularly important in the conduct of this debate. In the wrangle about definitions, the continuing dominance of Latin is conspicuous. In the New Testament the Greek verb *dikaioun* usually means 'to pronounce righteous'. Calvin emphasises this sense of being 'regarded as' righteous, or 'acquitted', in his discussion of the Trent decrees in his *Antidote* to Trent (VI, Decree 8), and it is to be found widely among the reformers. But the sense of the Greek had long been overlaid in the West by the weight of the Latin *justificare*, the Vulgate's rendering of *dikaioun*, which includes an actual 'making righteous'.[52] This emphasis is clear in the debates of the Council of Trent on justification. Vincentius de Leone, for example, in June 1546, proposed the definitions: 'justification is the making of righteousness, and to be justified is to be made righteous'.[53]

Both sides were highly conscious of the complexity of the questions of signification thus raised, and we find sophisticated use of the technicalities of signification theory as they touch on areas where grammar and logic overlap, in an attempt to get the epistemology right and to relate the *verbum* to the *res* correctly. The combatants employ the technical language of mediaeval signification theory freely and the bulk of the discussion is about the Latin and its usages. Some, bringing up the fashionable topic of the *chimaera*, argued that 'imputed justice' was an expression without reference, a *chimericum vocabulum*. It was replied that 'those who say that *imputatio* is a chimera with no corresponding reality (*nihilque correspondere sibi a parte rei*) are deceived. Taken passively *imputari* is like *ordinari, applicari, communicari*.'[54] At the same time, again in line with familiar mediaeval tradition, 'common usage' is set beside technical usage. It is, says Melanchthon, common

---

[52]   Cf. ARCIC II, *Salvation and the Church*, 14.
[53]   *Iustificatio est factio iustitiae et iustificari est iustus fieri, Acta CT* 5.264, 23 June 1546; cf. Contarini, *Confutatio*, 12.316.
[54]   *Documentos inéditos tridentinos sobre la justificación*, ed. J. Olazarán (Madrid, 1957), pp. 315–16. On *chimaera* literature, see *CHLMP*, pp. 794–5, and here pp. 130, 154.

usage to say (*usitate dicitur*) that 'to be justified signifies to become just instead of unjust' (*iustificari significat ex iniusto iustum fieri*). In this common usage to be unjust is to be guilty and disobedient and not to have Christ. To be just is to be absolved from guilt for the sake of the Son of God, and to lay hold by faith on the very Christ who is our justice.[55] This common or popular way of speaking has the same sort of authority as what Augustine or Anselm would have called *usus loquendi*. But there is also 'propriety' of usage, which is exact.

Thus Seripando explains that the word 'justification' (*justificationis vocabulum*) has a connotation or 'force' (*potestas* again, or *vis*, as in the mediaeval *vis verborum*) of righteousness of works (*iustitia operum*). In this sense a person is said to be justified if he lives justly and keeps the law. But he himself takes the view that this sort of righteousness is properly (*proprie*) called *sanctificatio*. He points to the Vulgate text of 1 Corinthians 1.30 for Biblical evidence for this position. Paul says that Christ was made (*factus est*) not only *iustitia* but *sanctificatio* for us. He also emphasises that we are called righteous (*denominamur ... iusti*) insofar as we are *aliquid Christi*, that is, insofar as we are his, his members, participating in his righteousness who alone is truly righteous.[56] The primary and proper sense of *iustificatio* for Seripando is that which makes our 'justice' Christ's, and he would prefer to use the word *sanctificatio* for holiness of life. Here he was in agreement with the principle of the Lutheran Formula of Concord, that the word 'regeneration' has exactly this double sense, including both 'the forgiveness of sins solely for Christ's sake, and the subsequent renewal which the Holy Spirit works in those who are justified by faith'.[57] The Lutherans, too, were anxious that terminological inexactitude should not blur a distinction between righteousness which is ours because we are Christ's and a personal growing in holiness.[58] Such instances of the combatants feeling their way in definition, and often coming close to a shared position, could be multiplied at considerable length. The debates are rich with them, and they reveal again and again the great difficulty of stating clearly and unequivocally a difference of position to which the parties could subscribe as being in language they could wholeheartedly own.

[55] *Confessio Saxonica, CR* 28.386–7. The 'qualities' theme recurs in the Formula of Concord, Solid Declaration, Art. 1, Tappert, p. 519.

[56] *De Iustificatione, Acta CT* 12.669.

[57] Art. 3, Tappert, p. 542.

[58] *Ibid.*, p. 543.

From logic – specifically, the *Categories* – are brought to bear various points about qualities, a topic familiar in fallacy-theory. Although justification is a new beginning in the individual (*inchoatur novitas*), Melanchthon explains in the *Confessio Saxonica* of 1551, we do not say that a person is just in this life because of new qualities (*novas qualitates*); we say that he is just because of the suffering, resurrection and intercession of Christ, who brings us life. It follows that we must understand as a correlative that the proposition 'we are justified by faith' implies nothing about our *qualitas*. We use a *particula exclusiva* (i.e. *sola*) and say 'by faith alone', because no merit of ours is involved. We meet further echoes of the *Categories* in one of Luther's disputations. 'To justify does not signify to accept, or to pronounce just, but it signifies the pouring in of new qualities.' Against this line of argument is first advanced Romans 4.3 and 4.5, where Paul speaks of the imputation of righteousness. *Ergo iustificare significat imputare.* Luther says that he does not like to hear righteousness or love called a 'quality' in theological discussion, although it is all right to do so if we are talking philosophy. It has been suggested that when Peter speaks of 'purifying their hearts by faith' (Acts 15.9), he means nothing other than pouring into their hearts new qualities. But even in Acts, says Luther, 'the vocabulary of purification is the vocabulary of imputation'. 'To purify the heart is to impute purification to the heart.' God purifies the Gentiles, that is he considers (*reputat*) them purified. That means that although they are really (*realiter*) still sinners, he counts them righteous, and then he begins to make them really righteous. 'First he purifies by imputing (*imputative*), then he gives the Holy Spirit, through whom we are purified in substance (*substantialiter*).' Faith purifies by the remission of sins; the Holy Spirit purifies by its effect (*per effectum*). 'This is the spiritual theology which the philosophers do not understand when they call righteousness a quality.'[59] Seripando takes up the idea of 'qualities' too, explaining that we can no more be called *iusti* as though the word referred to our substance than qualities can properly be thought substances just because they bear their names.[60] Our righteousness is imperfect not because the gift of grace is imperfect, but

---

[59] *WA* 39^i.98.16ff, 1536 *Disputation on Justification.*
[60] This is probably a reference to the mediaeval debate about denominatives. See D. P. Henry, *The Logic of St Anselm, passim.*

because we who co-operate with that grace are imperfect in our response.[61]

Thus to the questions about effect and power and authority in this area as elsewhere, must be added questions about the 'force of words', *vis verborum*, which are never far from the minds of those engaged in the sixteenth-century debates.

iv. THE LIMITS OF JUSTIFICATION

An article on justification was framed at Ratisbon in 1541. It strove to bring together the elements which had been thrust apart by efforts to construct definitions which would rule out one 'false' emphasis or another:

> Living faith is that which apprehends God's mercy in Christ and believes that the righteousness of Christ is freely imputed to oneself, and at the same time receives the promise of the Holy Spirit and also love ... But it remains true that we are justified, that is, accepted and reconciled to God by this faith insofar as it apprehends God's mercy and the righteousness which is imputed to us on account of Christ and his merit, not on account of the worth or perfection of the righteousness which is imparted (*communicata*) to us in Christ.

Calvin was willing to approve this formulation,[62] but Luther condemned it,[63] and so did Rome.

The Interim of 1548 sets out the steps of its own argument at length. It is suggested that when a person is justified three things happen immediately. His or her sins are forgiven; there is acquittal from the liability to eternal damnation; the Holy Spirit makes the individual no longer unrighteous but righteous, by purification of his or her heart, shedding love into the heart and inciting to good and just living (IV.1). In this light 'inherent righteousness' becomes simply God's gift – the real possession of the individual, but not of his own making (cf. IV.2). That does not bring an end to the war between concupiscence and holiness, but all our lives 'Christ ... by the communication of his own righteousness, renders the righteousness of the man partaking of it inherent, and so augments it' (IV.3–4). There is no incompatibility between this 'inherent righteousness to which we are renewed by the gift of charity' (IV.5) and a full

---

[61] *Acta CT* 12.669.
[62] *CR* 39.215.
[63] *WA Briefe* 9.406ff. (no. 3616) and 9.474 (no. 3645).

recognition that all merit is Christ's. The justified have peace with God through Christ (V.1) and are adopted as sons (V.2). The place of faith is described: God moves people's minds and wills to a detestation of sin (VI.1); he does so by the 'method' of faith (VI.2), and faith brings trust and hope, a hope which believes despite a recognition of one's utter lack of merit (VI.3). Justification is inseparable from sanctification (VI.4).

Calvin was an important influence in blocking the reception of this synthesis. He soon replied with a *True Method of Giving Peace and Reforming the Church* in which he blasts the whole.

The root of the difficulty was that even if these formulations could have been accepted as describing a justification in which all merit is Christ's, while allowing the individual a dignity and worth in God's eyes in his own right (thus shifting Luther's ground a little), as yet no way had been devised of admitting 'growth in holiness' into the scheme which would not bring after it the trail of entailments concerning the penitential system which Luther so much feared.

The mature Luther agrees with Augustine (who, he thinks, has alone preserved this teaching for us), that original sin is taken away in the sense that it is no longer counted against us. The serpent is still there, but its sting is drawn, as long as I remain in Christ. When I fall away, then it injures me. Original sin remains, he says, until death *quoad rem*, as a reality. But *quoad imputationem tollitur*, it is no longer imputed to us.[64] If there is still power in original sin, the problem of powerlessness cannot be said to be resolved at a stroke by justification.

At two related points Luther's 'decisive moment' in the Christian life, the initial commitment of faith, failed to meet the difficulties about powerlessness created by sin. It did so first in not containing a full account of the nature of the restoration of the sinner to the full working order of the human nature in which he was created; and secondly in not fully relating the salvation of the individual to the salvation of the community with which he is united when he becomes Christ's. It does not include the empowering for good which in fact the reformers acknowledged to be of the first importance in the Christian life, but which, in the Lutheran system, necessarily became something of an afterthought to justification.

The underlying question is again what 'counts' with God in the salvation of the individual. Whenever the reformers scent the imputation

[64]   *WA* 39^i.110.28ff.

of credit to man rather than God they reject it. But that does not mean that they do not see sanctification, growth in love and holiness, or 'quickening', as important, and indeed as necessary, in the sense that no-one who is saved will fail to experience it. Calvin's comments on the doctrine of 'mortification and quickening' make the point neatly. He explains that certain learned men of the past held that repentance consists of both mortification and quickening, and that they understood mortification as *contritio*, the grief and terror of the soul which comes to realise its sinfulness. Some have further divided this into two, a 'legal' form, such as was experienced by Cain, Saul and Judas, which leaves the sinner downcast and in fear of judgement: and a 'gospel' form, in which there is hope and a recognition of God's goodness. The 'quickening' which the mediaeval tradition wanted to make a part of repentance, seeing it as the joy of the soul which recognises by faith the mercy, grace and salvation obtained through Christ, Calvin prefers to regard as a consequence of repentance, and to describe it as the desire to live a holy life which springs from the new birth of the soul. Quickening is thus regeneration, the new life which follows death.[65] The concept here is sequential. The good which is the outcome of justification follows upon it, and does not form a constitutive part of it.

'Sanctification,' says Johannes Wollebius, 'is related to justification as light is to the sun. It is the free act of God, by which the faithful, who are engrafted into Christ through faith and justified through the Holy Spirit, are progressively set free from their innate sinfulness and restored to his image, so that they may be made fit to glorify him by good works.'[66] The question is whether this relationship of light to its source is to be understood on an analogy with the patristic interpretation of the image of the Trinity as sun, light and heat: that is, in such a way that the shining is itself justification. The answer of the Council of Trent is in the affirmative (VI, Canon 24), and it is a view shared by some of the reformers. Bullinger, for example, defines justification thus:

> To justify is as much as to say to 'quit from judgement' and from the denounced and uttered sentence of condemnation. It signifieth to remit offences, to cleanse, to sanctify, and to give inheritance of life everlasting ... This term ... is taken ... for the absolution

65 *Institutes* III.3–9.
66 Beardslee, *Reformed Dogmatics*, pp. 171–2.

and remission of sins, for sanctification, and adoption into the number of the sons of God.[67]

Sanctification, it is usually held, is a gradual change in the faithful, not an abrupt transformation. So if justification may be taken to include (rather than to give rise to) sanctification, it must itself be regarded as a process rather than an event. Calvin seems to concede as much in his commentary on Hebrews. The justice of God is communicated to us, he says, 'partly' when in free reconciliation we are regarded as just, and 'partly' when we are renewed by the Holy Spirit, so that we may live a holy life.[68]

[67] *Decades*, I.104–5; cf. III.336–7.
[68] *CR* 83.82, on Heb. 7.1.

6. The empowering of the will for good

The relationship of human free will to divine foreknowledge and grace had long been what Anselm of Canterbury called a *famosissima quaestio*.[1] The debate since Augustine had been chiefly concerned with the puzzle of the interaction of the three forces of 'will', 'power' and 'necessity', as Anselm describes them at the beginning of his *Cur Deus Homo*.[2] The concepts of human freedom of choice, divine grace, predestination and foreknowledge had consistently been recognised to make absolute demands, and the perennial problem was – and remains – to understand how they can be reconciled without diminishing the dignity and denying the fullness of being of either God or man. This way of posing the problem was in some degree determined by the preoccupation of philosophers from Aristotle's day with the puzzle of necessary and contingent futurity. 'Tomorrow's sea-fight' of Aristotle's *De Interpretatione* loomed over the debate.[3] When an omniscient and all-powerful God looks to the future it seems that he must determine the outcome of his creatures' lives by his very knowledge of what will happen to them. Augustine had developed a doctrine of divine grace which saw it as working irresistibly in those God chooses to save, and a doctrine of human free will which took away all its power to do good in its fallen state, and made it wholly dependent upon grace to enable it to work at all. The principle is stated in the Interim of 1548 (III.3), and by the Council of Trent.[4] Calvin says 'Amen' to this Canon in his *Antidote* to Trent.

Predestination was not in itself a topic central to the Lutheran debates. The Lutheran Formula of Concord says as much: 'no public discussion has developed among the theologians of the Augsburg Confession concerning this article'. But the Formula includes a note or two on the doctrine. It sees it as being of comfort when properly understood: that is to say, when it is recognised that God's foreknowledge is not a cause of anyone's being wicked, that God desires to save everyone, but not

1   *De Casu Diaboli*, 26, *Anselmi Opera Omnia*, I.274.
2   *Opera Omnia*, II.48–9.
3   Aristotle, *De Interpretatione*, 18ᵇ.
4   Trent VI, Canon 3.

everyone accepts his grace; and that we must always try hard to live according to the will of God, and not to consider ourselves free to do whatever we like because God accepts us as justified for Christ's sake.[5]

It is the idea of 'doing good' which concerns us here, for Luther's doctrine of the powerlessness of the fallen human will to do good, and of a justification which merely 'imputes' righteousness, are not on the face of it immediately reconcilable with this imperative to live a life in conformity with divine will; and remember that good works matter, even though they do not 'count'.

Augustine's concern over the relationship between a decisive faith and the importance of doing good arose in an altogether different context of controversy. His sixteenth-century readers made, on the whole, no allowance for the resulting difference of purpose between their writings on 'faith and works' and his. In the *De Fide et Operibus* and elsewhere, Augustine attacks a contemporary practice of teaching catechumens only the facts of faith, and reserving questions of life and discipline until after baptism. That meant that some were coming to baptism still living openly in serious sin, taking the view that amendment of life need begin only when they were baptised. Augustine insists that faith and works must always go together, that there can be no real faith where there is not a striving for amendment of life. His concern here was as much pastoral as theological. That pastoral emphasis is echoed in late mediaeval reflections on the subject of works, as the reformers were aware. Melanchthon quotes a passage from Jean Gerson on the spiritual life, in his *Apologia* for the Augsburg Confession,[6] deploring the danger to conscience which comes from wrong thinking on the problem of good works. One of the great strengths of the mediaeval penitential system at its best (and stripped of the undoubted corruptions with which it was shot through) lay in its teaching about the use of the will for good in those in whom the Holy Spirit is at work. It taught the believer to understand his task as a process of responding aright within the paths God laid down for him in life. It placed the emphasis upon a process, a growth in holiness, and it provided for the repair of slips and failings in a way which helped the believer to forgive himself, and to mend the hurt he did others. It recognised that 'mending' was the business likely to loom largest in individual lives. The emphasis was thus, for practical purposes, not upon the confrontation of human and divine will at the point of commitment,

[5]   Lutheran Formula of Concord, XI, Tappert, pp. 494–6, and cf. pp. 616ff.
[6]   Article 15.28, Tappert, p. 219, and Gerson, Lectio 2.iii.16 on The Spiritual Life.

nor upon the questions of election and predestination for good or ill, but upon the enabling of the will, by grace, to do good. In this way it was possible for Augustine's extreme position on predestination to form an acceptable background to the concentration of the penitential system upon what Augustine himself calls 'judgement now', the lifetime's testing and learning which forms a prelude to the final judgement.

The relationship of justification to growth in holiness seemed more imponderable to the reformers because of the preoccupation of both sides with power to justify or power to save. For Augustine and for the Western Middle Ages, good works are an effect of grace enabling the will to choose rightly, and integral to a process of justification. Repentance issues in what Thomas Becon calls 'a fervent and inward desire from henceforth to live godly and virtuously, and to frame our life in all points according to the holy will of God'.[7] Forgiveness and reconciliation with God must, it seemed to Bullinger, mean that we are no longer slaves in our wills, but free to do good.[8] The Formula of Concord insists more than once that the wills of the justified are empowered by grace to do good, that is, that there is a real change in man's situation of helplessness before the power of sin in man.[9] But there was a good deal of debate among Lutherans and others on this question of the power of the restored human will to do good, as the Formula of Concord itself freely acknowledges.[10] Some thought it necessary to deny that any freedom of the will to choose good can exist in man since the Fall, even in the justified. Other reforming communities were influenced by such anxieties.

Article 13 of the Anglican Thirty-Nine Articles says that 'works done before' justification, because 'they are not done as God hath willed and commanded them to be done', are not only 'not pleasant to God' but 'have the nature of sin'. The same theme is repeated in the Anglican Homilies. In the Sermon of Fasting we find the comment that however conscientiously we fast, 'so long as we keep ungodliness in our hearts' our fasting is not only 'unprofitable to us', 'but also a thing that greatly displeaseth Almighty God'.[11] It can even be said that those who 'think they have done

7 *Catechism*, ed. J. Ayre (Parker Society, Cambridge, 1843–4), p. 10; cf. *Anglican Homilies*, p. 374, on Repentance.
8 *Decades* III.305.
9 Tappert, pp. 472, 512, 533, 534, for example.
10 Tappert, p. 520, and cf. *CR* 21.658–9.
11 *Anglican Homilies*, p. 195.

much of themselves towards repentance, are so much the farther from God, because they do seek those things in their own works and merits, which ought only to be sought in our Saviour Jesus Christ, and in the merits of his death, passion and blood-shedding'.[12] The controversy is found widely among continental reformers, too.[13] In the case of works done 'after' justification the questions which arose concern the possibility of perfect observance of the law by the justified'[14] and whether the justified can ever sin again, whatever they do;[15] and whether, on the contrary, even the works of the justified are sins.[16]

Eck called this kind of thing a revival of the 'old Manichaean heresy'.[17] The theologians of Louvain supported in their 1544 Articles (11) the view which Trent was to endorse, that the free will of man is not dead since the Fall; nor does it survive in name only.[18] Yet if we take justification to be an event, so that the signification of the term excludes those elements loosely grouped under what came to be referred to as 'sanctification', there are a number of implications. It becomes necessary to distinguish between the status of works done before 'justification' and that of works done by the justified, as these reforming explorations acknowledge, and to confront repeatedly the paradox of the fallen powerless will and the imperative to live in obedience and conformity with the will of God. The reformers found, as Augustine had done, that although it was quite clear that the paradox could only be resolved in terms of the work of grace, it was far from easy to pin down the mode of grace's operation in the wills of the faithful.

Once we begin to give serious thought to the place of growth in holiness within the Christian life, we run at once into a complex of questions raised in the sixteenth century to do with the life of the individual in the Christian community. Those Christ makes his own through faith become members of his Body; they will normally be baptised as members of his Body, as the majority of the protestant reformers saw it. We must now turn to the implications of this corporate nature of the baptised believer's relationship with Christ.

12 Sermon of Repentance, p. 369.
13 Cf. Trent VI, Canon 7.
14 Cf. Trent VI, Canon 18 and Calvin's *Antidote*.
15 Cf. Trent VI, Canon 23.
16 Cf. Trent VI, Canon 25.
17 Eck, *Loci*, chapter 31, p. 313.
18 Trent VI, Canon 5.

PART III

Authority in the Church to reconcile

7. The saving power of the sacraments

> We are told that baptism '... gives ... initiates ... unites ...
> effects'. It has to be asked what is meant by 'baptism' where this
> sort of language is constantly used. Is it the actual performance
> of the rites? If so, the language seems at best hyperbole and at
> worst objectionable.
>
> Thurian (ed.), *Churches Respond to BEM*, vol. 1, p. 70.

This hostile reaction to the 1982 Statement of the World Council of
Churches on Baptism (the 'Lima' text) reflects the modern continuance
of suspicions of a number of reformers in the sixteenth century. If we say
that a sacrament has an effect, do we imply that the Holy Spirit is
somehow at the disposal of the Church, so that the mere 'performance'
of the rite 'guarantees' the effect, *ex opere operato*? The question can be
put in that way only if the Church is seen as in some sense standing over
against divine authority and laying claim to an independent power; with
its ministers endowed with a personal 'priestly power', and claiming that
'rites of the Church' infallibly bring about the operation of the gift of
grace. Such assumptions are to be found on both sides in the sixteenth-
century debates, and they largely dictate the shape of the discussion about
the role of the Church in salvation.

Luther was first and foremost concerned with the forgiveness of the
individual as he responds to God in faith. He was not able to offer in other
areas of contemporary theological vexation anything comparable in
clarity and simplicity with his great insight here. The Augsburg Confession
makes an attempt to describe the way in which Luther's concept of
justification as an event fits into the sacramental life of the Church, by
presenting this ministry of the sacraments alongside the ministry of the
Gospel as 'preparatory', instituted 'so that people might obtain the faith
which justifies', and as 'instruments by which the Holy Spirit is given and
the Holy Spirit produces faith'.[1] But the real difficulty lay in identifying
the place of the continuing work of the sacraments in the life of the
justified, that is, those in whom faith had already done its justifying work.

---

[1] Art. 5, Tappert, p. 31.

In the *Apologia* for the Augsburg Confession,[2] a key issue was whether the Church's sacramental ministry is 'necessary to salvation', for that would seem on the face of it to imply that justification is perhaps not by faith alone, and that there is a power vested in the Church without which no-one can be saved.

Mediaeval orthodoxy saw the sacraments as 'indispensable means', by which salvation was arrived at as an 'effect'. They were thus a 'remedy against sin'.[3] This was one of the areas in which the sixteenth-century reformers were suspicious that the sovereignty of God was at stake, the Holy Spirit being 'bound' by the actions of a Church which had become a largely human institution.[4] Martin Bucer went so far as to write in a letter of the 1520s that 'because we are justified by faith we must never seek salvation or righteousness in the sacraments'.[5] Yet the reformers, in the main, wanted to retain the sacraments of baptism and Holy Communion, as instituted by Christ, and as a result a certain tension was set up over the concepts of 'indispensability' and 'effect'.

Here we meet again the habit of thought ingrained in late mediaeval and in many sixteenth-century minds, which looked in this context for a power or authority operating as a 'cause'. In the discussion of causation the old Aristotelian habits proved irresistible; thinkers looked for final, formal, efficient and material causes, taking God as the final cause of salvation, and the justified soul as the matter or material cause upon which the final cause works. Aquinas, for example, speaks of Christ's Passion as the *causa universalis* of human salvation, which is 'applied' specifically.[6] We find such talk in Eck's *Loci Communes*.[7] Contarini tried to explain in these terms the different ways we may speak of 'being just'. (We may say that 'whiteness makes a wall white'. It does so as a *forma inhaerens*, an inherent form, and thus as a formal cause. Or we may say that the painter makes it white. He is an 'efficient' cause.[8]) But it is also natural to the reformers to approach matters in this way. There can be only

---

2   Art. 12.42, Tappert, p. 187 and 24.76, Tappert, p. 263.
3   *ST* III[a]6.63.a.1.
4   *WA* 39[i].186, Thesis 17, Disputation *De Potestate Concilii*.
5   *Correspondance*, Letter 49.5.
6   *ST* III.q.61 a.1 ad 3 and 52 a.1 ad 2.
7   For example, in chapter 31, p. 321.
8   *Confutatio*, p. 25.15ff.

one 'cause' of our reconciliation, says Calvin.[9] The Solid Declaration of the Lutheran Formula of Concord[10] speaks of the 'efficient cause', defining it in terms of the questions 'who works these things in us, from where man acquires these things, and how he comes by them'.

Calvin sets out with economy a difficulty about baptism in this connection. He suggests that there is a middle position between saying baptism is necessary to salvation and saying that it is not. The reformers, he explains, certainly consider it necessary. That is, they do not allow anyone to omit it out of neglect or contempt. So it is not optional. They maintain that it is the ordinary instrument of God's washing and renewal of the sinner, of communicating salvation to him. But he and his followers cannot see that God can be tied to baptism in such a way that he cannot effect salvation without it. If for some reason a person cannot be baptised, God can still act to save.[11]

There was no substantial difference between the mainstream reformers and their opponents on the question whether the sacrament was dependent for its validity upon the worthiness of the minister or the absence of corruption in the Church, at least in the case of baptism. That is partly because the problem was much older than the late mediaeval and sixteenth-century debates. Augustine had faced the difficulty in connection with baptism by schismatic ministers. He insisted that it is God who acts in baptism, and so even unworthy ministers may administer valid baptism, provided they do so in the name of the Trinity and with the intention to baptise.[12] Exactly the same rules were laid down by the Council of Trent,[13] and the principle is to be found in reforming documents too.[14] The 'effect' of the sacrament is thus seen to be brought about by Christ and to be in no way at odds with the doctrine that God alone is the author of salvation. This pre-existing 'settlement' to some extent took the pressure off the question of 'priestly power' in connection with baptism.

This general principle was not universally satisfactory, however. The anathemas of the Council of Trent outline a series of contemporary

---

9 *Vera ... Eccl. Ref. Rat., CR* 35.504.
10 Art. 2, Tappert, p. 535.
11 It is worth noting here that Canon 849 of Post-Vatican II Canon Law agrees that baptism in intention is enough where it cannot be administered in fact.
12 For example, *On Baptism against the Donatists*, I.i.1.
13 VII, *De Baptismo*, Canon 4.
14 Augsburg Confession, Art. 8; Thirty-Nine Articles 26, for example.

difficulties about the questions of 'power' and 'effect' in baptism, many of which were being raised not by the main reforming movements, but by radicals and extremists on its flanks. At one of these extremes lay a 'weak' doctrine of baptism, which sought to make it unnecessary (Canon 5) or to diminish the importance of one of its elements (Canon 2) or to allow its repetition (Canons 11, 13). At the other extreme lay a 'strong' doctrine of baptism, which saw it as so altering the believer that whatever sins he commits, he cannot afterwards lose grace (Canon 6), or that he is obliged only to keep the faith and not to try to obey God's law (Canon 7), or that he is under no duty to obey the precepts of the Church (Canon 8), or that he may make no vow after baptism (Canon 9), or that he need only recall his baptism to be discharged of all the sins he commits afterwards (Canon 10).

The material points for Calvin, and the ones to which he gives most space in his *Antidote*, are raised by Canons 7 and 10 of Trent on this subject. The Fathers of Trent, he says, are misreading Paul's teaching in Galatians 5.3, that by circumcision a man was obliged to keep the law of Moses. They make out a corresponding obligation imposed by baptism, to keep the law of Christ. But baptism is different, Calvin argues. It is indeed a covenant of mutual obligation between us and God, but its force is to make us sure of the free forgiveness of our sins and the perpetual gift of our adoption.

8. The penitential system and 'power to bind and loose'

i. FORGIVENESS SEALED AND RENEWED

The doctrine of justification by faith (with its insistence upon the freedom and completeness of the transformation of the individual's position before God) was not intended by Luther to conflict with the theology of baptism. But he did intend it to show that an elaborate penitential system was unnecessary, and its 'imposition' on the faithful dangerously likely to distract them from the great simple truth of their redemption. The new emphasis brought into clear view once more an anomaly which had in fact existed for many centuries.

As a rule, the first generations of Christians were baptised as believing adults, able to declare their faith for themselves and to make a deliberate choice in committing themselves to Christ. The response of faith and the rite of baptism went together without strain.[1] There was an emphasis in the first Christian centuries on the power of baptism to wash away sin and also its consequences; and a concomitant discipline which expected those who were baptised not to fall into serious sin again, for it would make a mockery of baptism to suggest that it could be repeated.[2] Not every community was willing to restore to fellowship those who did lapse, and where penitents were readmitted they usually had to demonstrate the sincerity of their repentance to the community so that there could be no doubt about it.[3] Penitents were marked by the wearing of special garments, and they performed various penitential acts. Their welcome back was a public act of the whole community, symbolising their return

---

1. Cf. *Anglican Homilies*, p. 311, on the Worthy Receiving of the Sacrament.
2. On the principle that baptism cannot be repeated, see Louvain 2, Trent VI, Canons 9 and 13. Formula of Concord, Solid Declaration, Art. 2.69, Tappert, p. 534. On the modern aspects of the question, see B-R (3), *Growth*, p. 136, and the Baptist Union of Great Britain and Northern Ireland, Max Thurian, ed., *Churches Respond to BEM* (Geneva, 1986), vol. 1, p. 71, para. 2.
3. Minor sins were confessed in the heart to God. Murder, apostasy, adultery, were serious sins which concerned the community. On the early debates as to whether reconciliation was possible, see B. Poschmann, *Penance and the Anointing of the Sick* (Freiburg, 1964).

not only to reconciliation with God, but also to the community of the Body of Christ. Restored penitents continued to suffer certain disabilities[4] as a sign of the seriousness with which the lapse from baptismal purity was regarded. Something of this practice lingered even in the sixteenth century. Zwingli makes a point of the public action of the community and of the committing of a public offence which needs such public reconciliation, in his account of the right use of excommunication.[5]

This strong doctrine of baptism sometimes led in early generations to its postponement until death seemed near, so that there should be the less risk of lapsing again into sin, and the once-for-all purification of baptism could bring the Christian to the threshold of eternal life free from all his sins. Though this practice was not encouraged by the Fathers, some argued for a return to it in the sixteenth century. But the same thinking could lead another way. If baptism was a divinely appointed means of freeing the believer from guilt, and from the penalty of eternal separation from God which must be the consequence of original sin, it was surely appropriate in the case of infants, who would otherwise be at risk of dying estranged from God? From the end of the fourth century it became usual in the West to baptise young children. So firm was the widespread confidence in the efficacy of baptism that Augustine of Hippo comments more than once in his writings against the Pelagians that, despite their claim that there is no such thing as original sin, they frequently take the precaution of having their babies baptised.

It was this change in practice which created the anomaly of a disjunction between the individual's consciously becoming a Christian by making a commitment to Christ, and his becoming a member of the Christian community in baptism. The natural sequence of the two key events was reversed. And it also meant that the issue of the power or effect of baptism was sharpened, and with it the question of the implications of the Church's authority to baptise.

Melanchthon was pleased to see that in the Confutation of the Augsburg Confession the Roman Catholics 'approve the ninth Article, where we confess that baptism is necessary for salvation; children are to be baptised; the baptism of children is ... efficacious for salvation'.[6] In the debate over infant baptism as it presented itself in the early sixteenth century, the Anabaptists were the prime challengers, as Melanchthon notes.

---

4   For example they could not be ordained.
5   Zwingli, *Defence*, Articles 31, 32.
6   *Apologia*, Art. 9, Tappert, p. 178.

Anabaptism began in Zurich, with the administration of believer's baptism under the leadership of Conrad Grebel and Felix Manz. This was a breach of the city's laws. The adherents of the movement proved disruptive in their exuberance, and they were expelled. The pattern repeated itself in other places, as Anabaptist evangelists founded new congregations by administering believer's baptism, and were then moved on by the authorities. The Anabaptists and other radicals who took a similar line about baptism[7] were, with some exceptions,[8] theologically unsophisticated. They preached a simple message of repentance, faith and baptism to new life. But implicit in their call was the fact that they disputed the existence of original sin. For that reason, they argued that the baptism of infants too young to have committed actual sins is useless. They were not prepared to allow that even for adults baptism confers automatic benefits. Zwingli recognises that the controversy they have stirred up has had some beneficial results. It has made it plain that the mere act of pouring water does not in itself wash away sin.[9] It has raised the question of the place of human response in faith and brought into focus other aspects of baptism, so that there is beginning to be a fuller picture of its totality.

Resistance to the Anabaptist case had the effect of strengthening the view of other reformers that infant baptism was not only permissible but of value; it also obliged them to think the theology through. The *Apologia* for the Augsburg Confession points out that if we do not baptise children (and at the same time hold that that is necessary for their salvation), we seem to imply that the Lord's promise of salvation does not extend to them.[10]

In a letter to Bucer in 1524, Zwingli outlines the *nodi* of the debate. First, some object that it does not say in Scripture that the apostles baptised infants. Yes, says Zwingli, there is guidance on this point in the Bible, for us to 'receive'.[11] Paul links baptism with circumcision (Romans 4.11), which is performed on infants. He baptised a whole family (Acts 16.33), in which it is most probable there were infants. Secondly, they contend that before the apostles baptised anyone, they enquired about their faith. No, says Zwingli, Scripture relates that the

7   See H. J. Hillerbrand, *Christendom Divided* (New York, 1971), pp. 72ff. The Melchiorites and the Mennonites, for instance, might be grouped with the Anabaptists in their rejection of infant baptism.
8   Such as Hubmaier, Denck and Hut.
9   Stephens, *Zwingli*, p. 201.
10 Art. 9, Tappert, p. 178.
11 *Recipere, Correspondance*, pp. 310–11, Letter to Calvin, 1524, p. 310.

apostles, like Christ himself, sometimes asked and sometimes did not. If it is objected that faith must precede baptism, Zwingli answers that only for those who are able to hear the Gospel preached is that a requirement; for infants, who cannot do so, there is no such constraint. He argues that the child grows in holiness the better for being baptised, and thus his faith matures.

In practice, most of the reforming communities retained infant baptism. The Augsburg Confession defends it on the ground that if children are thus offered to God they are received into his grace.[12] The Thirty-Nine Articles of the Church of England describe the baptism of young children as 'most agreeable with the institution of Christ' (27).[13] The practice of infant baptism is inseparable from a view of baptism as both a definitive (because unrepeatable and decisive) event, and a process. Though Luther and Calvin assert consistently that baptism cannot be 'lost' (which would make penance a second 'baptism'), there was as yet only a limited understanding of baptism as a process which works throughout the life of the believer, a view which makes the principal difficulty about infant baptism diminish, if not vanish altogether. If the gift of grace in forgiveness in baptism requires a personal response and commitment from an individual able to understand what is happening, it would seem on the face of it that there can be no means of baptising infants. But if baptism is understood as a lifelong process in which the rite itself is a decisive event, then it can be seen as perfected in the individual's response of faith as he or she grows older. Thus we may say that baptism is effective through personal response and still baptise infants. Baptism is then being viewed in the context of the Spirit's action upon the whole life of the individual and the Christian community. The 'community' context of baptism implicitly embraces this notion of 'process'. As Zwingli describes it, 'those who are born of Christian parents' are inheritors of God's promise that the Gentiles will be gathered into the people of God, and thus they are already members of the Church.[14] Because baptism takes place within the community of the Church and the response of faith of the individual is shared with the community, the act of God in baptism finds its response of faith not only from the one baptised but also from the community of faith which includes a child's family. The child thus grows up in his parents' faith within the Church of which he is now fully a

12 Art. 9, Tappert, p. 178.
13 Cf. Becon, *Catechism*, vol. I, p. 208.
14 *Werke* V.384 and VI.805; cf. Stephens, *Zwingli*, p. 212.

member by baptism. This principle is clear in outline in the Reformation debates, and it does a good deal to obviate difficulties about authority in the context of baptism for most of the reforming communities.

ii. *POENITENTIA*

It was never the teaching of the Church that penance is a second baptism, though Luther feared that many people thought so. The notion arose because of the problem raised by sins committed after baptism, which needed fresh forgiveness. The move to infant baptism had radically altered the picture here. Instead of the comparative rarity of individuals falling into serious sin after baptism, individuals whose reconciliation was properly a public affair, it became unlikely that anyone would go through life without committing some serious sin after baptism – though not perhaps the murder, adultery or apostasy which early Christian communities took particularly seriously. It was certainly morally impossible that anyone should live a lifetime after baptism without sinning at all. By the Carolingian period, the early Church's provision for dealing with penitents had been modified to deal with this new, routine need.

By the time of the Lateran Council of 1215, every Christian was obliged to confess his sins to a priest before coming to the Eucharist. It was understood that unless he did so, received absolution and carried out the penitential acts the priest enjoined on him, he could not know himself forgiven. It is not hard to see why confusion with baptism occurred in the minds of the faithful. Baptism left the individual clean of sin; penance left the individual clean of sin. There were other implications in popular understanding: that without priests to absolve them, people would perish in their sins; and without the greatest exactitude in recounting of sins and punctiliousness in the performance of penances for them, the individual might die unforgiven. Out of these arose the real abuses of the penitential system which incensed Luther. Melanchthon comments on these and other assumptions in his *Apologia* for the Augsburg Confession. 'Even the theologians', he says, 'admit that before Luther's writings the doctrine of *poenitentia* was very confused.'[15]

Luther's insight was prompted by a close study of the Bible's language of penitence. He explains in a letter to Staupitz that one sense stood out for him

[15]   Art. 12, Tappert, p. 183.

from a multiplicity of significations. The emphasis should, he thought, be not on the sense we translate into English as 'penance', but on 'repentance'. The first two of the Ninety-Five Theses and their *resolutiones* lay the foundation of Luther's theology of penance by distinguishing these two meanings of *poenitentia*. When Christ said *poenitentiam agite* he meant *transmentamini*. Strictly translated (*rigidissime transferri*) that means 'alter the whole direction of your mind'. He was speaking of the conversion of heart which takes place in repentance, and in which we must persevere as long as we live, making all our lives repentance. The word *poenitentia* cannot properly be said to refer to the sacrament of penance, Luther argues. First, the sacrament of penance is not continuous throughout our lives, but enacted at particular times. Secondly, it is external, and repentance must be inward. Thirdly, it can be pretended, but true repentance is always genuine and sincere. Fourthly, Christ gave no commandment about sacramental penance; it is established by bishops and ecclesiastical authority and it is subject to the changing whims of the Church. Finally, all the scholastics distinguish repentance from sacramental penance, regarding repentance as the *materia* or *subiectum* of the sacrament.

In their remarks on penance in their Article 3, the Paris theologians of 1544 recognise this difference between *poenitentia* ('penance') and *poenitentia* ('repentance'). They point out that when the Lutherans say that *poenitentia* is conversion to God born of loathing of sin and love of righteousness, they are not speaking of penance.[16] Calvin underlines the distinction when he claims that among the uses of the word *poenitentia* in Scripture none seems to him to have any reference to the rule that confession must be made to a priest and that some form of satisfaction must be made for penance to be valid.[17] It is on the basis of this difference of understanding of the term *poenitentia* that the Louvain theologians state that *poenitentia* (penance) is necessary after baptism for all the lapsed,[18] and the Augsburg Confession says that those who fall into sin after baptism can receive forgiveness of their sins afresh whenever they return to *poenitentia* (repentance).[19] One interpretation intends to make good works of no account; the other gives them a key place in the restoration of the sinner, as part of the sacrament of penance.

[16]   *CR* 35.10.
[17]   *CR* 35.10–11.
[18]   Article 3.
[19]   Article 12.

Luther's attempt to separate 'repentance' from 'penance' was perhaps workable with reference to the concept of a decisive event of conversion, the moment of justification by faith through repentance. But he himself stresses the continuance of *poenitentia* throughout a lifetime. Here it becomes much less easy to separate the two senses, because the attempt to make them distinct ignores the manner in which the 'sacramental' sense had been derived as a matter of pastoral practice from the idea of 'repentance'.[20]

The main thrust of both Luther's and Melanchthon's endeavour here was to offer people comfort for their fears that they had not done enough ('penance') to make up for their sins, by assuring them that that was not what was needed but 'repentance'. Melanchthon points to the endless questions which have been raised in the commentaries on Peter Lombard's *Sentences*. It has become impossible for people to grasp the essence of *poenitentia*, of what is needed for peace of conscience, he says.[21]

iii. CONTRITION AND SATISFACTION

Melanchthon explains in a treatise *On Penance* written in 1549 that complete conversion (*integra conversio*) includes the beginning of a new obedience. This is the source of the tangled misunderstandings which have arisen not only in the matter of the empowering of the will for good, but also of confusion and false opinions[22] over the power of this 'obedience' to save. The penitential system had long broken down conversion into a series of component elements: contrition, confession and satisfaction.[23] In the Smalkald Articles, Luther places the emphasis upon the third element, the making of satisfaction. 'In their teaching of penance', he says, 'the sophists ... instructed the people to place their confidence in their own works ... There was no mention here of Christ

---

20 W. Pannenberg, 'The *Confessio Augustana* as a Catholic Confession and a Basis for the Unity of the Church', in *The Role of the Augsburg Confession: Catholic and Lutheran Views*, ed. J. A. Burgess (Philadelphia, 1977), p. 27. 'Repentance is described [in the Augsburg Confession] as the constantly renewed actualisation of baptism. This view makes it difficult to do justice to the continuity of Christian existence founded in baptism ... it must be admitted that the abiding continuity of Christian being derived from baptism has not always been adequately expressed in protestant piety, proclamation and liturgy.'

21 Art. 12, Tappert, pp. 183–4.

22 *Multis labyrinthis et falsis opinionibus*, CR 23.647.

23 Cf. Seripando, *De Iustitia et Libertate Christiana*, pp. 92, 94.

or faith.'[24] Following a similar line of thought in the *Institutes*, Calvin contends that the division into contrition, confession and satisfaction puts all the stress on outward actions, ignores 'inner renewal',[25] and denies faith its proper place. This emphasis was unacceptable to the reformers on two main counts. They said that it denied that faith in Christ was the only thing with power to save; and that it made it impossible for people to enjoy the peace of mind Christ came to bring.

Luther had no quarrel with fasting, prayer and almsgiving in themselves. These traditional penitential works are enjoined by Christ.[26] Everyone agreed that the Christian ought to do good. The difference of opinion was over the value of man's good works in the sight of God, when set over against the faith which justifies. Eck said unequivocally that 'faith is not enough without works'.[27] Seripando argued that perfect justice must comprise both faith and works.[28] In putting all the emphasis on faith, he says, the reformers are ignoring one of the twin teachings of the Word of God, which speaks of both faith and obedience.[29] But it seemed to Luther that it was necessary to disjoin the two.

Thesis III.2 of the *Lutheran Disputation on Justification* of 1536 states that Paul clearly opposes faith to works (*opponit*). The debate begins with the assertion that opposites cannot be in the same subject at one and the same time. According to the thesis, faith and works are opposed to one another. So faith and works cannot be in the same person at one and the same time. Luther argues that 'justifying works' is a fictitious term, like *chimaera*, but faith has real existence; it is an *ens positivum*. That is why we can say with Paul that a person is justified by faith without works.[30] Calvin argues in his *Antidote* to the fourth of the Articles of the Paris theologians that faith is 'vain' if we allow any place to good works and the keeping of the law.[31]

Yet this absolute separation is seen, paradoxically enough, as a necessary concomitance. As Bullinger explains, 'faith alone' does not mean faith 'utterly destitute of good works', for 'wheresoever faith is, there also it sheweth itself by good works; because the righteous cannot but work

24 Smalkald Articles III.3, Tappert, p. 305.
25 *Institutes* III.2–4.
26 *WA* 1.532.
27 Eck, *Loci*, pp. 84ff.
28 *De Iustitia et Libertate Christiana*, Congressus Quintus, 1533, p. 57.
29 *Ibid.*, p. 49.
30 Romans 3.28; *WA* 39^i.82 and 84.
31 *CR* 35.12–13.

righteousness'.[32] Within the frame of this paradox, the Catholic theologians are able to say both that everything depends on the merits of Christ and that good works are necessary for salvation for all adults.[33] That is a claim that in fact the two are not incompatible.[34] Seripando sees works in this light as a *medium* or means by which man is led to salvation by grace. Works before grace 'do nothing', as Augustine proves, he says; works done under grace (*opera cum gratia*) do not themselves merit justification, but as a medium or means they are indispensable (*sunt media, sine quibus non perducitur homo ad eam*).[35]

In this struggle to grasp the relationship between faith and the good works from which it is agreed to be in practice inseparable (but from which Luther thought it most profoundly separated in the eyes of God), we find scholars engaged in the most delicate of balancing acts. 'Let us remember, that the reward is promised and great gifts are prepared for them that labour manfully', says Bullinger. 'To them that strive lawfully the garland is due ... Yet for all this we must not abuse these and such like testimonies touching the reward of works, nor the very name of merits, where it is found to be used of the Fathers; neither must we wrest it against the doctrine of mere grace'.[36]

Alongside the fear that a trust in the satisfactory power of works would displace faith in people's hearts ran a concern for the suffering of the terrified conscience. Every day, says Luther, people confess their sins and seek forgiveness. But real recognition of one's sinful condition must match in its pain and horror the awfulness of sin itself, or it is not true contrition.[37] In insisting in this way on the penitent's giving much more than a nod to the seriousness of sin, Luther was arguing against what he understood to be the late mediaeval teaching that something much less will do, the merest beginnings of repentance (*attritio*).

The doctrine of the terrified conscience led to extremes against which Roman Catholic respondents protested. The Louvain theologians argued that contrition, properly speaking, is sorrow over sin because one has offended God, not fear of Hell.[38] The Fathers of Trent made the same

---

32 *Decades* I.118.
33 Louvain 11.
34 'In adults faith is necessary above all things for justification'; 'works without faith cannot obtain justification', Louvain 8, cf. Trent VI, Canon 9.
35 *Acta CT* 12.640.
36 *Decades* III.344–5.
37 Cf. *WA* 39^i.84, Thesis 5.
38 Louvain 4.

point,[39] stressing the difference between a contrition made complete by love and an imperfect contrition or 'attrition'. The Augsburg Confession preferred to see contrition rather as 'terror smiting the conscience with a knowledge of sin'.[40] But, as Melanchthon acknowledges in his *Apologia*, it may not be easy for the 'terrified conscience' to judge whether it fears God for his own sake, or is running away from eternal punishments.[41] The danger which arose within the penitential system was of an anxious preoccupation with the number of works needed to placate God's anger.[42] It was here that the doctrine of assurance found its place in the Lutheran system.[43]

We must take a preliminary look here at the assumptions about the nature of 'satisfaction' which entailed these concerns about faith and works and about assurance. There was no dispute that justification must be deserved. The question was whether men and women can do anything for themselves to deserve it. At root all sides were in agreement here. The merit is Christ's and human efforts are of no worth in the sight of God in their own right. The Augsburg Confession says that no-one can be justified by his or her own strength, merits or works (4). In the *Confutatio* we find agreement that 'of themselves our works have no merit', but also the argument that God's grace makes those works worthy of eternal life.[44] Zwingli allows that because 'Christ is our righteousness' we may conclude that our works are good insofar as they are Christ's. But insofar as they are ours, they are neither right nor good. The Thirty-Nine Articles of the Church of England say that 'we are accounted righteous before God only for the merit of ... Christ' (11). The Trent Canons agree that no-one is justified except for the sake of the merits of Christ and that it was Christ who deserved our justification (VI, Canon 10). No-one can be justified by his own efforts, by the strength of human nature alone, but only with divine grace and through Christ (VI, Canon 1).

There are differences of emphasis here, but substantial agreement that only Christ 'deserves' salvation for mankind. The differences concern the understanding of the way in which Christ's merit becomes 'ours'. The principle Luther was anxious to stress was that his merit never belongs to

[39]   *Acta CT* 14.4.
[40]   Art. 12, cf. 20, para. 17.
[41]   Tappert, p. 183.
[42]   *CR* 27.446; C. E. Maxcey, *Bona Opera* (Nieuwkoop, 1980), p. 49.
[43]   See Poschmann, *Penance and the Anointing of the Sick.*
[44]   Part I, Art. 4; cf. *Apologia*, Art. 4, Tappert, pp. 107–8.

us but when we have faith it is imputed to us as though it were ours. The emphasis of the Trent Canons is upon the idea that the Christian's union with Christ makes Christ's merits those of the believer, so that, strictly in that sense, we can properly speak of human merits. That is to say, the good works of a justified man are the gifts of God in such a way that they are merits of the man himself, precisely because they are the merits of Jesus Christ, of whom he is a living 'member'.[45]

Alongside this account we might set that of the Roman Catholic apologist Contarini. Works done by those who belong to Christ must, he says, be different from those done before there is faith. When we are united with Christ, we are participants (*participes*) in the divine goodness. This is the principle outlined by Trent. It is in this sense, suggests Contarini, that we must read Christ's words in Matthew 19.17, 'If you wish to enter into life, keep the commandments.' Such obedience is satisfactory, not on its own account, but on Christ's account.

a. The penalty and the price

There was no substantial disagreement between reformers and their opponents that baptism remits the guilt of both original and actual sin once and for all.[46] But when the Christian falls into sin again after baptism, there is, said mediaeval theologians, a penalty to be paid, the *poena* to which, in the penitential system, *poenitentia* is seen as addressing itself. Eck, in supporting this view, explains that contrition and absolution restore the penitent to the forgiveness of his baptism by taking away the guilt, but that he ought to make satisfaction (*satisfacere debet*) for the penalty which is due.[47] This is the position to which the theologians of Louvain adhered in their Articles of 1544 (6), and the Council of Trent speaks of the liability to temporal punishment remaining.[48] It was here that the reformers attacked. Bullinger insists that 'Christ by his death hath taken away from us sinners both fault and punishment':[49] Calvin says the same.[50] It seemed to Luther that the rationale of the whole contemporary

45 Trent VI, Canon 32.
46 Cf. *Acta CT* 5.166: 'the death and Passion of the Son of God is applied by baptism' and is 'the remedy by which we are ... freed from sin'.
47 Eck, *Loci*, chapter 9, p. 125.
48 Trent VI, Canon 30.
49 *Decades* I.108.
50 *Institutes* III.4.29.

penitential system turned on this belief. It is standard teaching in the universities, he says, that no sin remains in those who are baptised, but that sins committed after baptism are actual sins which we must put away, and for which we must make satisfaction. That is the basis on which 'there have been many ways invented of reconciling'. 'We see this argument as the source and origin of all monasteries, masses, pilgrimages, invocation of the saints and such, with which people try to make satisfaction for their sins.'[51]

Mediaeval penitential practice took a strictly quantitative view of what was required to make satisfaction, so much penance for so great a sin; and also of what was appropriate recompense for persons in different circumstances. In Lanfranc's Winchester Canons of 1072, for example, distinction is made, among those who kill in battle, between the man who can testify to the number he has killed (a year's penance for each) and those, such as archers, who cannot be sure how many they have hit. An archer is to do penance for three Lents. Penance one day in every week as long as he lives (at the bishop's discretion) may be appropriate for the soldier who cannot remember how many he has struck. A man who intended to strike but failed to hit is to do three days' penance.[52] Hubert Walter, in his Westminster Canons of 1200, instructed priests to consider the circumstances of both the sinner and the sin; the time, place, occasion and present frame of mind of the penitent, in calculating the satisfaction due.[53] A variety of different kinds of factors were taken into account 'both in regard to God and the world'.[54] If anyone commits a fault unwillingly, he is not to be treated in the same way as someone who does it by choice and out of self-will.[55] Distinction should be made between rich and poor, freeman and slave, humble and proud, strong and weak, clergy and laity, in calculating what they must do to make up for their sins.[56]

The concept of reward was scrutinised carefully in the debate at Ratisbon in 1541. Caspar made notes on what was said, in which the concern for defining of terms is much in evidence.[57] He analyses various Scriptural texts which seemed to the disputants to have a bearing on the

[51] 1536 *Disputation on Justification*, Thesis IV.8, WA 39i.84.
[52] J. Johnson, *A Collection of the Laws and Canons of the Church of England* (Oxford, 1850–1), 2 vols., II.10–11.
[53] *Ibid.*, II.86.
[54] *Ibid.*, I.158 (725).
[55] *Ibid.*, I.428 (963).
[56] *Ibid.*
[57] *CR* 4.242ff.

question of earning God's favour. 'Blessed are those who suffer persecution for righteousness' sake. Your reward is in Heaven.' Here, it is argued, eternal life is clearly being described as a 'reward' (*merces*). One side said that *merces* does not mean 'due reward' (*debita*) in this context, but 'compensation' (*compensatio*) – a concept familiar to late antiquity in connection with the idea that those just men who suffer on earth will receive compensation in the life to come. If this is right, said the Protestants at Ratisbon, we cannot argue that Scripture teaches that we are rewarded for anything we do. We must not confuse paying a price for Heaven so that we buy a right to it as a reward, and the free gift of Heaven given us as a reward in compensation for the pains of this present life. But what about the term *praemium*, ask their opponents? They argue that in the Psalm, 'Judge me according to my innocence' (*secundum innocentiam meam*), it is evident that one's 'innocence', one's 'proper righteousness' (*propria iustitia*), is one's own, and that it merits eternal life as its reward, or *praemium*. There is no question of mere *compensatio* here. Their adversaries answer that *meam* ought to be read as referring not to a personal innocence, but to an innocency of ministry or calling (*ministerium*). Then there is the idea that the *causa* of God's giving salvation lies not in the 'reward' of that salvation, but in the promise of salvation. When Ezekiel says, 'Remember that I have worshipped you with a true heart', he is not expecting to be rewarded for his own merit, but putting his trust in God's promise.[58]

In the course of the discussions surrounding the Ratisbon Colloquy, much was said about the role of *vivificatio*, new life and obedience, as necessary to salvation. Caspar replies that the new obedience which follows on faith is necessary to eternal life, not because it is the price (*pretium*) which 'buys' eternal life, that is, a cause; but because it is the effect. Newness of life is inseparable from justifying faith (*novitas coniuncta fide*), in the sense that it necessarily follows it.[59] In the same way, the Augsburg Confession argues that justifying faith is bound to bring forth good works, and that these are necessary because they are what God wants, not because they earn justification. They are effects not causes.[60] The Thirty-Nine Articles of the Church of England say that good works follow after justification, and 'do spring necessarily out of a

---

58   *CR* 4.244–5.
59   *Ibid.*
60   Augsburg Art. 6, cf. Maxcey, *Bona Opera*, p. 278.

true and lively faith' (12). Here we are back in the arena of the discussion of the possibility of any good work being performed by a damaged human will, even one which is 'justified'.

b. The work of suffering

Luther says that the 'Papists' cannot teach correctly about repentance because they do not know what sin really is. If we understand that man's natural powers are taken away by sin, we can see that contrition cannot be something active (*activa*), but must be passive, a sorrow which is suffering. This was Luther's mature view, as he expresses it in the Smalkald Articles.[61] Melanchthon supports it in the *De Poenitentia* of 1549, with a similar emphasis upon sorrow and suffering in contrition. Both touch here upon the relation between a willing undertaking of penalties imposed within the penitential system, the willing acceptance of various sorts of unavoidable suffering in life, and the experience of forgiveness and repentance throughout a lifetime.[62]

The young Luther had no difficulty with the notion of a penalty remaining as an aftermath of sin throughout life in the form of the sufferings men and women endure: that hatred of self which is the concomitant of true inner repentance, the temptations of the Devil, persecutions and all forms of pain, of which the voluntary afflictions we endure in doing penance are perhaps to be regarded as one form.[63] His last thesis in the series is an exhortation to Christians not to look for a false peace, but to expect many tribulations before their entry into Heaven (95). So penalties of sin are felt in the sinner's life as a desire to mend what he has done wrong, as a suffering by which he grows in love and faith, and as a need for healing. Moreover, although repentance is met by full remission of the consequences of sin (35, 36, 37), the truly contrite soul wants to pay penalties for its sins (40). The third thesis states that if inner repentance does not show itself in outward mortification, it is nothing. Calvin, too, accepts that sometimes after guilt is taken away, God

---

[61] Smalkald Articles III.3, Tappert, pp. 304–5.

[62] As one modern author has put it, 'Knowing that we are forgiven does not remove our desire to express our sorrow ... the sacrament of penance gives us the opportunity to experience God's forgiveness in a way that is considerate of our condition ... this interplay between forgiveness and repentance can also be creative'. R. Strange, *The Catholic Faith* (Oxford, 1986), p. 92.

[63] Ninety-Five Theses, 4.

chastises his own, but not as a penalty, merely for the sake of admonition and correction.[64]

It is not perfectly clear in these accounts how far either thinker regards these penalties as 'due', that is, as in some sense owed to God in willing acceptance out of a desire to show the sincerity of repentance or a readiness to learn. The aggregation of all sorts of suffering, redemptive and educational and medicinal, is strongly Augustinian in both Luther and Calvin, as is the notion advanced by Luther in the Ninety-Five Theses that indulgences are wrong because they offer a *relaxatio* of penalties which are beneficial to us. But Bullinger is unequivocal that the 'afflictions' of 'discipline, chastisement … diverse sorts of punishments', 'howsoever they may be patiently suffered of the faithful, do not yet wash sins away, nor make satisfaction for misdeeds'.[65]

Here, then, in broad strokes, is the context of the discussion about authority in the Church in the matter of forgiveness.

iv. ABSOLUTION: THE PRIEST AS JUDGE

Melanchthon understood the historical origin of the penitential practice of making satisfaction for what it was: a relic of the rite of public penance in the early Church. He recognised several reasons why it was used at that time. The chastising of the lapsed served as an example to others, and it made a necessary hurdle for the penitent to leap so that he or she might be readmitted to communion in recognition that what had happened had been serious, but that it had been dealt with. The prime purpose of all this was, it seemed to him, to make satisfaction not to God but before the face of the community.[66] Calvin also explains that the Fathers understood satisfaction as made to the community, and he castigates the 'schoolmen' for misreading patristic authority on this point, citing Peter Lombard in particular.[67] The conception of a satisfaction made to the community presented no problems to the reformers; nor, in general, did the view that the leader of the community should exercise such a discipline. The problem lay in the exercise of what appeared a 'personal' power to bind

---

64 *Antidote* to Trent VI, Canon 30.
65 *Decades* I.110.
66 *Apologia* for the Augsburg Confession, Art. 12.113, Tappert, p. 199; cf. Gloss on Gratian, *Decretum* II, 24, q.3.18.
67 *Institutes* III.4.39.

and loose, vested in the priest seemingly independently of the action of the community. There was a further difficulty concerning what seemed the extension of the claim to jurisdiction far beyond the scope of the power of the keys in the early Church. In the Middle Ages, excommunication was used to bring recalcitrant princes to heel, and was therefore a political and civil as well as a spiritual penalty. It was threatened as a sanction where taxes were not paid as due to the Church, and it could thus be used to strike fear into ordinary people. This gave offence to reformers, who called it an abuse of power.

Luther wrote a *Sermon on the Ban*, published in 1520, in an attempt to get back to first principles, and help those who went in fear of excommunication and ultimately of Hell because they had not paid their ecclesiastical taxes. He explains that the Lord's Supper is 'a sign of the community of all saints'. To be excluded from the Supper is to be excluded from this fellowship. But he makes a distinction between the inward fellowship of union with Christ, which he insists no man, bishop or Pope – or even an angel – can take away, and the purely external act of formal exclusion from the Supper. If a man is inwardly alienated from God and his fellow Christians he excommunicates himself. The outward 'ban' should be used as it was in the early Church as an act of loving discipline, to bring the sinner to his senses, and never for vengeance or punishment. The intention should always stop short of ruin or death. Luther cites 2 Thessalonians 3.15, 'Do not look on him as an enemy, but punish him as a brother.' If, says Luther, it should happen that you are outwardly excommunicated, but know in your heart that you are in fellowship with Christ and your neighbour, there is no need for anxiety. God does not condemn you. On the other hand, those who are outwardly in communion with the Church but inwardly at odds with God and man should fear indeed. In all this, two principles should be borne in mind. The ban can never legitimately be used 'for money or for any other temporal matter'; and the power of excommunication does not mean, as some people think, a power to deliver souls to the Devil and deprive them of the benefits of the Church's love and intercession. The sinner remains within the Church's care.

The keys of binding and loosing, which Christ gave when he said to Peter 'Whatever you bind shall be bound in heaven', etc. (Matthew 6.18–19), have been misused and misrepresented, argues Luther. The words of Christ have been twisted. 'Bind' has been understood as 'command', 'forbid', 'legislate'. These false definitions have been used as a basis for claims to command absolute obedience on pain of eternal damnation. At the least this is bad practice in the interpretation of Scripture. One should not take a word out of context, without regard for the harmony of the interpretation given to it with the passage as a whole. And even if it were legitimate to do so, where in Latin or German can one find 'bind' meaning 'command' or 'decree'?[68]

Luther says that the binding and loosing Christ intended was rather 'an office, a power or command given by God through Christ to all of Christendom, for the retaining or remitting of the sins of men'. The keys unlock a heavenly not an earthly kingdom. They have nothing to do with worldly power and politics. Moreover, they should be used to 'bind' and 'loose' in connection with real sins; as it is, people of all conditions, bishops, monks, princes, noblemen and peasants, carry on with impunity with a multitude of shameful vices, stealing, ostentation, immorality.[69]

Luther thus attacked the architecture of the late mediaeval theology of the 'keys' by pointing to two respects in which it seemed to him wrong. It had been narrowed to focus on the Pope's personal possession of the keys as Peter's successor, when Luther believed Christ had given the gift to the whole Church. The Pope could even be said to have stolen the keys. And it had been widened to include claims to powers far beyond its original purpose, powers which had strictly nothing to do with sin. He further insisted (and he saw this as a result of such wrong thinking) that even where the keys were used for their proper purpose, they were not being used in a proper manner. Gross sinfulness was going uncorrected.

Luther was saying much that needed to be said here, and redressing an imbalance which had clearly arisen between the healing purpose of excommunication and its disciplinary role. The Catholic apologists show some remaining preoccupation with the concept of power. Eck angrily objects in his *Loci Communes* that excommunication is not inflicted on himself by the sinner, but is a *poena inflicta*, a penalty actually inflicted by the Church.[70] The Paris Articles of 1544 stress that the *potestas excommunicande* is granted by Christ *de iure divino* and *immediate* to the Church (21). 'For that reason', they say, 'the censures of the Church are greatly to be feared'.[71] There were significant vested interests here, both financially (for the Church would have been bankrupted if it could no longer

[68] *WA* 30[ii].465–507.
[69] *Ibid.*
[70] Eck, *Loci*, p. 238.
[71] *CR* 35.33.

enforce the payment of ecclesiastical taxes), and for the career civil servants of the hierarchy. Calvin reiterates several of Luther's points in his *Antidote* to this Paris Article. Excommunication should be used for 'edification' not for 'destruction'. If the Church acts as a tyrant and usurps legitimate judgement its judgements are empty; then we must not fear them.[72]

The act of excommunication remained a rare and exceptional use of the power of the keys, although it is discussed a good deal in the sixteenth-century debates. More commonplace, indeed universal, was experience of private penance, in which, not exceptionally, but as a matter of routine, every Christian is a penitent and small sins as well as large are laid before a priest. When the Council of Trent describes the use of the power of the keys in the context of penance as something 'received in the Church from the beginning',[73] it makes no distinction between public and private penance in this respect.

The sequence of events which had led to the rise of a system of private penance in the Celtic and Carolingian churches[74] had met a pastoral need. The Augsburg Confession retains provision for private absolution for the same pastoral reason, 'that we should joyfully comfort ourselves with absolution',[75] with the understanding that in their own practice the Lutherans are returning to purity of practice. That is to say, they are using absolution as 'comforting and necessary for terrified consciences'[76] and not making it conditional upon a tormenting anxiety about the enumeration of sins, and works done in satisfaction. The thrust of Melanchthon's argument is that private absolution is the 'voice of the Gospel sounding through the ministers' (*vox evangelii sonans per ministros*), of benefit to pious and tender conscience because it reassures them that the Gospel promises apply to them personally.

But difficulties arose for the reformers because of their broadly based disquiet over the penitential system at large, and because of the resentment of 'priestly power' which was inseparable from it. In these circumstances to call priestly absolution 'necessary' could be taken as implying that the Holy Spirit was enslaved to the power of the priests.

The rule that only a priest may give absolution was seen and resented as implying the possession of a personal power at an earlier date than the resentment of a 'sacerdotal power to consecrate' made itself felt.

72   *CR* 35.33–4.
73   Trent XIV, Canon 3.
74   See Poschmann, *Penance and the Anointing of the Sick.*
75   Art. 25.4.
76   *Ibid.*

Waldensians and Lollards in the Middle Ages insisted that laymen (and in Lollard practice laywomen too) had a right to perform all the tasks traditionally reserved to the clergy. The Anabaptists (and other radicals) of the sixteenth century followed them in taking the line that the baptismal vow gives every Christian authority to admonish his brother. Some have argued that the power of the keys has nothing to do with forgiveness, but merely changes eternal punishments into temporal punishments, says Melanchthon.[77] But that would make the priestly ministry one not of forgiveness but of wrath and punishment, which was clearly not God's intention. Others distort the principle of reconciliation with the community, and say that the power of the keys forgives sins before the Church but not before God. But that, says Melanchthon, would not bring peace to the terrified conscience.[78] These are errors arising from what he sees as a wrong doctrine of priestly power to absolve.

Calvin points out that private confession to a priest was not practised in the early Church, even though discipline was extremely strict and no quarter was given to sin. Innocent III's decree insisting on regular confession is, he says, a human imposition, binding consciences 'with a necessity from which God absolves and delivers them'. He sees it as yet another example of the institutional Church's usurpation of powers not vouchsafed to her by God, and as pastorally unfortunate in its consequences (because it encourages people to think that they can do what they like so long as they confess it).[79] It is certainly the case that the priest was seen as a judge,[80] and if that judgement was thought to be his own it did indeed look as though human imposition was involved. But Luther says that this 'judgement' which is an exercise of the power of the keys is 'a judgement of Christ himself'. If the sinner perseveres in his sin, he is certainly eternally damned for that reason. When the words of absolution are spoken, 'it has the same significance as if Christ himself passed judgement'. The implication is that it is Christ not the priest who binds or looses. Melanchthon agrees. 'We must believe the voice of one absolving as we should believe a voice coming from heaven', he says.[81] An alternative

---

77 So that good works done in the process of growing in holiness could be distinguished from those done in an effort to make satisfaction, which were really punishments willingly endured.

78 *Apologia* for the Augsburg Confession, Art. 12, Tappert, pp. 183–4.

79 *CR* 35.226.

80 Louvain 5; Trent XIV, Canon 9.

81 *Apologia* for the Augsburg Confession, Art. 12, paras 39, 40, and cf. Zwingli,

reforming position was to deny the element of 'judgement' in the human encounter. Zwingli says in one of the Articles in his *Defence* (52) that confession, whether made to a priest or to a neighbour, is no more than seeking advice, and Eck mentions the view that since James tells us to confess to one another,[82] we need not go to a priest.[83]

Hutchinson gives a more balanced account:

> As every private man forgiveth his brother, so much more the ministers of God's word have power to do the same, for to them belongeth forgiving and retaining, binding and loosing of the whole congregation.   To them Christ gave the keys of the kingdom of heaven. How then doth God only forgive sin? Truly, they are only ministers of ... forgiveness. Their forgiving and loosing is to declare the sweet and comfortable promises that are made through Jesus Christ in God's book to such as be penitent; and their binding ... is to preach the law, which causeth anger to such as be impenitent.

Importantly, we find here the notion of limitation of office which we shall meet later: 'Except thou repent', says Hutchinson, the minister 'hath no authority to forgive thee; for he is a minister of forgiveness only to such as repent and will amend. His commission stretcheth no further.'[84]

Defence, Art. 50, and Melanchthon, *Doctrina de Poenitentia*, 1549, *Werke*, vol. 5, p. 439.36.

[82]   Eck, *Loci*, chapter 8, p. 118.
[83]   Louvain 30, Trent XXV, *Decretum de Purgatorio*.
[84]   *Works*, ed. J. Bruce (Cambridge, 1842), PS, p. 96.

9. The Eucharist and authority to forgive

In 1367 the Bohemian dissident Milíc spoke of the *sacrificium Christi* of the Mass, and of himself as 'offering' it, with no sense that he was saying something which was potentially controversial (although he uses the expression in a sermon against Antichrist with much of which his successors among the sixteenth-century reformers could have agreed).[1] The debate about sacrifice became so central to the eucharistic controversy of the Reformation that it was the focus of a high proportion of the conversations of the Council of Trent on Eucharist and ministry, in 1547, 1551–2 and 1562.[2] Milíc also regarded the penitential system as having a natural and proper relation to the theology of eucharistic offering and sacrifice. This relationship between the Eucharist and the forgiveness of sins was already being explored in the earliest period of the Reformation debates by Kaspar Schatzgeyer, who died in 1527. He placed an emphasis on the action of the whole Church in the Eucharist, and on the function of the Eucharist within the Church's ministry of reconciliation in this life. In a series of works written in response to the Lutherans in the 1520s[3] he laid the groundwork of a theology of eucharistic reconciliation. But his death and a change in the focus of polemic, as Zwingli and Luther came into conflict and other preoccupations supervened, meant that his ideas were not taken further. The Trent Fathers perceived the interdependency of the Eucharist and penitential practice, but the topics were broadly separated in debate during the Council, and in the making of canons and decrees. This was determined in part, in the circumstances of current controversy, by the reformers' wish to retain the Eucharist but not the penitential system. Their particular concern was to deny any possibility that the Mass might be 'applied' by the celebrant for the benefit of particular individuals and especially as easing the penalty due for their sins. When

1   *F. Mencik, Milíc a dva jeho spisy z.r.1367, Prophecia et revelatio de Antichristo,* ed. V. Herold and M. Mráz (Prague, 1974), p. 329.
2   E. Iserloh, 'Das Tridentinesche Messopferdekret zu der Kontroverstheologie der Zeit', *Il Concilio de Trento e la Riforma Cattolica* (Rome, 1965), II.416ff.
3   *Replica contra Periculosa Scripta; Examen Novarum Doctrinarum; Tractus de Missa; Ecclesiasticorum Sacramentorum Assertio,* ed. E. Iserloh and P. Fabisch, C.Cath. 37 (Münster, 1984).

Robert Bellarmine came to sum up the debates at the end of the century, he identified these as the significant difficulties raised by the reformers.[4]

The chief preoccupations of reformers in the sixteenth-century debates in this area were the notions that priests were usurping Christ's unique priestly function, and that the Church was imposing on the faithful practices of merely human devising as though they were necessary to forgiveness; that the Church was trying to repeat Christ's unique sacrifice as though such repetition was necessary to forgiveness; that priests were claiming to 'make' a fresh Christ in each Mass, so that they might bring about the forgiveness of sins by his power; that this involved the possession by priests of a personal and exclusive power, linked to the power of the keys, to bring forgiveness to lay people.

Two *potestates* are given in ordination, said the Trent theologians, the *potestas offerendi*, in which lies the indelible character of ordination; and the power to remit sins, which makes the *character perfectior*.[5]

i. HUMAN INNOVATIONS AND MAN'S USURPATION OF CHRIST'S PRIESTHOOD

The Trent theologians began to explore the question of eucharistic sacrifice during the period at Bologna in 1547. Cochlaeus, Eck, Faber and de Castro drew up lists of errors found in the writings of the reformers, as did Seripando.[6] The pattern of working from *articuli* or *quaestiones*,[7] which was adhered to for the most part throughout the Trent debates (although there were also preparatory essays),[8] concentrated attention on the process of definition and on the formulation of propositions, perhaps to the detriment of the perception of the complex of problems as an interrelated whole. That was particularly unfortunate in this area.

---

4   Bellarmine, *De Eucharistia*, Books I–IV on the Real Presence; Book V on Sacrifice and related matters, such as whether the Mass benefits (*prosit*) both the living and the dead, whether it may be celebrated in honour of the saints, and liturgical points, in *Opera*, ed. X. R. Sforza (Naples, 1856–62).

5   *Acta CT* 9.25, cf. 31.

6   On the use which was made at Trent of the reformers' writings, see T. Freudenberger, 'Zur Benützung des reformatorischen Schriftums im Konzil von Trient', in R. Bäumer, *Von Konstanz nach Trient* (Munich, 1972), 577–601.

7   In 1562 the approach is by way of a list of questions rather than of errors, *Acta CT* 8.719, cf. H. Jedin, *Geschichte des Konzils von Trient* (Freiburg im Breisgau, 1970–5), IV[i].338 n. 11.

8   *Acta CT* 12–13.

Certainly at the stage in September 1562, when the doctrine and canons of the Council on the Sacrifice of the Mass were finally drawn up, the points made prominent by contemporary controversy were still shaping the theology.

The first edition of Calvin's commentary on Hebrews was published in 1549, two years after the first Trent debates on the Eucharist of 1547; two years before the discussions of 1551; and more than a decade before the Council's reconsideration of these and related issues in 1562. It is an unabashedly polemical work. Calvin contends that the author of Hebrews wrote with the overriding purpose of explaining the 'office' of Christ. That 'office' was to put an end to 'ceremonies'. The writer of Hebrews faced a difficulty in teaching the Jews of his own day what they had failed to understand, which is exactly parallel in Calvin's view to the difficulty reformers now have in making the 'Papists' understand the same points.[9] He proceeds throughout his commentary on a number of assumptions which had become familiar in debate since the 1520s, but which he brings together in making the connection between the discussion of 'rites' and 'ceremonies' and the controversy over 'priesthood and sacrifice' central to the interpretation of Hebrews.[10]

From a sixteenth-century viewpoint, the debates about transubstantiation and sacrifice meet on the question of priestly power in the ordained ministry. As a major reason for the revival of the challenge to the doctrine of transubstantiation in the later Middle Ages, this was sometimes obscured by the technical discussions of the logicians.

For Wyclif and the Lollards, for example, it was the notion that corrupt priests had power to 'make' the body of Christ which put the doctrine in an unacceptable light. Melanchthon echoes this line of thought when he explains that 'God is not to be bound where he does not bind himself'. That is to say, his presence is voluntary; it is not at the disposal of an individual invested with a power which enables him to perform a miracle at will with a piece of bread.[11] This power of the priest to produce the 'victim' to be offered was seen as coupled with a personal power to offer, in which lay people could not share. The dual *vis sacrificatoria* seemed to Julius Pflug in a letter of 1534 to be the nub of the matter. 'The

---

9   *CR* 83.6.
10 Luther's commentary on Hebrews was written early in his career as a reformer. It is contemporary with the Ninety-Five Theses, and Luther did not then see the difficulties picked up by Calvin.
11 See *CR* 4.263–4.

controversy on other matters might perhaps be dealt with more easily.'[12] Out of the *vis sacrificatoria* came the *vis applicationis*, the priestly power to determine by 'application' who should 'benefit' from the Mass.

The thrust of reforming objections was against an assumption which had grown up during the later Middle Ages that the Eucharist was chiefly the action of the priest, offering a propitiation to God in an analogy to the Levitical sin-offering in which the people who presented the animals to be offered took no part, leaving all to the priest. There were liturgical signs of this happening as early as the fifth century when the altar tended to be placed at the end of the church instead of in the middle, and the celebrant might have his back to the people. The sense of a mystery being enacted by the priest alone was deepened by the practice, as early as the end of the eighth century, of saying the prayer of consecration in whispers, and eventually in silence. The result was that the people's presence became dispensable – although the spiritual participation of the whole Church was never lost sight of. But when a priest celebrated a 'private' Mass to ask for mercy on behalf of someone who had died, he alone received the consecrated elements. Even in ordinary Masses it became usual for the laity to receive only bread. What began as a matter of convenience became a dogma, and it is perhaps of some significance that it was here that popular protest focussed among the Hussites, because it seemed to imply a further exclusion of the laity from a priestly privilege.[13]

This deep and pervasive resentment of spiritual and practical privileges, 'reserved' apparently to the priesthood,[14] underlies and informs much of the argument of the sixteenth century on the reforming side. That is not to say that it was always conscious. But it is important to bear this context of dissent in mind, as going back at least well into the twelfth century, and having a solid base of popular support which perhaps provided welcoming soil for the ideas of the sixteenth-century reformers in those areas where their views caught on quickly.

The theological *point d'appui* was the contention that the character of the Mass itself was being misunderstood. That is true, in the sense that the corporate nature of the celebration was being lost sight of – though

---

12   Pollet I.346, Letter 96.
13   Y. Congar, *Lay People in the Church* (London, 1957), pp. 230–2.
14   Cf. Johannes Eck, *De Sacrificio Missae*, ed. E. Iserloh, V. Pfnür and P. Fabisch, *C.Cath.* 36 (Münster, 1982), III.9, p. 174.

more by consequence of changes in practice than as a result of any change in doctrine. The relation in which the priest stands to the people as president of the Eucharist had been obscured and there was indeed a notion of a peculiar 'personal' power of priesthood. But it was not this misapprehension of the collective character of the eucharistic act to which the reformers characteristically addressed themselves when they said that the Church was misusing the Mass. They looked at the notion of sacrifice.

Johannes Eck reads the text *habemus altare* (Hebrews 13.10) as a clear statement by the Apostle that the Church has an altar and therefore makes sacrifice (*altare et ita sacrificium*). 'We have an altar of sacrifice in the Church and what shall be sacrificed there but the Eucharist, the Body and Blood of our Lord Jesus Christ?' he asks.[15] Calvin replies that this passage is to be understood anagogically. It compares the rite of the Old Law with the present state of the Church. It says, 'We have an altar, from which those who serve the tabernacle may not eat (*non habent potestatem edendi*).' 'Those who serve the tabernacle' are the ministers of empty rites. We, if we are to be in communion with Christ (*ut Christo communicemus*), must renounce such rites and separate ourselves from those who may not eat because they serve the tabernacle. He underlines the principle. If we retain such 'ceremonies', we shall not be participants (*participes*) in the sacrifice which Christ made once and for all.[16] Priests in the contemporary Church are thus being seen not as having power to sacrifice, but as conducting empty ceremonies, and so far not necessary that it is damnation to have anything to do with their rites.

Lutheran reformers altered the liturgy of the Eucharist so as to eliminate an offertory element.[17] Their intention in doing so was to return to what they believed to be an 'original' pattern, in which there was no notion that the Eucharist was a sacrifice. Emser discusses this Lutheran contention that it was only at some point after its institution that Holy Communion came to be thought of as a sacrifice (*coepit missa fieri sacrificium*). He argues that far from being 'made' a sacrifice in the liturgy, the Eucharist was a sacrifice from all eternity *in mente divina*. There was no innovation, no human imposition of something novel.[18] Eck sees this reforming

---

15 *Ibid.*, p. 74.
16 *CR* 83.191–2.
17 G. Rupp, *Patterns of Reformation* (London, 1969), pp. 141–3.
18 H. Emser, *Schriften zur Verteidigung der Messe*, ed. T. Freudenberger, *C.Cath.* 28 (Münster, 1959), p. 16, cf. Schatzgeyer, *Tractus de Missa*, p. 161.

practice as bringing desolation upon the Church.[19] Far from being innovative, the liturgy has been sanctified by continuing use in the Church from the beginning, that is, even from the time immediately following the death of the apostles.[20] It was intended that it should be used *in perpetuum*.[21] The apostolic custom (*apostolicus mos*) is what is still the custom of the Church today (*ecclesiae mos hodie*).[22] Emser cannot see that it can be right now, in the old age of the world, to make changes to what has always been received practice.[23] Schatzgeyer underlines the *grandis authoritas* of general and ancient custom, where it does not contradict or distort Scripture, and the benefit of avoiding *scissura* in the Church which comes from a common and universal practice in the celebration of Mass.[24]

Calvin goes as far as he does, in order to counter the view put forward by some moderates among the reformers that there is no need to reject the Mass altogether. Rites and ceremonies are things indifferent, or even beneficial, for they were 'introduced into the Church with good intentions for the sake of order and decorum'.[25] The Lutherans, considering this contention in framing the Formula of Concord, argued that any rites truly indifferent have no place in the worship of God;[26] and also that there is a danger that the acceptance of such rites may give the impression that there is nothing at issue between reformers and 'Papists'.[27] Richard Hooker, a generation later, disliked the idea that rites and ceremonies should be abolished just because they conform to Roman usage. It was Calvin's intention to make a separation between 'mere ceremonies' and sacraments, and to classify the action of the Mass with the former.[28] The idea was that ceremonies were not only demonstrably inadequate (omitting as they did a proper place for the proclamation of the Gospel, faith, prayer),[29] but also implied that there would be an automatic benefit *ex opere*

19   Eck, *De Sacrificio Missae*, I.5, p. 38.
20   *Ibid.*, II.3, p. 95.
21   *Ibid.*, pp. 79ff.
22   *Ibid.*, II.8, p. 113.
23   Emser, *Schriften*, p. 1.
24   Schatzgeyer, *Tractus de Missa*, p. 392.
25   Solid Declaration of the Formula of Concord, Art. 10, Tappert, p. 610.
26   *Ibid.*, p. 612.
27   *Ibid.*, p. 611.
28   *Acta CT* 7[ii].449.
29   *Apologia* for the Augsburg Confession, Tappert, p. 256.

operato. As Melanchthon puts it in the *Apologia* for the Augsburg Confession, the purpose of observing ceremonies ought to be that people may learn and be touched by faith and fear; that is the opposite of the notion that such ceremonies 'work' without moving or instructing the people.[30]

Melanchthon, like Calvin, links the concept of rites as unacceptable (because they seem to him to make a claim to an *ex opere operato* effectiveness) with a series of further notions which became commonplace among reformers. 'Ceremonies' are seen as a usurpation of divine rights by human authorities; as instituting new worship in the Church; which has no Scriptural warrant, and as an imposition upon the faithful.[31] The Lutherans were equally hostile to such *traditiones humanae*. Melanchthon calls them 'disorderly'.[32] The Solid Declaration sees it as an issue of Christian Liberty[33] and a submission to idolatry[34] to obey such 'commands of men'.[35] Calvin finds it indispensable to mix in human elements *quod nusquam Deus precepit*.[36] At issue, then, behind the debate about sacrifice at many points was the power-struggle about authority in the Church in which the reformers were engaged.

One of its most important effects was a tendency to separate the one sacrifice of himself made by Christ on the Cross on a single historical occasion; and the sacramental conveyance of the benefits of his Passion in the Eucharist.[37] Here it is of some importance that a great deal of weight was placed on Christ's death itself, so that (in this controversy at least) the broader context of his saving work tended to be pushed into the background.[38] Schatzgeyer, for example, turns over the question whether it is the bloodiness of the Passion which makes it uniquely a sacrifice and, elsewhere, whether it is possible to offer Christ if he cannot be 'crucified again'. These and related points are raised everywhere in the literature. It was argued that no human being could be a priest, for no-one could offer Christ now as he had once

30 *Ibid.*, p. 250.
31 *Ibid.*, p. 257.
32 *CR* 12.520.
33 *Ibid.*, p. 613.
34 *Ibid.*
35 *Ibid.*, p. 615.
36 *CR* 83.59, on Heb. 5.5.
37 Rupp, *Patterns*, p. 143, and cf. *WA* 18.62ff.
38 A point made implicitly in the Lima Statement of the World Council of Churches on the Eucharist, and see David N. Power, *The Sacrifice we Offer* (Edinburgh, 1987), p. 11.

offered himself; that to multiply Masses was to imply that what he had done needed repeating; that the idea that a fixed number of Masses eased the penalty of a fixed number of sins implied that his sacrifice needed adding to, as though it had not been quantitatively sufficient for all the needs of sinners.

Because of the preoccupation with priestly power, the central difficulty on this view lay in the connection between the concept of priesthood and this vexed question of sacrifice. Salmeron argued in the Trent debates that priesthood and sacrifice are so conjoined (*ita inter se coniuncta*) that neither can exist without the other.[39] Seripando refers to the point again in his preface to the Trent canons on ordination.[40] It was not in dispute that Christ the Great High Priest made once for all the sacrifice which made reconciliation possible. The issue was whether there remains any need or place for sacrifice, and consequently any room for priesthood's definitive sacrificial work of making satisfaction. In the reformers' view, to call the Eucharist a 'sacrifice' in this sense implied an addition to, or repetition of, what was accomplished once and for all by Christ. Melanchthon's concern, like Calvin's, is to identify the satisfaction which merits forgiveness with the *unica mors* of Christ, and not with the *ritus* of penance which are called 'canonical satisfactions', or with eucharistic sacrifice; and thus to eliminate any tendency to think that human beings can earn their way to Heaven. 'The death of Christ', says Bullinger, 'is a full satisfaction for our sins.'[41] Seripando, reflecting in the Trent debates on the Church's use of the word *satisfactio*, notes that it horrifies many people because it seems to arrogate to man what must be uniquely the work of Christ.[42] As the Anglican Becon (1513–67) puts it in his *Catechism*, 'The Holy Scripture declareth plainly ... that not another, but Christ himself offered himself a sacrifice ... and that by virtue of his one and alone sacrifice God is at peace with man.' 'Those who take upon them to offer Christ in their masses to be a propitiatory sacrifice unto God the Father for the sins of the quick and the dead, they show themselves to be more proud than Lucifer ... or than that most proud king, which said in his heart "I will climb up into heaven and exalt my throne above, beside the stars of God".'[43] Cranmer says that it dishonours the unique priesthood of Christ to plead remission of sins by an offering to the Father, for

---

[39] *Acta CT* 6ii.7, cf. 39.
[40] *Acta CT* 9.41.
[41] *Decades* I.108.
[42] *Acta CT* 12.633.
[43] Becon, *Catechism*, vol. I, p. 246.

Christ 'admits neither partner nor successor'.[44] There was a double concern here: both for the honour of Christ, and to resist the pride and usurpation which seemed to the reformers to be implied in the 'priestly act of sacrificing' as they understood it to be taking place in the contemporary Church.

Yet the need for a priest was not in question. There can be no hope for us before God without a priest, says Calvin.[45] However the text is construed in the Epistle to the Hebrews, that seems to him to be the Apostle's clear meaning. But Christ is unique in that he himself is both priest and victim, and it is that which makes it possible for him alone to soften God's wrath, as Calvin sees it. He can act on behalf of mankind because he is himself a man.[46] He alone among men is able to be the victim because he is sinless.[47] A victim is essential, says Calvin. A priest cannot be peacemaker between God and man (*pacificator*) unless a victim 'intercedes' (*nonnisi intercedente victima*).[48] (The term 'intercede' is of some note here.) The right of priesthood (*ius sacerdotii*, cf. *ius ... a Domino concessum*)[49] embraces two duties (*duo continet officia*), says Melanchthon. The first is propitiatory, to 'placate' God (*placare*, taken in a stronger sense than 'to please'). The second is to 'offer' to God (*Deo offere*).[50]

Reforming opinion regarded the offering of a victim as something more than the offering of gifts (*donorum oblatio*). Oblation has two meanings, says Calvin. In one sense it simply means the offering of gifts, as in the sacrifice of praise and thanksgiving which goes on in the Church today. But if it is taken to refer to the offering of a victim, then it is specifically a matter of expiation (*expiationis sacrificia specialiter designat*).[51] That is why, the reformers argue, if Roman bishops confer ordination with the purpose of making 'sacrifice' in this latter sense in the celebration of the Mass, they do so *in malum usum*, for there is no place for such work in the Church. Christ has already done all that is needed by way of propitiatory sacrifice.[52] So the *officium Christi* must be distinguished

---

44 *The Priesthood of the Ordained Ministry* (London, 1986), General Synod Report, Church of England, p. 53.
45 *CR* 83.57, on Heb. 5.1.
46 *Pro hominibus*, Heb. 5.1.
47 *CR* 83.93–4, on Heb. 7.26.
48 *CR* 83.58.
49 *CR* 83.59.
50 *CR* 12.501, Thesis 21.
51 *CR* 83.57.
52 *Acta CT* 7ii.449.

carefully from the *officium* of those ordained to 'priesthood' in the Church, says Calvin, making lists of points of comparison between Christ and human 'priests', in line with the distinctions he finds in Hebrews.[53]

ii. THE PROBLEM OF REPETITION: THE LAST SUPPER, THE PASSION AND THE EUCHARIST

The relationship between the Last Supper (coming first in time, before the Crucifixion), the Passion, and the Eucharist, was clearly perceived in the sixteenth-century debates as being the nub of the matter if the Eucharist was to be described as sacrificial; and if it was to be said to be in some manner conjoined with the Passion in effecting reconciliation and forgiveness. Schatzgeyer, for example, suggests that the words of the Lord at the Last Supper did not 'give' but only 'promised' the 'remission of sins', which was to take place 'through the oblation and shedding of blood on the Cross', and that that oblation is offered 'representatively' in the Mass.[54] He thus fixes upon the shedding of Christ's blood in the Passion as the key matter and relates the Supper and the Mass to that once and for all event by way of promise and fulfilment, respectively. The 'fulfilment' in Schatzgeyer's view consists in the fulfilment of Christ's intention by those who 'eat him in the sacrament' (*cum ipsum in sacramento manducamus*).[55] There are various difficulties about this account, of which the chief is that it may be taken to imply that Christ offered himself in the Last Supper only, as it were, in promise. Another possibility, put forward by Emser in reply to Luther, is that only on the Cross was the offering able to purchase (*offerebatur precium*), but that in the Mass the offering is perpetual (*offertur perennis*) and that in the Mass *iugiter coleretur per mysterium, quod semel offerebatur in precium.*[56] The Trent theologians found themselves unable to take a position on this point in the final debates of 1562. If Christ offered himself at the Supper, a problem arises about the need for, and the nature of, the sacrifice he made on the Cross; if he did not, what is the meaning of the words '*Hoc est corpus meum*'? The thrust of the Trent solution was to link the Supper directly with the Mass, and to say that the action of Christ at the Last Supper

---

53   *CR* 83.56.
54   Schatzgeyer, *Tractus de Missa*, p. 67.
55   *Ibid.*, p. 349.
56   Emser, *Schriften*, p. 18.

was to change bread and wine into his body and blood and to give himself in this way to his disciples, with the instruction that they should continue to eat and to offer him under the species of bread and wine.[57] The avoidance of the question whether he made an offering of himself at that time which was effectual as a sacrifice, involved glossing over a large body of Tridentine (and wider) debate on this point which turned on the elements of satisfaction and reconciliation[58] in the Last Supper, the Passion and the Eucharist.[59]

SACRIFICE AND RECONCILIATION

Thinkers of the sixteenth century did not in general have any difficulty with the idea of a God whose just anger requires propitiatory sacrifice before he can forgive and be reconciled with his people; any other view radically alters the basis of a theology of atonement on which both sides were fundamentally agreed. There was, however, no sense of contradiction in many Catholic minds between a conception of a justified divine anger and the view that Christ's self-offering to his Father was an act of mutual love, met on the Father's side by a corresponding giving which is felt by reconciled sinners as mercy and forgiveness. In the text of 1562 the Trent Fathers omitted the direct reference to divine anger which they had included in 1552, while retaining the notion of propitiation. Propitiation thus proved fully reconcilable with a God of mercy and not only with a justly angry God to whom sin is necessarily intolerable. And, most importantly, both 'mercy' and 'anger' theories may be contained within a doctrine of sacrifice.

It was important both to reformers and to Catholics that the Cross should be understood to have brought about something once and for all; which was not effected by the Last Supper; and which cannot be effected by the Mass as if it were a separate sacrifice.

The problem is to affirm the actual presence of the past redemptive event of the Passion in the celebration of the Eucharist, yet without prejudicing the uniqueness and decisiveness of that event. The thrust of

---

[57]   Cf. Power, *Sacrifice*, pp. 102–3.
[58]   Many classifications of sacrifice were tried. Eck, for example, points to the 'five kinds of sacrifice' in Leviticus 5, 6, 7 (I.2, p. 22, of the *De Sacrificio Missae*).
[59]   *Das Herrenmal* (Paderborh, 1978), Lutheran–Roman Catholic text on the Eucharist, points out that those who participate in the Eucharist are able to share in Christ's offering, and that Christians have nothing else to offer to God but Christ (repr. *Origins*, 8 (1979), 465–78).

the two main positions in the sixteenth century was in one case to envisage the 'memorial' as a mere bringing to mind, which specifically denies present or future reference; and in the other to see it as an actual making present of the historical event. The reformers who stressed the first said that the Eucharist is a *testamentum*, a legacy left us by Christ. Eck rejoins that the will only comes into effect with the death of the testator, and the death of Jesus was a sacrifice offered to God for our sin, 'and so his will includes this oblation' (*itaque testamentum, et hanc oblationem involvit*).[60] A number of devices were explored by Catholics in the sixteenth-century debates to find a way of understanding the *commemoratio* by which Christ commanded his disciples to perform the action of the Last Supper in remembrance of him, not only (*sola*) as a memorial of the Passion, but also as making the Passion a present reality.[61] One was the use of *quasi* or *ac si*. Anselm of Canterbury had used the concept of a *quasi aliquid* as a way of discussing sin and evil, which he, like Augustine, regarded as 'nothing'.[62] We find *quasi* explored in an analysis by one of the Trent theologians of the likeness between the Old Testament sacrifice of expiation involving two doves, and the twofold 'sacrifice' of the Passion and the Eucharist. The first dove's blood was shed for the sins of the people; the second was sent out to fly away with people's sins. Just so did Christ die as victim in expiation for our sins on the Cross, and in the Eucharist it 'is as though he were sent out, to carry away our sins' (*quasi dimittitur, ut secum portet ac deleat nostra peccata*).[63] The *quasi* here implies more than a vague 'as if'; it is human language stretched to its limits to accommodate a divine mystery.

The idea that the Mass is an 'image' (*imago*) of the Passion was not entirely satisfactory. The image of Caesar is clearly not Caesar himself,[64] although it was argued at Trent that the Mass is so perfect an image

---

[60] Eck, *De Sacrificio Missae* I.9, p. 59 and cf. III.2, p. 127. See, too, Bellarmine, *De Baptismo*, I.18, *Opera*, III.194, where baptism is described as a *testimonium sanguinis Christi effusi* which is found in the Eucharist.

[61] *Acta CT* 13.134, Tractatus 27.

[62] Anselm, *De Casu Diaboli, Opera Omnia*, I.248ff.

[63] *Acta CT* 13.134, on Heb.1.3; 9.12. Eck, in discussing the sacraments in general, suggests that they are *quasi cannales* for the application of Christ's merits (*Ad invictissimum Poloniae regem Sigismundum, De Sacrificio Missae* (Cologne, 1526), O³).

[64] Eck, *De Sacrificio Missae* I.10, p. 62; cf. Aquinas, *ST* III q.83.a.1, and Gabriel Biel, *Canonis Missae Expositio*, Lectio 85 F, ed. H. A. Oberman and W. J. Courtenay (Wiesbaden, 1963–), IV.101.

(*perfecta imago*) of the Cross that whatever applies to the one applies to the other (*quidquid convenit uni, convenit alteri*).[65] It was further suggested at Trent that since in an image there must be both identity with that of which it is an image, and difference (or it would not be an image but the thing itself), we may see the identity as consisting in the offering of the same victim, that is Christ, and the difference as lying in the distinct offering of each Eucharist. That is why the oblation comes after the consecration, so that when the offering is made it is the one crucified Christ who is offered.[66] There can, suggests Emser, in an earlier discussion, be no objection to the idea of repeated offerings, since Christ himself offered himself three times in one day, in the Supper (*figuraliter*), in instituting the Mass and on the Cross.[67] The device of allowing for the possibility of repeated offerings without implying a repetition of the one sufficient sacrifice is not, however, entirely satisfactory because it drives a wedge between Christ's self-giving and that in his sacrifice which is seen as effecting the reconciliation between God and man.[68] More important, perhaps, is the point made by Emser, as he discusses Zwingli's handling of various passages in the Fathers. Chrysostom, he argues, shows that an oblation may also be a *commemoratio*.[69] Here, too, we meet the idea that the victim offered is the same (*idipsum semper offerimus*), but the notion of the repetition of offerings in the Mass becomes in the context of *commemoratio* the understanding that the Eucharist is an offering of the 'true offering' made on the Cross and in no way a separate and further offering.[70] *Anamnesis* thus becomes not a simple recall, as Johannes Consilii argues, but a renewal and representation (*renovatio et repraesentatio*) of the thing known or the past event.[71] For Eck *repraesentatio* has a meaning in the eucharistic context which one Lutheran disputation acknowledges to be its 'grammatical' sense (that is, the natural sense of the language), which is 'to show something present and true' (*rem praesentem et veram ostendere*).[72]

65 Ricardus of Vercelli, *Acta CT* 6ii.437.41.
66 Ricardus, *Acta CT* 6ii.440.5.
67 Emser, *Schriften*, p. 17.
68 See Power, *Sacrifice*, pp. 69–70.
69 *Acta CT* 7ii.386.
70 Emser, *Schriften*, pp. 74–5.
71 *Acta CT* 7ii.513.34–5.
72 *WA* 39i.192–3.

We cannot pursue the idea of *repraesentatio* with its associations of 'making present' very far without coming to the question of the presence of Christ. Here we enter a much older debate, and perhaps because of its lengthier history, the question of Christ's bodily or other mode of presence in the consecrated bread and wine, or in the celebration as a whole, was, broadly speaking, treated in the sixteenth-century debates as a matter distinct from the question of sacrifice. We must look at it first in its own right, before we can attempt to set it in context in relation to the question of sacrifice.

iii. THE PRESENCE OF CHRIST

The topic was still sufficiently important in the particular questions it raised for Robert Bellarmine to think it helpful to give up half his treatise on the Eucharist to the subject. This continuing disjunction made it less obvious than it might otherwise have been that if the problem is seen as lying in a priestly power which is a usurpation, and which claims too much for human ministers, it is logical to oppose both the doctrine of transubstantiation and that of sacrifice as the reformers of the earlier sixteenth century understood them, because both appear to rest on large claims for the *vis* of the priest. On any other view, a doctrine of the real presence of Christ, whether of transubstantiation or not, would seem to make it necessary to accept that the Eucharist is sacrificial. Luther denied sacrifice but had no trouble with 'real presence'. The Zwinglians resisted both. But the failure to get to grips with the implication of one for the other resulted in a singular incompleteness in the treatment of both topics during the century. It would not be true to say that the two are never linked. Iudocus Clichtoveus, for example, says that it is correct to infer (*recte colligi*) from Melchisedek's *offering* of bread and wine that the body of Christ is truly contained (*vere contineri*) in the sacrament of the Eucharist.[73] But at Trent the matter of Christ's presence was debated separately in 1551, and a set of canons constructed to meet various reforming contentions and to insist that Christ's body and blood are 'truly, really and substantially present' and that Christ is not merely *impanatus*, somehow contained in what remains bread.[74]

---

73   Iudocus Clichtoveus, *De Sacramento Eucharistiae contra Oecolampadius* (Paris, 1526), I.4, p. 14.

74   *Acta CT* 7[i].116ff. The theologians of Paris in their 1544 Articles made a classic statement of the doctrine of transubstantiation: 'Every Christian is bound to believe that in the consecration of the Eucharist bread and wine are converted into

In the eleventh century the doctrine of transubstantiation was framed in terms of Aristotle's *Categories*. Everything has a substance which cannot change without the thing ceasing to be what it is. Attributes or qualities of the substance may change. Bread may change in appearance and smell when it grows mouldy, without ceasing to be bread. But to suggest that the reverse can happen, and the substance change while the attributes remain the same, seemed to Berengar of Tours an affront to common sense. It was in response to his challenge and in the terms he had set for the debate that the doctrine of transubstantiation was formulated. The twelfth century saw some tinkering with the theory, some speculation about the question of what would happen if worms or mice ate the consecrated bread. But there was no serious assault on it again until the thirteenth and fourteenth centuries, when the academic study of logic had progressed far enough to make the technical issues interesting again, at a more sophisticated level than they could be examined at in the eleventh century. The sixteenth-century debates had nothing to add to the sophistication of these discussions, and indeed the pronouncements of the Council of Trent avoid going into technicalities of this sort as far as possible.

The paradox of physics and metaphysics to which Berengar of Tours and his fourteenth-century successors had addressed themselves largely gave way to more recent concerns in the sixteenth-century debates. The Trent canons insist that both bread and wine contain the whole Christ, for the pressure to allow communion in both kinds to the laity had implied that they were being denied him in his fulness (Canon 3). Christ is said to be present not only when he is received (*dum sumitur*) but objectively in the bread and wine after consecration (Canon 4), because the reformers had been arguing that Christ is present only to the faith of the believer. But

> the true body and blood of Christ, the species (accidents) of bread and wine remaining, and under these species the true body of Christ is contained, which was born of the Virgin and suffered on the Cross' (*CR* 34.14, Article 5). The Paris theologians made no attempt to explain the physics and metaphysics. Their proof is simply that this was a resolution of a Council held under Gregory VII, and their discussion is concerned with the weighing of authorities on this matter. Ambrose supports them, 'and the Master of the Sentences', Peter Lombard, 'alleges this as a certainty'. 'His citations must be held to be authentic.' Patristic authorities which seem to go the other way must be considered in the light of the fact that they spoke before the time of Gregory VII. Only one of the many *questiunculae* of the mediaeval debate is referred to. If the consecrated bread were to be eaten by worms or otherwise corrupted, it would miraculously return to ordinary bread; the body of Christ could not suffer in that way.

we find old battles being refought too. In answer to the objection that Christ's body cannot be in many places if it is physically present (a contention we meet in the eleventh century too), Innocent III is cited. The most important innovation of the sixteenth-century debates was the adoption of the phrase *realis presentia*. It is used as early as the late fifteenth century by Pico della Mirandola. It covered all that the doctrine of transubstantiation was designed to protect, implying a presence which was not merely figurative (*nonfiguralis*).[75] But it contained something more: the possibility of a conceptual link with the idea of 'representation'. 'Christ is very present (*praesentissima*) to the Church in the Mass', says Schatzgeyer, 'not figuratively but really, *per recordationem et repraesentationem*.'[76]

The thrust of the reformers' attack on the doctrine of transubstantiation was twofold. It was held that it encouraged the believer to think in a materialistic way, first that the 'present Lord' is a body rather than a person,[77] and secondly that his presence is somehow 'confined to the elements'.[78] It is important that the Augsburg Confession does not deny that 'the body and blood of Christ are truly present' (Article 10), since it underlines the fact that the Lutherans were closer to the Catholics than Zwingli on this point. In one of the papers drafted in connection with the Council of Ratisbon in 1541, we meet the explanation that Christ's presence is not a matter of physical change (*conversio physica*) in the bread, or of local fixing (*localis inclusio*).[79] The Council of Trent made it plain, by including a reference to the presence of Christ's soul in its first canon on the subject, that the doctrine of transubstantiation did not intentionally emphasise a 'bodily' conception of the presence of Christ to the exclusion of a sense of his presence as a person.

---

75   J. de Montclos, *Lanfranc et Bérengar* (Louvain, 1971).
76   Cf. *Acta CT* 7ᶦ.
77   L–RC dialogue, Eucharist (49), *Growth*, p. 204.
78   ARCIC I Eucharist (6), *Growth*, p. 74.
79   This preoccupation with 'how' Christ is present is specifically set aside again and again in recent ecumenical dialogues involving Roman Catholics, Lutherans and Anglicans; it is the fact not the mode of his presence which is seen as important, 'God acting in the Eucharist effects a change in the inner reality of the elements.' The term 'transubstantiation' 'should be seen as affirming the fact of Christ's presence and of the mysterious and radical change which takes place. In contemporary Roman Catholic theology it is not understood as explaining how the change takes place.' ARCIC I E 6.12 and footnote, p. 71; A–L Pullach (68), p. 23, 'Both communions affirm the real presence of Christ in ... the Lord's Supper, but neither seeks to define precisely how this happens.' Cf. R–RC (70), *Growth*, p. 45; L–RC Eucharist (51), *Growth*, p. 204.

Nevertheless, there was a tendency for both sides to become fixated on the topic of the mode of Christ's presence as understood in the traditional terms of the transubstantiation debate. Reformers proposed two ways out of the impasse.[80] The first was to regard the presence of the Lord as subjective. *Fiat nobis.* Let it be 'to us' the body and blood of Christ. Christ is present to the eye of faith, and only the believer receives him. In one sense this was not a new emphasis. But 'worthy receiving' had formerly been coupled with a doctrine of Christ's objective presence, and not seen as constituting a necessary condition of that presence for the recipient. The penitential system was linked to the idea that the communicant should come to Mass with his sins forgiven and in right relationship with God so as to be a worthy recipient. Since 1215 it had been mandatory that everyone should communicate once a year at Easter and the penitential system of Lent had been a time of preparation to ensure that everyone came as a worthy recipient. The sixteenth-century Book of Common Prayer in the Church of England echoes that emphasis in its exhortation to the faithful to come to Holy Communion only when they have confessed their sins before God, are in love and charity with their neighbours, and are resolved to lead a new life in obedience to God's law. The two aspects of receiving worthily and in faith are linked in the Interim of 1548, and Gropper commented at Trent that the *effectus* of the Eucharist seems to him, as Cajetan remarked, to be a 'response' to the devotion of the recipient (*respondet ... devotioni*).[81]

A second way of keeping out of the hornets' nest of the transubstantiation debate was to argue that 'in the Eucharist there is no body and blood of Christ as a real thing' (*res vera*), but only as a sign (*tantum ut in signo*).[82] This 'article' was carefully considered by the Trent theologians. They examined the words of consecration used by Jesus and recorded in the Gospels and in 1 Corinthians 11, in the light of current thinking about figurative language in Scripture. If this had been meant figuratively, they suggest, it would have borne one of two distinguishing marks. It would either be clear from the absurdity of the literal meaning that it was meant figuratively; or there would be some indication in the text that what followed was intended to be taken figuratively. 'If someone wanted

---

[80] On the Catholic side here, see in particular Louvain 13 and 14 (1544) and Trent XIV, Canons 7 and 8.
[81] *Acta CT* 7[ii].446, cf. Cajetan, *Opuscula*, II, Tract 3, *De Missa Celebratione* (1510).
[82] *Acta CT* 7[iii].3.

to signify that man is an animal', they argue, resorting to a standard Aristotelian and mediaeval example, 'he could not express it more clearly than in these words: "Man is an animal." When, then, the Lord said, "This is my body", he could not explain in clearer words his true presence (*vera praesentia*).' They are aware of objections made by the Zwinglians that *est* as a copula does not always perform the same function, and they do their best to deal with this problem too.[83] A battery of skills in the interpretation and identification of figurative language is brought into play. Calvin tackles the article of the Paris theologians on transubstantiation along similar lines, but including elements of Augustinian sign-theory and the importance of the sign in the sacrament having some similitude, some likeness to the thing it signifies.[84]

iv. IN THE PERSON OF CHRIST

The insistence of the transubstantiation debate upon an understanding of the change as taking place in a particular manner threw a strong emphasis in the West upon the words of consecration, and thus upon the power of the priest to bring about that change as he uttered them. Reformers who wanted to deny transubstantiation, with all that it seemed to them to imply, argued that the words do not 'consecrate matter' but simply 'teach the people' (*ad materiam consacrandam; ad populum instruendum*).[85] They belong, in other words, to the ministry of the Word. That, objects Bellarmine, is not an adequate account of the matter because it does not explain the *vis eucharistiae*,[86] the power of the Eucharist.

With this notion of a eucharistic 'power' or 'force' we come to the heart both of the debate about sacrifice, memorial and the relation of the Last Supper, the Cross and the Mass; and of the dispute about the real presence of Christ.[87] Both turned on the conception of a 'priestly power' to which we have been brought back again and again.

The *potestas consecrandi*, like the power of binding and loosing, is, says Gabriel Biel, irremovable (*inauferibilis*) even where a priest or bishop is suspended, excommunicated or degraded.[88] In this sense it is

83   *Acta CT* 7[iii].4.
84   *CR* 35.14–15.
85   Bellarmine, *De Eucharistia*, IV.12, *Opera*, III.421.
86   *Ibid.*, p. 54.
87   See pp. 180ff.
88   Biel, *Canonis Missae*, Lectio 2, I.15.

certainly a 'personal' power. Yet, suggests Iudocus Clichtoveus, the priest speaks not in his own person, but Christ's, when he says the words of consecration (*non quidem in sua sed Christi loquentis persona*).[89] Thus it is Christ himself who, acting through the priest, is the source of the *vis eucharistiae*, just as he is of the *vis* of baptism.[90] That is why, as Augustine had convincingly argued in the case of baptism, the unworthiness of the minister does not invalidate the sacrament. A number of misunderstandings on this point made reformers object to the doctrine of an *ex opere operato* efficacy of the sacraments. Bellarmine explains that the *virtus* or *vis* of the Spirit is not contained in the sacraments as in vessels (*in vasis*); the sacraments are merely instruments in the Lord's hands.[91] During the Trent debates Antonio Ricci complains that 'the heretics' impute many opinions to the Catholics which are quite foreign to them (*a nostra sententia sunt alienissima*). We do not speak of *ex opere operato* as though we meant that the sacraments operated automatically, he explains; we mean that Christ works in us.[92]

But to speak in the name of Christ is also – and supremely in the Eucharist – to speak in the name of his Body the Church.[93] Eck says the priest prays *in persona Ecclesiae*.[94] Alexander de Bononia says in the Trent debates that the chief 'offerer' of Christ in the Mass is the Church, and that the priest offers on behalf of the Church as her minister.[95] Schatzgeyer had made the same point, that the *sacerdos sacrificans* does

---

[89] Clichtoveus, *De Sacramento Eucharistiae*, I.22, p. 76. Eck puts his finger on a major limitation imposed on this debate by the preoccupation with sacrifice, and its connection with a personal priestly power of the ordained ministry. The Eucharist is not like other sacraments, in that the priest is sharing in a corporate act. He himself communicates, whereas he cannot baptise or absolve himself (*De Sacrificio Missae*, III.5, p. 155). Priestly action in the Eucharist is directed towards communion, a celebration of that union of Christ's people with their Lord, which is one with Christ's own reconciling work. The priest who forgives *in persona Christi* (2 Corinthians 2.10) when he declares absolution, also offers in the Eucharist *in persona Ecclesiae* (Eck, *De Sacrificio Missae*, III.9, p. 174). Cranmer emphasises that the use of the first person plural in ancient liturgies presupposes that the action of the Eucharist is communal (*The Priesthood of the Ordained Ministry*, Faith and Order Advisory Group (London, 1986), p. 52).

[90] *Acta CT* 8.744.

[91] Bellarmine, *De Baptismo, Opera*, III.23.

[92] *Acta CT* 7ii.467.

[93] Schatzgeyer, *Tractus de Missa*, p. 247.

[94] Eck, *De Sacrificio Missae*, I.3, p. 27 and Schatzgeyer, *Tractus de Missa*, p. 263.

[95] *Acta CT* 6ii.459.

not offer as a 'private person' (*persona privata*) but as a *minister Ecclesiae*, himself an instrument as the sacrament itself is an instrument. He receives the sacrament *ut privata persona in fide*, in faith, and as an individual, but in offering *in persona Ecclesiae* that which he consecrates *in persona Christi* he 'represents and renews in the Spirit' (*repraesentat ac in spiritu renovat*) the oblation made by Christ on the Cross.[96]

Thus there is no such thing as a private Mass. 'Every Mass is public', says Bellarmine; the celebrant acts as a *publicus minister* and 'for the common and public benefit of the whole Church' (*pro communi et publica utilitate totius Ecclesiae*).[97] The Tridentine decree explains that this is so because of the public nature of the priest's ministry, and also because of the spiritual communion of the people of God in the Eucharist.[98] On this understanding of things, the 'priestly power' of consecration is inseparable from the action of Christ and the action of the Church. Schatzgeyer goes so far as to suggest that on the Cross itself Christ was offered by the Church, so that we may say that the Church offered him *in propria persona* in the Passion and celebrated the *memoria* of this offering daily in the Eucharist.[99] If it is argued that we cannot offer Christ but only our thanks and praise, Schatzgeyer answers that even the Church's thanks and praise are not her own to offer. We have nothing to offer of ourselves. The Church's offering of Christ in the Passion and now in the Eucharist, in a *recordatio* and *repraesentatio* of that one historical event, is indistinguishable from Christ's own offering of himself (*aliud non est quam*), and that in itself shows that it is not a repetition of that event.[100]

This is of some importance – although Schatzgeyer argues along an unusual line in conceiving of the Church as offering Christ in the Passion itself – in bringing together conceptions of a propitiatory sacrifice made present in the Eucharist, with the sacrifice of praise and thanksgiving in which the reformers saw the true *eucharistia*. It also provides a means of uniting with these the people's sacrifice of broken and contrite hearts. In the Trent debates Pflug did not carry everyone with him on the question whether consecration is the *pars principalior*.[101] But this kind of talk underlines the importance of seeing the

---

96 Schatzgeyer, *Tractus de Missa*, pp. 68 and 227.
97 Bellarmine, *De Baptismo*, I.3, *Opera*, III.23.
98 Power, *Sacrifice*, p. 25.
99 Schatzgeyer, *Tractus de Missa*, p. 48.
100 *Ibid.*, p. 223.
101 *Acta CT* 7[ii].628, and Lectio 15, p. 120.

Eucharist as the action of the whole Church and not as solely the action of the priest, and others were as anxious as Pflug to see the priest as president of a celebration in which he acts *in persona Christi* and *in persona Ecclesiae* and not as a private person having a power which is his alone.[102]

The debates at Trent move from the notion that the Mass is a sacrifice to the understanding that 'in this divine sacrifice which is made in' (*peragitur in*) the Mass, the same Christ (*idem ille Christus*) is 'contained' (*continetur*) and unbloodily sacrificed, who on the altar of the Cross 'once bloodily offered himself'.[103] The difference is seen as consisting in the uniqueness of the historical event, which was, because there Christ died in blood and agony, the definitive and unrepeatable sacrifice which made reconciliation possible. The Mass is a celebration 'in' which this same sacrifice is not merely recollected but present. It is propitiatory, not in its own right as a separate sacrifice (a repetition or addition to the original sacrifice) but 'through' (*per*) the unique sacrifice on the Cross which is 'in' it, so that 'if' (*si*) the recipient comes to God in the Eucharist 'with fear and reverence', 'contrite and penitent' and 'in fulness of faith' (*plenitudine fidei*), he may obtain mercy and find grace.[104] For the sake of that great and unique sacrifice God sets our sins aside (*dimittit* not *remittit*)[105] in the Eucharist in response to our faith and not in any way as an automatic action at the behest of the priest. The sacrifice is always the same one; it simply differs in the mode of its offering (*ratio offerendi diversa*), and that is why it can be offered 'for' (*pro*) the dead as well as the living and 'for' (*pro*) sins, penalties and so on, because what is being pleaded is not a fresh sacrifice but the sacrifice which is sufficient for the sins of the whole world.[106] It is in this way that the faithful are seen as participating in Christ's self-offering.[107]

v. APPLYING THE WORK OF CHRIST

The purpose (*finis*) of priesthood, says Calvin, is to be a means by which people may come to God,[108] that is, to be an instrument of God's

---

[102] *Acta CT* 7ii.628.
[103] *Acta CT* 8.910, 1562 Decree and Canons.
[104] *Ibid.*
[105] *Ibid.*
[106] *Ibid.*
[107] On prepositions, compare Schatzgeyer, *Tractus de Missa*, p. 45 and *passim*.
[108] *CR* 83.53.

reconciliation with man.[109]   This is the heart of priesthood, and it is the crux both of the notion that in the presidency of the Eucharist the ordained minister speaks *in persona Christi*, and of the understanding that he also acts *in persona Ecclesiae*, on behalf of the (collective) priesthood of all believers, making it possible for them to exercise their priesthood together.

Chrysostom emphasised the way in which the action of the Eucharist points beyond this life. 'When you see the Lord sacrificed and lying before you ... are you not straightway transported to Heaven?' he asks.[110] The late mediaeval emphasis is rather different. Gabriel Biel, for example, stresses that the 'new sacrifice' of the Eucharist, instituted by Christ himself, is to last 'to the end of the world'.[111] This is Schatzgeyer's position. The Eucharist is a sacrifice of the Church militant as distinct from the Church triumphant (*prout contra triumphatricem distinguitur*).[112] That does not mean that it is not an earnest of Heaven. Christ gave himself in the Eucharist as a token, sign and seal of his promise that just as he has given himself to us *in via*, so we shall possess him in Heaven for eternity. Nevertheless, it is now in this life that we have need of the reconciliation of which the Eucharist is one instrument.

'It is always the blood of Christ which cleanses', says Bellarmine, but it is 'applied' *per varia instrumenta*, through various sacraments, or by faith alone, or by martyrdom.[113]   In baptism 'the Passion of Christ' is applied (*applicatur*) to wipe out all blame and all punishment.[114] It was non-controversial that an application of Christ's saving work on the Cross occurs in connection with baptism (although some reformers preferred not to speak of the 'effect' of baptism as an instrument of the forgiveness of sins). In absolution the ordained minister declared God's forgiveness to the penitent and again Christ's work on the Cross could be seen to be 'applied'. It is of some significance here that Ockham's case for denying that sin is remitted *per sacramentum eucharistiae* was that the communicant must come to Mass having been already absolved,[115] that is, as having had such application

109   *CR* 83.57.
110   *De Sacerdotio*, ed. J. A. Bengel (Leipzig, 1894), III.iv.175.
111   Biel, *Canonis Missae*, Lectio 36 F, II.45.
112   Schatzgeyer, *Tractus de Missa*, p. 187; cf. p. 263.
113   Bellarmine, *De Baptismo*, I.18, *Opera*, III.194. Cf. Aquinas' application *ad singulares effectus*, that is, to meet specific human needs (*ST* III q.61 a.1 ad 3 and 52ᵃ q.1 ad 2).
114   *De Baptismo*, I.12, p. 183 and *De Poenitentia*, *Opera*, III.731.
115   Quaestiones in IV Sent., *Opera Theologica*, VII, ed. R. Wood *et al.* (New York, 1984), p. 221.

already made to him. The Eucharist itself was not easily seen by the reformers of the sixteenth century as an occasion for 'applying' the *causa universalis* of our salvation because of resentment of a number of corrupt practices associated with the system of indulgences, where payment was taken for the saying of Masses for the dead, and because of the widespread resentment of 'priestly' claims to a *vis applicationis*.[116] The preoccupation with sacrifice was important here, too, as focussing attention on the argument that the Mass cannot bring about forgiveness by being propitiatory, and cannot be a 'work of satisfaction' (*opus satisfactorium*) for that reason.[117]

There would seem to have been two main areas of difficulty here. The first lies in the notion of the special priestly *vis*, which is an extension of the power to consecrate and to offer, or power to determine to whom and in what manner the *effectus* of the celebration shall apply.[118] It is this which Luther attacks as early as 1518, claiming that it is arrogant for the priest to think he can 'take God captive' and decide whom he will forgive; the most the priest can do, he says, is 'reverently' to place the matter *in arbitrium Dei*.[119] The second difficulty lies in the notion that the action of the Eucharist can be limited or made specific, parcelled out, as it were, to such categories as 'sinners not yet reconciled with God'; the righteous, that they may continue *in iustitia*; those in purgatory, that they may 'by the power of this sacrifice' (*virtute huius sacrificii*) be more speedily purified of their sins.[120] Within this area lies the question whether what counts is the measure of the recipient's faith or the *mensura* of Christ's gift.[121]

It is in connection with this second that the two traditionally main aspects of the ordained ministry of reconciliation come together: much turns on one or two cardinal principles of the mediaeval penitential system. Satisfaction, as brought about by Christ's death, is seen by Antonius Delphinus in the debates of 1547 at Bologna (in a manner reminiscent of Anselm of Canterbury's theology of atonement) as

---

116 Cf. *Acta CT* 7[ii].445.
117 *CR* 12.502.
118 Power, *Sacrifice*, p. 73 suggests the outline which sees Christ as himself, through the priest, transforming the bread and wine into his body and blood, while the priest merely has power to focus the Church's offering and the application of the fruits which come from Christ's saving action.
119 Sermon I, *De Passione Christi*, 1518, *WA* 1.297. Cf. Schatzgeyer, *Tractus de Missa*, p. 267.
120 Schatzgeyer, *Tractus de Missa*, p. 267.
121 *Ibid.*, p. 303.

consisting in the paying of a debt to an offended divine honour.[122] It is an act of reparation, an actual paying back. This heritage of a doctrine of satisfaction which associates it with debt strongly colours both the soteriology and the eucharistic doctrine of the Reformation debates. For the Catholic side it endorsed the fundamental distinction normally made in the penitential system of the later Middle Ages between the fault (*culpa*) and the punishment (*poena*) of sins. Reconciliation with God is a forgiving of sin in which remission of fault and of penalty go together, and baptism is the sign and seal of this complete forgiveness. But if the forgiven sinner sins again, there is an assumption in penitential practice that punishment is due, even though the fault may be freely forgiven when he repents and acknowledges his sin. That is to say, some amends ought to be made to demonstrate the sincerity of his repentance and to pay the debt he owes. We have seen how penitential codes from at least Carolingian times consistently quantify such punishments and at the same time regard them as commutable. Thus something other than the stated penalty may be offered instead and God's honour still be satisfied.

It was a key point of the penitential system that 'remission of guilt' (*remissio culpae*) and 'remission of penalty' (*remissio poenae*) are distinct and separable, 'so that the first does not necessarily imply the second', as Schatzgeyer puts it.[123] The death of Christ on the Cross is sufficient to take away all guilt and all penalty for the sins of the whole human race, as both reformers and their opponents agree. 'Christ ... offered himself a sacrifice unto God his Father to appease his wrath kindled against mankind through sin; and ... by the virtue of his one and alone sacrifice God is at peace with man, favoureth and loveth man, and accepteth man for righteous in his sight', as Becon puts it.[124] His death 'abolishes all guilt' and 'all penalty' which is due as a result; it is *sufficientissima*, says Schatzgeyer.[125] The penitential system's way of putting it takes account of the place of faith. Schatzgeyer explains that this 'abolition of guilt' takes place 'in those who have contrite hearts (*convertuntur ad cor*), are moved by faith to repentance and trust in hope in the mercy of Christ'.[126] The difference between his and Becon's position,

122   *Acta CT* 6ⁱⁱ.606.
123   *Tractus de Missa*, p. 319.
124   *Catechism*, p. 246.
125   *Tractus de Missa*, p. 273.
126   *Ibid.*, p. 275.

and perhaps between those of the two sides in general, lies in the distinction of 'penalty' from 'guilt' and the view that although the guilt of sin is forgiven once and for all in the believing and baptised individual, freely and as often as the sinner repents of sins committed afterwards, God may require a form of satisfaction for the sins of the lapsed.[127] Temporal penalty is not always 'squared' with guilt (*non quadrat*), says Schatzgeyer, and that is why God can ask us to show by some token that we take it seriously. He who is forgiven less loves less (Luke 4.47)[128] is the Scriptural principle advanced here.

The distinction within the penitential system of penalty from guilt was necessarily associated with a belief that the penalty was not only temporal, that is, due in this life, but also quantitative. There was a difficulty here to which the reformers of the sixteenth century were quick to point. If Christ's merits are infinite and his satisfaction on the Cross all-sufficient, there seems no place for finite and specific applications of his redeeming work in particular celebrations of the Mass. One answer advanced to this was that the 'making present' of his sacrifice in the Mass has a finite value, as being only a particular celebration, and cannot be equated with his full offering.[129] But that makes a separation between Eucharist and sacrifice which runs counter to much else in the system of explanation we have been looking at. Another possibility canvassed at Trent is that the effect of the Eucharist may be seen as twofold. It is intercessory, so that the Church is seen as entering into the movement of Christ's self-offering by joining to it her own sacrifice of prayer, praise and thanksgiving. Thus the Church appeals to divine mercy and God grants a forgiveness which goes beyond man's just deserts.[130] It is also an act of pleading the merits of Christ and it thus obtains forgiveness *per modum satisfactionis*,[131] as

127 *Ibid.*, p. 282.
128 *Ibid.*
129 Cf. Power, *Sacrifice*, pp. 41–2, and Schatzgeyer, *Tractus de Missa*, p. 299.
130 *Acta CT* 6ii.608–13.
131 Cf. Power, *Sacrifice*, p. 82. It was something of a commonplace among the reformers that the Roman Church taught that Christ's death satisfied only for original sin, and that Masses were sacrifices designed to make satisfaction to God for the actual sins committed after baptism. The Confutation of the Augsburg Confession says that this reflects a misunderstanding. That is not Catholic teaching. Masses do not wipe out sins; but the Mass can take away the penalty due for sin (*delet poenam pro peccato debitam*); it can supplement or complete satisfaction (*satisfactiones supplet*) and confer an increase of grace and comfort us in our need (*Confutatio*, Tappert, p. 163).

an act of divine justice. It is this latter 'mode' of application of the Eucharist which makes it possible for a Mass to be said for the sins of a particular individual in what may be thought of as a quantitative way.[132] The first rests on the free gift of God;[133] the second on human action to earn it.[134] There are difficulties about this too – not least that it brings us again into the area of the debate about faith and works.

Schatzgeyer gives a large part of his *De Missa* to the penitential system, in recognition of its relevance here. Private Masses, in which communion was not received by the faithful (although they might be present), were celebrated from a period between the end of the fifth and the eighth centuries, and as the practice of commutation of penance grew, Masses were accepted in lieu of works of penance.[135] It is of some significance here that their 'value' would seem not to have lain primarily in the notion that they were quantitative applications of Christ's sacrifice. The saying of Psalms would do.[136] They were 'works' rather than 'sacrifices', or at least, rather than 'propitiatory sacrifices' in their own right. (It is worth commenting in this connection perhaps that, along with the Psalms, they might be seen as having a thanksgiving or intercessory purpose.) There is a clear conception of a special function for 'applied Masses' by the end of the Middle Ages. Gabriel Biel, for example, says that 'Christ instituted this sacrament to be frequently repeated, so that it might be a memorial sign of his Passion and so that it might be a remedy against the daily sins of the soul.'[137]

The conception behind the private Mass was not only that of special application, but also of the work of the Mass in relation to an individual soul, rather than the community. It is perhaps paradoxical that this preoccupation with the salvation of the individual is echoed among the

---

132   Cf. Power, *Sacrifice*, pp. 42–3.
133   *Acta CT* 7ii.477. Marianus Rocha argues that we do not deserve it, but intercede or ask God that through the merits of Christ our Redeemer, which we offer in the Eucharist, he may grant us mercy.
134   It should be emphasised perhaps that the system of indulgences stands outside the penitential system, because the granting of an indulgence is understood to be a remission of the temporal penalty of forgiven sin, and not a part of the process of forgiveness.
135   C. de Vogel, 'Une mutation cultuelle inexpliquée: le passage de l'eucharistie communautaire à la messe privée', *Revue des sciences religieuses*, 54 (1980), 231–50.
136   *Ibid.*, p. 245.
137   *Canonis Missae*, Lectio 36 F, II.44.

reformers, in their stress upon the importance of his receiving, in faith, what only 'worked' for him personally if he did so. The reformers' concern was to get away from the idea that automatic benefits were to be had from the saying of the Mass, whether or not the individual who benefited had a saving faith.[138] The Anglican Homily Concerning the Sacraments instructs the faithful in making their communion 'to apply [Christ's] merits to thyself'. 'Herein', it continues, 'thou needest no other man's help, no other sacrifice or oblation, no sacrificing Priest.'[139] The notion that there might be an application to those not participating in faith is equally ruled out by Melanchthon in the *Apologia* for the Augsburg Confession.[140] The need to deny any automatic priestly power of application, or any limiting of the forgiveness made available through Christ's Passion by the intention of the celebrating priest can be seen here to be encouraging the making of a different set of distinctions which were again working against the conception of the Eucharist as an action of the community with Christ.

Let us take one or two instances of this failure by both sides to explore fully the implications of a doctrine of forgiveness within the Eucharist. Despite his reservations about the possibility of specific application, Luther held that there is an *effectus* of forgiveness, which is brought about by the saying of the words of consecration. 'By [the] words "for you" and "for the forgiveness of sins" … the forgiveness of sins, life and salvation are given to us in the sacrament, for where there is forgiveness of sins, there are also life and salvation … the eating and drinking do not in themselves produce … such great effects … but the words "for you" and "for the forgiveness of sins" ', he wrote in the Small Catechism he framed for the use of ordinary households in 1528–9.[141] In the Larger Catechism of the same period, designed for the use of the clergy, he emphasises again that it is the words 'for you and for the forgiveness of sins … through which this [forgiveness] is imparted'.[142] This focussing upon the utterance of certain words, although it shifts attention away from the protracted debates of many centuries upon the words *Hoc est corpus meum* etc., still fails to take the eucharistic action of the community as a whole or to place the president's role in context within it, and it fails to address the question of the relationship

---

[138] Power, *Sacrifice*, p. 56.
[139] Concerning the Sacraments, *Anglican Homilies*, p. 310.
[140] Tappert, p. 256.
[141] *Ibid.*, p. 352.
[142] *Ibid.*, p. 449.

between this 'imparting' and the idea of 'application'.[143]

On the other side, an important distinction between the 'effect' and the 'fruit' of the Mass, familiar in the later Middle Ages, does not seem to have been followed through in the sixteenth-century debates, perhaps because the 'fruits' belong to a devotional tradition rather than to the arena of academic theology. Aristotelian principles of cause and effect were advanced in the debates on justification, as well as in the discussion of the efficacy of the Mass. The devotional writers prefer to speak of 'fruits' which are not solely a remission of the temporal penalties due for forgiven sins, but a matter of visible growth in holiness. Schatzgeyer lists twelve of these 'fruits': newness of life (*vivificare*); kindling (*inflammare*); the gift of patience; healing; strength, and so on.[144] Like Eck,[145] he links this actual change in the faithful to the 'renewal and representation' of Christ's Passion which takes place in the Eucharist. 'Through' (*per*) the action of the Mass which makes present Christ's self-offering, *ac si in cruce pateretur*,[146] newness of life becomes real to his people.[147]

vi. RECEIVING

We have noted that the Lateran Council of 1215 laid down as a rule what was already accepted practice, that the faithful should receive communion at least once a year at Easter, and that they should first confess and do penance, so that they might come to the Eucharist with contrite and pure hearts.[148] The same insistence on confession before the *sumptio eucharistiae* is to be found in the Trent debates.[149] The underlying intention is identical with that of the reformers, when they emphasise the importance of receiving in faith and not 'unworthily', but they set aside the formal provisions of the penitential system in favour of a simple confession to God in the heart.

---

143 *Acta CT* 7ii.445.
144 Schatzgeyer, *Tractus de Missa*, p. 347.
145 *De Sacrificio Missae*, I.10, p. 64.
146 Schatzgeyer, *Tractus de Missa*, p. 347.
147 Power, *Sacrifice*, p. 131.
148 'Grant us therefore, gracious Lord, so to eat the flesh of thy dear Son Jesus Christ, and to drink his blood, that our sinful bodies may be made clean by his body and our souls washed through his most precious blood', Book of Common Prayer of the Church of England, Holy Communion.
149 *Acta CT* 7i.143.

The act of physical 'receiving' is central here. Gabriel Biel provides a commentary on the late mediaeval debate about the relationship of consecration to communion. He quotes Alexander of Hales' view that since 'consecration is for the purpose of communion' (*propter communionem*), communion is greater than consecration, and mentions the argument that since the laity receive the consecrated elements they should be able to consecrate them too, for otherwise they are allowed the greater but not the lesser part of the Eucharist.[150] Schatzgeyer prefers to link oblation and communion, as complementary in the fullness of the Eucharist.[151] But throughout such debates the Catholic position is clear: the Mass is not 'communion only', as some of the reformers argue when they protest that it involves no oblation and that nothing is objectively brought about by the saying of the words of consecration.[152] At Trent Johannes Consilii presses the view that the most precious body of Christ 'is not only received' (*non tantum sumitur, ut sacrilegi isti volunt*) but is also consecrated and offered before being received.[153] Thus it is not the case that the bread and wine become the body and blood of Christ only when they are received by the faithful,[154] and it is an error to say that nothing but faith is required to make a valid Eucharist.[155]

But in Catholic practice the physical receiving of the people was certainly complemented by a 'spiritual receiving'. Can we believe, asks Eck, that those not present at the communion, but who would wish to be present, are not included?[156] To say that the Mass cannot benefit those who are absent (including the dead) is to imply that they have no communion with us, argues Schatzgeyer.[157] It is perhaps legitimate to link this spiritual action of the people of God with talk among the reformers of the sacrifice of praise and thanksgiving, which is seen as a spiritual sacrifice.[158]

---

[150] Biel, *Canonis Missae*, I.41.
[151] *Tractus de Missa*, p. 225.
[152] *Ibid.*, p. 269.
[153] *Acta CT* 6[ii].507.
[154] Schatzgeyer, *Tractus de Missa*, pp. 189–97.
[155] *Ibid.*, pp. 110–13.
[156] Eck, *Loci*, p. 397.
[157] *Tractus de Missa*, p. 267.
[158] Tappert, p. 252.

We have come some way from the kinds of authority questions raised by the debates about text, testimony and the use of formal reasoning, into the area of the Church's sacramental authority and the function of that authority in the economy of salvation. It will be plain that again and again disquiet in this arena focussed among the reformers upon the role of the ordained minister, and in particular upon the 'priestly' functions. That cannot be separated from the question of the structures through which order in the Church is seen to operate, and that is what we come to next.

PART IV

Authority in the visible community

10. *Visible and invisible*

In *The City of God* Augustine develops two related ideas. The Church includes all the elect, those who have already died, those still living and those yet to be born, in a bond of unity which transcends the ties of this life. It is therefore a community whose invisible reality is only imperfectly and partly embodied in its visible presence on earth. Secondly, because the human community on earth includes members of both 'cities', and because (as Augustine held) only God knows who are his elect, the ostensible Church membership here and now is in fact a mixed community.[1] Wheat and tares grow together until harvest. The principle is echoed in Thomas Becon, Anglican reformer and Homilist, in his *Catechism*; he points out that 'This word "Church" in the Holy Scripture is taken not only for the fellowship or company of the good and faithful, but also of the wicked and unfaithful.'[2] Augustine saw it as essential[3] that the earthly community should preserve its unity as one body, saints and sinners together; no-one should presume to have special knowledge which enabled him to say who were God's people and who were not. There was thus a built-in tension in Augustine's ecclesiology. Visible and invisible Churches have different constitutions.

The difficulty Augustine threw into relief arises in part from a doctrine of election which denies that anyone but God can know who are the elect. The Lutheran stress on assurance, and later Calvin's doctrine of the assurance of election, should in principle have bridged the gulf between 'invisible' and 'visible' conceptions of the Church by making it possible to say who were truly Christ's. But in a Church divided in its visible body, the tendency was the other way: to create self-defining 'saved' communities of the 'invisible' Church, 'gathered believers' made locally visible. Among the most extreme adherents of this line of thought were radical communities of separatist brethren. The Confession of Faith produced at Schleitheim in 1527, for example, speaks of 'God's obedient children ...

---

1 Cf. Melanchthon, *CR* 12.434.
2 Thomas Becon, *Catechism*, p. 41.
3 And his encounters with Donatist schismatics in north Africa made it necessary to emphasise it.

who have been and shall be separated from the world in everything ... We shall not have fellowship with ... the wicked ... By this is meant all popish and anti-popish works and church services, meetings and church attendance, drinking houses, civic affairs, the commitments made in unbelief and other things of that kind.'[4] These and other more moderate bodies could be seen as set over against a community whose membership was defined by baptism, and was thus wholly visible because heads could be counted even if vocations could not.

Study of the Fathers did not do all that was hoped of it to clarify matters. In a series of *Questions and Answers*, Pilkington (*c*.1520–76), one of the Anglican Reformers, tackles a catena of texts, from Augustine, Cyprian and Jerome, all asserting that the Church is a visible company of people which continues from the time of the apostles by a perpetual succession in one faith under Christ its Head; in which there is a succession of bishops; and outside which there is no salvation. He seeks to show that there is a difference between a 'papistical' and an 'apostolical' succession, and that it is the 'Papists' who have 'divided themselves from this Church of Christ', so that to keep apart from them is in fact to belong to it.[5] Even if we allow for a good deal of special pleading of this sort, there were real difficulties in determining a solid patristic position on this question of the identity of the Church, because circumstances made Augustine and others emphasise different considerations from those which preoccupied the sixteenth century. Augustine's view of predestination as a mystery necessarily opaque to the elect was coupled with a sacramental theology not yet subjected to the profound stresses of late mediaeval developments. Augustine taught that grace operates in the Church by direct action of God through an ordained ministry which acts as a channel. So the Church does not exercise a separate or vicarious power in the administration of the sacraments, but a *ministerium* of God's power. In this way, Augustine keeps in balance the relationships of the individual and God; and of the community as a whole with God and with one another. God works directly in the individual in and through the community, and there is no rivalry in Augustine's mind between the action of grace in the Church and the action of grace in the heart. Nor is there any anomaly in saying that the sacraments are effective for some and not for others. In the mixed

---

[4] See John C. Wengen, 'The Schleitheim Confession of Faith', *Mennonite Quarterly Review*, 19 (1945), 243ff.

[5] *Works*, ed. J. Scholefield (Parker Society, Cambridge, 1842), pp. 617–19.

Church on earth God's grace secretly touches his elect. The same view of *ministerium* enables him to answer the Donatists' claim that only a minister in communion with the Holy Spirit (that is, in their Church) could administer the sacraments validly. 'It is Christ who baptises.' We shall see as we go on how late mediaeval developments shape the sixteenth-century debates on the implications of all this, but it needs mentioning here because it has a bearing on the question of order and structure in the visible Church.

Much of Augustine's ecclesiology was worked out in response to situations of emergency. *The City of God* was written at a time when educated pagans were asking why, if Christian teaching was right, their God had allowed a Christian Empire to be overrun by unbelievers. In north Africa itself, Augustine worked for many years to try to resolve the problem of the schism of the Donatists. These two circumstances led Augustine to emphasise first the eschatological dimension and, secondly, the importance of unity in the Body of Christ; he argued that division is itself the worst heresy.[6] These, *mutatis mutandis*, are sixteenth-century concerns too. There is a sense of the *senectus mundi* about in sixteenth-century apocalyptic,[7] and a pervasive consciousness of the pain of schism. Partly because of this superficial likeness in circumstances, the reformers often read Augustine as though he were the first Protestant; and just as mediaeval readers had coloured his words with their own experience, so reformers now took him to be speaking for their own time. Conservatives took him for their own spokesman too, as Pilkington complains. But Augustine's world differed from that of the Middle Ages in a number of practical respects. His was still a Roman frame of reference. Concepts of power and authority in the Church owed a good deal to Roman secular thinking, but they lacked quite the coloration of the regal and princely which they were to get from the Germanic peoples. Above all, there was as yet nothing exactly comparable with the intermeshing of interests which was to arise in feudal society, where ecclesiastical lords were also feudal lords. It was above all out of these developments in the Church in Western society in the centuries after Augustine that there arose the ecclesiological and sacramental abuses the reformers confronted in the early sixteenth century.

Although both sides in the sixteenth-century debates could subscribe to the doctrine that 'there is no salvation outside the Church', they could do so only on the basis of different conceptions of the Church. When

6   On the context, see H. Chadwick, *Augustine* (Oxford, 1986).
7   See R. Bauckham, *Tudor Apocalypse* (Abingdon, 1978).

Boniface VIII promulgated the doctrine in the Bull *Unam Sanctam* of 1302, he understood the Church to be a visible body on earth, with the Pope at its head, a hierarchy of ordained ministry and a laity identifiable by baptism. The task of the Church, thus understood, was to help the baptised come to eternal life by making provision for their souls' needs on earth, and especially by making it possible for them to deal with the consequences of sin in their lives. An alternative view was already abroad. Movements of popular dissent from at least the twelfth century criticised the corruption they saw among some of the clergy and the claim of the Church to a plenitude of power[8] which was increasingly regarded as domination requiring blind obedience. This prompted the development of an alternative ecclesiology which located the centre of gravity of the Church not in the hierarchy but in the community as a whole, and thus compounded the difficulties about 'visibility'. Theories on this basis are to be found in academic circles as well as in grass-roots movements.[9] Peter d'Ailly[10] emphasised the organic unity of the Church and William of Ockham saw it as the body of the faithful.[11]

This revolt had the effect of linking the idea of a 'visible' Church in people's minds with that of dominion by a hierarchy and the overwhelming of the humble and weak. The campaign for the 'popular' and 'free' Church was also for this reason usually envisaged as a campaign for an 'invisible' Church.

The historical roots of the disputes of the Middle Ages, here as elsewhere, lay in a series of power-struggles: between Church and state in the Investiture Contest of the late eleventh century and its aftermath; between the people and their spiritual rulers in succeeding centuries; and finally between powerful interests within the hierarchy, in the Conciliarist movement. The reformers of the sixteenth century drew attention to the way in which the power and sovereignty of God himself was sometimes being lost sight of in all this. If the Church claimed that her sacramental ministry was indispensable to salvation, was the power of God not being tied down to the sacraments? To the assertion that the one true catholic

---

[8]   See the oeuvre of the late W. Ullmann on these developments.

[9]   There is a full bibliography in K. M. Capalbo, '*Politia Christiana*: the ecclesiology of Alvarus Pelagius', *Franciscan Studies*, 35 (1986), n.1.

[10]   Peter d'Ailly's *De Potestate Ecclesiastica* is printed in Jean Gerson, *Opera Omnia*, ed. E. du Pin (Antwerp, 1706), II.925–60. In this treatise he sets out his final position.

[11]   See J. B. Morrall, 'Ockham and Ecclesiology', in *Medieval Studies Presented to Aubrey Gwynn*, ed. J. A. Watt *et al.* (Dublin, 1961), 481–91.

Church of Christ on earth is the visible community of the baptised under the hierarchy, or even that it consists in that hierarchy alone, Calvin answers that the Church is visible where Christ is to be seen.[12]

The central paradox was outlined by Luther in a disputation of 1542: 'The congregation of the Church is such that unless the Holy Spirit revealed it, we could not comprehend it, for it is in the flesh and visible; it is in the world and is seen in the world; yet it is not in the world ... and no-one sees it.'[13] What was at issue was the way in which the visible and institutional Church, with its manifest corruptions and human failings, could be at the same time that holy thing which is united with Christ as the body to the Head, in a mystery hidden from mortal eyes. The Interim of 1548 tries to bring the two together. It explains that the 'Church is ... composed of saints and though spiritual and invisible, yet it is also perceptible to the senses'. It says that 'to this same Church belong the bishops ... the Word of God ... the sacraments ... the keys of binding and loosing ... the power of coercing by excommunication ... calling to ecclesiastical offices ... the right of making canons' (IX.5). There is an attempt to link the invisible and the visible, to present the Church in the world as identifiable by outward signs and as a channel of 'the invisible grace of God' (XIV.1–2). It is acknowledged that bad men as well as saints are mixed in among the members (IX.7). There is an insistence that 'those things which pertain to the sensible and external part of the Church ought to be subservient to the perfecting of saints' (IX.7). But there is no real resolution of the paradoxical elements.

The questions to do with the 'visible' Church which presented themselves most forcefully in the sixteenth-century debates were the matters of sacramental 'effect' and 'power to reconcile' at which we have been looking, and a series of difficulties over order and structure which had, ultimately, the same resistance to an idea of 'priestly power' at the heart of them. In what follows here there cannot be space to do more than indicate where the most vexing of these concerns about the authority of the ordained ministry lay.[14] The theology of the Church's formal

12 *Antidote* to the Paris Articles of 1544, *CR* 35.31–2.
13 *WA* 39ii.149.
14 A–L Pullach (53), *Growth*, p. 20. We still hear echoes of the old difficulties with the paradox of the invisible and holy Church and the visible and fallible. Baptists and Reformed have suggested that the Church is 'first and foremost an event, rather than an institution', but reserving the principle that 'it becomes concrete in

structures is in any case especially sensitive to the need to make adjustments appropriate to time and place and it would not be possible to project a pattern which would work in detail always and everywhere from an analysis of these sixteenth-century disputes. We can, however, see certain broad principles emerging clearly in areas of continuing importance today.

the local congregation' (B–R (36, 37), *Growth*, pp. 149–50). This notion of the Church as something in continual movement has been transforming the issue by shifting the pillars of the paradox. 'Visible unity' can be seen as coming 'from the one grace of the Spirit of God dynamically present among Christians even in their divided condition (D–RC, *Growth*, p. 156).

11. *The two swords and the political analogy*

Melanchthon proposed a compromise in the matter of the powerlessness of the human will to do good, which was later adopted by the framers of the Lutheran Formula of Concord of 1577. He says that although man's will cannot choose the good in spiritual things (because without the help of the Holy Spirit it cannot even understand what is good), it is possible for human beings to identify what is reasonable in 'external, temporal and civil affairs'.[1] This anomalous and imperfectly accounted for exception reflects a more pervasive difficulty experienced by the reformers in accommodating secular rule and civil affairs within the religious sphere, and balancing the authority of Church and state. Luther and Melanchthon were among a number of reformers who decried the habit of thinking about the Church's authority in a political way.[2] The Pope is not a magistrate, says Luther, seeking to separate spiritual and temporal jurisdiction as being of different sorts, and to get away from the political analogy.[3] 'Human polities are bound to a certain succession; they have their laws and power to interpret their laws; they have degrees of persons, kings, dukes; they also have their glory ... the Church is not such a polity.'[4] The particular difficulties involved were in part a matter of contemporary vocabulary. As nineteenth-century debates might emphasise 'duty' and today's language might be of 'responsibility' and 'service', as a democratic model replaces a paternalistic or imperial one; so for the sixteenth century the key concern was with notions of princeliness and magistracy, and their application to the government of the Church.

i. ORDER

Yet there is a problem deeper than that of verbal usage in the relations of Church and state. It can never be possible for ecclesiastical government to throw off all political associations.

1   Augsburg Confession, Art. 18 and *Apologia*, Art. 18.4; cf. Tappert, p. 512.
2   *WA* 39^{ii}.177.
3   *WA* 39^{ii}.42, Disputation of 1539.
4   *WA* 39^{ii}.147.

They cry out upon us at this present everywhere, that we are all heretics, and have forsaken the faith, and have with new persuasions and wicked learning utterly dissolved the concord of the Church; … that we … live … without any regard or worshipping of God; that we despise all good deeds; that we use no discipline of virtue, no laws, no customs; that we esteem neither right, nor order, nor equity, nor justice; … that we labour and seek to overthrow the state of monarchies and kingdoms, and to bring all things under the rule of the rash inconstant people and unlearned multitude; that we have seditiously fallen from the catholic church, and by a wicked schism and division have shaken the whole world, and troubled the common peace and universal quiet of the Church.[5]

The Anglican Bishop John Jewel (1522–71) wrote a defence of the reformed Church in England in 1562. He sees the thrust of the complaints against the reformers as lying in the fear that reform has disrupted order. In the same year the Anglican Homilies were in the final stages of preparation for the 1563 edition.[6] Among those in Book I is 'An exhortation concerning good order and obedience to rulers and magistrates' which seeks to counter much the same anxieties as those to which Jewel addresses himself, but which gives a more explicit account of the theory of order on which Jewel and Cranmer alike rested their case. The Homily links heavenly and earthly, supernatural and natural order:

Almighty God hath created and appointed all things in heaven, earth and waters, in a most excellent and perfect order. In heaven he hath appointed distinct and several orders and states of Archangels and Angels. In earth he hath assigned and appointed Kings, Princes and other Governors under them, in all good and necessary order. The water above is kept, and raineth down in due time and season. The sun, moon, stars, rainbow, thunder, lightening, clouds, and all birds of the air, do keep their order … All the parts of the whole year … do continue in their order … And man himself also hath all his parts both within and without … in a profitable, necessary and pleasant order. Every degree of people in their vocation, calling and office, hath appointed to them their duty and order: some are in high degree, some in low … so that in all things is to be lauded and praised the goodly order of God; without the which no house, no city, no commonwealth,

---

[5]　Jewel, *Apology*, ed. J. Ayre (Parker Society, Cambridge, 1848), vol. I, pp. 53–4.
[6]　Which reissued the Homilies of Book I (published in 1547 and prepared mainly by Cranmer), and added a further series.

can continue and endure, or last. For, where there is no right order, there reigneth all abuse, carnal liberty, enormity, sin, and Babylonical confusion. Take away Kings, Rulers, magistrates, Judges, and such estates of God's order ... and there must needs follow all mischief and utter destruction both of souls, bodies, goods and commonwealths.[7]

Among the many assumptions which underlie both the Homily and Jewel's comments, we might single out two here. The first is that spiritual and temporal order ultimately form a single system within God's providential order. The second is that order necessarily involves – and is indeed principally characterised by – a pattern of rule and subordination to rule.

The first notion is in tune with a fundamentally Aristotelian approach to the theory of causation, in which there is no causal boundary between physical and metaphysical. All order is orderly because the first principle of order imposes order upon it. Anselm, Aquinas, and later Hooker, explore a theory of divine ordering in a Christian universe in which eternal order is seen as a harmony in which all things are held in balance and proportion without chafing. This eternal harmony is built into the created structures of the world, including our humanity, as natural law. Earthly law, or order, is seen as an appropriation of that order by human beings as intelligent (rational) creatures, responding to the contingencies of life, and in the case of Christian order, this appropriation is understood to be guided by the Holy Spirit. But because of the disruptive effects of sin not only in the lives of individuals but upon the whole creation,[8] order is seen as having corrective work to do in the world. Human beings need order and structures to preserve the 'common peace' in Church and state and avoid 'Babylonical confusion'. Aquinas sees human laws and structures as in part mutable, as needs change and vary in different places at different times, but as answerable always to the natural law which governs created things and the divine law which is eternal.

This way of thinking made it natural in the Middle Ages to apply parallel if not similar criteria to the adjudgement of right order in Church and state. (Anselm uses *rectus ordo* for both spheres indifferently.) The Church was tempted to think of its power in a political way and to use a political vocabulary, and the state to blur the lines between spiritual and temporal jurisdiction in defining the powers of princes. The laying out of those lines

7 *Anglican Homilies*, pp. 72–3.
8 Genesis 3.17–19.

was the difficult task of the contenders in the Investiture Contest of the late eleventh and twelfth centuries; we can see something of the delicacy of the balance arrived at, in an account of an agreement of 1107 in England, 'That for the future none be invested by the King, or any lay hand, in any bishopric or abbey, by delivering of a pastoral staff or ring', but on the other hand, the archbishop concedes that no-one who is elected to any prelacy 'shall be denied consecration upon account of the homage which he does to the King'.[9]

ii. TWO SWORDS

The whole matter was made prominent and contentious by the effort made by Gregory VII (d. 1085) to alter a longstanding balance of power. The state had had supremacy (for practical purposes) throughout most of Europe since the time of Constantine. Gregory employed canonists to make collections of legal texts to bear out the contention that, on the contrary, God's gift of authority to bind and loose made the Church supreme over all secular powers. In the last years of his life, Bernard of Clairvaux (d. 1153) wrote a letter in five books, the *De Consideratione*, for Pope Eugenius III who had been one of his monks. He wanted to encourage him to understand the supreme seriousness of the responsibility now laid upon him. Bernard revived a notion used by Gelasius I (492–6) that secular and spiritual power are the 'two swords' of the Gospel. He argued that both swords were entrusted by God to the Church and secular rulers were merely 'lent' the sword of temporal power by the Church at coronation.

There followed a protracted late mediaeval debate about the source of the temporal ruler's authority (whether it was directly from God, or through the Pope, or from the people of the realm, or by some combination of these).[10] It could be argued both that the Pope has an intrinsic right to do as he will in temporal affairs without bowing or even referring to any other authority,[11] and that, since Aristotle says the state is a product of nature, the secular ruler has a natural autonomy in exercising his authority.[12]

---

9   Eadmer, *Historia Novorum*, ed. M. Rule, Rolls Series, Book IV (London, 1884).
10   W. D. M. McCready, 'Papalists and Anti-Papalists', *Viator*, 6 (1975), 241–74, lists the key theorists on the matter of the source of authority in Church and state, especially pp. 241, 244.
11   M. Wilks, *The Problem of Sovereignty in the Later Middle Ages* (Cambridge, 1963), p. 265.
12   McCready, 'Papalists', p. 242.

The Church's consistent position was that spiritual power is 'simply the greater' (*simpliciter maior*), as John of Paris puts it.[13] This trend reached its apogee in 1302 in the Bull *Unam Sanctam* issued by Boniface VIII during his quarrel with the King of France, which claimed that it was necessary to salvation to be subject to the Roman Pontiff and that the two swords were his to wield directly (or to direct to be wielded on his behalf, in the case of the temporal sword). The 'two swords' theme remained a commonplace and came naturally to Luther's mind.[14]

Even without the initiative of Gregory VII, such concerns would have made themselves felt, and the Church could not have avoided thinking of its powers in contemporary political terms. Within the feudal system which operated throughout most of northern Europe in the high Middle Ages there was a deep entanglement of financial interests, legal and jurisdictional rights, going back far beyond the eleventh century. We find Frankish and Anglo-Saxon Kings enacting penitential canons, for example, and everywhere bishops and abbots were also barons, holding landed estates of the king. In late mediaeval England there remained notorious conflicts in the areas where canon and civil law overlapped. Professional lawyers urged the superior authority of the King-in-Parliament. Henry VIII's ecclesiastical revolution of the 1530s made it possible to get rid of the exemption of the clergy from the jurisdiction of the civil courts (which had provoked such bitterness in the late twelfth century under Henry II); but at the cost of leaving Parliament legislative authority in ecclesiastical matters. The laity were also affected directly by the battle over jurisdiction, especially in matters of marriage discipline and the maintenance of Church property.[15]

Thomas Erastus (1524–83), a Swiss theologian alarmed at the direction of certain Calvinist teaching, put into a coherent form a theory of local and national jurisdiction. He proposed that in a state where there is a single Church, the civil authorities ought to exercise jurisdiction over both secular and ecclesiastical matters. There were Carolingian precedents in the matter of synodical government. In accordance with such a policy of *cuius regio, eius religio* we see the German princes at work, convening

---

13   *Ibid.*, p. 245, and see John of Paris, *Tractatus de Potestate Regia et Papali* (Paris, 1942), chapter 5. See, too, Hudson, *The Premature Reformation*, pp. 362–7 and on 'dominion', pp. 360–2.
14   *WA* 39ii.83.
15   For example, Grosseteste, *Letters*, ed. H. Richards Luard, Rolls Series (London, 1861), Letter 72, pp. 205ff.

meetings, receiving documents with dedicatory epistles from theologians and churchmen, lending their authority to theological statements. Papal and episcopal authority was loudly questioned by the reformers, but only the Anabaptists and a few other fringe groups denied civil authority. Zwingli spoke for the main body of the reforming movement when he said that 'temporal' authority 'derives strength and affirmation from the teaching and work of Christ', and that all Christians owe obedience to that authority.[16]

The great exception to this kind of thinking were the radicals. This relatively small and highly varied individualistic body of reformers was to appear in one form or another in most of the areas touched by the Reformation. Its leaders were often men who had been drawn to Luther or Zwingli and who had come to find them too moderate. Carlstadt had been Dean of the Theology Faculty at Wittenberg before he broke away. Thomas Münzer had been a minister at Zwickau in 1520, where he had been for a time an adherent of the Wittenberg programme of reform. By 1521 he was in Bohemia, publishing the *Prague Manifesto*. In it he called on the people of Prague to accept the new faith, with the threat that if they did not do so, God would see that they were smitten by the Turks within a year.[17] A year or two later he had moved on to Allstedt in Saxony, and was publishing pamphlets against Luther.

Certain teachings were characteristic of such radicals. Münzer used Joachim of Fiore, but a general apocalypticism was widespread. Those who responded to the call were God's saints. They would be persecuted and they would suffer. They must not defend themselves or resist. 'The Gospel and its adherents are not to be protected by the Sword, nor are they thus to protect themselves ... True Christian believers are sheep among wolves, sheep for the slaughter; they must be baptized in anguish and affliction, tribulation, persecution, suffering and death.'[18] God would intervene directly in history to make his will plain. Melchior Hofman, who appears in Sweden in 1526, in north Germany in 1527, in Alsace in 1529, in east Friesland in 1530, similarly taught believers' baptism, rejection of oaths and non-resistance as a Biblical teaching. He too was thinking in apocalyptic terms. The Melchiorites lived in expectation of Christ's imminent return to destroy his enemies. They were content to wait in patient suffering in the meantime.

16   Zwingli, *Defence*, Articles 34, 35, 37.
17   *Thomas Münzers Briefwechsel*, ed. H. Böhmer and P. Kim (Leipzig, 1931), p. 142.
18   Conrad Grebel, Letter of 1524 to Thomas Münzer, in *Spiritual and Anabaptist Writers*, tr. George Hunstanton Williams (Philadelphia, 1957), pp. 83–5.

Such groups made local secular authorities nervous. In some cases there was good cause. Radical revolutionaries broke away from the pacifists and non-resisters. Jan Matthijs of Haarlem took over the government of Münster in Westphalia in 1534 with his followers; he was killed, but he was succeeded by one Jan of Leiden, who had himself crowned and set up in polygamy. Even the peaceable radicals, because of their refusal to fit into society, were persecuted and driven underground. Ordinances were made denying them citizenship and freedom to worship.

The result was to encourage them to think of themselves as martyrs, to identify with the suffering Christ, to walk with joy along the hard road before them. In fact they were mostly nothing like the threat the authorities thought. Their talk of the overthrow of society was commonly apocalyptic and other-worldly. Nevertheless, they refused to regard themselves as belonging to secular society at all, and that in itself set a dangerous precedent. They made daily life strictly a Christian and not at all a secular business. An important exception was the Hutterite communities in Moravia. There the authorities proved to be more tolerant, and it was possible for the Hutterites to develop a structure which would unite their communities. They became communist in the sense of holding goods in common, and they made their religious communities in some measure also civil communities.[19]

The reformers of the sixteenth century, then, retained – with some exceptions – a solid regard for the importance of secure and princely government, and were inclined to give the temporal sword a certain pre-eminence of jurisdiction if that diminished the absolutist claims of a 'papal monarchy'. That brings us to the second of the assumptions of Cranmer and Jewel with which we are concerned here, and the one of greatest importance for the failure of the Reformation debates to resolve contemporary difficulties: that is, a conception of order as constituted by a pattern of 'subjection' to government. Benedict of Mantua suggested at Trent that order is a *potestas et praeeminentia in ecclesia Dei*; that there has always in human society been a *potestas* directed to a supernatural end and a *potestas* which has a political purpose; and that their omnipresence indicates that they are not inventions of men but of divine institution.[20] Whitgift stresses the need for 'right government of the Church' in co-operation with the government of the state.[21] Only in this

---

[19]   See Hillerbrand, *Christendom Divided*, pp. 84ff.
[20]   *Acta CT* 9.12.
[21]   Whitgift, *Cartwright*, p. 17.

way, he argues, can 'confusion' and 'disorder' be avoided. William Laud declares that the Church of England 'believes ... that our Saviour Christ hath left in his Church, beside his law-book the Scripture, visible magistrates and judges – that is, archbishops and bishops, under a gracious king, to govern both for truth and peace according to the Scripture'.[22] This contemporary view of the right and necessary association of Christ and Caesar in government carried with it at that time a view of 'order' inseparable from a rather narrow conception of hierarchy and degree as involving dominion and subjection. Whitgift speaks of 'degree and order one under another'.[23]

A significant legacy of the habit of thinking in political terms about the nature of authority in the Church was the vocabulary used to describe bishops and priests: *praepositus, rector, praelatus*. Luther makes the link explicitly. In a disputation of 1542 he argues against the following syllogism: 'there can be no obedience where there is no power. We must obey the Church. Therefore there must be power in the Church.' Luther replies: 'We are speaking of pretorial and political power (*praetoria et politica*), which ought not to be in the Church.'[24] This terminology (and cognate terms) was in use among the Latin Fathers, who, in the *inopia verborum* of early Christian Latin, borrowed from the vocabulary of government. Augustine speaks of the *praepositi* by whom the Church is 'governed' (*gubernatur*).[25] For Gregory the Great, *rector* was an uncontroversial term. Mediaeval usage came to prefer *praelatus*, again with a clear connotation of a legally conceived jurisdiction and obligations of government not wholly distinct from those of the secular world.

Auctoritas often became synonymous in the ecclesiological debates with a *potestas* conceived of as absolute dominion. This was a direct consequence of the developments which had been taking place in Church–state relations since the eleventh century. Popes had wrestled with Emperors for a temporal as well as a spiritual supremacy,[26] and in the process ecclesiological apologetic had come to see Christian authority largely in terms of control over subordinates. The association of authority in the Church with this limited understanding of the nature of its power

---

22   Laud, *Fisher*, p. 234.
23   *Cartwright*, p. 18.
24   *WA* 39ii.177.
25   E.g. *De Civitate Dei* XX.9, and see J. Todd, ed., *Problems of Authority* (London, 1962), pp. 150–3.
26   Capalbo, '*Politia Christiana*', again gives a convenient bibliography.

on an analogy with the temporal power has thrown a long shadow, from which we are only now beginning to emerge, and which threatens still to muddy the conception of a 'hierarchy' in the Church.[27]

Whatever legislative powers with reference to the Church reside in the Church's own authoritative structures must be given some legislative extension by secular authority if they are to have force in society and be endorsed by society as right, customary and reliable. Every local Church exists in a secular community, and must govern its life in ways which are appropriate to the circumstances in which it finds itself. Every Christian is also a citizen living under secular law. Throughout the later mediaeval centuries the running battle continued over this matter of the respective jurisdictions of secular and ecclesiastical courts, as over rights to Church holdings of lands and goods.

Luther reached a point where he repudiated any form of legally constituted Church, and with it the whole of canon law. The Wittenberg jurists were nervous of this line of argument and inclined to ignore it,[28] and ideas of legitimacy continued to be important but not always clearly defined in reforming communities.[29] Luther's arguments on this point of 'law' are at their most heated in his writing on the papacy, and compounded, as we might expect, of what we may call 'Antichrist' elements, and perceptions of real difficulties. He argues, for example, within the 'Antichrist' frame, that the Pope is outside the law (ανόμος) because he not only wants to be above all law, but also wishes all laws to be false. 'The Pope is such a monster that he wishes to be without law, and so to speak, *exlex*, when even the angels are under God's law.'[30] 'Whoever acts entirely on his own whim, without laws, is a tyrant. The Pope does exactly what he likes. Therefore the Pope is a tyrant', is presented as an argument in a 1539 disputation. Luther comments that a tyrant is self-appointed (*in sua ordinatione*); the Pope has a sort of ordination, but it is against the law

27 See, for example, Strange, *The Catholic Faith*, pp. 45 and 68.
28 On Luther's repudiation of any legally constituted form of the Church at one stage, see W. Elert, *The Structure of Lutheranism* (St Louis, Miss., 1962), tr. W. A. Hanson, p. 256.
29 Thirty-Nine Articles, 23, and Trent III, 1546, on the notion of a Council *legitime congregata*. A recent Lutheran–Roman Catholic Dialogue speaks, without defining terms, of both 'legitimacy' of papal ministry and 'legitimate traditions of the Lutheran communities', together with their 'rights of self-government'. *Papal Primacy in the Universal Church* (Minneapolis, 1974).
30 *WA* 39ii.82.

of nature.[31] If it is argued that we must not resist magistrates and princes, so we must not resist the Pope; that is true, says Luther, so long as the magistrate or prince is acting legitimately, but the Pope is not doing so. (And anyway he is not a magistrate.[32]) Luther concedes that the bishops of Rome once had the same *ius* as other bishops.[33] But that was 'at the time when there were (true) bishops of Rome'; he holds that Gregory the Great was the last who was not a usurper. Now the bishop of Rome claims to be bishop of the world; *ius* to decree laws lies with bishops collectively, in council, and not with a single bishop, so he cannot have any such *ius* as he asserts.[34] Luther also looks at the notion that 'laws are validated by approval' (*leges valent approbatione*). A syllogism is constructed in disputation to the effect that if papal laws are received by the Church, they are valid. Luther says that the minor premiss is questionable. 'The books and groans of many good men show how the Church approves these laws!' he exclaims.[35]

It may be helpful here to borrow terminology from the seventeenth century and speak of a contrast between an 'ascending' and a 'descending' authority. In the English controversy of the seventeenth and eighteenth centuries over the place of episcopacy in the ordering of the Church, George Hickes (1642–1715) read in the New Testament a picture of bishops as having power 'to coerce or compel their subjects ... to obey them', and saw them as 'spiritual princes' and 'their dioceses principalities'.[36] Thomas Brett, in *An Account of Church-Government and Governours* published in 1701, agrees that 'The New Testament does so plainly assert a Government in the Church, and so apparently distinguish the Members of Christ's mystical body into Governours and Governed, that one would think this Matter could not admit of a dispute.'[37] These instances are of course contributions to just such a debate, and we see here

---

31   *WA* 39ii.55.
32   *WA* 39ii.56 and 60.
33   Cf. Calvin on Hebrews 7.11, *CR* 51.88, on the link between *legislatio* and *sacerdotium*.
34   It is in line with Luther's general principles here that in practice Lutheran doctrinal decisions acquired legal status through the action of the princes of Germany, who played the part in this of 'emergency bishops' (L–RC, 1981 (54), *Growth*, p. 265). But that raises other difficulties.
35   *WA* 39ii.85.
36   George Hickes, *On the Christian Priesthood and on the Dignity of the Episcopal Order* (Oxford, 1847–8), vol. 2, p. 301.
37   Chapter 1, p. 1, citing Ephesians 4.11; 1 Corinthians 12.28; Romans 12.4; Hebrews 13.7.

the results of the polarising of what John Owen (1616–83) calls 'descending' and 'ascending' theories of the means by which a Church is constituted and governed. 'To constitute a ... Church by descent', he says, 'it must be supposed that all Church power is vested in ... officers, namely archbishops, and from them derived ... by a distribution of power.'[38] By the 'ascending' theory we constitute a Church by becoming 'members by our own voluntary consent'.[39] These were not novel conceptions.[40] We find them everywhere in the sixteenth-century debates, and not always with any clear attempt at reconciliation. The Tyrolean revolutionary Michael Gaismir, for example, suggested in 1526 both that the people of God ought to 'act in unity and always by mutual decision' and that they must 'faithfully obey the authority set over [them]'.[41] The emphasis of many centuries in the Church had been upon the conceptions of dominion and subjection inseparable from a 'descending' theory and from the twelfth century such movements as that of the Waldensians, and in later generations the Lollards, had proposed as an alternative some form of voluntary association with a democratic system of government.

As we go on we shall see these notions of 'ascending' and 'descending' authorising being presented again and again as opposed, or as alternatives, rather than as being complementary, and indeed intimately and subtly interdependent. We shall find an implicit assumption that 'descending authorising' involves the possession of private personal power, while 'ascending authorising' is 'corporate'. And most important of all, we shall glimpse an underlying conviction that subjection to authority is a restriction of freedom, while Gospel liberty demands an absence of structural constraints upon the people of God. This last view is challenged by Seripando in the paradox which forms the basis of his little book on Christian righteousness and Christian freedom. 'The Christian is everyone's servant, ... subject to all; the Christian is everyone's lord, utterly free and no-one's subject.'[42]

---

38 *Of Schism*, p. 188.
39 *Ibid.*, p. 197.
40 Although for Owen the idea of voluntary consent had overtones of the 'social contract'.
41 Michael Gaismir, *Landesordnung*, in M. Klaasen, *Michael Gaismir* (Leiden, 1978), p. 131.
42 *De Iustitia et Libertate Christiana*, p. 39.4ff.

12. Making ministers

i. THE PRIESTHOOD OF ALL BELIEVERS

One of the most far-reaching of the perspectives of the Second Vatican Council was to view the Church 'from the starting-point of baptism', so that the ordained ministry is seen not as possessing a 'higher power' but as 'a service at the centre of the Church community'. To say that 'the greatest day in the life of a Pope is not that of his election or coronation, but the day on which he receives that which the Greek Fathers call the holy and unbreakable seal of baptismal regeneration',[1] is to reverse the assumption which was causing difficulty in the late Middle Ages and the sixteenth century: that that which is common to all is of less value than that which is committed only to some. For that carries with it its concomitant problems of resentment, and a sense of alienation among those who are not ordained. That had been and remained the nub of the problem about the authority of the ordained ministry in the Church.

Waldensians in the twelfth century, Franciscan factions upholding the virtues of poverty from the thirteenth,[2] a growing number of critics both within and outside the ranks of the clergy, contrasted the simplicity of Jesus' life with the pomp and display and wealth of the higher clergy. While the Church was the only alternative to a military career for the well-born, and the higher offices in the Church were filled with scions of the nobility, there were bound to be many who entered the Church from worldly motives. The Church was unavoidably involved in the running of landed estates, and in political and military obligations within the feudal system. In these circumstances the situation was beyond straightforward reform, even if much could have been done to curb the buying of preferments and other financial malpractices. But in any case, resentment of corruption was only a part of a more broadly based

---

1   Suenens, *Dossier*, ed. J. de Broucker (Dublin, 1970), p. 14, and *Co-responsibility in the Church*, tr. F. Martin (London, 1968), p. 31.
2   See G. Leff, *Heresy in the Later Middle Ages* (Manchester, 1967), 2 vols., on the poverty debate, and for a recent view of sixteenth-century developments, C. Haigh, 'Anticlericalism and the English Reformation', *The English Reformation Revised*, ed. C. Haigh (Cambridge, 1987), 56–74.

anticlericalism which – for Wyclif quite explicitly – embraces Pope, clergy, monks and friars alike. Wycliffite polemic is addressed to all four categories as having usurped for themselves rights and privileges and powers and wealth which ought to be shared in the community; and as having compounded their wickedness by at the same time arrogating to themselves the claim to a higher sanctity than could be aspired to by any lay person.

Resentment of a claim to higher sanctity was certainly still rankling in the sixteenth-century debates about the taking of monastic vows. Luther contends that no vow is proper or even possible for Christians after baptism.[3] It cannot restore baptismal purity, although, he says, 'on the authority of their St Thomas [Aquinas], such people boast that a monastic vow is equal to baptism. This is blasphemy.' Anyone who 'believes he is entering upon a mode of life that is better than that of the ordinary Christian' when he becomes a monk is in error, and he is arrogant indeed if he thinks he is superior because he 'proposes by means of his work to help not only himself but also others to get to heaven'.[4]

There had been a long process of legislative reinforcement of a difference of 'estate' between clergy and laity, to which lay as well as ecclesiastical authority contributed. In 725 an English law-code expresses the principle that when a member of the clergy is killed his 'worth' is to be calculated for purposes of punishment not only on the basis of his birth, but also on the basis of his orders. 'For whatever is consecrated, orders, and God's hallowed house, ought diligently to be honoured, for the fear of God.'[5] In 960 we meet the rule that no lawsuit between priests should be held before 'secular men'; clergy should be tried only before their 'equals'; 'or let them lay their cause before the bishop, if there be a necessity'.[6] By the high Middle Ages it had come to seem unfitting that such distinction should not be apparent even in dress. Legatine Constitutions of Otto (1237) insist that 'laymen take great scandal at the unclerical habit of clergymen' and find it improper for them to be clothed like soldiers.[7]

This clericalism had the consequence of making the laity feel that they

3   Cf. Pilkington, *Questions and Answers*, p. 621, 'All vows following [baptism] which are contrary to that, not only may and ought to be broken, but it is wicked to keep them.'
4   *De Votis Monasticis*; Smalkald Articles III.14, Tappert, p. 316; cf. Augsburg Confession, Art. 27.
5   Johnson, *Laws and Canons*, I.156.
6   *Ibid.*, I.413.
7   *Ibid.*, II.161.

were being treated as second-class citizens of the city of God.

The dual resentment – of a claim to superiority; and of greed, corruption, abuse – underlies not only the reformers' resistance to the idea of a priestly 'power' in the sacramental life of the Church, but also their arguments about the need for a fundamental reordering of the Church's ministerial structures. The chief theme of the debate, the notion of 'the Priesthood of all believers', brought together the question of the sacramental office of the ordained ministry and this matter of hierarchical order. The use of the term 'priest' itself for the ordained minister became controversial among reformers for reasons we have already explored in connection with the debate on the Eucharist.[8] But 'priest' (*sacerdos*) was not rejected as an appropriate term for the common Christian ministry, for the New Testament gives clear warrant for such a usage. The protestant reformers described all Christians as 'equally priests' (*ex aequo sacerdotes*), with an 'equal power' (*potestas*).[9]

Luther's case in *Concerning the Ministry* (the treatise he wrote for Bohemia in 1523) is set out like this: Christ is our High Priest, and through union with him we are all priests, without rite of ordination, and without having a special character impressed on us. The primary office of ministry, the ministry of the Word, is, he says, common to all Christians.[10] There is no other baptism than the one which any Christian can bestow; no other remembrance of the Lord's Supper than that which any Christian can observe; there is no other kind of sin than that which any Christian can bind or loose; any Christian can pray; any Christian may judge of doctrine. These make up the royal and priestly office.[11] The emphasis

---

[8]   It is instructive that the word *pontifex* did not generate a similar row, although the term features prominently in the Vulgate text of Hebrews in connection with Christ's unique High Priesthood.

[9]   Cf. *Acta CT* 7[ii].348.

[10] 1 Peter 2.9: 'You are a royal priesthood that you may declare the wonderful deeds of him who called you out of darkness into this marvellous light.'

[11] Luther was prepared to use the term 'priest' for the ordained ministry, but he thought that according to the New Testament, 'minister', 'deacon' 'bishop', 'steward', 'presbyter' were more acceptable (*WA* 12.170ff.). Among the questions debated at Trent was that of the end or purpose (*finis*) of ordination. A contrast was drawn between a loose usage (*usus totalis*) of the term *sacerdos* and its more 'proper' sense (*proprius usus*). Taken broadly, it covers the tasks of teaching, praying, baptising, judging, blessing, consecrating, sacrificing, which are the responsibilities of those who are ordained. But strictly speaking it is said to refer to the two aspects which were under discussion in the debate about the difference

here was upon the equality of individuals, not upon the collective character of the 'Priesthood of all believers', that is, their shared participation in the single Priesthood which is unique to Christ.

The debate about the Priesthood of all believers caused a reaction which sharpened the conviction on the Roman Catholic side that ordination somehow superseded baptism, so that the ordained minister could be seen after his ordination as having, as it were, proceeded to a higher degree (as though he were now a Doctor of Divinity and not a Master of Arts, and his 'first degree' was put in the shade). One significant consequence of this habit of thought was to blur the recognition that an ordained minister was still, and primarily, a member of the laity, one of the *laos* or people of God. Another was to encourage a separation of baptism in its relation to commitment to Christ and membership of the fellowship of his Body (*koinonia*) from baptism seen as a commission for ministry and thus as involving admission to participation in the community's corporate authorising – the aspect the reformers were anxious to stress. We see these disjunctions and one-sided emphases reappearing again and again as impediments to the resolving of the question of ordained ministry in a manner satisfactory to both sides in the sixteenth-century debates.

Both sides in the sixteenth century could broadly agree that 'every power which was in the college of the apostles is now in the Church'.[12] The difference of opinion was about the distribution of that power (with its connotation of 'dominion') in the Church. When the Lutherans said that order requires structure in the use of power, the reformers accepted that principle. But they said that the ordained ministry had, not a special or higher power, but a licence to 'use' a power which belongs to all Christians equally.[13] This *usus* is what is bestowed by popular assent (*plebis assensu*) and taken away by the same means.[14] Thus the baptismal base was being regarded as the source of ministerial authority in the Church in a way which not only stresses that the will of the people alone confers power, but also retains control of that power in the hands which have so entrusted it.

between bishop and priest: 'judging' and the 'consecrating and sacrificing' of the celebration of the Eucharist (*Acta CT* 7[ii].457).

12 *omnis ... potestas quae fuit in collegio apostolorum, est nunc in ecclesia* (*Acta CT* 9.25).

13 Cf. *Acta CT* 7[ii].461.

14 *Ibid.*

ii. MAKING MINISTERS

Despite their concerns over the pattern of existing ministry, the protestant reformers – apart from certain extreme factions – did not want to do away with a special ministry. Even the radicals, for the most part, had pastors. Menno Simons, founder of the Mennonites, a Roman Catholic priest who had come to think the Church wrong about transubstantiation and about infant baptism, had renounced the Roman Catholic Church in 1536 and married. He became a 'bishop' of a brotherhood arising from an offshoot of the Melchiorites.[15] The Schleitheim Confession of Faith defines the office of pastor in the Church as, 'to read, to admonish and teach, to warn, to discipline, to ban in the Church, to lead out in prayer for the advancement of all the brethren and sisters, to lift up the bread when it is to be broken, and in all things to see to the care of the body of Christ, in order that it may be built up and developed, and the mouth of the slanderer to be stopped'.[16]

Melanchthon was able to see ministerial office as the living nerve of the Church.[17] He acknowledged the dependence of order in the Church upon the existence of such a ministry and its recognition by some orderly means. The Augsburg Confession states that no-one shall preach publicly in the Church or administer the sacraments unless regularly called (14). Calvin puts it like this:

> No sound Christian makes all men equal in the administration of the Word and sacraments, not only because all things ought to be done decently and in order, but also because, by the special command of Christ, ministers are ordained for that purpose. Therefore ... no man who is not called may take the honour upon himself.[18]

If such a ministry was to be compatible with a doctrine of the 'equality of priesthood' of all believers, its constitution needed to be rethought. Some of the protestant reformers explored the possibility of reconsidering the nature and intention of ordination, and the ways in which 'legitimate calling' could be recognised.

An immediate prompter was the experience of the Bohemians. As a result of the Hussite upheavals of a century before, they were without a bishop who could ordain ministers for them, and it had become the

---

15   *Reformers in Profile*, ed. B. A. Gerrish (Philadelphia, 1967), pp. 198ff.
16   Ed. John C. Wengen, *Mennonite Quarterly Review*, 19 (1945), 243ff.
17   Cf. *CR* 12.490, Thesis 8.
18   *Antidote* to Trent VII, Canon 10, *CR* 35.496.

practice to send ordinands to Italy. There they were obliged to forswear Hus's teaching that the laity should receive both bread and wine in the Eucharist, and to do so with the intention of breaking their oath when they returned to Bohemia, so that they could minister to the congregations there in the way Hus had encouraged. In *Concerning the Ministry*,[19] Luther assures the Christians in Bohemia that they need not send young men to Italy to be ordained. Ordination is, he says, an action of the local Church, an entrusting of an office to an individual approved by the people.

Luther describes for the Bohemians the procedure they should adopt in making ministers. First they are to pray, individually and together, for the guidance of the Holy Spirit. This is a great undertaking, and its seriousness rather than its novelty ought to be the striking thing about it, for it is the practice of the New Testament communities. Then they should meet and elect one or more who are thought worthy and able. The leaders of the community are then to lay hands upon them, and commend them to the people, and in this way they become their ministers or pastors.[20] No indelible change takes place in those so appointed and it remains at the community's disposal to replace them with other ministers given pastoral charge in the same way. The elements in this process were immediately controversial at the points of the initiative taken by the local community and above all by its people as a whole; and the substitution of local 'leaders' for bishops; and in the challenge to the permanence of ordination.

There was a tendency in the Trent debates to look for constitutive elements in ordination, or 'key' moments, rather than to ask how the action of the Holy Spirit, the ordaining bishop and the whole community may be seen as working together. Thus, for example, we find an investigation of the role of the priests present, who lay their hands on the ordinand too. Can it then be 'only the bishop' (*solus episcopus*) who ordains? Perhaps the pressure may be taken off this point by saying that the order is conferred (*ordo traditur*) not by the laying on of hands but by the giving of the chalice?[21] On the contrary, says another contributor, the imposition of hands is not only 'apostolic' but 'necessary' in making a priest.[22] Perhaps it is the moment when the bishop says, 'Receive the

---

19   *WA* 12.169–95.
20   *WA* 12.193–4.
21   *Acta CT* 7[ii].450–1.
22   *Acta CT* 7[ii].457.

Holy Spirit' which counts.[23] These were not new considerations, but they were greatly sharpened by the reformers' challenge because it made it essential to be able to pinpoint that which is constitutive for ordination so as to show that it involves something more than mere appointment to a temporary office in the community.[24]

Because he believed that such appointment to an office in the community was not permanent, Luther created a stress in the traditional logic of ordination by implying that the Holy Spirit guided the community into a short-term not a settled choice. To say that the service of ordination is 'only a ceremony' was to say that it was not a sacrament, and that the minister therefore received no 'indelible character' as a result of ordination. Zwingli and his party were in agreement with Luther here. In his Articles of 1525, Zwingli dismisses the idea of a special character in ordination, and he says elsewhere that if a minister does not carry out his responsibilities, 'he is no longer a priest'.[25] These were principles specifically proposed as a way of resisting a conception of a power which was not only a personal possession, but was also one which could never be taken away, and was not answerable to the community. Yet both sides held that a *potestas* is given to Christians sacramentally. The Lutherans saw baptism as 'ordination to ministry'.[26] The Trent theologians could find no warrant for this in Scripture or tradition,[27] and it was their view

[23]   *Acta CT* 7[ii].448.

[24]   In the rite of ordination in the Book of Common Prayer of the Church of England (1662 revision) candidates are presented to the people and provision is made for the bishop to ask the people if they know of any 'impediment or notable crime' in the candidate. Each candidate is asked if he believes himself to be 'truly called' by the Holy Spirit. The bishop lays hands on the candidate with the declared intention of ordaining him to the priesthood; 'Receive the Holy Ghost for the office and work of a priest in the Church of God, now committed unto thee by the imposition of our hands.' The bishop does this as one acting within the universal Church ('the Church of God'). Cranmer's paper on the doctrine and discipline of the Church (1538) is quite clear that Scripture gives a divine institution for such orders (*Remains*, p. 484) and Becon emphasises that it is also necessary for the candidate for ordination to 'submit himself to the judgement of the congregation, either to be admitted or refused' (p. 319). Here there is a bringing together of human and divine authorising in ordination with an emphasis upon both the universal and the local church in which the minister is to serve.

[25]   Zwingli, *Werke* II.438, and Article 61 of the Articles of 1525. See, too, Stephens, *Theology*, p. 275 and Gogan, *Common Corps*, p. 155.

[26]   *Acta CT* 7[ii].461–2.

[27]   *Acta CT* 7[ii].462.

that a special *potestas* for ministry is given sacramentally at ordination.[28] There is, then, in fact no question for either side that the commission for ministry is sacramental, or that it is indelible. When Luther claimed that ordination is neither indelible nor a sacrament, he was referring to appointment to a 'special' ministry, and the real question concerns the relation of that special ministry to the ministry of all the faithful, rather than its indelibility or sacramental character, which is actually not in dispute.

iii. EPISCOPAL ORDINATION

The Trent Fathers found the same contentions in Calvin's writings as in Luther's that if bishops alone (*soli episcopi*) confer 'priesthood' (*sacerdotium*), they do it *illegitime*, for the true agent (*agens*) and conferring authority (*conferens*) is the people.[29] It is the people who have *auctoritas et potestas* from God to ordain.[30] In reaction it was insisted that the *ius ordinandi* lay with bishops alone. Since Titus was made a bishop without the people's consent, that consent cannot be necessary,[31] it is argued.[32]

Soli episcopi was used equivocally to mean both that 'bishops alone' have the necessary power and that bishops may act alone, that is, without the consent of the people being constitutive for ordination. The first notion is explored in the Trent debates on ordination, in an attempt to define the power which distinguishes a bishop from a priest. Both equally can consecrate the body and blood of Christ,[33] but the bishop alone is said to have powers of governance (*gubernatio*) in Christ's mystical Body, the Church.[34] This includes a power to ordain (*fideles...ad sacra ordinare*).[35] The power to ordain would seem to make the bishop a *sacerdos perfectus*. He is compared with a full-grown man, who is able to beget others like himself, while a priest is like a boy who does not possess the power to do so.[36] The second notion is inseparable from the first as long as the 'power'

---

28 *Acta CT* 4[ii].164.
29 *Acta CT* 7[ii].448.
30 *Acta CT* 7[ii].348.
31 *Acta CT* 9.33.
32 Cf. Melanchthon on the Titus question, *CR* 12.490, Thesis 12, and *CR* 8.430 on episcopal ordination.
33 *Acta CT* 9.33 and 42.
34 *Ibid.*
35 *Acta CT* 7[ii].460.
36 *Acta CT* 9.31.

involved is conceived of as the personal possession of the bishop, and his to entrust to those he ordains. This limited concept of a power which is dominion, and which is a personal possession, dogs the debate at every point, and makes it almost impossible for the combatants on either side to begin to see their way to a solution in which 'dominion' is in balance with 'service' and 'personal' with 'corporate' authorising.

Much necessarily depends in the debate on the question whether the authority to ordain entrusted to bishops comes from God. There was discussion at Trent as to whether it is derived from the Church (*ex ordinatione Ecclesiae*) or is of the nature of orders by divine institution (*ex natura ordinis et consecrationis per divinam institutionem*). The matter had been raised in earlier generations.[37] The Trent debates favoured the latter view.[38] That would make the jurisdiction which includes the power to ordain a proper and inalienable power of bishops, but not a priestly power unless entrusted to a priest by his superior.[39] Scripture seemed equally balanced here. On the one hand, it cannot be said that any superior powers of an episcopal sort were given by Christ when he 'made the apostles priests' at the Last Supper, saying, 'Do this …' etc.[40] On the other hand, Christ's own priesthood 'according to the order of Melchisedek' must be a *sacerdotium episcopate* (Psalm 109 and Hebrews 6 and 7). It can be nothing less, for Christ is Lord. That would imply that the prime and perfect sacerdotal order is that of bishops, and the remainder of the priests 'were instituted and created to assist the bishops',[41] and that would mean that bishops had their powers *ex ordinatione Ecclesiae*, but also *iure divino*.

The very framework of this discussion at Trent in the period between 1551 and 1562 was a result of a habitual disjunction in thinking. The Lutheran controversy had in some measure reinforced this, by encouraging a view of the institutional Church of the day as a human rather than a divine institution.[42] It was this which made sense of the contention that a rite of the Church might be a 'mere' ceremony[43] and the making of

37   Cf. Petrus de Palude, *In Sent.* IV d.24 q.6 and 3 (Venice, 1493), fo.130ʳ.
38   *Acta CT* 7ⁱⁱ.440.
39   *Acta CT* 7ⁱⁱ.468.
40   *Acta CT* 9.57.
41   *Acta CT* 9.72.
42   J. Massner, *Kirchliche Uberlieferung und Autoritat im Flaciuskreis* (Berlin/Hamburg, 1964), p. 20.
43   *Acta CT* 7ⁱⁱ.449 and cf. 348.

ministers by such a rite a matter of human not divine ordering. As we have seen, Luther thought that the guidance of the Holy Spirit could be sought and acted upon without the ensuing entrusting of ministerial responsibility being anything other than a human arrangement to meet the temporary needs of a local congregation, although Melanchthon is clear that authority to ordain is a direct gift of God to the Church.[44] In making a separation, even for purposes of discussion, between 'the ordination of the Church' and *ius divinum*, the Trent Fathers were postulating what is fundamentally the same notion. They were saying that the Church could act authoritatively without her authority being at the same time Christ's own authority. That this possibility could even be envisaged was itself a result of the habit of thinking of power in the Church as the personal possession of those to whom it was entrusted. An incomplete and imperfectly balanced theology of power and authority in the Church was, then, ironically enough, capable of resulting in a similar disjunction in the thinking of theologians on both sides in the sixteenth-century debates.

Luther departed from established practice in proposing ordinations without bishops. But that did not replace the unitary effect of ordaining episcopally, with a popular consent conceived of as 'universal' in the same way. What was missing here was a conception of the participation (directly or indirectly) not only of the local but also of the wider community of the Church in the making of ministers. It had been of the essence of the mediaeval doctrine of ordination that what Luther scathingly calls 'papal ordinations' had in fact been a means of holding discipline, teaching and a common sacramental life together throughout the Church in the West through the exercise of the episcopal ministry of oversight. Local popular assent to the choice of a minister (although at a pinch it may be said to represent the consensus of the whole body of the faithful) is conceived of by Luther as having reference to the needs of a particular community. The difference is pointed out in the Trent debates, where the possibility is mooted that 'the consensus of the whole Church' is not necessary in ordination, although the consent of those who have a direct local concern in the matter is a most important factor (*potissimum*).[45]

The traditional view had been that a priest was ordained as a minister in the Church of God. It was also understood that although he must have

---

44   *CR* 12.489, Thesis 5.
45   *Acta CT* 7[ii].441.

from the beginning a particular community to serve, he would remain an ordained minister if he moved elsewhere. Episcopal ordination secured that universality, because the bishops formed a brotherhood stretching backwards in time to the apostles and horizontally across the Christian world. The fourth-century *Canones Apostolorum* already insist that a bishop should be consecrated by at least three other bishops, in token that he was to be a minister with responsibilities directly to the universal Church.

It would not be fair to suggest that the Trent Fathers wanted to exclude altogether any role for the people. Seripando's preface to the canons on ordination says only that popular consent or the choice of a secular authority (*magistratus*) cannot be said to be 'required' in such a way that without it no ordination can be orderly.[46] Another of the theologians of Trent says that there is a 'proper place' (*locus proprius*) and an office of the people (*officium plebis*) in ordination. They are to bear witness to the holiness of life and good behaviour and worthiness of the candidate, and to give their consent, and receive him as their guardian and leader.[47] It remained the conservative view that within the structure of the Church's order something more was needed: a special ministry commissioned by the Holy Spirit, through the whole Church and not merely locally, and with responsibilities which reflected a lifetime's commitment to the service of the community.

---

[46]   *Ita requiri, ut sine ea irrita sit, Acta CT* 9.42.
[47]   *Ut consentiant ordinatum et eum recipiant in custodem et ducem, Acta CT* 7ii.453.

13. *Higher authority*

i. OVERSIGHT AND DISCIPLINE: OFFICE OR POWER?

Although Luther's recommendations to the Bohemians were offered as an emergency solution, he took the underlying theology to have more than interim force. The local focus prominent in Luther's attempts to solve the Bohemian problem, and in the 'gathered churches' of some branches of the reforming movement, rests on the best authority. The local church as a territorial entity under the leadership of one *presbyteros* or *episcopos* was the fundamental unit of Church organisation in the early Church. The territorial principle of 'one priest one church'[1] is insisted upon throughout the Middle Ages. No priest is to abandon the church 'to which he has been blessed and married'.[2] To give a church two rectors would be 'spiritual bigamy'.[3] No-one may preside in two bishoprics and no-one may receive in his diocese any priest who does not belong there.[4] But such strictures in the mediaeval period were always understood within the context of the wider Church, a community extending through time and throughout the world.

Difficulties about 'order' in its wider structural sense quickly became apparent in Lutheran and other reforming communities, as they began to discover that in escaping from the 'tyranny of clerical dominion' they were in danger of losing something of that order which had from very early times been inherent in the visible structure of the Church.

The new worshipping communities which gathered round the reformers soon found a practical need for a ministerial office which included a power of governing in a larger sphere than that of the local congregation and which could exercise discipline. Luther complains about the Anabaptists in a treatise against *Infiltrating and Clandestine Preaching*

---

1 Legatine Constitutions of 1237, Johnson, *Laws and Canons*, II.159. Some of the material which follows is used in a revised form in *Episcopal Ministry: The Report of the Archbishops' Group on the Episcopate* (London, 1990).

2 Johnson, *Laws and Canons*, I.413 (960).

3 Langton's Constitutions 1222, Johnson, *Laws and Canons*, II.107.

4 Johnson, *Laws and Canons*, II.8 and 14, and Lanfranc's Winchester Constitutions, Bodleian Library, Oxford, MS. Jun.121, fos. 2b–4a.

228 Problems of authority in the Reformation debates

written in 1532.[5] He protests not only about the content of their preaching – and that of other extremists who were getting a hearing in Lutheran communities – but also about the people, who are 'too untamed and forward' in their claim to a right to listen to any preacher they choose. He saw advantages in the exercise of an 'oversight' by appointed 'visitors', who would fulfil what he saw to be the original function of bishops in the Church by guaranteeing a proper order.[6] Zwingli, too, discovered, as a result of the invasions of the Anabaptist preachers, a need for a way of ensuring order and discipline by a higher authority.[7]

Luther's view of bishops remained ambivalent. He accepted the need for oversight and conceived of a 'true' *episcope*. But he thought it inconceivable that such bishops should exist in the Church as he knew it. 'If the bishops were true bishops and were concerned about the Church and the Gospel, they might be permitted, for the sake of love and unity, to ordain and confirm us and our preachers … However, they neither are nor wish to be true bishops. They are temporal lords and princes who are unwilling to preach or teach or baptise or administer communion or discharge any office or work in the Church.'[8] It was, then, at least for Luther, the failures of the episcopal system in the contemporary Church, not primarily any theological objection, which created the difficulty about bishops. Zwingli's concept of the minister as 'guardian' concedes the principle of oversight, too, in a limited sense.[9]

In the English Becon's *Catechism* there is an exploration of the ways in which ideas of 'service' may be balanced against the notion of 'power' as dominion which Luther thought to be wrongly exploited in practice in the contemporary Church. Becon places the emphasis on the bishop's role as 'spiritual pastor'. He is 'minister of Christ' because he is 'Christ's servant and ambassador'. He is 'dispensator of the mysteries of God' because he is God's steward, that is to say, communicator of 'the heavenly riches and most blessed treasures of God … to such as the Lord hath committed to his spiritual charge'. He is able to perform this service as

---

5   *WA* 30[iii].518–27.
6   *Instructions for the Visitors of Parish Pastors in Electoral Saxony, WA* 26.195–240.
7   Zwingli hoped much of government by council here (Stephens, *Zwingli*, pp. 270ff.).
8   Smalkald Articles III.10, Tappert, p. 314.
9   Stephens, *Zwingli*, p. 275 and Article 31 of Zwingli's *Defence* of 1525, and *Werke* II.438 and 440.

'an officer in the Church of Christ at the appointment of God' and Scripture calls him an 'overseer or superintendent'[10] because God has committed him to a 'sword'.[11] For Becon, then, the notion of pastoral 'service' is inseparable from the ministry of oversight. Numerous criticisms of the Middle Ages, directed towards prelates who flaunted their wealth before the poor and behaved without humility, were not about a mere matter of style, but a comment about an anomaly between the behaviour of such bishops and their proper position in the community they ought to 'serve'.[12]

As 'chief pastor', it seemed to Becon, the bishop is both the servant of the community and responsible for exercising discipline on its behalf, not as an act of dominion, but in the interests of an order which has recently been felicitously described as 'love in regulative operation'.[13] Because of the nature of the contemporary crisis, the concept of an ordered liberty of this sort was not easily brought into focus in the sixteenth-century debates. The definition of 'obedience' had to be got right if it was to be possible to understand as constitutively Christian a regulative authority in connection with which we might properly use the words 'obedience' and 'discipline', without these terms carrying the pejorative and inappropriate associations with which they had become encumbered. There can be no objection to a concept of obedience in Christian faith. Eck quotes Paul: *omnia subiecit sub pedibus eius*,[14] and none of his protestant opponents would have wished to deny that the Church is a community which consciously seeks to submit to Jesus Christ. The difference between them lay in the understanding of obedience of one Christian to another within the ministerial order of the Church.

It was usual in the fourteenth and fifteenth centuries to couple sacramental and jurisdictional authority in speaking of bishops.[15] At Trent, jurisdiction is defined in terms of 'governance'.[16] Late in the sixteenth century, Archbishop Whitgift of Canterbury argues that there is 'an equality of all the ministers of God's Word *quoad ministerium*', that is, in their ministry, but 'degrees and

10   Cf. Peter Lombard, *Sentences* IV Dist. 24, c.15 (145).
11   *Catechism*, pp. 317–19.
12   Cf. Johnson, *Laws and Canons*, II.86, Hubert Walter's Canons at Westminster, 1200.
13   A–R, 82.
14   Eck, *Loci*, p. 17.
15   Peter d'Ailly's *De Potestate Ecclesiastica* is in J. Gerson, *Opera Omnia*, II.925–60.
16   E.g. *Acta CT* 9.25.

superiority' among them 'touching order and government' (*quoad ordinem et politiam*).[17] This was no raw dominion but essentially a legal power, and thus subject to the constraints of the laws it served. That is another way of expressing the principle of limited office, a jurisdiction which serves a purpose in the community and cannot go beyond that.[18]

The idea of 'office for a purpose' is adumbrated in the Confutation of the Augsburg Confession. Certain powers (*potestates*), of defining, discerning, decreeing, are said to be necessary in that they assist in and lead to the achieving of an end: *ad praefatum finem expediunt aut conducent.*[19] There is a hint of the same idea in Coverdale.[20] We may speak, then, in a way not anachronistic for the sixteenth century, of jurisdiction as a 'power'; but strictly as a power needed for the effective fulfilment of an office.[21] This way of looking at it safeguards much of what concerned Luther. Jurisdiction is seen as both limited, and inseparable from responsibility to the people whom the office is to serve. There was sound precedent for saying that such jurisdiction is always (structurally speaking) exercised within the community. As Augustine puts it, 'I am a bishop for you and a Christian with you.'[22] Anything else, says one of the Lutheran disputations, is a usurpation because it is to 'sit in the Temple of God' *tamquam sit Deus*, 'as though one were God'.[23]

---

[17] Whitgift, *Cartwright*, pp. 535–6.
[18] Cf. *Acta CT* VI^{iii}.164. Eck, *Homilies*, Vol. IV, Hom. 13.3, Calvin, *Antidote* to Trent IX, Canon 9 (also Calvin's reflections on *officium* in his Commentary on Hebrews). Some uncertainty about the signification of 'office' here is evident even in the Trent debates. Johannes Gaglio remarks that the subdiaconate seems 'more an office than a power', for example, and thus separates 'power' and 'office' in a way which links 'power' with 'order' and emphasises by contrast the humbler and impermanent nature of an 'office' (*Acta CT* 9.25 and cf. *Acta CT* 7^{ii}.348). But it is suggested elsewhere in the debates that even office confers power, 'a certain superiority to those who are subject' (*superioritatem quandam ad subditos*).
[19] Art. 28, cf. *C. Cath.* 33, p. 199.
[20] *Remains*, p. 336.
[21] Cf. ARCIC II 16.
[22] *Vobis sum episcopus, vobiscum Christianus.* *Sermo* 340.1, *PL* 38.1483; cf. *Enarrationes in Psalmos* 126.3.
[23] *WA* 39^{ii}.67. Since ordained ministers are also members of the laity, they can have authority only 'within' and 'among' the Christian faithful. Cf. *Codex Iuris Canonici* (Vatican, 1983), Canon 207.1.

ii. HEADSHIP ON EARTH

For mediaeval thinkers the notion of monarchy carried a strong association which is perhaps best illustrated by the story of the Fisher King in the Arthurian cycle. The King is identified with his people, so that his sickness is theirs, his triumph theirs. When he is ill, the whole community decays. Even the crops fail. Eck states the principle in his *Loci Communes* as though it applied to Peter in the same way as to the Emperor: *Petrus gessit personam Ecclesiae, sicut imperator Germaniae.*[24] The Pope is the Church in his own person, just as the Emperor is Germany. Luther is, consciously or not, echoing this tradition when he says, 'The Pope cannot err without bringing great harm upon the whole Church.'[25] Zwingli makes use of the same idea with a different slant. He borrows from political theory of classical Rome to say that 'The Church's condition is that of her members, just as a state's fortunes are those of her citizens.'[26] Despite the shift of emphasis from head to members there is a clear persistence of the concept of a collective destiny of those who are held together in such an ordered unity, a destiny which reaches deeper than superficial fortunes in war or prosperity. The idea that Peter in some sense was the Church in his own person (*Petrus gessit personam Ecclesiae*) needs to be linked, too, with the assumption that the ordained ministry 'is' the Church (perhaps preserved in the expression used of someone ordained, 'he entered the Church').[27] All these variations on the theme – Eck's, Zwingli's and this last – reflect a mystique of corporate identity profoundly feudal and at the same time traceable in city-states and systems of collective monarchy in both the classical and the mediaeval world; but which is supremely a notion of 'the prince' on whose welfare all members of the body-politic depend.

This kind of assumption about the nature of monarchy is present pervasively, whether consciously or unconsciously, in the debates about papal monarchy of the first half of the sixteenth century, as much in civic-minded Italy as in prince-ruled Germany. Most of the reformers were

24 Eck, *Loci*, p. 56.
25 Cf. *WA* 50.96ff., *Ioannis de Monarchia Disputatio*, 1537, with Luther's *Postfatio*, col. 99.
26 Zwingli, *De Peccato Originali* (1526), *Quorum eadem est ecclesia, horum eadem est conditio, non aliter quam qui eiusdem sunt rei publicae, fortuna quoque eadem est, Werke* V.385.2.
27 Cf. Paris Article 18, *CR* 35.29.

solidly in favour of secure and princely government but felt very differently about papal 'monarchy'. There were practical and political reasons for the respect for secular lordship, in the climate of controversy which was dividing the Church and presenting new problems of ordering and authority. In Germany, and especially in England, the role of the prince as magistrate and protector in a local reformed Church was crucially important for its being regarded as 'legitimate'. But it has to be conceded that there were inconsistencies. Nevertheless, Luther at least was prepared to countenance a form of earthly leadership in the Church which could be entrusted to a secular ruler, but was not a primacy.

Yet in all this it was not in dispute that the Church was in need of a single Head who guarantees her unity; it was simply that the reformers believed that because the Church has such a Head in Christ, she needs no head upon earth. Reason, clear definition, the avoidance of misleading analogies and the historical record of the Papacy prove the point, says Luther (among others).

It thus proved very difficult in practice to keep a clear mind about the difference between arguments for and against primacy as a guarantee of unity and primacy as experienced in a late mediaeval Church ruled by Rome. One of Luther's earliest writings on the Papacy, *On the Papacy in Rome* (1520), was a reply to a treatise of the Leipzig Franciscan, Augustine Alveld. Alveld had contended that the Papacy has power over all Christendom *iure divino*. He argued that every earthly community needs a physical head under Christ its true Head, if it is not to fall apart. The head guarantees its unity. Since the whole of Christendom is a single community on earth, it must have a single head, who is the Pope. Luther attacks both the premisses and the conclusion. If a common head is needed to maintain unity, why not a common woman, a common city, house, country? The reasoning of Alveld's argument derives from experience of secular affairs, says Luther. Since the survival of human communities in the temporal sphere is dependent on human law, we cannot argue from this weaker law to the action of divine law in providing the Christian community with a head in the Papacy. It would perhaps be acceptable to have a *caput in Ecclesia* such as the Pope, a primate on earth, says Luther, if it were possible to find a good one. But it is not, and in any case, the Church has no need of a bishop to rule the whole world because it has its Head in Christ.[28]

---

28   Cf. *WA* 39ii.89.

Zwingli says that power and dignity are Christ's alone, and that anyone who claims these for himself is a usurper.[29] In replying to Article 23 of the Paris theologians, Calvin concentrates in his *Antidote* on the argument that unity requires a single Head, and that that Head is Christ alone.[30] He argues against papal primacy on Scriptural grounds. 'Scripture often reminds us that Christ is our universal Head; it never mentions the Pope.' Paul says that Christ governs (*gubernare*) the Church through his ministers (Ephesians 4.11). 'And yet the context demands that one should be named above all; ... he there sets out a mode of unity (*modus unitatis*) in which the faithful are united with Christ.' In commendation of unity he names one God, one faith, one baptism (Ephesians 4.5). If primacy was his intention, why does he not add one Pope as ministerial head (*caput ministeriale*)?[31] The Pope probably thinks the Holy Spirit is tied to Rome, comments Luther. 'But if he could produce reliable evidence to prove it, he would have done so.'[32]

The Paris theologians of 1544 were concerned to establish that there is a special place for Peter in the Church, and to make a secure link between Peter and the bishop of Rome as his successor.[33] This brought into the discussion much comment on the historical record of the Papacy in its second millennium. Luther was able to make a good deal of this history in attacking both the office and the institution of primacy, and we are thrown again and again into the maelstrom of Antichrist literature.

Hysteria had been waxing on and off since the thirteenth century on the subject of Antichrist. Luther's own dissatisfaction and dissent only gradually came to centre on the notion that the Papacy was the embodiment of Antichrist. When he published his Ninety-Five Theses he was moved by anger against abuse of the system of indulgences, but he located that abuse in malpractice by individuals who were exploiting the system for personal and financial ends. He spoke of the Pope with a respect not as yet obviously touched with irony, and with the implication that he believed that once the Pope understood what was going on in his name, he would put a stop to it. The response to his Theses and the ensuing events convinced him that nothing was to be achieved in that way; and in a short time he began to write tirades in which there is no restraint at all

29 Zwingli, *Defence*, Art. 17.
30 *CR* 35.37–8.
31 *Antidote* to Paris Article 23, *CR* 35.37.
32 *Against the Roman Papacy*, 1545, *WA* 54, Part I.
33 Paris Articles, 13, *CR* 35.35–6.

of language or sentiment, and of which the Pope is unequivocally the subject. Once launched, Luther let rip against the Papacy in streams of the crudest obscenities of language he allowed himself on any subject (and the obscenity extended to published Lutheran cartoons).

The points of substance which Luther wanted to make were a mixture of ideas current from the later Middle Ages among dissenters,[34] and views he himself had arrived at as a result of his first brushes with the Church's officialdom. To regard the Pope as Antichrist implied for Luther not only that he has no real authority among Christians, but also that he is intent on bringing as many souls as possible to Hell. 'The Pope positively seeks the souls of the whole human race', says Luther. 'That is, he wishes above all that every soul should be subject to his blasphemies and come by his efforts (*propter eum*) to Hell.'[35] The hysteria which Luther helped to whip to a new fervour gave heat to the posing of the question: what is the warrant for the view that it is God's intention that there should be a single human head of the Church on earth?[36]

Giles of Rome, who was influential in the framing of the text of the Bull *Unam Sanctam* of 1302 which marked a culminating point in the claims to plenitude of power by the mediaeval Papacy, had drawn a parallel between divine and papal authority. 'Just as' (*sicut*) God rules in the realm of all created things, so the supreme pontiff, God's vicar, does so in the government of the Church and the realm of the faithful. The implication is that God entrusts the government of the Church in this world directly and absolutely to the head of the Church on earth. This was enshrined in canon law in the principle that the Pope had a direct jurisdiction over the whole Church. As Giles of Rome puts it, 'the bearer of a plenitude of power can do directly and immediately himself what he normally accomplishes through a secondary cause'.

In fact this was a special case of the 'jurisdiction as ordinary' which the bishops all had in canon law, inherent in their office, and making them principal minister in their dioceses and requiring them to punish where necessary any who needed correction; it gave them authority over the clergy in their dioceses, such that they granted licences to those who were to serve there and received in return their canonical obedience. But in

---

34 See R. K. Emmerson, *Antichrist in the Middle Ages* (Manchester, 1981).
35 *WA* 39ii.55.
36 Luther, *Against the Thirty-Two Articles of the Theologians of Louvain*, 50 and 51; cf. Sykes (ed.), *Authority*, pp. 245–6.

relation to the Papacy it posed two kinds of problem in the late mediaeval and sixteenth-century context.

The first question is that of the Pope's appearing to be above the law. This 'animal without halter and bridle', this 'man above the law', ought to bridle himself and live by the laws, says Giles of Rome.[37] The twenty-third of the Paris Articles of 1544 insists on the universal immediate jurisdiction of the Pope. This was read by the protestant reformers in the sixteenth century as a claim to open-ended and unlimited dominion, interfering with the spheres of office of other bishops and in local churches by virtue of 'immediacy' and extending throughout the Church by virtue of 'universality'. This suspicion is inseparable from Luther's and Melanchthon's nightmare of an ecclesiastical authority which behaves like a temporal tyranny.[38] It filled them with such fear for the security of Christian freedom that it overrode for them the argument that a single head of the Church on earth may be a helpful practical focus of unity among Christians. Even if such a head were chosen directly by the people, Luther cannot see that he would guarantee their unity. 'Suppose', says Luther, putting the case at its most extreme,

> that the Pope would renounce the claim that he is the head of the Church by divine right …; suppose that it were necessary to have a head … in order that the unity of Christendom might be better preserved against the attacks of sects and heresies; and suppose that such a head would then be elected by men and it remained in their power and choice to change or depose this head.

He argues that only confusion could result. Those who chose their leader thus would not all continue to adhere to him. There would be more sects and divisions than ever.[39] (Luther took this to indicate not that the

---

[37] *De Ecclesiastica Potestate*, ed. R. Scholz (Weimar, 1929), 3.9, p. 190.

[38] Luther's defence of Thesis 22 of the Ninety-Five Theses had included the contention that at the time of Gregory the Great the Church of Rome had no jurisdiction over the Greek Churches. He cites the Fathers as further examples of Christians who had not been under the authority of the Pope. As early as 1520 Luther was tackling the Petrine texts, and other passages of Scripture, arguing that it cannot be right to say that Aaron, for example, is a figure of the Pope. He is the type of Christ, says Luther. The High Priest of the Old Testament was not allowed to own any part of Israel. He lived instead from the gifts of the people. But the Roman See strives to gain ownership of the whole world. The old High Priest was a subject ruled by kings. But the Pope wants to have his feet kissed, and he wants to be king over all kings. That was not the example Christ set.

[39] Smalkald Articles II.4, Tappert, p. 299.

principle of crude popular election was wrong, but that that of primacy on earth was mistaken.)

The second question is that of the relationship between the Pope as himself a bishop among bishops, and his powers 'over' all other bishops. This was the question to which Luther and others addressed themselves in putting the view that all bishops are equal.

The patristic inheritance did not speak with one voice here; neither is there agreement on Peter's place. Augustine's emphasis is upon the notion that Peter personifies the Church.[40] Thus it was to 'Peter as the Church' that the keys were given by Christ. Cyprian had preferred the view that all the apostles received the keys equally with Peter, and that Peter possessed a *primatus inter pares*.[41] But for Leo the Great, as for Augustine, *Petrus ipse* has a special place, and for Leo that means that Peter is a source of *firmitas*.[42]

As a first step away from the deadlock of late mediaeval debate on the relationship between universal primacy and local and collective episcopal oversight, the Lutherans revived the idea of equality among bishops. Luther sets out his case in 1520 in *On the Papacy in Rome*. Matthew 16.18–19 contains the reference to Peter as the rock and the gift of the keys. On the basis of this text, says Luther, the keys have been held to be Peter's alone. But Christ was speaking to all the apostles when he told them that what they bound and loosed on earth would be bound and loosed in Heaven. He argues from this and other passages that all the apostles were 'equal in power' to Peter. The same points are made in a debate of 1539 ('He commends them all equally to go into the world ... Peter could not preach everywhere'),[43] and in Part I of *Against the Roman Papacy* in 1545.

In the context of the late mediaeval and sixteenth-century debates about supremacy, primacy and conciliarity appeared alternatives. The conciliarists were opposed to those who favoured a theory of papal monarchy.[44] Nicholas of Cusa (1401–64), for example, changed his mind. He argued at first that the Pope is simply one member of the universal Church. That Church can be represented only by a General Council. So such a Council will bind the Pope by its decrees. Later, he

[40] Y. Congar, *L'ecclésiologie du haut moyen âge* (Paris, 1968), p. 139.
[41] *De Catholicae Ecclesiae Unitate*, 4.
[42] E.g. *PL* 154.48ff.
[43] *WA* 39ii.70.
[44] Nowell, *Catechism*, p. 115 and see p.v. on its status; McCready, 'Papalists', p. 269.

took the view that it was necessary to subordinate the Council to the Pope. This debate had its political as well as its ecclesiological roots, but here as elsewhere we find reflected the preoccupation with power in the Church conceived of as a domination over subordinates.

Luther argues that the Petrine texts are being misread by the Catholics not only with respect to the Pope's power to rule, but as an argument for primacy which he does not find in the texts.[45] Peter is not singled out, he says, as unique among the apostles. All that is given to him is given him on behalf of the community and not to his person alone. All the apostles are equal according to Paul in 1 Corinthians 3.4–8, says the Smalkald League in the treatise on the power and primacy of the Pope of 1537.[46] In his Smalkald Articles Luther had given a historical account of the situation in the early Church as he understood it. The churches 'did not choose to be under' the Bishop of Rome 'as under an overlord', he says. They 'chose to stand beside him as Christian brethren and companions, as the ancient councils and the time of Cyprian prove'. Luther pointed to Cyprian's calling Pope Cornelius 'brother', on more than one occasion. 'But now no-one dares to call the Pope "brother"', he says; everyone must address him as 'most gracious lord', as if he were a king or an emperor.[47] Luther's conclusion is that 'the Church cannot be better governed and maintained than by having all of us live under one Head, Christ, and by having all the bishops equal in office and diligently joined together in unity of doctrine, faith, sacraments, prayer, works of love, and so on'. Jerome says that the priests of Alexandria governed in that way, and the apostles did the same. The Pope 'will not permit such faith, but asserts that one must be obedient to him in order to be saved'.[48] The Smalkald League's treatise (which Luther did not sign because he was ill) expatiates with some bitterness on this: 'What the papists mean when they say that the Roman bishop is above all bishop by divine right' is that 'all bishops and pastors throughout the whole world should seek ordination and confirmation from him because he has the right to elect, ordain, confirm and depose all bishops'.[49]

---

45   *On the Papacy in Rome*, 1520; cf. Eck, *De Primatu Sedis Apostolicae et Petri*, pp. 55, 56. Cf. Strange, *The Catholic Faith*, pp. 68–73, on the Petrine texts.

46   *On the Power and Primacy of the Pope*, 4, Tappert, p. 321; 6, Tappert, p. 323.

47   Smalkald Articles, II.4, paras 1–2, Tappert, p. 298.

48   *Ibid.*,, paras 9–12, Tappert, p. 300.

49   Tappert, p. 320: 'Besides, he arrogates to himself the authority to make laws concerning worship, concerning changes in the sacraments, concerning doctrine.

The issues touched on here abut onto the area of 'power-struggle' within the ambit of the formal structural arrangements for preserving order in the Church with which we have been concerned in these chapters. But their real importance lies in their implications for decision-making in matters of faith, which we come to last.

He wishes his articles, his decrees, his laws to be regarded as articles of faith or commandments of God, binding on the consciences of men, because he holds that his power is by divine right, and is even to be preferred to the commandments of God [and that] it is necessary to salvation to believe all these things.'

PART V

The authority of common sense

14. *A decision-making body*

Underlying both the debates about practice and the doctrinal debates on matters of authority lay questions of another order about the authority on which the authoritativeness of any statement about authority is to be judged. These were of particularly acute concern in the sixteenth-century debates, as reformers pressed for reliance upon 'Scripture alone'. Inseparable from the question of the primacy of Scripture was a complex of difficulties at this level to which sixteenth-century scholars gave a great deal of attention as they struggled to define the way in which Christ is to be made in practice the ground of all truth in Christian believing, and to understand the manner in which that truth might be expressed in the words and experience of the community of his people first and supremely in Scripture, and also in the continuing life of the Church. Problems of authority at this level lie behind all that was said in our opening chapters about the status of the written and intellectual resources on which the sixteenth-century combatants drew in their debates. We have seen how there grew up a tendency to think in terms of a 'power-struggle' between the divine gift of Scripture and the rival authorities of human scholarship, human fancy, human reasoning, human opinion, human tradition, and above all a 'human' Church authority. Contemporary work on the text of the Bible in Greek and Hebrew challenged such simplifications at innumerable points, and a good many individuals found themselves at times exasperated (Erasmus), or unable to reconcile a scholarly with a partisan position (Eck). We have met cross-currents everywhere, the tug of one consideration against another, warring against the seeking of a consonance with Scripture and the forming of a common mind. In all these ways there arose blurring of distinctions between theological questions to do with the nature of Christian authority, matters of practical concern in the running of the visible community, and the implications of these questions of a higher order about the authoritativeness of any sort of theological pronouncement.

It was a special concern of the reformers of the sixteenth century that there must be no overriding of Scripture in any conciliar decree, or any other pronouncements of the Church. That would immediately invalidate it. Nor, says Article 21 of the Anglican Articles, should anything be added to

Scripture. Councils cannot make anything 'necessary to salvation' which is not shown in Scripture to be so. One of the stumbling-blocks of greatest importance in the failure of the Ratisbon meeting of 1541 was a disagreement over this point. The reformers said that the Fourth Lateran Council of 1215 had made pronouncements on penitential practice which went beyond Scripture in these ways. Melanchthon said that he was prepared to 'respect the holy Councils, as long as they do not conflict with the Word of God', 'but this rule must be kept; if an angel from Heaven were to teach anything other than the Gospel, he would be anathema'. Wollebius put the principle succinctly in a later generation. 'The authority of a Council is as great as its conformity with Scripture.'[1] This particular preoccupation of the Reformation debates – central though it is – takes us only part of the way. It does not contribute to the answering of the question how this conformity with Scripture is to be judged or agreed.

Of supreme importance in all this in the sixteenth century was the contemporary tendency to conflate 'human' and 'merely human' in speaking of authority in the Church, and to associate 'merely human' with the tyranny of a dominant clerical class. Paradoxically, this results at the same time in calls for the removal of all 'human' claims to authority in the Church and demands that any human authority should be shared by all, and not remain the prerogative of a privileged few. In attempting to determine what might be the legitimate concern of any such decision-making body of the faithful two further ideas were frequently not clearly separated in the sixteenth-century debates: that of 'authority to establish the truth', and that of the role played by various parts of the whole people of God in constituting a decision-making body in terms of faith. The first has to do with our question of the authority on which the authoritativeness of any statement about authority is to be judged – in short, it is a 'truth-question'; the second with what are in a sense 'political' aspects of the power-struggle of the late Middle Ages and the sixteenth century in the Church.

We must now look at some of the directions in which the debates about decision-making ran, and the challenges the reformers posed to existing assumptions about powers of decision-making in the Church invested in her officers.

The first printed collections of Councils (by Merlin, Paris, 1525; Peter Crabbe, Cologne, 1538, with a second edition in 1551; Laurentius Surius,

---

1   Beardslee, *Reformed Dogmatics*, p. 150.

Cologne, 1567) contained a great many inaccuracies.[2] Surius says that he has tried to correct errors. But the English reformers comment more than once that they know that they are working with faulty texts.[3] Bullinger gives a list of conciliar creeds at the beginning of the *Decades* (1557) in which there are mistakes in the dates of all six General Councils.[4] One result of this insecure scholarly base was that it was not easy for anyone in the sixteenth century to arrive at a balanced and informed picture of what constitutes a Council and what its function is. Surius, for example, saw his own exercise as a means of combating the novel heresies of the day. A Carthusian, he dedicated his book to Philip of Spain. The dedicatory letter contains the assertion that 'the doctrine of the catholic Church is always one and the same' (*perpetua una atque eadem, et semper sui similis permansit*). This must be so, because its author is not the feeble wit of man, but the Holy Spirit, unchanging truth (*incommutabilis veritas*) 'which is God himself'. He rests his case on the documents. He prefaces the texts of conciliar acts with a series of authorities: the letter of Photius to Michael, Prince of Bulgaria, on the seven ecumenical Councils; Isidore on the origin of General Councils and on the mode of holding them;[5] the Glossa Ordinaria on the 'Councils' of Acts 1, 6, 15, 21 – with Acts 15 held up as setting the pattern for future Councils (*plenaria conciliorum forma*); the *Canones apostolorum*; eight books of *Constitutiones apostolicarum* by Clement of Rome, and so on. Surius was not in a position to judge of the doubtful authenticity of some of these pieces. He simply used them to lay the foundation of what seemed to him a solid case for the consistency of teaching about doctrine to be found in the canons and decrees of Councils 'general, provincial and particular', as he puts it.

The notion that Councils are preservers of unity in matters of faith[6] (and therefore of the organic unity of the Body of Christ), and that *ipso facto* they are instruments for condemning heresies,[7] was a commonplace on which

---

2   See S. L. Greenslade, 'The English Reformers and the Councils of the Church', *Oecumenica*, 1 (1976), 96–7, on the texts the reformers used and their shortcomings.

3   *Ibid.*

4   See *Decades* I.12–35, and cf. *The Writings of John Bradford*, ed. A. Townsend (Parker Society, Cambridge, 1848), 2 vols., I.371 and *The Writings of John Hooper*, ed. S. Carr (Parker Society, Cambridge, 1843), 2 vols., II.533.

5   *Ordo de celebrando concilio.*

6   Philpot, *The Examinations and Writings of John Philpot*, ed. R. Eden (Parker Society, Cambridge, 1842), p. 397.

7   William Whitaker, *A Disputation on Holy Scripture*, ed. W. Fitzgerald (Parker

all sides could agree in the sixteenth century.[8] It was for that reason that so many looked to the calling of a General Council as a means of resolving the troubles in which the Church found herself.[9] But it was again a function of the incompleteness of conciliar theory, and of imperfect access to the sources, that idealism and enthusiasm turned so easily to disgust and disillusion in reforming minds. Calvin grieves in the Preface to the *Antidote* to Trent over what he sees as the failure of the Council of Trent to do what was hoped of it in this respect. 'When many corruptions were seen in the Church, when grave disputes on doctrine had arisen, a Council was long and ardently desired by many who hoped that by this means all evils would be ended.'

Certain polemically heightened issues tend to dominate the discussion. Article 21 of the Anglican Thirty-Nine Articles speaks only of General Councils, and has in mind chiefly those which all could agree were 'Ecumenical'. Its preoccupation is with their summoning ('General Councils may not be gathered together without the commandment and will of Princes'), with their potential for error ('they may err') and with their authority ('Things ordained by them as necessary to salvation have neither strength nor authority, unless it may be declared that they be taken out of holy Scripture').[10]

The power to summon Councils had by long tradition been associated with the question of what made them 'legitimate' and gave them authority at least as legislative bodies.[11] Early Councils set a precedent for valid calling by ecclesiastical officers alone, and also for valid calling by, or only by, secular rulers. The rule of holding Councils or synods regularly was tied in Carolingian times to local and territorial needs, as Western Europe settled into kingdoms. Hincmar of Rheims was acutely aware that the division of the Church into areas under different secular rulerships posed a question about its own unity. He insisted that the Church

---

Society, Cambridge, 1849), p. 449.

8   Cf. H. Chadwick, 'The Finality of the Christian Faith', *Lambeth Essays on Faith*, edited by the Archbishop of Canterbury for the Lambeth Conference of 1968 (London, 1969), 22–31.

9   *The Acts and Monuments of John Foxe*, ed. J. Pratt (London, 1877), 5.138–42, gives the text of 'A Protestation in the Name of the King, and the whole Council, and Clergy of England, why they refuse to come to the Pope's Council, at his call', in which a General Council's constitution is roughly defined.

10 The question of the force of conciliar and primatial decrees can be answered in part in terms of 'legislative' power (but cf. Calvin on Hebrews 7, *CR* 51.84ff.).

11 Cf. Melanchthon, *CR* 12.396, and *Reformatio Legum Ecclesiasticarum*, 14, ed. E. Cardwell, *Synodalia* (Oxford, 1842), I.6.

remained one holy people.[12] Nevertheless, the lives of the Hispano-Visigothic, Frankish and English Churches were independently regulated and royal power was intimately involved in their governance. It was widely found practical in the circumstances of this settling process to hold frequent Councils of bishops, even annually, as Boniface recommends in a letter to Cuthbert of Canterbury in 747.[13] We find similar exhortations to hold synods once a year in Lanfranc's Winchester Constitutions of 1077.[14] Milíc laments the failure to hold such meetings in his own time.[15]

This nascent pattern of local provincial government in the West in the early Middle Ages was not seen to be at odds with loyalty to the See of Rome. Boniface stresses in the same letter the unity of his provincial synod with the one Church, and its subjection (*subiectio*) to the Roman Church and to Peter and his Vicar. It was a revival of a system of conciliar government known to have been used in earlier Christian centuries, and it is of some significance that it coincides with the establishment of Roman primacy on a firm footing in the West.

In the reforming furore of the sixteenth century there was sometimes a denial of the right of bishops or Pope to summon Councils because that had become associated with the claim that any meeting so summoned would receive the automatic guidance of the Holy Spirit, and its decisions would accordingly carry direct divine authority as well as legislative authority. It was argued among the reformers that Councils called by a Pope could not be free to deliberate;[16] the bishops who come to it are all the Pope's men and must vote as he directs.[17] There were attempts to show that, apart from the earliest Councils, a secular sovereign had normally conferred validity upon the proceedings by his summoning of the Council and by his ratification of its decrees.[18] In the 'letter of Photius' which Surius includes in

12 *De Coercendo et Exstirpendo* I, Congar, *Ecclésiologie*, p. 143.
13 Congar draws a parallel with the early years of the Church in the United States of America when seven provincial Councils were held between 1829 and 1849 as the young Church there 'found itself' as an ecclesial body (*Ecclésiologie*, p. 132).
14 Johnson, *Laws and Canons*, II.9.
15 *F. Mencik, Milíc a dva jeho spisy z.r. 1367, Prophecia et revelatio de Antichristo*, p. 320.
16 Foxe, *Syllogisticon*, p. 138, and see Greenslade, 'English Reformers', pp. 101, 104; Bullinger, *Decades* IV.45; Rogers, *Exposition*, p. 204; Jewel, *Apology*, II.108 and I.410; Tyndale, *Works*, I.272, in Parker Society editions, also the opening of Luther's *Against the Roman Papacy*.
17 Jewel, *Apology*, I.205.
18 Rogers, *Exposition*, p. 205.

his *Concilia* much is made of who was president of the Council in each case and whether the Emperor was *praesens et favens*.

The membership of Councils was also widely discussed in the search for what validates or confirms their decisions. Three points commonly arose here: whether it is important that the council should consist of 'good men';[19] whether a larger number carries more weight than a smaller number; whether a Council must be 'representative' of the whole Church. The last two points are interrelated. Latimer says that larger numbers are not necessarily better; it is not a matter of a majority decision.[20] There was some awareness here of a patristic sense that a Council should have the widest possible base (a theme of the 'Photius' text with its painstaking inclusion of the numbers for those present at each of the ecumenical Councils), but apparently there was no strong feeling in favour of the universality for which Cyprian and Celestine I had pressed.[21] 'Representativeness' is a much more complex matter in sixteenth-century eyes. Ignatius had argued at the turn of the first century that the whole Church entrusted to a bishop is present in his person.[22] This sense seems less strong in the sixteenth-century debates.

The formal structures of decision-making in the mediaeval Church were predominantly of the 'descending' sort, and maintenance of the truth, like the correction of error, was regarded as a duty almost entirely of higher authority in the Church.[23] The petition of the English Lower House of Convocation to the bishops in 1554 took this view in attempting to restore 'all bishops and other ecclesiastical ordinaries ... to their pristine jurisdiction' and to endorse their powers 'against heretics and false preachers'.[24] Such thinking shows that if the concept of the guardianship of the Church's verbal expression of the faith has from the first been associated with the ministry of 'oversight', it has been seen not

19 *Remains*, I.299. But Cranmer says error is still possible, and see Foxe, *Syllogisticon*, p. 139.
20 *Remains*, I.288; cf. Greenslade, 'English Reformers', p. 101.
21 Henry Chadwick, 'The Status of Ecumenical Councils in Anglican Thought', *Orientalia Christiana Analecta*, 195 (1973), 393, cites Cyprian, Ep. 55.6, a letter written to Rome to ask whether their consensus can be added to that of the African bishops. Pope Celestine is cited (p. 394), Ep. 18.1, *PL* 50.506A, to the Council of Ephesus, 431.
22 *Ibid.*, p. 393, citing Ignatius, Ad Eph. 1; Ad Magn. 2; Ad Trall. 1.
23 Cf. *WA* 39ii.147.
24 Cardwell, *Synodalia*, II.434.

only as a personal but also as a collective responsibility. This has normally been exercised in the formal framework of a Council[25] but which is in principle also collegial,[26] that is, a perpetual responsibility of the bishops together, even when they are not assembled in council.

In the context of the late mediaeval and sixteenth-century debates this question of decisive decision-making by those with oversight in the community, and especially by the Pope, presented itself in familiar forms, in the context of the discussion of 'power'. Peter Lombard suggests that although every bishop and priest has the power of the keys to bind and loose in absolution, not all have the *altera clavis*, the 'other' key, of discerning truth from falsehood in matters of faith (*scientia discernendi*).[27] Luther refers to this second key in his treatise on *The Keys*, published in 1530. Papal claims to plenitude of power, he says, include assertions of rights to issue commands, to prohibit in Heaven and on earth, to enthrone and dethrone kings and emperors, to command even the angels, to empty

25 The vocabulary of conciliarity is very ancient. From the earliest times Christians met to consult together when there were differences, or when decisions needed to be made. Conciliarity can never be separated from collegiality. All 'Councils' are episodes in a continuing collegial life. They are meetings in person of those who live in perpetual brotherly fellowship. The principal differences between the terms 'conciliarity' and 'collegiality' as they are used in what follows is this: the first refers to the exercise of consultation in the Church on particular occasions and the second to a continuous common reflection and action, as of those who share their lives in Christ, and it is on this understanding that the terms are taken here.

26 Cyprian suggests that episcopal collegiality involves a special form of pastoral responsibility which we may describe as a *communis cura*, a shared or joint pastoral care. The notion is found in Bede (Hom. II.15, *PL* 94.218–19 and cf. Hom. II.16, *PL* 94.222, cf. Congar, *Ecclésiologie*, p. 141). The term 'collegiality' is used in contemporary parlance in a variety of senses. It is taken in the documents of the Second Vatican Council to describe the relationship instituted by Christ among his apostles (cf. Luke 6.13; Vatican II, *De Ecclesia* III.18). This relationship has long been seen as visibly continued among the bishops of the Church. Hincmar of Rheims (c. 806–82), for example, uses it for the bishops of a province (*PL* 126.30D, *MGH Epp.* VIII.149.19, to Nicholas I (864)). The Bohemian reformer Milíc speaks of 'brother bishops' (*F. Mencik, Milíc*, pp. 319, 320). As a permanent 'college' in brotherhood, the bishops are seen as constituting a *coetus stabilis*. This is a particular use of the term for an enduring bond among equals which is the classical sense of *collegium*. In mediaeval usage, *collegium* can refer to the bond of all the faithful (*collegium ecclesiae*; *collegium fidelium qui sunt templum dei*), and episcopal collegiality belongs within the context of this universal bond of collegiality in the community.

27 Sent. IV, Dist. 19.1 (105).i.

purgatory. These are the keys of binding and loosing. The second key, the key of knowledge (*clavis scientiae*), is the Pope's assertion of 'power over all law, canon and secular, and all doctrine, divine and human', all questions of faith.[28] The emphasis in other words was upon two notions not always clearly separated in the sixteenth-century debates: that of a personal (as opposed to corporate) authority of oversight and that of a direct 'bindingness' (*firmitas*) inherent in that authority, and linked to the idea of Peter as the Rock.[29]

i. INERRANCY

A principal argument advanced by the Roman Catholic side in support of the view that a primate is necessary, was that only in this way could pure doctrine be preserved. The case is put in one of the Lutheran disputations: the power which acts to preserve pure doctrine must be retained in the Church. The power of the Pope was instituted for this purpose. Therefore it must be retained, and experience shows that this *monarchia* has been useful to the Church. Luther replies robustly. 'Monarchy is no use for pure doctrine. It is a destroyer of doctrine.'[30] Another argument cited Cyprian's teaching that the only reason there are heretics in the Church is that not everyone obeys one supreme *sacerdos*. But Cyprian was not speaking of the Roman Pontiff, is the reply, but of individual bishops; for it is right that there should be a leading *sacerdos* in individual churches, so that there may be no schisms.[31] These and other debating points reflect the opposing views we met in the general context of ministry: that primacy is necessary and constitutive for the unity of the Church and a guarantee of its continuance in faithfulness to Christ; and the belief that the Church needs no head but Christ. But they also reflect the prejudices implicit in the two positions. On the reformers' side there is the objection to papal 'monarchy'; on the side of their opponents the belief that without firm leadership there will be confusion and division.[32] In the circumstances of the time, there was justice in both misgivings.[33]

---

28 *WA* 39ii.465–507, *Works*, 40.357.
29 Cf. Congar, *Ecclésiologie*, p. 138 on Leo the Great's view here, and p. 147, on that of Odo of Cluny, *PL* 133.711–13.
30 *WA* 39ii.83.
31 *WA* 39ii.89.
32 Paris Articles, 20.
33 On the origins of the concept of papal infallibility, see B. Tierney, *Origins of Papal Infallibility, 1150–1350* (Leiden, 1872). On the principle that infallibility 'is not

In the last mediaeval centuries we begin to meet the idea that the Church is a structure like a legal corporation, a moral body with authority residing in all its parts taken together. But there are substantial ecclesiological differences on this point in late mediaeval minds. Jean Gerson regarded Councils as assemblies of the universal episcopate, but not as representing the whole body.[34] The Faculty of Theology at Paris had in mind a Council of bishops in framing an article which stated that such a Council is 'a full and adequate representation of the Church'.[35] When Luther argued that the Church is not bound to bishops but to the Gospel, he was contending that a Council of bishops carried no automatic authority derived from such episcopal 'representativeness'.[36] Calvin preferred to substitute for the notion of episcopal representation the rule of Christ-centredness as making a Council authoritative. In his *Antidote* to the article of the Paris theologians in 1544, he says that we should look not to episcopal membership, but to Christ's presence with those who are gathered in his name.

In the thirteenth century, Innocent IV's master at Bologna, the canonist Huguccio, envisaged that *in extremis* the corporation would possess the

the private possession of the Pope; it is rather ... a gift which belongs within the Church'; 'Rome seems to make judgements which are about as right and as wrong as anyone else's', see Strange, *The Catholic Faith*, p. 75.

[34] Jean Gerson, *De Auctoritate Concilii*, ed. Z. Rueger, *Revue d'histoire ecclésiastique*, 53 (1978), p. 787. Cf. Conrad of Gelnhausen, *De Congregando Concilio* III, ed. E. Martène and U. Durand, II.1217–18. The term 'Council' has traditionally been reserved for meetings of unusual importance and seriousness, involving the whole Church, or a major area of the Church, and convened to discuss matters of high moment. The Greek root which gives us 'synod' has sometimes been regarded as interchangeable with the Latin root which gives us *concilium*, but in recent usage in some (for example Anglican) quarters it has come to refer to regular meetings of a constitutional body of three 'houses' of bishops, clergy and laity. Such a synod differs from a Council in having in it by constitution direct representatives of the full *collegium* of the Church, whereas, historically, Councils have varied in this respect, sometimes consisting of bishops only, sometimes of bishops and clergy, or bishops, clergy and laity. It also differs from a Council in being not a special or emergency but a routine gathering (cf. *Codex Iuris Canonici* (Vatican, 1983), Canon 440). It can thus be seen as in a sense a 'constitutional' body rather than an occasional one.

[35] Paris Articles, 22, *CR* 35.34–5.

[36] Two ways of understanding 'representatively' are attacked. Grammatically, 'representatively' signifies 'to show something present and true' (*rem praesentum et veram ostendere*), and so the bishops acting representatively are the true Church. Secondly, it is argued that the bishops are the true Church because they sit in the apostles' place, *WA* 39i.192–3.

authority of its leadership.[37] In the same period clericalism was already entrenched in the Western Church, with distinction of dress, education, and the practice of celibacy making the clergy a visibly separate estate. These conceptions, as we have seen, encouraged the view that the *Ecclesia* can be identified with the ordained ministry. At issue here is whether a Council of the Church's leaders, or the Pope alone as head of the Church on earth, can in some sense constitute the Church, and act and speak in a manner which is binding on the whole community. We still find in the Paris Articles of 1544 the assertion that it is one of the *principia fidei* that the Church cannot be separated from the hierarchy (18).[38] Their argument is not only that a ministry with responsibility for order is constitutive for the Church (a notion with which a number of reformers would have had little difficulty), but that it is itself the Church. The understanding here was that membership of the community by baptism was necessary for salvation, but only membership by ordination enfranchises, by conferring a role in the decision-making process. Writing on the Thirty-Nine Articles of the Church of England in the 1580s, Thomas Rogers speaks of the notion of an 'ordinary power annexed to the state and calling of popes, bishops and clergymen',[39] which guarantees right interpretation and right teaching. Eck sustains a tradition that while lay members may be present at Councils as 'witnesses, as defenders, as advisers, to make suggestions and carry out decisions', they may not join in the decision-making by voting.[40] It could be deemed unnecessary for them to do so.

Eck, putting the conservative view in the sixteenth century, says that when the leaders and *potiores*, the more powerful persons of a province, decide something (*aliquid statuunt*), the whole province is said to have decided it, because they represent those subject to them (*subditos suos*).[41] This is a kind of representing which acts on behalf of, and which implies that in some sense the bishops 'are' the Church, carrying their subjects with them as a king carries his people in committing his country to war or peace. Luther contends that it is empty to talk of such 'representing' in the Christian community. A representation is, he says, like a picture. We do not say that a picture of a man is a real man. Indeed, a picture may

---

37 Cf. Gogan, *Common Corps*, p. 29.
38 *CR* 35.29.
39 Rogers, *Exposition*, p. 194.
40 Eck, *Loci, De Conciliis*, Propositio secunda, pp. 40–2.
41 Eck, *Loci*, p. 32.

be misleading,[42] as when the Devil represents himself as an angel of light. His point is that representing does not have an effect; it cannot enact a decision. And far from constituting the reality of that which they represent, these 'representatives' are mere shadows.

In Luther's view, bishops, even when meeting in council, are just private citizens of the City of God. 'Bishops met in council can err, just like other men', says one of the Theses of a debate of (?) October 1536. Their meeting together (*congregatio eorum*) has no intrinsic *autoritas*.[43] Even if bishops have, by chance, the promise of the Holy Spirit as individuals, because they happen to be holy, they do not have it by virtue of their office, individually or collectively.[44] At issue in all this was first the assumption that, as Nowell puts it in his *Catechism* of 1570,[45] Councils serve the need for a means of settling matters of faith, taking 'away controversies that rise among men' and 'stablishing ... the outward governance of the Church'. Eck puts it even more strongly. 'Take away the authority of councils and everything in the Church will be ambiguous, doubtful, hanging fire, uncertain'.[46] Second was the question whether a Council's decrees could have any force at all if it was not properly summoned, or its work not properly ratified, or its membership in some way lacking. The question whether a properly convened Council necessarily has the guidance of the Holy Spirit was the subject of much debate at Wittenberg and elsewhere.[47] Most urgent of all, however, seemed the principle that Christ is present where two or three are gathered in his name. Did it follow that Christ must be the president of any true Council?[48]

It seemed evident to those who framed the Thirty-Nine Articles that sometimes Councils have erred, even that their definitions can contradict one another. Councils cannot make a rule of faith, says Jewel.[49] It was argued that no-one's faith could be 'bound' by a Council, unless what it

---

42 Compare *Ego ecclesiam virtualiter non scio nisi in Christo, repraesentative non nisi in Concilio, WA* 1.656, and B. Löhse, 'Luther und die Autorität-Roms in Jahre 1518', in *Christian Authority: Essays Presented to Henry Chadwick*, ed. G. R. Evans (Oxford, 1988), p. 152.
43 *Disputatio, De Potestate Concilii*, Theses 12, 13, *WA* 39ⁱ.181ff. and 184.
44 *Ibid.*, p. 188, Argument against Thesis 5; *ibid.*, pp. 189–90, 195, 195–6, 196.
45 P. 115.
46 Eck, *Loci*, p. 38.
47 *WA* 39ⁱ⁻ⁱⁱ.
48 Cf. e.g. Jewel, *Apology*, II.995.
49 *Ibid.*, II.996.

said could be confirmed out of Scripture.[50] The point was emphasised because a lengthy debate among continental reformers had made it a prominent matter of concern. To take a sample from Wittenberg, 'Those who meet together in Christ's name cannot err', says one disputation, 'But a council and bishops meet together in the name of Christ. Therefore council and bishops cannot err.' The first premiss is proved from Matthew 18.20. Where two or three gather in his name, Christ is in the midst of them. The second is proved from a definition. To meet together in Christ's name is nothing else than to meet and discuss the business of the Church with a desire to find out the truth. The bishops certainly do that, and so they can be said to meet in the name of Christ.[51] In response, it is argued that the second premiss is misleading. To say, 'We meet in Christ's name' is not necessarily to do so. If they really meet in Christ's name what they say will be in accordance with his Word. At the Council of Constance the bishops acted in their own name, not Christ's. Even if the Council is composed of holy men, many holy men, even angels, they are not to be believed because of who they are, but because they speak according to the Word of God. (Both Christ and Paul warn against the respecting of persons.) It is not the meeting of particular persons but conformity with Scripture which is the guarantee against error. 'Even the holy can make mistakes.' And there is no guarantee in majorities. If I see one man holding the right view I ought to embrace what he says and abandon the many who are wrong.

Again: if the argument is put that Councils sometimes find themselves preserved from error because there is one man present who is holy, it must rest on the belief that human merit justifies, for certainly if someone saves many others in a Council from error by his merit, it would be a small matter for him to be the author of his own salvation. (It was smartly pointed out in the debate that 'saving' is not the same as 'justifying'.[52])

If we cannot show that it is the persons of the bishops who guarantee against error, perhaps we can show by the argument that the bishops 'constitute' the Church that it is impossible for them to err. 'The Church does not err. The bishops are the Church. Therefore the bishops do not

---

[50] See Chadwick, 'Ecumenical councils', p. 401 and Tyndale, *Works*, III.99; Becon, *Catechism*, pp. 391–2; Cranmer, *Miscellaneous Writings*, II.36; Rogers, *Exposition*, p. 210, in Parker Society volumes.
[51] WA 39i.189–90.
[52] WA 39i.195.

err.'[53] The first premiss rests on 1 Timothy 3.15. The second is supported
by a further argument. The successors of Peter are the Church. The
bishops are the successors of Peter. Therefore the bishops are the Church
(Matthew 16.18, with patristic supporting material). But, says the
argument in reply, the rock is faith. The text applies to the elect, who stand
upon the foundation of Christ. The bishops do not stand upon him as their
foundation, and so 1 Timothy 3.15 does not apply to them, and we may argue
that it is 'faith', not *regimen* or power to rule, which makes Christians.

On the other side, various proofs were advanced to support the view
that the Church cannot err at all, and *a fortiori* not in council. It was
axiomatic for the theologians of Louvain in 1544 that 'the Church cannot
err in matters of faith'.[54] Eck says that the Church is the Bride of Christ
and has the *magisterium* of the Holy Spirit always guiding her.[55] The
Paris theologians of 1544 make the same point. The Holy Spirit cannot
err and so, *per consequens*, neither can the Church.[56] There is also the
argument from history which we met in the debate over the Vulgate. It is quite
inconceivable, says Eck, that the Church could have been in error for a
thousand years 'as the Lutherans rave'.[57] If the Church was not protected by
an 'invincible shield' from error, the Paris theologians say, 'we should already
have been overcome a hundred times by the Lutherans who press us with
strong arguments which have the appearance of truth on their side'.

What was at issue in all this was the nature of the ultimate guarantee that
the Church would never lose the faith which had been entrusted to it. At
two points the theology of the sixteenth century was relatively undeveloped:
in the understanding of the role of the voice of the whole people of God,
the *consensus fidelium*; and in the area of 'reception'. Here help might
have been found on a number of knotty and unresolved points concerning
the validity and authority and universality of Councils, their capacity for
error and their dependence upon Scripture; it is only when the work of
Councils is set in its full context within the order of the Church and the
continuing process of reception that the tensions begin to relax and the
question of 'finality' becomes manageable.

53 Argument 13, against Thesis 12 in the same disputation.
54 Article 21.
55 Eck, *Loci*, p. 20.
56 *CR* 35.30.
57 Eck, *Loci*, p. 20.

As a rule in the Middle Ages the laity had been thought of as passive recipients of a ministry done 'to' them or on their behalf by those who were ordained. This was entirely in harmony with mediaeval thinking about God's intentions in the political and social spheres. Labourers in the fields were seen as created for a humbler place in this world than their secular overlords.[58] Thus the laity could be thought of as simple souls, children in the faith, of whom God required a less sophisticated understanding, and to whom he had committed humbler spiritual gifts.

A number of factors made this seem a reasonable position for several centuries after the end of the Roman Empire, with its major changes in social and educational patterns. In Augustine's day educated pagans and lay Christians included some of the leading intellectuals of the Empire. But gradually education was confined to monks and the clergy, and until perhaps the twelfth century lay people had little opportunity of studying Scripture or learning theology. Pressure seems to have come first from the articulate middle-class laity which began to make its appearance in the twelfth century.[59] They and their successors in the later Middle Ages – notably the Lollards in England and the Hussites in Bohemia – coupled the demand for access to the Bible in their own language, as Latin declined as a vernacular in the West but persisted in liturgy and in academic and theological use, with their rampant anticlericalism.

Among the sixteenth-century radicals it was often the case that members, and even leaders, were of some simplicity theologically, believing only that they must follow Jesus and do as he commanded, even if it led them to suffering and death. Few could answer their accusers with a coherent theology of any sophistication.

Eck scathingly pointed to the Lutherans' attempts to meet the need to provide something at the level of understanding of the general populace. 'They seek to dispute not among the learned and lettered and those who know something about theology (*in theologia exercitatis*), but before the ignorant, common laity, whose capacity does not extend to the judgement of this sort of mystery of faith.'[60]

---

[58]   Both the Princess in the folk tale of the princess and the pea and Perdita in Shakespeare's *The Winter's Tale* exemplify the belief that some are innately of a higher and finer nature than others.

[59]   Brian Stock, *The Implications of Literacy* (Princeton, 1983), explores twelfth-century developments.

[60]   Eck, *Loci*, p. 281.

It was already apparent that there were deep flaws in this attempt to classify Christians. On the one hand, argues Hervetus in the Trent debates, it can be held that Scripture ought to be kept from the people because it needs learned study if it is to be understood. On the other hand, is that not to say that we must not cast pearls before swine; and that implies that Christ died for people who are mere beasts.[61] Whitgift reflected in some uncertainty on the mediaeval tradition which envisaged the laity as a humbler and lowlier class of Christian, of whom less was required by God and who could not be expected to make a useful practical contribution to the Church's authorising. 'The inequality of ... persons, and great difference betwixt them, both in godliness, zeal, learning, experience and age ... ought to be well considered.'[62] The hierarchical habit of thought died hard, and a concern for social order made reformers who asserted the equality of all Christians in their common priesthood as believers stop short of egalitarianism or democracy or radical social reconstruction. It proved in practice no easy matter to make a clean separation between temporal and spiritual here, any more than in the higher spheres of government. Issues of power and authority conceived of as 'dominion over' were hard to distinguish from power to determine truth.

There was the further difficulty that the strains imposed on clear thinking by pervasive anticlericalism tended to obscure the fact that the clergy are also members of the *laos*, and to present as alternatives a corporate decision-making and a decision-making by those with special responsibilities of leadership. In contending that no special power is bestowed in the making of ministers, and no duty of obedience to the decision of higher authority consequent upon it, Luther also argues that the people of God in their local congregation have the right and authority to judge all teaching. His own community, he says, does not need a Council, 'for by God's grace our Churches have now been so enlightened and supplied with the pure Word and the right use of sacraments that we do not ask for a council for our own sake'.[63] Calvin says that Paul gives the method of making community decisions on matters of faith in 1 Corinthians 14.29. Everyone may take part in judging the truth of what is said to them. If there is disagreement between churches, Calvin says it should be settled by rational discourse, and agreement reached by

61 *Acta CT* 12.535.
62 Whitgift, *Cartwright*, pp. 29ff.
63 Tappert, p. 290.

discussion. The *pastores* of the community involved can then 'come together' (*coeant*) in carrying out what is decided, in an informal and, by implication, egalitarian Council of equals. Both were pressing for an extreme version of a doctrine to which Thomas More could subscribe as readily as he.[64] But in so doing, Luther in fact sets the laity as the Church of God (*Ecclesia seu laicos*) over against the *sacerdotes*,[65] and in his own way he is making the very distinction he is challenging.

The preoccupation with the notion that authority in matters of faith rests with a hated ecclesiastical hierarchy encouraged a concentration in the debates of the reformers upon a 'power-struggle' model of decision-making in the Church. The bulk of intellectual effort on both sides went into attacking and defending Popes, bishops and Councils; and into the attempt to prove that they had or had not erred in their pronouncements. We hear relatively little of the *consensus fidelium*, and what is said is limited by the same pattern of assumptions: that we are dealing with 'power to decide', and with pronouncements which, once made, are 'binding' and irrevocable.

This is where more thought was badly needed on the scope and nature of reception. There was some notion that it might be a constitutive factor in the 'making' of a 'decision' in a matter of faith, and some understanding that that would interfere with the idea that conciliar decrees were necessarily 'final' at the time they were issued. The Anglican Calfhill, in 1565, touched on the principle of retrospective ratification through subsequent assent by the faithful. But when he asks 'what moved the faithful to refuse the second of Ephesus and willingly embrace the Council of Chalcedon?', he answers in terms of their examining their decrees by Scripture.[66] He does not explore the way in which the judgement of the community makes this 'examination'.

Aristotle saw consent as a principle of verification.[67] For Euclid and Boethius alike, the *communis animi conceptio* is a truth attested by

---

64   'All the crysten people whom we call the chyrche', More, *Dialogue*, lxxviii[r] AB, ed. W. E. Campbell (London, 1927), p. 142.

65   *WA* 39[i].30.

66   James Calfhill, *An Answer to John Martiall's Treatise of the Cross*, ed. R. Gibbings (Parker Society, Cambridge, 1846), pp. 10ff., 155ff.

67   On the history of consent, see K. Oehler, 'Der Consensus Omnium', *Antike und Abendland*, 10 (1961), 103–29. The following paragraphs are used, with some modification, in my *Authority in the Church: a challenge for Anglicans* (Norwich, 1990), pp. 91–3.

universal acceptance,[68] as being apparent to all reasonable minds. Hooker comes close to a significant development of this idea in his notion that reason ought to be used by the Christian as an instrument on which to test his growing understanding of the truth.[69] Henry Hammond, among other seventeenth-century authors, explored this idea of 'right reason' as 'appointed ... judge of controversies'.[70] This operation of reason does not alter anything; it is not a creating of truth or a legitimising of a decision. It is a process of recognition of a truth which already exists,[71] and which compels by simply being right.

Christian consensus is corporate in a sense beyond what Cicero envisaged in remarking that what all peoples accept is natural law.[72] Isidore speaks of *consentire in unum*.[73] Hincmar of Rheims in the ninth century sees it as a sign of the unity of the Church that there should be consent and *consonantia*.[74] Thomas More speaks of the *consentientis authoritas*, the authority of consent, and Erasmus thinks it wrong to dissent from the *sententia consensuque Ecclesiae*.[75] We can seen this authority as that of God in the Church, and at the same time as a function of communication among the Christians, a living interplay, in which there is perpetual mutual correction and room for growth in understanding. The 'effect' of consensus is, then, the growth of individual and corporate understanding, rather than the creation of truth. It operates both intellectually in 'judgement', and spiritually, in an embracing of the truth discovered. (Even though everyone cannot be expected to judge theological technicalities, all can judge whether a doctrine, as explained in non-technical terms, corresponds with their own faith.)

The nature of Christian authority is thus such that it 'involves' rather than 'imposing on' minds and hearts. The notion of reception as an active welcoming rather than a passive acquiescence is adumbrated in the Middle Ages. The conception of an active 'receiving' is put forward in the eleventh century by Anselm of Canterbury. In his *De Casu Diaboli*

68 Boethius, *De Hebdomadibus*, p. 40.
69 See J. E. Booty in Sykes (ed.), *Authority*, pp. 94–118.
70 Hammond, *Of Fundamentals, Works* (Oxford, 1849), vol. 2, p. 29.
71 ARCIC A I E 3; cf. A II 27, *Growth*, p. 113.
72 Oehler, 'Consensus'.
73 *Etymologiae*, ed. W. M. Lindsay (Oxford, 1911), VI.16.12–13.
74 Hincmar of Rheims, *De Praedestinatione*, 38.1, *PL* 125.419.
75 More, *Responsio*, p. 198.27; Erasmus, *Letters*, 6.206.

he tries to answer the question how some angels were able to persevere in righteousness while others were not. If God gave some perseverance and not others, it would seem that he condemned some to fall, and that would make him the author of evil. Anselm's explanation is that God gave perseverance to them all, but only some accepted it; that is, it was by their own active response that they received it.[76]

Although the word 'receive' was in use in the sixteenth century in the general area of what we should now call 'reception',[77] it was not yet an established technical term. But the notion of an active 'embracing' is clearly present. 'In general councils, whatsoever is agreeable unto the written word of God we do reverently embrace.'[78] 'Whatsoever also is grounded upon God's written word, though not by our common and vulgar terms to be read therein, we do reverently embrace.'[79] 'We must not only hear and understand ... but also with stedfast assent of mind embrace ..., heartily love, ... yield ourselves desirous and apt to learn, and to frame our minds to obey.'[80]

The essence of this 'active welcoming' is that it is not an individual but a collective act of the people of God. It shifts the recent emphasis of the word *consensus* from its use in, for example, Aquinas, where it is merely an agreement of the will to sin or to marriage and so on, to the idea of shared understanding: *con-sensus*. Thus Melanchthon is able to define the Church as: *homines amplectentes Evangelium*,[81] people collectively embracing the Gospel. In the same spirit the Church of England's Thirty-Nine Articles urge that the Creeds 'ought *thoroughly* to be received and believed'.

So reception is a response, an active welcoming by the people of God. That is, it is not simply the submission of obedience to a duly constituted authority, a passive acquiescence. It is both intellectual, an active exercise of the judgement, and a consent of the believing mind and heart. It is a recognition. 'By "reception" we mean the fact that the people of God acknowledge ... a decision or statement because they recognise in it the apostolic faith. They accept it because they discern a harmony between

---

76 Anselm, *De Casu Diaboli*, 2–3, *Opera Omnia*, I.235.
77 For example, Cardwell, *Synodalia*, II.492; More, *Dialogue*, ed. Campbell, p. 111; Rogers, *Exposition*, p. 198.
78 Rogers, *Exposition*, pp. 210–11.
79 *Ibid*, p. 201.
80 Nowell, *Catechism*, p. 117.
81 *CR* 24.401, cf. 406 and 409.

what is proposed and the *sensus fidelium* of the whole Church.' What is being recognised is the voice of the Holy Spirit, 'that through that definition, whether it was of a synod or a primate, the authentic, living voice of faith has been spoken in the Church, to the Church, by God'. It is of the essence of this recognition that it will always be consonant with Scripture. Because it is fundamentally an act of recognition, reception does not create truth or legitimise the decision. It is the final indication that such a decision has fulfilled the necessary conditions for it to be a true expression of the faith. But our receiving has a positive, vital effect.[82] It is a real 'testing'.[83] There is a living continuous process in creative tension with that which is eternal in Christian truth.

[82] ARCIC A I E 3, and H. Chadwick, in General Synod of the Church of England, *Report of Proceedings* (February 1985), 16.1, p. 75.
[83] Cf. *Articuli Cleri*, 1558, *recepta et probata*, Cardwell, *Synodalia*, II.492.

15. Decision-making in a divided Church

i. THE PROBLEM OF THE MIXED COMMUNITY

We have been arguing that as a member of a believing community the Christian holds his faith in fellowship with all the faithful, saying not only 'I believe' (*credo*) but 'we believe' (*credimus*).[1] The conception that it is faith which is central to the Church's apostolicity was not new among the reformers. It was already well developed in the Carolingian period.[2] Christianus of Stavelot, a contemporary of Hincmar of Rheims, says that everyone who believes and confesses the faith with Peter deserves to be called an apostle as much as he.[3] So important is the collective confession of faith by believers that Luther argues that it is this which makes the Church identifiable as a visible community.[4] But it was also apparent to the reformers that the machinery for the collective expression of the faith has not always worked smoothly, either in Councils,[5] or through the offices of those with a responsibility for oversight. Why has there frequently been imperfect consensus, periods of learning from mistakes, and so slow and patchy a growth in understanding? A reason for this to which Augustine could subscribe as readily as a modern commentator is that in the deep structures of decision-making human needs and failings are accepted and allowed for, and the mode of our learning together is in tune with the enabling of our growth in holiness through living together

---

1 Cf. L. T. Johnson, *Decision-Making in the Church* (Philadelphia, 1983), p. 29, and on corporate believing, A. Harvey, *Believing in the Church* (London, 1981), p. 44. 'Insofar as I am a member of the Church, I associate myself with a "corporate believing" ... any individual who consciously associates himself with the Church' is recognising 'that by so doing, he is making his own personal understanding of the faith to a certain extent subservient to the collective activity of attention to, and interpretation of, Scripture which is an essential part of corporate believing.'

2 Congar, *Ecclésiologie*, pp. 128–9.

3 *PL* 106.1396–7, Congar, *Ecclésiologie*, p. 144.

4 *Propter confessionem coetus Ecclesiae est visibilis, WA* 39ii.161.

5 Rogers, *Exposition*, pp. 208–9, Proposition III, gives a list of councils which have done harm, from the 'Council gathered to suppress Christ and his doctrine' (John 9.22; 12.42; 11.47) to that which 'caused the apostles to be beaten and commanded them also that they should not preach in the name of Jesus' (Acts 5.40), and a series of others.

in the faith. If God never forces his people's consent, it must be the case that, though the Church has a commission to preach the Gospel to all the world and the promise that Christ will always be with his disciples and the Holy Spirit guide them into all truth,[6] 'the Spirit's guidance is not irresistible and that the Church in history has not necessarily at all points been perfectly responsive to its infallible Guide'.[7]

Augustine was led to hold that the Church visible in the world includes among the baptised many who are not of the City of God. He could come to no other conclusion in the face of the Donatist challenge. The Donatists claimed to be the pure and undefiled community of the holy. The Catholic Church was manifestly no such thing, and yet Augustine was clear that it was the true Church. He concluded that it is a 'mixed' Church, in which wheat and tares grow together until the Last Judgement. In this teaching dissenters and reformers in the later Middle Ages found a principle on which they could distinguish between the true Church of the faithful and the institutional Church in which they saw abuse and corruption. Boniface VIII's declaration that there is no salvation outside the Church[8] was intended to apply to the institutional Church. Wyclif and Hus[9] accepted the notion only as applying to the community of the predestinate, the invisible true Church, and although Wyclif did not see the need for the dissolution of the Church as a visible temporal society, his sixteenth-century successors were driven further, and some communities took a radical line on the matter of wheat and tares. 'We do not concede to the papists that they are the Church ... the Church is holy believers and sheep who hear the voice of their shepherd', says Luther in the Smalkald Articles.

A clear appreciation of the alternatives is to be found in the contrast between the present-day Reformed and the Baptist traditions as it strikes one twentieth-century Commission:

> The Reformed tradition emphasises the aspect of the community of salvation and thus the thought of the Church as also a mixed body (*corpus permixtum*), cf. Mt. 13.24–30, 47–50. ... The Baptist tradition emphasises the ... thought of the Church as 'gathered believers' committed to the task of proclaiming the gospel to each individual.[10]

6   John 16.13.
7   McAdoo, in Sykes (ed.), *Authority*, p. 73.
8   *Unam Sanctam*, 1302.
9   Gogan, *Common Corps*, pp. 51–2.
10 Cf. Mt. 28.16–20. B–R (8), *Growth*, p. 138

The first model sees the Church as a community within which the individual grows to his full stature, where the baptism of infants is appropriate and which couples with the Church's mission to those who are outside the community altogether, a mission working within. The second envisages membership of the Church as a matter of commitment of faith, marked by baptism of adult believers, so that there are no tares but only a gathering of wheat. These 'gathered believers' go out in mission to bring others to Christ. (Much hangs here on the doctrine not held by Augustine that the elect know who they are.)

The Lutheran community pioneered its way through partially unmapped territory in this area. Luther himself was inclined to take the robust, even rough and ready view that the true Church and the false, Abel and Cain, once mixed together, were now unmixing into Papists and reformers. The Augsburg Confession defines the Church as the congregation of saints.[11] Melanchthon defends his Augsburg formulation by referring to the Apostles' Creed and to the spiritual character of the Church as the 'people of God' and kingdom of Christ.[12] In the Lutheran disputations we find theses to the effect that the saints are 'believers' in the Gospel, 'reborn' in the Holy Spirit and 'beginners' in obedience.[13] But there is also the concession that mixed in among them are 'hypocrites'.[14] These profoundly complicate the attempt to equate those who are justified by faith with those who hold and witness to the apostolic faith, and whose consensus accordingly carries authority as the *consensus fidelium*. These hypocrites say that they believe. Even if we can say that the Church is the congregation of saints, there is still, then, a difficulty about the collective witness of all who call themselves Christians. And if the Church is a mixed community, there will certainly be the difficulty that good and bad doctrine, true and false faith will always be mixed together in the Church. At least that can be expected to be so after the apostolic age when the development of doctrine has been seen as under special protection and – as Melanchthon (ironically) thought – 'not yet tainted with Platonic opinions'.[15]

---

[11] Article 7. Zwingli seems to be saying much the same in *Defence*, Article 8; cf. *The Accompt and Confession of the Faith* (Geneva, 1555), p. 21. For a fuller analysis of 'models of the Church', see Avery Dulles, *Models of the Church* (New York, 1974). See, too, Confutation of the Augsburg Confession and Melanchthon's *Apologia*, Article 7, Mt. 13.47.

[12] Confutation, Article 7.8, 7.14, 7.16ff.

[13] *WA* 39ii.146.

[14] *Ibid.*

[15] *CR* 11.786, *De Luthero et Aetatibus Ecclesiae.*

Thomas More draws attention to another aspect of the matter, a point often referred to by the reformers' opponents. 'The chyrche is and must be of one beleue and have all one faythe ... But as for amonge heretyques there be as many dyvers myndys almoste as there be men.'[16] If adherence to the faith is constitutive for the true Church, how, he asks, can the many sects of the reformers all claim to be the true Church? He argues that the true Church must on these grounds be identified with the institutional and visible Church which is able to declare a clear and single faith. Linked with this question was a point raised by Luther himself. If, as he came to believe, the visible and institutional Church was now under the control of Antichrist, so that it could not be held to have the true faith, where was that faith preserved? Where was the Church of the faithful in the period before the reformers began their work? He suggests that 'the Church was always there' (*semper fuit Ecclesia*), even among the Papists, for true baptism always remained, and the true text of the Gospel was preserved miraculously by God's action. There were therefore many who were taught by Scripture about the benefits of Christ's passion, and who made right use of their baptism. These, since they were truly members of the Church, were saved.[17]

Much of the energy of the combatants in the sixteenth-century debates was directed towards the resolution of this complex of difficulties.

There was thought by some to be a case for the argument from force of numbers. It is put succinctly in one of the Paris theologians' Articles of 1544. If one man's authority is enough to constitute proof (*ut ad probationem sufficeret illud*) in the school of Pythagoras, how much more sufficient for the purpose is the agreement of many masters?[18] The same notion was tested in connection with 'many bishops' in the Lutheran disputation *De Potestate Concilii* of 1536.[19] The bishops as a class (*in specie*) had and have the Holy Spirit, not *in individuo*, it is proposed. But, it is answered, that is like saying that a multitude will always win by force of numbers. The Turks are a great multitude and more powerful than the Council. So the Turks are the Church. The king of the Scythians is more powerful than the king of the Turks. So he is the Church. In any case, one cannot argue from person to thing (*a personis ad rem non valet argumentum*). This is the argument which counts: 'Here is Christ with his

---

16   More, *Dialogue*, lxiii[rc], ed. Campbell, pp. 132–3.
17   *WA* 39[ii].167, Disputation of 1542.
18   *CR* 35.5.
19   Argumentum 10, against Thesis 5.

Church.' Then the conclusion is true, 'Christ has authority and his Word, not a multitude or a small group.' Therefore what we must do is to analyse faithfully, carefully and logically whether Christ has spoken or not. If he has spoken, we must accept it, if not we must reject it.[20]

In such debates there was an implicit exploration of the dictum of Vincent of Lérins. Yet the rules *quod ubique, quod semper, quod ab omnibus* were being put under intolerable stress by the events which were dividing the Church. The first and most obvious sense in which the *dictum* was tested to breaking point in the sixteenth century concerns 'place'. Luther argued for the importance of the local congregation, a community (*gemeyne*) in which the pure Gospel is preached and the sacraments administered – notes of the Church almost universally adopted by the reformers.[21] Thomas More, in his *Responsio* to Luther, says that the Church of God is one (*una est ecclesia Dei*) and those who separate themselves from it, even if they form a congregation, can be no more than a *conciliabulum diaboli*.[22] He describes an enquirer, 'E', who sets out to verify what he hears preached in one local church by travelling through many Christian nations to see if he finds everywhere 'the same faith, the same teachings regarding what is necessary for salvation'.[23] If Luther says that the Christians of Italy, Germany, Spain, France and so on are outside the Church, he is either arguing that the Church is nowhere, or, like the Donatists, he is reducing it to a gaggle of two or three heretics whispering in a corner.[24] But he concedes that it is not easy to find a 'perfyte perswasyon and byleve' which is 'receyued thrughe crystendome', although Christians in many places may concur.[25] The argument from what is received everywhere had, for practical purposes, temporarily broken down, and the best which can be advanced by way of warrant from ubiquity is some such formula as 'Hereunto subscribe the churches in

20 *WA* 39ⁱ.194, *De Potestate Concilii*, 1536.
21 Tappert, p. 503.
22 More, *Responsio*, p. 119.30–2. It is worth noting that Luther could not have subscribed in 1541 to the view that 'a theological teaching remains a theory of individuals as long as it is not affirmed and adopted by the whole people of God' (L–RC on the Eucharist, 1978, *Growth*, p. 212). But modern Lutherans would place a renewed emphasis upon the importance of a consensus of 'all parts of the Church' and 'all believers', over time (Thurian (ed.), *Churches Respond to BEM*, vol. 1, p. 31).
23 More, *Responsio*, p. 191. Cf. a similar example in Fulke, *Defence*, p. 56.
24 *Responsio*, p. 119.21–3.
25 More, *Dialogue*, ed. Campbell, pp. 111 and 182.

Helvetia, Wittenberg, Bohemia'[26] – or that this is 'the judgement of our godly brethren in foreign countries'.[27]

In the case of time we come up against Luther's contention (endorsed vigorously by Calvin, *Institutes*, Prefatory Letter to the King of France, 5) that in the 'matter of judging teachings' one 'should not care at all about ... old precedent, usage, custom' even if it 'lasted a thousand years'.[28] The kind of thing he had in mind is More's argument that the cult of saints and images which has been allowed for generations by common consent is warranted by usage, and that this custom is a stronger proof even than the miracles associated with them that such worship is right.[29] More argues in reply that Christians are bound by the past. Where past generations have arrived at consensus we must remain true to their position, however many now want to abandon it.[30] He cites Augustine's view that what is held by the whole Church as a matter of invariable custom is rightly held to have been handed down by apostolical authority.[31] We must follow 'the direction of the church ... which all times could point at', presses the English recusant Edmund Lechmere[32] in a later generation. More looks to find continuity from the time of Christ's Passion *in haec usque tempora*, the Church remaining in unity of faith *per tot secula*.[33] Luther's community is not only a 'rivulet' flowing away from the universal Church but a break in continuity. Where does Luther think the Church has been in the ages before him? When in the past have Luther's views been the Church's views?[34] Nowell, in his *Catechism*, speaks of 'custom' as 'at this day received in our churches' as something derived from 'the ordinance of the apostles and so of God himself'.[35]

This shake-up of assumptions about continuity of *consensus* in time forced new thinking which has borne fruit since. In More's *Dialogue* there is already some recognition that opposing views may coexist in the

26 Rogers, *Exposition*, p. 193.
27 *Ibid.*, p. 190.
28 Luther, *Assembly*, WA 11.408f.
29 *Dialogue*, ed. Campbell, p. 32.
30 *Ibid.*, p. 111.
31 Augustine, *On Baptism against the Donatists*, IV.xxiv, 32.
32 Lechmere, *A Relectio of Certain Authors* (Douai, 1635), English Recusant Literature, vol. 126, p. 3ᵛ.
33 *Responsio*, p. 191.
34 *Ibid.*, p. 193.
35 Nowell, *Catechism*, p. 116.

Church for centuries and then merge in a single voice which must be heard as that of Christ. For that reason a recently arrived at consensus may be no less binding than an old one. 'Yf there were any thyng that was peradventure such that in the chyrche somtyme was doubted and reputed for unreveled and unknowen; yf after that the holy chyrche fall in one consent upon the one syde eyther by common determynacyon at a generall counsayle or by a perfyte perswasyon and byleve … receyued thrughe crystendome' it is established as Christian truth.[36] In a notable nineteenth-century usage of the term 'reception' Pusey spells out one implication in a letter to Manning. The Council of Trent 'might', he postulates, 'by subsequent reception, become a General Council'. That would mean that 'it might be so now virtually, although' as yet 'unrecognised as such by the whole Church, but in a state of suspense'.[37] A simpler expression of the same idea, with a broader application, is to be found in the Final Report of ARCIC I. The process of reception may be 'gradual' (that is, running through time) as decisions come to be seen in perspective through the Spirit's continuing guidance of the whole Church.

A similar shaking out of assumptions is to be seen in the case of the principle of unanimity. Wyclif states comfortably that it is the nature of every creature to know God to be his *superior* and to want to help other creatures to work together as one.[38] More describes the Holy Spirit's method of bringing about *consensus* among his people, as he 'enclyneth thyr credulyte to consent in the byleuying all in one poynt whiche is the secret instyncte of god'.[39] Heretics do not disrupt this pattern for their dissent is transient in the continuing history of the Church.[40] Nor is it necessary for all Christian people to be present to vote in order to register their consent. A Council is the Church in microcosm; we cannot all meet but we can do so through our representatives.[41] But against this picture of a community in concord we need to set More's assertion that in no action of a multitude is unanimous consent required:[42] Edmund Lechmere

36   *Dialogue*, ed. Campbell, pp. 111 and 182.
37   In R. H. Greenfield, 'Such a Friend to the Pope', in *Pusey Rediscovered*, ed. P. Butler (London, 1983), p. 174.
38   *Opera Minora*, p. 327.30ff.
39   *Dialogue*, ed. Campbell, pp. 157–8, but cf. Pilkington, *Questions and Answers*, pp. 625ff., and Jewel, *Apology*, I.76.
40   *Dialogue*, ed. Campbell, pp. 132–3.
41   *Responsio*, p. 626.
42   *Ibid.*, p. 608.

goes further. The truth of the community's assertions, he says, 'dependeth not upon the approbation of everie one that is in her communion ... if some of them do chance to forgo the truth and leave it, there is power to the rest to define the matter and condemn them'.[43]

In connection with the principle of agreement *ab omnibus* the reformers ran into difficulties which make their pronouncements seem sometimes contradictory. Melanchthon can say both that the *coetus* is catholic which embraces the consensus of the Church[44] and that sometimes an individual or a small group is mandated by God to speak the truth against centuries of accepted teaching and a majority view in the Church. Those individuals who have a *mandatum Dei* must speak up. Luther dared to do it. Our congregations (*nostrae ecclesiae*), says Melanchthon, follow him rather than the *consensus* of so many centuries.[45]

The Augsburg Confession, the Lutheran Formula of Concord, the Calvinist confessions of faith,[46] the Church of England's Thirty-Nine Articles, the Zwinglian *Confessio Tetrapolitana* of 1530,[47] the *summa doctrinae* of the Strasbourg Synod of 1539,[48] may all be described as *consensus* documents. The *Confessio Tetrapolitana*, for example, agreed by the cities of Constanz, Memmingen, Lindaw and Strasbourg, drawn up in a bilingual version and in response to Imperial orders, was intended to put an end to divisions by agreeing on a common statement of doctrine. But these confessional formularies were challenged from within as well as from outside the communities whose faith they sought to express, and they remained in some degree in the melting pot of sixteenth-century 'articles' with the disputation theses and other loci to which they bear an unavoidable family likeness.

Some of these documents were drafted by individuals (Melanchthon's Augsburg Confession; Farel's (not Calvin's) Geneva Confession of faith

43 Lechmere, *Relectio*, p. 4.
44 *CR* 24.398; cf. Trent IV, Decretum Secundum.
45 *CR* 4.671; cf. Sebastian Castellio, *De Arte Dubitandi*, ed. D. F. Hirsch (Leiden, 1981), p. 3, for criticism of this view. Rogers, like Melanchthon, believes that 'to interpret the word of God is a peculiar blessing, given by God only to the Church and company of the faithful, though not to all and every one of them' (*Exposition*, p. 193).
46 Conveniently collected in a recent volume by O. Fato *et al.* (Geneva, 1986), and see *La vraie piété*, ed. I. Backus and C. Chimelli (Geneva, 1986), for Farel's Geneva Confession of Faith of 1537.
47 M. Bucer, *Deutsche Schriften*, ed. R. Stupperich (Gütersloh, 1954), vol. 3, pp. 37ff.
48 *Ibid.*, vol. 6ii, pp. 214ff.

of 1537). Others were the result of corporate effort. The Wittenberg Concord of 1536[49] was drafted by Melanchthon, with the aid of others present, and individuals contributed their own understandings of the issues. (Bucer, for example, underlines the points on which his party concedes or sustains certain positions.[50]) The corporate effort in this case was felt to lead to agreement, but with the rider that 'since we who are assembled are few, and it is necessary to refer the matter on both sides to our superiors, we cannot yet congratulate ourselves on having reached agreement'.[51]

What was happening here was a pressure of circumstances which made it necessary to look more deeply into the implications of what Vincent of Lérins had said. In the debates of the sixteenth century we see a good deal of wrestling with the anomalies. (Among the results is the 'at all times and in all places' of the Lutheran Summary Formulation already quoted.) Only much more recently have new formulations of the principles begun to emerge along lines which are not divisive but reconciling; a conception of unanimity as corporate believing in which individual insights are pooled, a conception of 'always' as involving the embrace of fluctuation and change and even periods of continuance in error only slowly corrected, an understanding of 'everywhere' as including both a monolithic universality and full recognition of the autonomous identity of local communities.

ii. THE FAILURE OF COMMUNICATION

Cardinal Michael Sylva reflected at the Council of Trent, in the debates of 1546, on the desirability of free consultation between those of opposing views. He describes an ideal encounter, in which Lutherans and Roman Catholics would 'freely say what they thought' (*libere dicerent sententias*) and listen to one another's points of view, so that the truth might emerge the more clearly.[52] But Campeggio argued against him that experience shows that no good comes of allowing heretics to put their case before Councils. He points to 2 Timothy 2.14, with its rule that those who ignore warnings about their errors are to be avoided thereafter.

The difficulty at issue here is that the 'heretics' of the sixteenth century would not be joining in the consultations of the Council as equal

---

49   *CR* 3.75–80.
50   *CR* 3.75.
51   *CR* 3.76.
52   *Acta CT* 12.447ff.

members; they would come before it, as it were, to give evidence at a trial of their opinions. The problem was touched on by Isidore in the sixth century. He sees the gathering of bishops in council as designed to protect the Church against heresy, and, paradoxically, the presence of heresy as making it difficult or impossible for them to gather for that purpose.[53] The same difficulty was raised by sixteenth-century reformers about the holding of a 'free' Council in contemporary circumstances.

In the Smalkald Articles which Luther composed in 1537 he divided the topics into three categories. Some articles could be conceded for the sake of peace; a second group was non-negotiable; a third set might be negotiated. The assumption on which Luther proceeded here was that peace was to be had only by bargaining, by give and take on both sides. There is barely a hint in the sixteenth-century debates of the notion of an agreement arrived at by mutual consent and without the need for either side to make concessions.

This picture of the task in hand was imposed by contemporary circumstances. Loyalty to party positions became so strong that it was and long remained natural to speak of 'our' definition of, for example, grace, and to contrast it as with that of an enemy.[54] It was not easy in practice to separate this way of thinking and speaking from the imperative to be loyal to the truth. The party label could become shorthand for the truth.

The reformers were aware of steering a course between Scylla (the institutional Church) and Charybdis (extreme factions such as the Anabaptists).[55] Confessional documents which linked church loyalty or party loyalty with a doctrinal position provided a flag to which supporters could rally and a point of reference to prevent inadvertent drifting away from the truth.

> The primary requirement for basic and permanent concord within the Church is a summary formula and pattern, unanimously approved, in which the summarized doctrine commonly confessed by the churches of the pure Christian religion is drawn together out of the Word of God … we pledge ourselves again [said the Lutherans in drawing up their Formula of Concord in 1577] to those … common confessions which have at all times and in all places been accepted in all the churches of the Augsburg Confession.[56]

53 *Etymologiae* VI.16.2–3, Congar, *Ecclésiologie*, pp. 134–5.
54 Benedict Aretius, *Theologiae Problemata* (Berne, 1604), col. 79.
55 Melanchthon in particular was anxious on the subject of the Anabaptists. See his *Loci Communes* XXI, and Articles 12, 16 and 17 of the Augsburg Confession.
56 Formula of Concord, Solid Declaration, Summary Formulation, Tappert, p. 503.

They made their pledge after decades of division and dispute within the Lutheran ranks and with a fervour made the greater by these earlier failures.[57]

It was thus as more or less identifiable parties that the combatants tended to meet when attempts were made in the 1530s and 1540s to mend the breaches in the Church.

Commonly, articles were drawn up by both sides, and there was an attempt to settle disputed questions by debate between the parties, with intervals for withdrawal while each side conferred over what was to be conceded or defended.[58] Here the disputational procedure ran into a serious methodological difficulty. The mediaeval academic disputation and its sixteenth-century equivalent was presided over by a Master who had authority to 'determine' the result. It was not designed for use between opponents who could agree on no mutually acceptable superior authority. (A president, perhaps a prince or his representative, was a different thing.) Again and again in the *reportationes* of the Wittenberg Disputations we see Luther stepping in genially or firmly to quash a conclusion falsely drawn. At Ratisbon in 1541 the lack of this sort of *magisterium* quickly proved fatal.[59] The situation was further complicated where the opposing parties met on the assumption on each side that it alone represented the true Church, so that the presumption even of equality was illusory, and the adversarial pattern indispensable to the mediaeval disputation became polemical.

Luther notes the characteristically adversarial nature of the thesis method in the preface to his collected disputations. 'For nearly twenty years', he says, he has been discussing certain topics with all his energies (*summis viribus et studiis*), against great abominations and profanations.[60] It is a matter of warfare. There are enemies. George Witzel wrote to Pflug, chief drafter of the 1548 Interim, to enrol himself as a *miles theologicus*, a theological soldier ready to fight, if not with the body, then with the mind, in the cause of truth.[61] This heritage of the mediaeval academic

---

57 See Tappert, pp. 463–4, for a brief account of how the text was put together in 1577 out of a long series of failed attempts to unify the Lutheran factions.

58 For a detailed account of the procedure at the Colloquy of Augsburg in 1530, see J. Wicks, 'The Lutheran *Forma Ecclesiae*', in *Christian Authority: Essays Presented to Henry Chadwick* (Oxford, 1988).

59 Cf. *CR* 4.208ff., 268, 349, 414.

60 *WA* 39^i.2.

61 Pollet II.742, Letter 354. On comparisons between the disputation and the tournament, see *CHLMP*, p. 22.

disputation makes its mark everywhere in the sixteenth-century debates. Calvin wrote *Antidotes* to the Articles of the Paris theologians of 1544 and to the pronouncements of the Council of Trent, on the principle of returning enemy fire. But a new note was present in the Reformation disputations. Mediaeval academic contests could certainly be acrimonious, and few holds were barred when it came to debunking one's opponent's opinions. But formal rules which imposed a certain stateliness and artificiality kept the temperature relatively cool. Luther and Calvin and their followers and sympathisers reached a pitch of fury where they did not hesitate to accuse the Church authorities of 'pretence', deliberate misrepresentations of truths of faith for base ends. Their opponents returned the accusation.[62]

The habit of thinking of one another as enemies increasingly got in the way of clear thinking for both sides. Thinkers in both camps not uncommonly sustained opinions with which the other side could agree, and one does not perhaps misrepresent Calvin to suggest that there is a note of embarrassment in his 'Amen' to certain of the Trent clauses, especially where he covers himself with bluster, and a 'Here they state what anyone could see', or 'This is a fine concession'. On the reformers' side in particular the great simplicities of what Chemnitz calls 'purified doctrines' were emphasised, so that we find talk of 'only Scripture', 'only faith', and so on; and of conflict with fundamentals. Polemical exchanges encouraged this tendency to stress black and white contrasts. This polarisation of positions, coupled with the notion that a string of abuses must follow from taking up the wrong position, made it difficult for either side to see fully into the implications of the intimate interrelationship of truths of faith which their work was in fact bringing to light, sometimes for the first time. The anti-theses match the theses of debate,[63] and the very method and structure of the discussion tend to discourage consensus.

The idea of attempting to reach not *determinatio* but consensus *was* broached. Calvin was known to speak of *consensio* as the end in view.[64] A *concordia* was arrived at by the ministers of the Church at Strasbourg in 1542, for the practical conduct of church life.[65] The most successful

---

62   Ambrosius Catharinus Politus, *Apologia pro Veritate Catholicae et Apostolicae Fidei et doctrina adversus impia ac valde pestifera Martini Lutheri dogmata* (1520), ed. J. Schweizer, *C. Cath.* 27 (Münster, 1956).
63   Cf. Tappert, p. 507.
64   *CR* 35.693ff.
65   Bucer, *Deutsche Schriften*, vol. 3, pp. 224ff.

experiments in consensus theology were the confessional formularies framed by several of the reforming communities, most notably the Lutheran Formula of Concord which resolved half a century of internal warfare.

The call for a General Council was slow to get a response. 'We despair', wrote Julius Pflug, bishop of Naumberg, in 1534. 'While it is put off the sects are growing and there is a danger that they may spread all over the Christian world. Some people are putting their hope in private meetings.'[66] A letter written to Pflug five years later speaks of the deferred hope of the General Council which has been awaited for nine years at least.[67] In the meantime a series of 'private meetings' was held. The disagreements of the Zwinglians and the Lutherans, for example, led to pamphlet warfare up to the Marburg Colloquy of 1529 and the Wittenberg Concord of 1536. Even at the 1536 meeting Luther showed himself suspicious of the motives of the Zwinglians and disinclined to believe them sincere, and there was a tendency for the parties to withdraw in order to consult.[68]

When he heard that a General Council was at last in prospect, Bucer wrote a *Dialogue in Preparation for Union*,[69] and in due course the Elector called the Lutherans together at Schmalkalden so that articles could be drawn up to present the Lutheran view to the Council when it met.[70] Luther agreed to prepare a Confession for this purpose. He had long wanted to change the emphasis of the Augsburg Confession at certain points where he thought Melanchthon had minimised real differences; and he was now anxious to draw up a definitive account of his own teaching before he died.[71] Melanchthon himself contributed a treatise on the power and primacy of the Pope and something *On the Power and Jurisdiction of Bishops*.[72] The primary purpose of these efforts was to set out the reformers' case clearly and cogently. As with the withdrawals to consult at Wittenberg in 1536 the assumption was that each party had a case, a distinctive position, and that this was to be compared with the arguments of the other side to 'determine' where the truth lay.

Something closer to the idea of meeting and talking across party

[66]   Pollet I.346, Letter 96, October 1534, para. 3.
[67]   *Ibid.*, I.463, Letter 131, 1539, para. 3.
[68]   E. G. Schwiebert, *Luther and his Times* (St Louis, Miss., 1950), pp. 695ff. and 737–8.
[69]   *WA Briefe* 7.145–6, note 2.
[70]   Schwiebert, *Luther*, p. 739.
[71]   *WA* 50.161; *WA Briefe* 7.605, 614; *CR* 3.156ff.
[72]   *WA* 50.176, *CR* 3.271, 286–8.

divisions was attempted in the 1540s. A meeting was held at Hagenau in 1540, under the presidency of King Ferdinand. Calvin attended it with the theologians of Strasbourg. Melanchthon was ill, and Wittenberg was represented by Cruciger, Myconius and Menius. The Catholic contingent included Fabri, Cochlaeus and Nausea.[73] The meeting quickly ran into major difficulties about establishing a *modus conciliandi*, a basis on which decisions could be mutually arrived at. It was eventually decided to meet again at Worms in October and there to proceed on the basis of 'Scripture, as truly, plainly and commonly understood by the apostolic and Christian Churches'. The Worms meeting was deferred, with its task uncompleted, to Ratisbon in 1541.[74] There it proved impossible to make the *modus conciliandi* work, because there was no means of agreeing what was 'truly, plainly and commonly understood'.

The group which met was made up of Bucer, Melanchthon and Pistorius on the reformers' side, Gropper, Eck and Pflug on the Catholic side. Eck, as had happened before, proved something of an embarrassment. He ranted and tried to lay down the law,[75] and thus created hostility to his often sound and scrupulous judgements. One commentator speaks of his *apoplexia*. 'Conjure up a picture of a rude sophist ... crowing among illiterates, and you will have half an idea of Eck', says Calvin.[76] Melanchthon, by contrast, gave an impression of moderation[77] but that, too, was unpleasing to some observers. Calvin was to speak scathingly of *moderatores* a few years later, because he saw mediation as compromising with the truth.[78]

Several comments by observers and contemporaries suggest reasons why the Ratisbon talks failed. Among the broadest in their implications are remarks about slipperiness in the formulations. 'That *farrago* satisfied neither side, both because it contained certain innovations, and because much of it was obscure, improperly expressed and inexact

---

[73] See F. Lau and E. Bizer, *A History of the Reformation in Germany to 1555*, tr. B. A. Hardy (London, 1969).

[74] P. Vetter, *Die Religionsverhandlungen auf dem Reichstag zu Regensburg 1541* (1889), pp. 89ff. On the failure of the Ratisbon talks, see too D. F. Wright (tr.), *Commonplaces of Martin Bucer* (Abingdon, 1972), pp. 42–4.

[75] *CR* 4.252.

[76] *CR* 9.217, Letter 309, and Pollet II.235, Letter 176, from Pflug and Gropper to the Presidents of the Colloquium, complaining about the accusations Eck had made against them. Cf. Calvin, *Letters*, 273, *CR* 39.146.

[77] *CR* 39.216.

[78] *CR* 35.612, *His iactis fundamentis*.

(*flexiloqua*)'.[79]   Melanchthon and Bucer 'composed formulas about transubstantiation which were ambiguous and foggy, so that they might see whether they could satisfy their adversaries without conceding anything (*nihil dando*)'.[80] This kind of criticism reflects both the tradition of exactness in definition at which we have been looking in this study, and a fundamental mutual mistrust and suspicion which was a serious block to progress even where there was a real desire to reach agreement. Even in this apparently sincere wish there was ground for suspicion. A letter of Caspar written in May remarks, 'It is not to be hoped that they would all suddenly change their minds ... so that they would seek a pious and sincere concord out of love of truth; and yet I understand that some, who have great authority with the Emperor, too, try with all their might to bring about agreement on all articles of controversy.'[81] The record of failure presented a serious difficulty here. Melanchthon comments in one of his letters on the Ratisbon colloquy that there are too many former and recent examples of the way such talks run into difficulties about 'ambiguous' and slippery (*flexiloqui*), foggy and fallacious articles which are destructive of truth and do not heal the Church but rather make things worse.[82]

Experience had not yet taught the need for unlimited patience in such negotiations. Cruciger notes that 'because it was not possible to come to agreement (*convenire*) quickly and immediately' on certain articles, there was pressure to move on to other matters.[83] Nor was it altogether clearly understood that a process of emendation and modification of the formulas might be the way to a solution rather than a recipe for obfuscation and compromise.[84] Neither side was wholly willing to be content with convergence where consensus was as yet impossible, with a formulation 'not contrary to our confession, but not as yet determined and concluded' so as to be fully acceptable to all,[85] in the expectation that that would prove to be a stepping-stone to full agreement.[86] These were lessons which could not be

---

[79]   *CR* 4.332.
[80]   *CR* 39.217, Letter 309.
[81]   *CR* 4.252.
[82]   *CR* 4.330.
[83]   *CR* 4.259.
[84]   *CR* 4.252. Calvin's fear of compromise is especially marked in the *Vera Eccl. Ref. Rat.*, *CR* 35.594–7.
[85]   *CR* 4.264, Reibisch to Medler, May 1541.
[86]   A recent example is the Authority texts of ARCIC I, which are taken to represent convergence rather than consensus.

learned in a short meeting, but which have emerged in more recent discussions only over a period of years, as members of ecumenical commissions have met repeatedly and grown together in trust as well as in thinking.[87]

At the root of the difficulties at Ratisbon was the assumption that the parties were adversaries meeting to fight a contest for the truth. Again there was much withdrawing to compile or to answer articles.[88] This methodological disincentive to come together as a single group, rather than as two groups drawn up in battle lines, was compounded by the failure of the proposed '*modus conciliandi* by Scripture'. The question of authority in the Church proved an insurmountable stumbling-block for that reason.[89] Even if it were possible to agree on a definition of the Church, Calvin commented, there was inevitably disagreement about *power* in the Church (*potestas*).[90] Yet contemporaries were puzzled and distressed by the failure of the Ratisbon talks; a vast worried correspondence travelled across Europe amongst reformers and their opponents alike.

In 1547 the Council of Trent adjourned to Bologna. In 1548 the Emperor Charles V promulgated an Interim Declaration of Religion agreed between Protestants and Catholics in an attempt to establish religious unity in Germany while 'Trent is suspended in confusion', as the Prefatory Letter puts it. The document was largely the work of Julius Pflug with the collaboration of Helding and Johann Agricola, who had studied under Luther at Wittenberg, had been presented at the Leipzig Disputation and had lectured at Wittenberg. (There had been an estrangement between them, however, over Antinomianism.) The Interim was intended to be a provisional settlement which would keep the peace until the Council of Trent had finished its deliberations. It conceded two practical points to the Protestants: communion in both kinds and clerical marriages. But on other matters it strove for a 'fuller concord on controverted points'.[91] That this was something new in form is attested by the fact that it proved impossible to attack it as Calvin had done with the Paris Articles of 1544 and as he went on to do with the Decrees and Canons of Trent, that is, by writing an *Antidote* to the articles point by

---

87 See my *Doing Theology Together* (Norwich, 1986).
88 Bucer's publication of the documents of the Colloquy (Strasbourg, 1541) gives the series.
89 *CR* 4.253.
90 *CR* 39.215. Cf. *WA Briefe* 9.406ff., Letter 3616 and p. 474, Letter 3645.
91 Prefatory Letter to the Interim, and cf. *CR* 35.612 for a mention of *loci*.

point. When Bullinger persuaded him to write a refutation of the Interim, Calvin found it most convenient to do so in a book on *The True Method of Reforming the Church*. The motives which gave the Interim its form were subtly different from anything which had gone before. Pflug was genuinely distressed by the confusion in his diocese (*Ecclesia mea misera ... convulsa*).[92] Melanchthon, always a moderate and anxious for real rapprochement, wrote to express his willingness to help in any way he could, recalling their encounter at Ratisbon and giving a detailed list of points which, he says, change very little what was done at Ratisbon.[93] The Interim failed partly because of Calvin's resistance to it, and partly because of the timing; the pronouncements of Trent were soon to overshadow it.

We need not look far for other underlying reasons for the failure of the attempts at making peace before the end of the Council of Trent. As we shall see again and again, the adversarial method of the mediaeval disputation had the disadvantage that it encouraged the polarising of opinions, black and white, for and against, on issues which could be categorically stated as propositions or theses, even if within those limitations it fostered exactness in analysis. Into the disputations of even the young Luther and others a note of exasperation began to enter. Combatants gave way to personal abuse, allowed themselves to become aggressively defensive of their own motives. It has to be said that Luther himself was a prime offender in this, although he clearly felt himself justified by the failure of the authorities to acknowledge the existence of the corruptions he was pointing out. There was in any case a tradition, now some centuries old, which regarded the Pope as Antichrist,[94] and it was natural for Luther and other reformers to fall in with it as they became more and more frustrated and angry. Calvin's *Antidote* to Trent contains a good deal of this sort of writing.[95] The result was an admixture of bluster and fury with the clear exposition of the arguments on either side and a tendency to lose sight of the change and development in thinking which was going on in the opposing camps.

One might quote Luther's or Calvin's fulminations at length, but it is

---

92 Pollet III.95.6–7, Letter 375.
93 Cf. Bucer to Pflug, 13 April 1548, *ibid.* III.80, Letter 374.
94 See W. Bousset, *The Antichrist Legend* (London, 1896), and Bauckham, *Tudor Apocalypse*.
95 To take one or two examples of Calvin's language in the *Antidote* to Trent (VII), he speaks sarcastically of 'these holy fathers', says 'they are dishonestly deluding us', that 'they ignorantly wrest' the evidence to their purposes.

perhaps more instructive to consider the effect of polemical method on a cooler mind. Something of the resulting sensation of being bruised and unjustly treated echoes in Melanchthon's *Confessio Saxonica* of 1551, which, like the Augsburg Confession, was offered in the hope of reconciliation. He sets out to explain how the reformers came to take the position they did. We did not, he says, embrace this doctrine with wicked intent (*prava cupiditas*); nothing could be more wicked than knowingly to oppose the truth. That is the sin against the Holy Ghost. When we saw the clear truth we gave thanks for it.[96] Nor did we seek new opinions for the sake of novelty.[97] It all began with indulgences.[98] Luther's propositions were *pie et modeste scriptas* and were intended merely to instruct (*erudiendas*) and warn (*commonefaciendas*). But they were opposed. Because Luther could not abandon the 'defence of the truth' he was forced to write more, and to go further into many parts of the doctrine.[99] Melanchthon tries to make it plain what Luther was contending against. 'There are books', he says, which have been in circulation for three hundred years, which teach that remission of sins can be deserved by human efforts. This huge investment of time and thought in the teaching of a doctrine 'against the Son of God' was what Luther confronted,[100] with all its implications.

Melanchthon was the most moderate of men in his attempts to bring about reconciliation between the opponents; indeed Luther was none too pleased with him for 'treading softly' in the framing of the *Confessio Augustana* in 1530.[101] But even he is unable to avoid caricaturing the views of the other side. Their way of thinking, he says, is like this: 'I shall believe when I have enough merits.' They do not say, 'I believe that remission of sins is freely and certainly given for the sake of the Son of God, not on account of our merits or any deserving of ours.' It is, ironically, on the basis of such inherently hostile and often crude statements of the position of opponents that attempts were made to get things clear, so that there might be no *ambiguitates*.[102] Yet Melanchthon was trying to be fair, and

96   *Confessio Saxonica*, p. 84.9–13.
97   *Ibid.*, p. 84.30.
98   *Ibid.*, p. 84.31–2.
99   *Ibid.*, pp. 84.36 – 85.3.
100   *Ibid.*, p. 85.33ff.
101   On Melanchthon's treading softly, see V. Pfnür and H. Schütte, in J. A. Burgess (ed.), *The Role of the Augsburg Confession: Catholic and Lutheran Views* (Philadelphia, 1977), pp. 4–6, 51–2.
102   *Confessio Saxonica*, p. 90.18–25 and p. 93.8ff.

was indeed doing his best to refrain from complaining about the unfairness with which he felt his own side had been treated. His honest intention was to get the essence of the two positions clear so as to show where the truth lay.

One cannot shout abuse with subtlety. Polemic is inimical to exactitude and it encourages oversimplification. At the same time it heightens the impression of the importance of what is at stake (not a small point but the whole of Christian truth; not a word, but a complete summary of the Gospel). Calvin was not unaware of these effects of the adversarial approach when it was infused with hostility. 'I come to that obstacle which prevents many in our own day from coming closer to Christ.' He is speaking of the proliferation of 'contrary opinions' even among the reformers, and the 'bitterness' of the 'conflicts' which result. 'This throws people into doubt', he comments, and not only within the walls of schoolrooms but in books too there are multitudes of embattled opinions (*pugnantibus sententiis*).[103] He has in mind particularly the *opiniones* of late mediaeval scholasticism, but as brought forward into his own day, and infecting debate on theological matters on every side. Yet his own response was, in effect, to go further into the polemical and adversarial corner occupied by the reformers in these wars. We should, he says, be willing to suffer anything rather than be deflected by a hair's breadth from true doctrine. We must resolutely determine not to listen to terms for peace which mingle the figments of men (*hominum figmenta*)[104] with the pure truth of God. In this spirit supporters wrote to urge him to 'repudiate' 'papal dogmas' and 'invented innovations'.[105] He himself uses the language of repudiation and declares with a note of triumph that when he repudiated transubstantiation this was 'in no way tolerable to our adversaries'.[106]

The Trent theologians, although they speak of *heretici*, are rarely guilty of the polemical extremes of the reformers.[107] It is clear how different things might have been if hostility had not clouded and distorted the issues in this way if we look, for example, at the agreement *De Sacramentis* arrived at among the reformers in 1549.[108] A series of peaceable *responsiones* to proposed articles was exchanged between Bullinger and

---

[103]   Calvin, *De Scandalis* (1550), *CR* 36.56–7.
[104]   *CR* 35.593.
[105]   *CR* 35.182–3.
[106]   *CR* 39.215, Letter 308.
[107]   *Acta CT* 6iiii.406ff.
[108]   *CR* 35.693ff.

Calvin. Even so, the furthest the system allows the participants to go is mutual agreement. 'I agree with what you say', says Calvin. 'All that you say is true, and agrees beautifully (*pulchre congruunt*) with our opinion.'[109] But there is no more than a shaking of hands between the parties in token of a *determinatio* not quite appropriate between equals, where there is no recognised *magister* to settle matters. They are not able to make a statement together.

iii. DECISION-MAKING

The full operation of the processes we have been examining requires a united Church. That includes those for rescue in emergency. In a divided Church they can proceed only imperfectly, and we have seen some of the problems presented by a failure of convergence in the sixteenth-century debates. One result is that it becomes necessary to take a view of what a Church or Communion may do or decide on its own account in a situation of division, without further prejudice to the unity of the Body of Christ. Is there, in short, a place for independent authorising in matters of faith or of order?

In Augustine's eyes schism was heresy, indeed the worst of heresies, because it involved a breach of the unity of the very Body of Christ. The sixteenth-century debates put a new complexion on the matter for the reformers. Secession from a visible and institutional Church which requires obedience to rules of merely human devising seemed in certain circumstances not only justified, but a duty of true Christians. The ecclesiological controversies had made it in any case a matter of opinion whether this constituted schism at all.[110]

There had come to be a clear though not always consistent distinction in some reforming minds between the fundamental truths of faith, laid down by Scripture and unchanging, and the 'rites' of the institutional Church. These Calvin sees as 'superstitions', 'superinduced on the pure ordinances of the Lord' by 'human presumption'. His objection to these rests on two grounds, of which we have already seen something in considering the relationship of Scripture and the Church. They overlay with 'various and discordant additions' the great simplicities of the faith. 'All the godly complain, or at least regret', for example, 'that in baptism

---

[109] *CR* 35.704.
[110] All this takes a stage further the Wycliffite readiness to countenance resistance to spiritual authority wrongly exercised. See Hudson, *The Premature Reformation*, p. 366.

more is made of the chrism, the taper, the salt ... than the washing with water'. What is visibly a 'rite' in the administration of the sacraments has its counterparts in teaching in the traditions of the Church.[111] The second objection is that they are merely human additions. More briefly the Church of England's Thirty-Nine Articles condemn what is 'vainly invented' (22); Luther opposes divine to human ordering.[112] Sixteenth-century protestant understanding of tradition is thus highly charged with the assumption that tradition is human, superfluous and opposed to the divine.

It is here that resentment about papal exercise of the first of Luther's two 'keys', the key of binding and loosing, overlaps with feeling against the use of the second, the key of discerning truth from falsehood in matters of faith. These are seen not only as additions, but as additions imposed by force and on pain of eternal damnation, and thus as falling within the 'disciplinary' sphere of the keys as well as in the sphere of judgement about matters of faith. The Paris theologians insist upon obedience to the *constitutiones Ecclesiae* in their Articles of 1544, and Calvin replies with angry insistence that the Christian obeys only one Lord, and that is God.[113] Luther refers to 'the miserable plague of human teaching' inflicted by Pope and bishops, and claims that human teaching always takes away from God's commandments and adds its own commandments.[114] Zwingli too inveighs against human traditions.[115] Against this scathing talk of human tradition the *Loci Communes* of Eck state, upholding the disjunction between human and divine, that 'the human constitution of councils and pontiffs is to be preserved' (XIII, Axiom 1)[116] and 'the Church's constitutions, rites and ceremonies are to be observed equally with divine laws' (XIII, Axiom 2).[117] The Council of Trent denies that penitential satisfactions are 'traditions of men' (XIV, Canon 14). The result was a separation and opposition in the combatants' thinking which made it possible for Melanchthon to lay down this rule (*regula*) at the time of the Council of Ratisbon: 'The authority of the Word of God is greater than that of any man, any bishops, any synods, or the

111   Calvin, *Antidote* to Trent VI, Canon 13.
112   *On the Papacy in Rome, WA* 6.277ff.
113   *CR* 39.39–40, Article 24.
114   *Against the Spiritual Estate of Pope and Bishops*, 1522 (*Works*, vol. 39.239ff.), *WA* 6.277ff.
115   Zwingli, *Defence*, Article 9.
116   Eck, *Loci*, p. 146.
117   *Ibid.*, p. 149.

whole Church.'[118] The Bible was being set over against this 'merely human' Church as though they were rival authorities. 'The principal respect ought to be given to the Church after God and his Word',[119] conceded moderate Protestants at Ratisbon, but even here the authority of Bible and Church are seen as distinct, even as alternatives.

The second ecclesiological implication, then, is that the Church is 'human' and the Word 'divine'; and this reinforces the first, that to divide the Church is not necessarily to be a heretic.

Luther argued that because 'rites' in the Church are of human devising, they do not have to be the same everywhere.[120] This variability is contrasted with the immutability of the fundamental truths of faith, which have the sanction of a divine origin.[121] Luther's case rests upon a series of polarisations which we have already met: a separation of a 'human' Church from a 'divine' authority, a contrasting of a truth once and for all delivered with subsequent 'additions' and 'impositions'. Above all, there is no room here for the notion of a diversity arising from complementary perceptions of a single and immutable truth. There is thus no way through to a principle which is proving of the first importance in modern ecumenical discussion, and which must be the ultimate justification for the preservation of an ecclesial identity based on the 'special insights' of a particular leader or movement. That is to say, Luther did not explore the possibility that the reformers were offering a necessary corrective and important insight but not a full account of apostolic truth.

Nor did he disentangle systematically an implicit confusion in his use of the term 'rites'; he deserves some criticism for failing to do so because he understood very well that liturgy is also theology. The debate about 'rites' was set on foot precisely because the reformers believed that the Church was teaching the people theological errors through its rites (especially in the Mass,[122] in the penitential system and in encouraging the veneration of images, for example). It was apparent to both sides in the debates that the claim to the right to vary rites and ceremonies was also a

---

[118]   *CR* 4.349.
[119]   Bucer, *Ratisbonensis Acta* (Strasbourg, 1541).
[120]   Cf. Solid Declaration, Art. 10, Tappert, p. 612.
[121]   *WA* 50.379ff., especially p. 380.
[122]   Hubert Walter's Canons at Westminster (1200) stress the importance of the exact and proper saying of the canon of the Mass; a not unimportant reason is that to fail to do so is to foster error (Johnson, *Laws and Canons*, II.84).

claim to authority in deciding matters of faith. The point is made explicitly by William Beveridge (1637–1708). He suggests that the Church's authority extends to two things, 'the decreeing of ceremonies' and 'the determining of controversies'.[123] It was therefore disingenuous of Luther to propose so sharp a distinction between 'rites' and matters of perennial Christian truth.

The thinking of the reformers here had important consequences. It is particularly clear in the sixteenth-century formularies, Articles and liturgy of the Church of England that liturgy and theology are inseparable. Yet we find the Articles maintaining that such 'traditions' as rites and ceremonies are at the disposal of the Church in different places to decree as appropriate to local needs.[124]

A further area of potential confusion lay in the attempt to distinguish between the immutable and fundamental truths of faith, and lesser truths, which could be held as a matter of opinion, and on which one Christian could legitimately differ from another.[125] Among the *Propositiones* of Luther listed by Leo X in 1520 was the notion that it is neither sin nor heresy to disagree with a papal pronouncement (provided it has not been endorsed by a General Council), especially in something 'not necessary to salvation'.[126] Some use has been made in modern ecumenical contexts of the notion of a 'hierarchy of truths', in an attempt to allow in this way for differences between Christians in separated communions. As a device for holding together real contradictions that cannot be satisfactory, because it is incompatible with the unanimity which is inseparable from consensus. It is also a disincentive to the patient effort to discover a common position. We should not today want to say that the province of authorising in divided communions is limited to matters low in a 'hierarchy of truths', or that the contribution of special insights must be restricted to such areas.[127]

There is, however, a real duty to meet differing local needs in patterns of worship, and to express the common truth in ways conformable to different cultural circumstances. Something of this sort is adumbrated in the Church of England's Thirty-Nine Articles, in the statement of Article 34 (1571) that decrees about rites and ceremonies must meet two tests.

---

123   *Ecclesia Anglicana*, p. 118 (*Works*, vol. 7); cf. Article 20 of the Thirty-Nine Articles.
124   Article 33 of 1552; Article 34 of 1571.
125   On the history of these debates, see B. J. Verkamp, *The Indifferent Mean* (Ohio, 1977).
126   Denzinger 1478/768, in Denzinger and Schönmetzer, *Enchiridion Symbolorum*.
127   See W. Henn, *The Hierarchy of Truths according to Y. Congar, O.P.* (Rome, 1987).

The first is conformity with Scripture, and the second that they should be established locally by common authority (*publica auctoritas*). The reasons given reflect both contemporary preoccupations (there should be obedience to local and secular authority) and a concern for Scriptural principles (obedience here is a way of deferring to the consciences of weaker brethren).[128] The underlying rule is that obedience to local regulations in matters of rites and ceremonies is a way of preserving order, and an expression of mutual respect within the community.

This is to recognise the legitimate existence of both traditions which are 'customs of the Church produced by the frequent and long-continued usage of the great part of the community' and which are rightly precious to that particular group of Christians; and traditions of the Church universal, that is, of the whole community over time. There must be room for variety in practice without prejudice to theological consensus.

The difficulty is to define the limits of that variation which must operate if there is not to be a consequent division in matters of faith.[129] Patterns of life and worship in the Church, though locally variable, are ultimately inseparable from questions of unity of faith with the whole believing community of the universal Church, so that each communion affirms its catholicity by joining with the whole Church in authorising the great central truths of faith. The truth once and for all delivered is, at the same time, also maintained and living and growing in the Church. Fundamentals cannot be separated from the fullness of Christian believing, so that we should aim, not to distinguish central truths for universal agreement and leave the rest to local licence, but to seek a consensus on all matters, which embraces the full range of understanding represented in variations of local practice and emphasis.

If these principles are right, perhaps we may conclude that there are two proper spheres for independent authorising in matters of faith within a communion in a divided Church. It is the place of each ecclesial body to word the truths of faith apprehended by the whole community in ways comfortable and natural and appropriate to the style and character of the communion, and which may be used in its common life and worship; but always with a care not inadvertently to set up a barrier to other Christians. It is also the duty of each such body to correct error and misunderstanding and to work towards unanimity with the *consensus fidelium*.

128 Cardwell, *Synodalia*, I.14, 30, 49.
129 Cf. the text of my *Authority in the Church: a challenge for Anglicans* (Norwich, 1990), chapter 8.

We must therefore carefully separate a sense of corporate identity based on common norms of worship and on common life within a communion, from the expectation that members of any separated communion will share a common faith which somehow distinguishes them from other Christians (so that we may say 'Lutherans believe ...' or 'Anglicans believe ...'). That cannot be right. Everything we know about faith endorses the view that it unites us to the whole Body of Christ's faithful people through Christ, and is thus a corporate believing with the universal community. Matters of doctrine must thus be regarded as always the responsibility of the universal Church and never at the disposal of a local or a separated community without reference to the whole under Scripture.

All this has clear implications for authorising in matters of faith and practice within individual provinces, and within the particular churches, or individual dioceses, and, with certain restrictions, for individual congregations. An ecclesial community may, within the structures of its order, legislate for its own people. It may do so freely in matters which cannot be divisive in relation to other communities or communions, provided its actions are consonant with Scripture and are acceptable to the local faithful, causing no difficulty to tender consciences. In all matters of faith and worship where there is known to be imperfect consensus as yet in the universal Church, the diocese or province, or the whole communion or ecclesial body, must be prepared in charity to 'defer to the common mind'.[130] That may mean being patient; it may mean seeking to lead the common mind into agreement; there should never be precipitate action to force others into conformity with a *fait accompli*. In practice such action has sometimes been taken, and situations created in which some are unable in conscience to accept the resulting position as compatible with universal faith and order. Here again the rule of charity operates. No communion, province or diocese should respond in a manner likely to lead to division. Solutions must be sought which reconcile and foster the growth of common life. Where this purpose is paramount and anger and resentment are not allowed to confuse the real issues, we may go on in faith that the Lord, whose intention for his Church is that it should be one with him, will bring about a right resolution of differences. Deference to the common mind means a willingness to accept that one may be wrong, and to grow in understanding, as well as a pooling of special insights into the fullness of the truth.

[130]   Lambeth, 1948, p. 84.

Conclusion: the unity we seek

> We do not seek unity because we can approve of one another. We seek it because, when we refuse to do so, we treat with contempt the immeasurable kindness of our Lord who has accepted us as we are in order that he may make us what he would have us be. (A–R, 123b)

In the last analysis, perhaps we must say that the sixteenth-century debates failed in the attempt to convince and persuade opposing parties that there was a common truth upon which they could continue to build a common ecclesial life, because the urge to unity was simply not strong enough. The doctrine of the Church which Augustine held made schism the worst of heresies. The sixteenth century did not share that priority. The adversarial character of the debates made for polarisation, and the opposition of elements which we should now see as complementary in the balanced ecclesiology of a united Church. Classic principles of formal 'order' were reinforced in the Roman Catholic community to the point where rigid rules were imposed as a condition of membership. The reformers tended to place the emphasis on the individual's relationship with Christ, with a correspondingly undeveloped theology of community; and with the strengthening of notions of Scriptural primacy and rights of private judgement in interpretation, over against the community's *consensus* expressed through time. There was a danger of imbalance on one side in favour of what can be called 'descending' authorising and on the other in favour of an 'ascending' authorising; on one side a preference for a central and on the other a prejudice in favour of a 'diffused' authorising. The Reformation debates left these imbalances unredressed.

We see as a result a further imbalance, in the form of preoccupation with one or more overriding concerns. Calvin stresses, for example, in his *True Method of Reforming the Church* that we must be careful in defining terms, so that nothing taints or 'mingles with' the notion of a gratuitous reconciliation. That sort of thing made for cautiousness and mutual suspicion in the sixteenth-century debates. Concordance of ideas is frequently suspect. It seems to Calvin to be usually the result of failing to recognise differences of signification between terms used in Scripture, and bringing passages together artificially (*ut suum inde concursum stabilant*).[1]

---

[1] CR 35.594.

285

One of the most important aspects of today's ecumenical bringing together of what once seemed contrasting viewpoints is the understanding of ways in which the Church may be *both* visible and invisible, *both* an ordered human society in which the fullness of human possibilities can be realised and a mystery fully present only to God; how the decisive events of committing oneself to God in faith and of baptism may be at the same time part of a single process; how justification by faith may go hand in hand with growth in holiness in which the individual and his actions are of real worth in the sight of God. Thus we avoid the polarisation and the danger of falling into absurd extremes of which one sixteenth-century author wrote in describing two opposing errors, of those 'that presume of themselves, thinking to be justified by themselves, by their owne strength and righteousness, without the help and grace of God'; and of those who 'pretending their owne infirmitie and weaknesses do no good deedes and trust and presume onely to be saved by God's grace and mercie though they live ungodly'.[2] John Wesley commented on the same phenomenon. 'I fell among some Lutheran and Calvinist authors, whose ... accounts magnified faith to such an amazing size that it quite hid all the rest of the commandments. I did not then see that this was the natural effect of their overgrown fear of popery, being so terrified with the cry of merit and good works that they plunged at once into the other extreme.'[3] Wesley himself was unable 'to reconcile this ... either with Scripture or common sense'. By embracing in a single account what once seemed contradictories we may begin to find that we are no longer walking a tightrope between 'certain errors and misguided developments' in the late mediaeval Church and 'extreme reforming movements'.[4]

It is here that the debates we have been examining are of the first importance. Much that stands in the way of process towards consensus today has to do with mutual misunderstanding about authority questions in their sixteenth-century forms. Christians on all sides need the clearest possible picture of what was said and what was thought to be at stake in the period when the Church in the West became divided. Old sensitivities about the keys and the swords are still alive. Nevertheless, there are changes of attitude which give good ground for hope.

[2] Reginald Pole, *Treatie of Justification* (Louvain, 1569), Preface.
[3] John and Charles Wesley, *Selected Prayers*, ed. F. Whaling (London, 1981), pp. 99–101.
[4] A–L Pullach (28), *Growth*, p. 17.

The leading ideas of the Second Vatican Council, which have been taken up throughout Christendom, and which have radically altered the terms of the debates we have been examining, are ecclesiological. Baptism is seen as of central importance. It is by baptism that the faithful are incorporated into the Church and which makes all Christ's people his ministers; and baptism is an existing bond uniting all Christian people even where they belong to separated communions.[5]

The deep root of Luther's resistance to talk of *ius divinum* in the Papacy is the ecclesiological implication that other Christians, Russians, Greeks, Bohemians, who are not in communion with Rome are not Christians at all, that being under Roman authority somehow creates Christians.[6] The language of *ius divinum* was used again by the First Vatican Council in the late nineteenth century, and at that date it was still read by Protestants as implying the claim that no Christian community which does not acknowledge the leadership of Rome can belong to the Church of God.[7] The Second Vatican Council does not see the Church as coextensive with the Roman Catholic Church or exclusively embodied in that Church.[8] Mutual respect between ecclesial communities rests upon a respect for the ministerial gifts of all the baptised people of God. The same respect for the whole people of God and all its members underlies the new emphasis upon a balance of collegiality and primacy, and between the responsibility of oversight and the recognition of the contribution of lay ministry. Thus the resentments and (often justified) sense of their ministry going unrecognised, which prompted Waldensians and Lollards and Lutherans alike to voice an aggressive anticlericalism, century by century from the high Middle Ages, become unnecessary.

The second of the great transforming conceptions of Vatican II is that of the pilgrim Church.[9] This ancient notion of a people travelling home to God became briefly overlaid, during the centuries with which we have been concerned, with a static picture of an inerrant and unchanging Church. The emphasis of Vatican II is upon growth and renewal.

It is in the context of these concepts of a profound existing unity through baptism and of an onward movement towards a fuller realisation

---

5 *Lumen Gentium*, 11, 15.
6 Luther, *On the Papacy in Rome*. On the point at issue, see ARCIC A I 24 and A II 10ff.
7 ARCIC A II 11, 12; cf. Tappert, p. 320.
8 *Lumen Gentium*, 8; *Unitatis Redintegratio*, 13.
9 *Lumen Gentium*, 6, 8.

of the being of the Church that one recent ecumenical commission tries
to express the idea of a communion *in via*:

> We see ourselves as having a communion *in via*. The unique unity
> of the one Church of God is the goal. We are already on the way;
> we have taken the first step in faith through baptism which is also
> the call to that final unity. Now we have the task of giving external
> expression to the communion *in via*.[10]

In this study we have been looking at the difficulties of a period in the life
of the Church which, despite the apocalyptic expectations of many
contemporaries, did not prove to be the final age. It is important that we
should not now remain captured in the prison of the terms and the frame
of reference of the sixteenth-century debates in which this period reached
its crisis. We need to recognise that a large proportion of the difficulties
which are voiced today about going forward to unity are the legacy of
attitudes and assumptions of the sixteenth century, and perhaps above all
of the adversarial method which encouraged the polarisation of seeming
opposites: Scripture and tradition, faith and works, and so on. It is here
that 'Protestants' are called on to make a leap as courageous as that of
Vatican II and to overcome their fear of losing what was so bravely and
honestly struggled for, four hundred years ago.

A third step with enormous implications was taken by the Second
Vatican Council in speaking of *plures christianae communiones*.[11] The
Council makes a distinction between the divisions of the early Church,
which Paul condemns,[12] and those of later ages in which there were faults
on both sides and the Church was divided into estranged ecclesial
communities. But those who believe in Christ and are baptised are not
wholly separated. They are *in quadam communione*, although that
communion is not complete. The barriers to full communion are seen as
in part doctrinal, and in part to do with questions of discipline and
structure which remained unresolved in the sixteenth century (partly
because the division of the Western Church removed the immediate
pressure of the need to settle them). This has broken new ground in
making possible the mutual recognition of separated Churches, for on
both sides the sixteenth-century combatants insisted again and again that

[10] D–RC, *Growth*, p. 164.
[11] *De Oecumenismo*, Preface, 3.
[12] 1 Corinthians 1.11ff., 22.

their opponents were not the true Church – in a tradition which goes back to the late mediaeval Antichrist literature with its insistence that the Pope is Antichrist and a usurper and his Church a false Church. The major development of recent decades here is the perception of the Church in terms of the New Testament concept of *koinonia*. This gets behind the late mediaeval and sixteenth-century preoccupation with the difference between a Church conceived of as a hierarchy with power to govern the faithful and a Church conceived of as the community of the faithful as a whole. A central conception of *koinonia* in the New Testament puts the sovereignty of God at the heart of things. *Koinonia* is a gift of the Holy Spirit, a reality itself divine, and which is itself a participation. This *koinonia* is conceived of as a communion of individuals who have a relationship to Christ as their Head, and a relationship to one another which is dependent on that primary relationship.[13] Christ is the Head of a unifying structure formed by living relationships held in a pastoral discipline of love and mercy.[14] This is helpful in shifting concern away from the now stale and perhaps ultimately insoluble dilemma of the 'visible' and 'invisible' Church – insoluble because of the difficulty about 'knowing oneself elect' which lies at the heart of it – to a conception of a living fellowship.

As we move towards a deeper universal *koinonia*, we need to treat the issues with sensitivity to values for which many have been martyred, but we also need to be clear about the difference between the positive and the negative in individual confessional traditions. Structurally and organisationally as well as doctrinally there was great diversity among reforming groups. As a result, the conception of a common enemy proved easier to hold onto in the sixteenth century than a sense of common identity, and when internal harmony failed, the 'errors of Rome' presented a unifying target.[15] The Lutherans suffered long and bitter internal conflicts before 1577 and among the Reformed controversy was still going on during much of the seventeenth century. Thus, on the negative side there is a heritage of hostility and mutual suspicion, a self-definition by contrast with others, which still sometimes echoes in contemporary comments. Loyalty to the memory of a founder was helpful in providing a sense of identity. Luther, Calvin and later Wesley for the Methodists are

13 Cf. 1 John 1.3.
14 Cf. 1 Corinthians 6.10–11.
15 Beardslee, *Reformed Dogmatics*, p. 6.

290 Problems of authority in the Reformation debates

cases in point. But this, too, has its negative implications as carrying with it some risk of diverting minds from the centrality of Christ, encouraging nostalgia and obscuring the historical reality. The Summary Formulation of the Solid Declaration of the Formula of Concord looks back to a 'period when people were everywhere and unanimously faithful to the pure doctrine of the Word of God as Dr Luther of blessed memory has explained it'. The Zwinglian *Confessio Tetrapolitana* which is roughly contemporary with the Augsburg Confession makes a historical claim too. For ten years, it says, the 'doctrine of Christ' has been treated throughout Germany in a manner 'more sure and more clear' (*certius et luculentius*) than ever before and only the wiles of Satan have created division of opinion. The positive contribution of the confessional traditions which identified themselves in the sixteenth century and after now begins to appear in a different light, not as unique possession of the whole truth, but as shared possession of that truth together with special insights to put into the common pool of Christian understanding.

It was not easy for the reformers to see themselves, in the excitement and challenge of the time, as standing at a certain stage in a continuing sequence of unfolding understanding, or to envisage that it would go on beyond them. There was a sense of having discovered final truths. Calvin insists again and again that true Christians must not let go of these truths or give any quarter to the opposition. Melanchthon describes how Luther has come with a special mandate from God to right wrong thinking and how his substantial following demonstrates the rightness of what he is teaching.[16]

In entering thus into a climate of growing anger and excess we must try to keep, in our own day, a detachment which was rarely possible for the combatants. Their anger proved a barrier to the finding of a solution, and we have to get behind it if we are to see why they failed in the enterprise dearest to the hearts of reformers and conservatives alike: of bringing all Christendom to peace under one Christ.

Both methodologically and in terms of content then, the sixteenth-century debates must be seen as constituting only an interim stage and as making a contribution in a continuing process. But if the divisions of the sixteenth century were a *culpa*, it is possible to begin to see them as a *felix culpa*. They have shown up serious faults in the system as it was developing in the West in the later Middle Ages. They have been

16 *CR* 4.671, *CR* 11.786.

corrective. The Council of Trent was not able to make a statement with the reformers because the Church was divided and the division in its turn consisted in part in the inability of the Christians of Western Europe to speak with a common mind at that time.[17] Mutual misunderstanding had reached a point where the anathemas of the Council's canons could only be directed as against enemies of the truth. After Trent the Roman Catholic Church could refer to a clear statement of its position on the controverted issues; by 1577 the Lutherans could point to their Formula of Concord, the Anglicans to the Thirty-Nine Articles, and so on. Attitudes became entrenched. That is not to say that there were no further efforts at rapprochement, but after the Council it could hardly be expected that Reformers and Counter-Reformers should soon sit down together to try to make the kind of common statement which has been attempted in recent decades.

Doctrinal definition has often been arrived at in the course of the Church's history as a result of persistent questioning by individuals who were eventually rejected as 'heretics'. Such 'theologising against error' was clearly recognised as a branch of theology in the Middle Ages from at least the twelfth century.[18] Something of the sort was clearly in the minds of the Trent theologians when they spoke of *heretici*, and of the reformers when they attacked the *papistae*. But hindsight indicates that something rather different was happening, a confrontation of communities with what can perhaps best be described as different angles on orthodoxy, rather than of orthodoxy and heterodoxy. These ecclesial communities have proved to be parts of a whole, and their doctrines complementary and also contributions to a whole theology.

The realisation that this was so has come gradually and unevenly. In the Roman Catholic Church a number of abuses were already acknowledged by the Council of Trent; a high proportion of its pronouncements are concerned with reform. The Church was in fact changed inwardly by the comments of the reformers; theology became sensitive not only in protestant quarters to any implication that the sovereignty of God was being treated lightly, or sacred objects, sacred rites and clerical powers allowed to get in the way between the faithful and Christ. Vatican II is the product of mature reflection on the events of the sixteenth century and their aftermath.

17 Cf. Whitgift, *Cartwright*, pp. 12–13 on the tension between warfare and brotherly love.
18 See my *Alan of Lille* (Cambridge, 1983).

It is as yet a weakness of the ecumenical progression towards consensus that what is emerging is an ideal rather than an actual picture[19] of the reality of the Church. But that does not invalidate what is being discovered. It is important to get the theology right so that there may be a point of reference and a picture of the goal which is set before us. 'The reception of the word of God in faith is the basis of the unity of the community.'[20] Where that reception is incomplete or fragmented there cannot be unity in life and worship. It is for that reason that ecumenical theological endeavour has an indispensable part to play in the achievement and maintenance of unity among Christians because it is an important means of arriving at consensus. But perhaps the most important thing of all is the evidence of the working of the *consensus fidelium* which must ultimately be the ground of unity in the Church in today's ecumenical theological process. Commissions working independently are coming to harmonious conclusions. Popular movements for local unity are coming much of the way to meet them. A remaining task is the patient removal of those stumbling-blocks which remain as a result of the failure of the sixteenth-century debates, and it is to this labour that this study has tried to make a contribution.

---

[19]   ARCIC A I, Preface, on the 'distinction between the ideal and the actual' as 'important for the reading of our document and for the understanding of the method we have used'.

[20]   See P. Duprey, 'A Catholic perspective on Ecclesial Communion', in *Christian Authority: Essays Presented to Henry Chadwick*, p. 11, note 25.

Select bibliography

Sources

(No bibliographical details are given for classical and patristic texts which exist in several modern critical editions.)

Abelard, Peter, *Dialectica*, ed. L. M. de Rijk (Assen, 1970)

Aegidius Romanus (Giles of Rome), *De Ecclesiastica Potestate*, ed. R. Scholz (Weimar, 1929)

Agricola, Rudolph, *De Inventione Dialectica Lucubrationes* (Cologne, 1539)

Ailly, Peter d', *De Potestate Ecclesiastica*, in J. Gerson, *Opera Omnia*, ed. E. du Pin (Antwerp, 1706), II. 925–60

Albertus Magnus, *In Sententias*, ed. R. Spiazzi (Turin, 1964–5), 2 vols.

Alexander of Hales, *Summa Theologica* (Florence, 1924–), vol. 1

Alexander de Villa Dei, *Doctrinale*, ed. D. Reichling (Berlin, 1893)

Andre, Antoine, *In Quatuor Sententiarum Libros opus longe absolutissimum* (Venice, 1578)

Anglican Homilies, The (London, 1833, repr. Sussex, 1986)

Anselm of Canterbury, *Opera Omnia*, ed. F. S. Schmitt (Rome/Edinburgh, 1938–68), 6 vols.

Apostolicae Curae, Acta Leonis XVIII (Vatican, 1867), XVI. 258–75

Apuleius, *Perihermeneias* in *De Philosophia Libri*, ed. P. Thomas (Stuttgart, 1970)

Aquinas, Thomas, *In Sententias* (Venice, 1586)

 Quaestiones Quodlibetales, ed. R. Spiazzi (Turin, 1956)

 Summa Theologiae, ed. P. Caramello (Turin, 1962–3), 3 vols.

 Quaestiones Disputatae, ed. R. Spiazzi (Turin, 1964–5), 2 vols.

Aretius, Benedict, *Theologiae Problemata* (Berne, 1604)

Aristotle, *De Interpretatione; Categoriae*, ed. H. Tredennick (London, 1962)

Augustine, *De Baptismo contra Donatistas*

 De Civitate Dei

 De Doctrina Christiana

 De Magistro

 Sermones

 De Spiritu et Littera

Aureoli, Peter, *Super Primum Sententiarum*, ed. E. M. Buytaert (New York, 1956)

Backus, I. and Chimelli, C., *La vraie piété* (Geneva, 1986)

Barbaro, Ernolao, *Epistolae, Orationes et Carmina*, ed. V. Branca (Florence, 1943)

Bebel, Heinrich, *De Institutione Puerorum* (Strasbourg, 1513)

Becon, Thomas, *Catechism, Works*, ed. J. Ayre (Parker Society, Cambridge, 1843–4), 3 vols.

Bede, *De Schematibus et Tropis*, ed. C. Halm, *Rhetores Latini Minores* (Leipzig, 1863)

Bellarmine, Robert, *De Controversiis Christianae Fidei adversus huius Temporis Haereticos* (Venice, 1587)

Opera, ed. X. R. Sforza (Naples, 1856–62), 6 vols.

Liber de Locis Communibus, Fragmenta Inedita, ed. S. Tromp (Rome, 1935)

Bereira, Bento, *Commentariorum et Disputationem in Genesim* (Lyons, 1594–1600), 4 vols.

Bernard of Clairvaux, *Opera Omnia*, ed. J. Leclercq, H. Rochais and C. Talbot (Rome, 1958–80), 8 vols. (vol. 3 contains *De Consideratione*)

Beveridge, William, *Works*, ed. J. Bliss (London, 1843–8), 12 vols.

Beza, Theodore, *Epistolam D. Pauli Apostoli ad Galatas notae, ex Concionibus Casparis Oleviani exerptae, et a Theodoro Beza editae* (Geneva, 1578)

Abraham sacrifiant, ed. and tr. K. Cameron, K. M. Hall and F. Higman (Geneva, 1967).

Biel, Gabriel, *Questions on Justification*, ed. C. Feckes (Aschendorff, 1929)

Canonis Missae Expositio, ed. H. A. Oberman and W. J. Courtenay (Wiesbaden, 1963–), 4 vols.

Defensorium Obedientiae Apostolicae et alia Documenta, ed. and tr. H. A. Oberman, D. E. Zerfoss and W. J. Courtenay (Cambridge, Mass., 1968)

Collectorium circa quattuor libros Sententiarum, ed. W. Werbeck and U. Hofmann (Tübingen, 1973)

Boethius, *Theological Tractates*, ed. H. F. Stewart, E. K. Rand and S. J. Tester (London, 1973)

Boethius of Dacia, *Modi Significandi*, ed. J. Pinborg and H. Roos, *Opera*, I (Copenhagen, 1969)

Quaestiones super Priscianum Minorem, Opera, IV

Bonaventure, *In Sententias, Opera Omnia* (Florence, 1882–), 1–

Boyle, Robert, *Cogitationes de Scripturae Stylo* (Oxford, 1665)

Brassicanus, *Institutiones Grammaticae* (Strasbourg, 1508)

Brett, Thomas, *An Account of Church-Government and Governours* (London, 1701)

Bricot, Thomas, *Textus Totius Logices* (Basle, 1492)

Tractatus Insolubilium, ed. E. J. Ashworth, *Artistarium*, 6 (Nijmegen, 1986)

Brito, Radulphus, *Quaestiones super Priscianum Minorem*, ed. J. Enders and J. Pinborg, *Grammatica Speculativa*, 3 (1980)

Brito, William, *Summa Britonis sive Guillelmi Britonis Expositiones*, ed.
   L. W. Daly and B. A. Daly (Padua, 1975)
Bucer, Martin, *Acta Ratisbonensis* (Strasbourg, 1541)
   Deutsche Schriften; *Opera Latina*, ed. R. Stupperich (Gütersloh,
   1954–)
   Commonplaces, tr. D. F. Wright (Abingdon, 1972)
   Correspondance, ed. J. Rott (Leiden, 1979)
Budé, Guillaume, *Opera Omnia* (Basle, 1557), 4 vols. (repr. Farnborough,
   Hants, 1966)
Bullinger, Johann, *Decades*, ed. T. Harding (Parker Society, Cambridge,
   1849–52), 4 vols.
Buridan, John, *Perutile Compendium Totius Logicae*, with John Dorp's
   commentary (Venice, 1499, repr. Frankfurt, 1965)

Caesarius, *Dialectica* (Cologne, 1559)
Cajetan, Tomás de Vio, *Opera Omnia quotquot in Sacrae Scripturae
   Expositionum Reperiuntur* (Lyons, 1639), 5 vols.
Calixt, Georg, *De Praecipuis Christianae Religionis Capitibus
   Disputationes* (Helmestadt, 1648)
Calov, Abraham, *Systema Locorum Theologicorum* (Wittenberg, 1655–
   77), 12 vols.
Calvin, Jean, *Opera, CR 29 – 87*
   In Librum Psalmorum Commentarius, ed. A. Tholuck (Berlin, 1836),
   2 vols.
Cardwell, E. (ed.), *Synodalia* (Oxford, 1842), 2 vols.
Cassiodorus, *In Psalmos*, ed. M. Adriaen, *CCSL* 97, 98 (Turnhout, 1958)
Castellio, Sebastian, *De Arte Dubitandi*, ed. D. F. Hirsch (Leiden, 1981)
Celtes, Conrad, *Opera*, ed. A. Rutland (Serapeum, 1870)
Chemnitz, Martin, *Examen Concilii Tridentini* (1565–73)
   Loci Theologici (Frankfurt, 1591)
Cicero, *De Inventione*
   De Oratore
   Orationes
   Topica
Clement of Alexandria, *Stromateis*, ed. O. Stählin (Leipzig, 1905–60),
   vols. 2, 3
Clichtoveus, Iudocus, *De Sacramento Eucharistiae contra Oecolampadius*
   (Paris, 1526)
Codex Iuris Canonici (Vatican, 1983)
Colet, John, *An Exposition of St Paul's Epistle to the Romans*, ed. and tr.
   J. H. Lupton (London, 1873)
   Confutatio der Confessio Augustana, ed. H. Immenkötter, *C. Cath.* 33
   (Münster, 1979)

Contarini, *Confutatio Articulorum seu Quaestionum Lutheranorum*, ed. F. Hünermann, *C. Cath.* 7 (Münster, 1923)

Coverdale, Miles, *Remains*, ed. G. Pearson (Parker Society, Cambridge, 1846)

Cradock, Samuel, *The Harmony of the Four Evangelists* (London, 1668)

Cranmer, Thomas, *Remains*, ed. H. Jenkyns (Oxford, 1833), 4 vols.

Writings on the Lord's Supper, ed. J. E. Cox (Parker Society, Cambridge, 1844)

Miscellaneous Writings and Letters, ed. J. E. Cox (Parker Society, Cambridge, 1846)

The Works of Thomas Cranmer, ed. G. E. Duffield, *Reformation Classics* (London, 1964)

Dante, Alighieri, *Monarchia*, ed. E. Moore and P. Toynbee, *Le Opere di Dante Alighieri*, (Oxford, 1963, 5th ed.)

Documentos inéditos tridentinos sobre la justificación, ed. J. Olazarán (Madrid, 1957)

Donne, John, *Sermons*, ed. G. R. Potter and E. M. Simpson (Berkeley, Calif., 1953–62), 10 vols.

Doughty, Thomas, *A brief discoverie of the crafte and pollicie* (1621), ed. D. M. Rogers, English Recusant Literature, 62 (London, 1971)

Duns Scotus, *Commentaria Oxoniensia, ad IV Libros Magistri Sententiarum*, ed. P. M. F. Garcia (Florence, 1912)

Opera Omnia, ed. A. Sepinski (Vatican, 1960)

Eck, Johannes, *Disputatio Viennae Pannoniae Habita* (1517), ed. T. Virnich, *C. Cath.* 6 (Münster, 1923)

Enchiridion Locorum Communum, ed. P. Fraenkel, *C. Cath.* 34 (Münster, 1979)

Enchiridion of Commonplaces, tr. F. L. Battles (Grand Rapids, Mich., 1979)

De Sacrificio Missae, ed. E. Iserloh, V. Pfnür and P. Fabisch, *C. Cath.* 36 (Münster, 1982)

Eckhart, Meister, *Prologue to the Book of Commentaries*, tr. A. A. Maurer (Toronto, 1974)

Enchiridion Symbolorum Definitionum et Declarationum, ed. H. Denzinger and A. Schönmetzer, 36th ed. (Herder, 1976)

Erasmus, *Annotationes in Novum Testamentum* (Antwerp, 1516)

Opus Epistolarum, ed. P. S. Allen, H. M. Allen and H. W. Garrod (Oxford, 1906–58), 12 vols.

Enchiridion Militis Christiani, ed. H. and A. Holborn, in *Ausgewählte Werke* (Munich, 1933)

Erasmi Opuscula, ed. W. K. Ferguson (The Hague, 1933)

Opera Omnia, ed. J. H. Waszink *et al.* (Amsterdam, 1969–), vols. 1–
Collected Works, ed. and tr. R. J. Schoeck *et al.* (Toronto, 1974–),
vols. 1–
*Apologia Respondens ad ea quae Iacobus Lopis Stunica Taxaverat,
Opera Omnia*, vol. 4 (Amsterdam/Oxford, 1983)
Estius, Guilielmus, *Annotationes Aureae in Praecipua ac Difficiliora
Sacrae Scripturae* (Coloniae Agrippinae, 1622)
Étienne, Robert, *see* Stephanus, Robertus

Faber Stapulensis, Jacobus, *Commentarii in omnes D. Pauli epistolas,
libri xiiii* (Cologne, 1531)
Commentarii in Epistolas Catholicas (Antwerp, 1540)
Commentarii initiatorii in quatuor evangelia (Cologne, 1541)
Fasciculi Zizaniorum, ed. W. W. Shirley, Rolls Series, 5 (London,
1858)
Fabri, Johannes, *Malleus in Haeresim Lutheranum* (1524), ed. A. Naegele,
C. Cath. 25 (Münster, 1952)
Ficino, Marsilio, *Dionysii Areopagitica Episcopi Libri Duo* (Venice, 1538)
Opera Omnia, 2 vols. (Basle, 1561 and 1576)
Commentary on Plotinus' *Enneads*, in *Plotini Enneades*, ed. F. Creuzer
and G. H. Moser (Paris, 1896)
The Philebus Commentary, ed. and tr. J. B. Allen (Berkeley, Calif.,
1975)
Fisher, John, *Opera Omnia* (Würzburg, 1697)
The English Works of John Fisher, ed. J. E. B. Mayor, The Early English
Text Society (London, 1876)
Flacius Illyricus and the scholars of Magdeburg, *Historia Ecclesiastica
Integram Ecclesiae Christianae Conditionem, inde a Christo ex Virgine
nato, iuxta seculorum seriem exponens* (Basle, 1559–74)
Fournier, Jacques, *Registre d'Inquisition*, ed. J. Duverney (Paris, 1965)
Foxe, John, *Syllogisticon* (London, 1563)
Acts and Monuments, ed. J. Pratt (London, 1877), 5 vols.
Fulke, William, *A Defence of the Sincere and True Translations of the
Scriptures into the English Tongue* (London, 1583), ed. C. H. Hartshorne
(Parker Society, Cambridge, 1843)

Gagny, Jean, *Clarissima et facillima in quatuor Sacra Iesu Christi
Evangelia necnon in Actus Apostolicos Scholia* (Paris, 1552)
Gaismir, Michael, *Landesordnung*, ed. in M. Klaasen, *Michael Gaismir*
(Leiden, 1978)
Gelnhausen, Conrad of, *De Congregando Concilio*, ed. E. Martène and
U. Durand, *Thesaurus Novus Anecdotorum* (Paris, 1717, facs.
Farnborough, Hants, 1968–9), 5 vols., III

Gerard of Bologna, *Summa*, ed. P. de Vooght, *Les sources de la doctrine chrétienne* (Brussels, 1954)

Gerhard, Johann, *Loci Theologici*, ed. Preuss (Berlin, 1863)

Gerson, Jean, *Six sermons de Jean Gerson*, ed. L. Mourin (Paris, 1946) *Oeuvres complètes*, ed. P. Glorieux (Paris, 1960–), vols. 1– *De Auctoritate Concilii* ed. Z. Rueger, *Revue d' histoire ecclésiastique*, 53 (1978)

Gilbert of Poitiers, *Commentaries on Boethius*, ed. N. M. Häring (Toronto, 1966)

Giles of Rome, *see* Aegidius Romanus

Goffe, Thomas, *Deliverance from the Grave* (London, 1627)

Gower, John, *Confessio Amantis*, ed. R. A. Peck (New York, 1968)

Gregory the Great, *Moralia in Job*, ed. M. Adriaen, *CCSL*, 43 (Turnhout, 1969), 3 vols.

Gropper, Johannes, *Briefwechsel*, ed. R. Braunisch, *C. Cath.* 32 (Münster, 1977)

Grosseteste, Robert, *Letters*, ed. H. Richards Luard, Rolls Series (London, 1861)

Growth in Agreement: Reports and Agreed Statements of Ecumenical Conversations on a World Level, ed. H. Meyer and L. Vischer (Geneva, 1984)

Gundissalinus, *De Divisione Philosophiae*, ed. L. Baur, *Beiträge zur Geschichte der Philosophie und Theologie des Mittelalters* 4 (1903)

Hacket, John, *A Century of Sermons* (London, 1675)

Hafenreffer, Matthias, *Loci Theologici* (Tübingen, 1603)

Hegius, *Invectiva in Modos Significandi*, ed. J. Ijsewijn, *Forum for Modern Language Studies*, 7 (1971), 299–314

Himmel, Johann, *Syntagma Disputationum Theologicarum Methodicum* (Erfurt, 1630)

Hooker, Richard, *The Laws of Ecclesiastical Polity*, ed. W. Speed Hill (Cambridge, Mass., 1977)

Hugh of St Victor, *De Sacramentis Ecclesiae*, *PL* 176, and tr. R. J. Deferrari (Cambridge, Mass., 1951)

Hus, John, *Super IV Sententiarum*, ed. W. Flajshans and M. Kominkova, *Opera Omnia* (Prague, 1903), vol. 2 *Letters*, tr. M. Spinka (Manchester, 1972)

Hutchinson, John, *Philosophical and Theological Works*, ed. R. Spearman and J. Bate (London, 1748–9), 12 vols.

Hutter, Leonard, *Compendium Locorum Theologicorum* (Wittenberg, 1610)

Jewel, *Apologia Ecclesiae Anglicanae*, vols. I and II, ed. J. Ayre (Parker Society, Cambridge, 1848), *Works*, vols. 3–4

John of Ragusa, *Oratio* at the Council of Basle, *Concilia*, ed. N. Coleti (Venice, 1781), vol. 17

John of Salisbury, *Metalogicon*, ed. C. C. J. Webb (Oxford, 1929)

Johnson, J., *A Collection of the Laws and Canons of the Church of England* (Oxford, 1850–1), 2 vols.

Knox, John, *The History of the Reformation of Religion within the Realm of Scotland*, ed. C. J. Guthrie (London, 1905)

Lambeth Conferences, The First Five (London, 1920)

Latimer, Hugh, *Sermons and Remains*, ed. G. E. Corrie (Parker Society, Cambridge, 1844–5)

Latomus, Bartholomew, *Lucubrationes in Ciceronis Orationes* (Basle, 1539)

Ennarrationes in Topica Ciceronis (Strasbourg, 1539)

Adversus Martinum Bucerum Defensio (Cologne, 1545)

Latomus, Jacobus, *De Trium Linguarum et Studii Theologici Ratione Dialogus* (Antwerp, 1519)

Opera, ed. J. Latomus jr (Louvain, 1550)

Laud, W., *The Conference between William Laud and Mr Fisher the Jesuit, Works*, vol. 2 (Oxford, 1849)

Lechmere, Edmund, *A Relectio of Certain Authors* (Douai, 1635), English Recusant Literature, 126 (1973)

Luther, Martin, *Opera* (Wittenberg, 1545)

Werke (Weimar, 1883–1983), 102 vols.

Briefwechsel, ed. E. L. Enders (Stuttgart, 1884–), 17 vols.

Vorlesung über den Hebräerbrief, 1517–18, ed. J. Ficker (Leipzig, 1929)

Vorlesung über den Hebräerbrief nach der Vatikanischen Handschrift, ed. E. Hirsch and H. Rückert (Berlin, 1929)

Luthers Werke, ed. E. Vogelfang (Berlin, 1955–), vols. 1–

Works, tr. J. Pelikan (St Louis, Miss., 1958–), vols. 1–

Maldonatus, Johannes, *Commentarii in Quatuor Evangelistas*, ed. J. M. Raich (Mainz, 1874)

Martin, Gregory, *A Discoverie of the Manifold Corruptions of the Holy Scriptures* (Rheims, 1582)

Martin of Dacia, *Quaestiones super Librum Topicorum Boethii* (Copenhagen, 1961)

Matthew de Janova (Mateje z Janova), *Regulae Veteris et Novi Testamenti*, vols. 1–4, ed. V. Kybal (Innsbruck and Prague, 1908–13), vol. 5 ed. O. Odlozilik and V. Kybal (Prague, 1926)

Melanchthon, *Opera Omnia*, ed. C. G. Bretschneider and H. E. Bindseil (Halle/Brunswick, 1834–), *CR* 1–28

Werke, ed. H. Engelland *et al.* (Gütersloh, 1951–), vols. 1–
Melanchthon on Christian Doctrine: Loci Communes, ed. and tr. C. L. Manschreck (Oxford, 1965)
Mencik, F., *Milíc a dva jeho spisy z.r. 1367, Prophecia et revelatio de Antichristo*, ed. V. Herold and M. Mráz (Prague, 1974)
Mirandola, Pico della, *Opera Omnia* (Basle, 1557), ed. C. Vasoli, and repr. Hildesheim, 1969
Conclusiones, ed. B. Kieszkowski (Geneva, 1973)
More, Thomas, *Dialogue*, ed. W. E. Campbell (London, 1927)
Complete Works, ed. J. M. Headley (London/Yale, 1963–), vols. 1–

Nebrija, A., *Grammatica* (Lyons, 1520)
Neobarius, Conrad, *Compendiosa Facilisque Artis Dialecticae Ratio* (Strasbourg, 1536)
De Inveniendi Argumenti Disciplina Libellus (Strasbourg, 1536)
Nicholas of Cusa, *De li non aliud*, ed. and tr. J. Hopkins (Minneapolis, 1983)
Nicholas of Dresden, 'Master Nicholas of Dresden, The Old Colour and the New', ed. H. Kaminsky, D. L. Bildeback, I. Boba and P. N. Rosenberg, *Transactions of the American Philosophical Society*, 55 (1965), 5–93
Nicholas of Lyre, *Biblia cum Glossa Ordinaria et Expositione Lyre Litterali et Morali necnon Additionibus ac Replicis* (Basle, 1498), 6 vols.
Nowell, Alexander, *Catechism*, ed. G. E. Corrie (Cambridge, 1853)

Ockham, William of, *Opera Theologica*, ed. G. Gal, S. Brown *et al.* (New York, 1967–), vols. 1–
Opera Philosophica, ed. P. Boehner *et al.* (New York, 1967–), vols. 1–
Quaestiones Variae, ed. G. I. Etzkern *et al.* (New York, 1984)
Origen, *Werke*, ed. P. Koetschau *et al.* (Leipzig, 1899–1914), 12 vols.
Osiander, *Gesamtausgabe*, ed. G. Müller and G. Seebass (Gütersloh, 1981)
Owen, John, *Works*, ed. W. H. Goold (London/Edinburgh, 1851)

Parsons, Robert (N. D.), *Review of Ten Public Disputations or Conferences, held within the Compass of Four Years, under King Edward and Queen Mary* (St Omer, 1604)
Paterson, William, *The Protestants Theologie*, ed. D. M. Rogers (London, 1976)
Paul of Venice, *Logica Magna*, ed. N. Kretzmann *et al.* (London, 1979)
Peter Lombard, *Sententiae Spicilegium Bonaventurianum* (Florence, 1971–81), 4 vols.
Peter of Spain, *Tractatus (Summulae Logicales)*, ed. L. M. de Rijk (Assen, 1972), with Versor's *Expositio* (Cologne, 1522)
Pflug, J., *Correspondance*, ed. J. Pollet (Leiden, 1969–82), 5 vols.

Pilkington, James, *Works*, ed. J. Scholefield (Parker Society, Cambridge, 1842)

Pole, Reginald, *Treatie of Justification* (Louvain, 1569)

Politus, Ambrosius Catharinus, *Apologia pro Veritate Catholicae et Apostolicae Fidei*, ed. J. Schweizer, *C. Cath.* 27 (Münster, 1956)

Porphyry, *Isagoge*, *PL* 64

Prideaux, John, *The Christian Expectation* (Oxford, 1636)

Priscian, *Institutio Grammatica*, ed. H. Keil, *Grammatica Latina* (Leipzig, 1855–80), vol. III

Ramus, Peter, *Scholae Grammaticae* (Paris, 1559)

Raymundus de Sabunde, *Theologia Naturalis* (1502)

Reuchlin, Johannes, *Vocabularis breviloquus* (1486)
  De Arte Praedicandi (1508)
  In Septem Psalmos (1512)
  De Accentibus (The Hague, 1518)
  Lexicon Hebraicum (Basle, 1537)

Rhegius, Urban, *Loci Theologici*, ed. J. Freder (Frankfurt, 1545)

Rhetorica ad Herennium (anon.), ed. H. Caplan (London, 1954)

Ridley, Nicholas, *Works*, ed. H. Christmas (Parker Society, Cambridge, 1841)

Rijk, L. M. de (ed.), *Logica Modernorum* (Assen, 1967), 2 vols.

Rinucci, Alemanno, *Lettera ed Orazioni*, ed. V. R. Giusiniani (Florence, 1953)

Rogers, Thomas, *An Exposition of the Thirty-Nine Articles*, ed. J. J. S. Perowne (Parker Society, Cambridge, 1844)

Sanderson, Robert (ed.), *Logicae Artis Compendium* (Bologna, 1984)

Schatzgeyer, Kaspar, *Replica contra Periculosa Scripta*; *Examen Novarum Doctrinarum*; *Tractus de Missa*; *Ecclesiasticorum Sacramentorum Assertio*, ed. E. Iserloh and P. Fabisch, *C. Cath.* 37 (Münster, 1984)

Semler, Johannes Solomo, *Paraphrasis Evangelii Johannis cum notis* (Magdeburg, 1771)
  Philosophia Scripturae Interpres (Magdeburg, 1776)

Seripando, *De Iustitia et Libertate Christiana*, ed. A. Forster, *C. Cath.* 30 (Münster, 1969)

Simon of Dacia, *Opera*, ed. A. Otto, *Corpus Philosophicorum Danicorum Medii Aevi*, 3 (Copenhagen, 1963)

Stapleton, Thomas, *Promptuarium morale super Evangelia Dominicalia* (Antwerp, 1593)
  Relectio Scholastica, Opera (Paris, 1620), vol. 1
  A Fortress of the Faith first Planted among us Englishmen (St Omer, 1625)

Stapulensis, Jacobus Faber, *Commentarii initiatorii in quattuor Evangelia* (Cologne, 1541)

Staupitz, *Tübinger Predigten*, ed. G. Buchwald and E. Wolf (Leipzig, 1927)
Stephanus, Robertus (Robert Étienne), *Phrases Hebraicae Biblia utriusque Testamenti* (Geneva, 1557), vol. 3
Stillingfleet, W., *The Council of Trent Examined*, 2nd ed. (London, 1688)

Tertullian, *De Pudicitia*
Thomas of Erfurt, *Grammatica Speculativa*, in Duns Scotus, *Opera Omnia* (Louvain, 1639)
Tichonius, *The Book of Rules*, ed. J. Armitage Robinson (Parker Society, Cambridge, 1895)
Trithemius, *Opera Historica*, ed. M. Freher (Frankfurt-am-Main, 1601, facs. London, 1966)
Tyndale, William, *Works*, ed. H. Walter (Parker Society, Cambridge, 1848–50)

Valla, Lorenzo, *Dialecticae Disputationes contra Aristotelicos* (Cologne, 1499, 1531)
Elegantiae de Lingua Latina (Lyons, 1501)
Collatio Novi Testamenti, ed. A. Perosa (Florence, 1970)
Repastinatio Dialecticae et Philosophiae, ed. G. Zippel (Padua, 1982)
Vermigli, Peter Martyr, *In Epistolam S. Pauli ... ad Romanos, Commentarii* (Zurich, 1568)
Vives, Juan Luis, *Adversus Pseudo-Dialecticos*, ed. Majans, *Opera Omnia* (Valencia, 1782–90), vol. I, tr. R. Guerlac (Reidel, 1979)
Voetius, G., *Selectae Disputationes Theologicae* (Utrecht, 1648–9)

Walton, Brian, *Prolegomena to the Polyglot Bible* (Cambridge, 1828), 2 vols.
Wesley, J. and C., *Selected Prayers*, ed. F. Whaling (London, 1981)
Wyclif, John, *De Civili Dominio*, ed. R.L. Poole (London, 1884)
De Ecclesia, ed. J. Loserth (London, 1886)
De Veritate Sacrae Scripturae, ed. R. Buddensieg (London, 1905)
Opera Minora, ed. J. Loserth (London, 1913)
Ps. Wyclif, *Wycliffite Tracts and Treatises* (London, 1845)

Zwingli, H., *Werke*, CR 88–101

Modern works

Aland, K., *Martin Luther's Ninety-Five Theses* (St Louis, Miss./London, 1967)
Althaus, P., *Die Prinzipien der Deutschen Reformierten Dogmaatik im Zeitalter der Aristotelischen Scholastik* (Darmstadt, 1967)
Armstrong, B. G., *Calvinism and the Amyraut Heresy* (Wisconsin, 1969)

Ashworth, E. J., 'The Treatment of Semantical Paradoxes from 1400–1700', *Notre Dame Journal of Formal Logic*, 13.1 (1972), 34–52
'Andreas Kesler and the Later Theory of Consequences', *Notre Dame Journal of Formal Logic*, 14.2 (1973), 205–14
Language and Logic in the Post-Medieval Period (Dordrecht, 1974)
'The Structure of Mental Language: some problems discussed by early sixteenth century logicians', *Vivarium*, 20 (1982), 59–82
Aston, M., *The English Iconoclasts* (Oxford, 1988)
Avis, P., *The Church in the Theology of the Reformers* (London, 1981)

Backus, I. D., *The Reformed Roots of the English New Testament: the Influence of Theodore Beza*, Pittsburgh Theological Monographs (Pittsburg, 1980)
Backus, I. D. *et al.*, *Logique et théologie au xvi⁰ siècle: aux sources de l'argumentation de Martin Bucer* (Geneva, 1980)
Baptism, Eucharist and Ministry, Faith and Order Paper, 111, World Council of Churches (Lima, 1982)
Bataillon, M., *Erasmo y España*, tr. A. Alatorre, 2nd ed. (Mexico City, 1966)
Bauckham, R., *Tudor Apocalypse* (Abingdon, 1978)
Bazan, B. C. *et al.* (eds.), *Les questions disputées, Typologie des sources du moyen âge occidental* (Turnhout, 1985)
Beardslee, J., *Reformed Dogmatics* (Oxford, 1965)
Bentley, J. H., 'Erasmus' *Annotationes in Novum Testamentum* and the Textual Criticism of the Gospels', *Archiv für Reformationgeschichte*, 67 (1976), 33–53
'New Testament Scholarship at Louvain in the Early Sixteenth Century', *Studies in Mediaeval and Renaissance History*, N.S. 2 (1979), 51–79
Humanists and Holy Writ (Princeton, N.J., 1983)
Benz, Ernst, *Wittenberg und Byzanz* (Marburg, 1949)
Bischoff, B., 'The Study of Foreign Languages in the Middle Ages', in *Mittelalterliche Studien* (Stuttgart, 1967), 2 vols., vol. 2, pp. 227–45
— 'Das griechische Element in der abendländische Bildung des Mittelalters', *ibid.*, pp. 246–75
Bizer, E., *Luther und der Papst* (München, 1958)
Bludau, A., *Die Beiden Ersten Erasmus-Ausgaben des Neuen Testaments und Ihre Gegner*, Biblische Studien 7, 5 (Freiburg, 1902)
Böhmer, H. and Kim, P. (eds.), *Thomas Münzers Briefwechsel* (Leipzig, 1931)
Booty, J. E., 'The judicious Mr Hooker and Authority in the Elizabethan Church', in Sykes, ed., *Authority in the Anglican Communion*, pp. 94–118
Bornkamm, H., *Luther's World of Thought*, tr. M. H. Bertram (Missouri, 1958)
Bousset, W., *The Antichrist Legend* (London, 1896)

Brandt, A., *Johann Ecks Predigtatigkeit* (Münster, 1914)
Brann, N. L., *The Abbot Trithemius (1462–1516): The Renaissance of Monastic Humanism* (Leiden, 1981)
Breen, Q., 'The terms "loci communes" and "loci" in Melanchthon', *Church History*, 16 (1947), 197–209
Brightman, F. E., *What objections have been made to English Orders?* (London, 1898, repr. London, 1958)
Brod, M., *Johannes Reuchlin und sein Kampf* (Stuttgart, 1965)
Brooks, P. N. (ed.), *Seven-Headed Luther* (Oxford, 1983)
Bühler, F., 'A Lollard Tract: On Translating the Bible into English', *Medium Aevum*, 7 (1938), 167–83
Burgess, J. A. (ed.), *The Role of the Augsburg Confession: Catholic and Lutheran Views* (Philadelphia, 1977)
Butler, C., *The Theology of Vatican II* (London, 1967, revised, 1981)

Cambridge History of the Bible, The, ed. P. R. Ackroyd *et al.* (Cambridge, 1963–70), 3 vols.
Cambridge History of Later Medieval Philosophy, The, ed. N. Kretzmann, A. Kenny and J. Pinborg (Cambridge, 1982)
Capalbo, K. M., '*Politia Christiana*: the ecclesiology of Alvarus Pelagius', *Franciscan Studies*, 35 (1986)
Caplan, H., ' "Henry of Hesse" on the Art of Preaching', *Proceedings of the Modern Language Association*, 43 (1933), 340–61
'A Late Mediaeval Tractate on Preaching', *Studies in Rhetoric and Public Speaking in Honour of James Albert Winans*, ed. A. M. Drummond (New York, 1962), 61–90
Chadwick, H., 'The Status of Ecumenical Councils in Anglican Thought', *Orientalia Christiana Analecta*, 195 (1973)
Augustine (Oxford, 1986)
'Augustine and Tyconius', *Colloquy* 58, Centre for Hermeneutical Studies in Hellenistic and Modern Culture, Berkeley, California (Berkeley, Calif., 1989)
Chadwick, W. O., *From Bossuet to Newman* (Cambridge, 1957)
Chrisman, M. U., *Strasbourg and the Reform* (Yale, 1967)
Clark, F., *Eucharistic Sacrifice and the Reformation* (London, 1960)
Colish, M., *The Mirror of Language* (Nebraska, 1983), revised
Collins, B., *The Sacred is Secular: Platonism and Thomism in Marsilio Ficino's Platonic Theology* (The Hague, 1974)
Congar, Y., *Lay People in the Church* (London, 1957)
L'ecclésiologie du haut moyen âge (Paris, 1968)
'Valeur et portée oecuméniques de quelques principes hermeneutiques de Saint Thomas d'Aquin', *Revue des sciences philosophiques et*

théologiques, 57 (Paris, 1973), 611–26
Thomas d'Aquin: sa vision de théologie et de l'église (London, 1983)

Davies, H., *The Worship of the English Puritans* (London, 1948)
Davies, H., *Like Angels from a Cloud* (San Marino, 1986)
Deanesley, M., *The Lollard Bible* (Cambridge, 1920)
Dekkers, E., 'L'Église devant la Bible en langue vernaculaire: ouverture de principe et difficultés concrètes', in *The Bible and Mediaeval Culture*, ed. W. Lourdeaux and D. Verhelst (Louvain, 1979), 1–15
Dickey, M., 'Some Commentaries on the *De Inventione* and the *Rhetorica ad Herennium* of the Eleventh and Twelfth Centuries', *Mediaeval and Renaissance Studies*, 6 (1968), 1–41
Dulles, Avery, *Models of the Church* (New York, 1974)
Duprey, P., 'A Catholic Perspective on Ecclesial Communion', in *Christian Authority: Essays Presented to Henry Chadwick*, ed. G. R. Evans (Oxford, 1988)

Ebeling, G., 'Hermeneutik', *Die Religion in Geschichte und Gegenwart*, 3 (1959) 249–50
Evangelische Evangelienauslegung (Darmstadt, 1962)
Eells, H., *Martin Bucer* (New Haven, Conn., 1931)
Eisenstein, E. L., *The Printing Press as an Agent of Change* (Cambridge, 1979)
Elert, W., *The Structure of Lutheranism* (St Louis, Miss., 1962), tr. W. A. Hanson
Elie, H., 'Quelques maîtres de l'université de Paris vers l'an 1500', *Archives d'histoire doctrinale et littéraire du moyen âge*, 18 (1950–1), 193–243
Elswijk, H. C. van, *Gilbert Porreta* (Louvain, 1966)
Emmerson, R. K., *Antichrist in the Middle Ages* (Manchester, 1981)
Empire, P. C. and Murchy, T. Austin (eds.), 'Papal Primacy and the Universal Church', *Lutherans and Catholics in Dialogue*, 5 (Minneapolis, 1976)
Emser, H., *Schriften zur Verteidigung der Messe*, ed. T. Freudenberger, *C. Cath.* 28 (Münster, 1959)
Evans, G. R., 'The "Secure Technician": Varieties of paradox in the writings of St Anselm', *Vivarium* 13 (1975)
Old Arts and New Theology (Oxford, 1980)
Augustine on Evil (Cambridge, 1983)
Alan of Lille (Cambridge, 1983)
The Language and Logic of the Bible: the Earlier Middle Ages (Cambridge, 1984)
The Language and Logic of the Bible: the Road to Reformation (Cambridge, 1985)
Doing Theology Together (Norwich, 1986)
The Thought of Gregory the Great (Cambridge, 1986)

Anselm (London/New York, 1989)
Authority in the Church: a challenge for Anglicans (Norwich, 1990)

Forbes, A. P., *An Explanation of the Thirty-Nine Articles* (Oxford and London, 1867), 2 vols.
Fraenkel, P., '*Testimonia Patrum*: the function of the patristic argument in the theology of Philip Melanchthon', *Travaux d'humanisme et renaissance* (Geneva, 1961), 46
De l'écriture à la dispute (Lausanne, 1977)
Frederick, P. W. H., *John Wycliffe and the First English Bible* (Fremont, Nebr., 1957)
Freudenberger, T., 'Zur Benützung des reformatorischen Schriftums im Konzil von Trient', in R. Bäumer, *Von Konstanz nach Trient* (Munich, 1972)

Geanakoplos, D., *Greek Scholars in Venice* (Cambridge, Mass., 1962)
Girardin, B., *Rhétorique et théologie: Calvin, le commentaire de l'Épitre aux Romains* (Paris, 1979)
Glorieux, P., 'Le chancelier Gerson et la réforme de l'enseignement', *Mélanges offerts à Étienne Gilson* (Toronto, 1959), 285–98
Goff, Jacques le, *La naissance du purgatoire* (Paris, 1981)
Gogan, B., *The Common Corps of Christendom*, Studies in the History of Christian Thought, 26 (Leiden, 1982)
Goldsmith, V. F., *A Short-Title Catalogue of Spanish and Portuguese Books 1601–1700 in the Library of the British Museum* (London, 1974)
Graebner, A. L., 'An Autobiography of Martin Chemnitz', *Theological Quarterly*, 3 (1899), 472–87
Grant, R. M., *The Letter and the Spirit* (London, 1957)
Gray, H. H., 'Valla's *Encomium of St Thomas Aquinas* and the Humanist Conception of Christian Antiquity', *Essays in History and Literature ... Presented to Stanley Pargellis*, ed. B. Bluhm (Chicago, 1965), 37–51
Greenfield, R. H., 'Such a Friend to the Pope', in *Pusey Rediscovered*, ed. P. Butler (London, 1983)
Greenslade, S. L., *The Work of William Tindale* (London, 1938)
'The English Reformers and the Councils of the Church', *Oecumenica*, 1 (1976)

Hagen, K., *A Theology of Testament in the Young Luther: the Lectures on Hebrews* (Leiden, 1974)
Hebrews Commentary from Erasmus to Beza, 1516–1598 (Tübingen, 1981)
Hägglund, H., *The Background of Luther's Doctrine of Justification in Late Mediaeval Theology* (Philadelphia, 1971), first published in

Lutheran World, 8 (1961), 24–46

Haigh, C., 'Anticlericalism and the English Reformation', *The English Reformation Revised*, ed. G. Haigh (Cambridge, 1987), 56–74

Haikola, L., *Gesetz und Evangelium bei Matthias Flacius Illyricus* (Lund, 1952)

Haller, J., *Concilium Basiliense: Studien und Quellen zur Geschichte des Konzils von Basel* (Basle, 1896–1936), 8 vols.

Halliburton, John, *The Authority of a Bishop* (London, 1987)

Hamm, B., *Frömmigkeitstheologie am Anfang des 16 Jahrhunderts* (Tübingen, 1982)

Hargreaves, H., 'Popularising Biblical Scholarship: the Role of the Wycliffite *Glossed Gospels*', in *The Bible and Mediaeval Culture*, ed. W. Lourdaux and D. Verhelst (Louvain, 1979), 171–89

Harvey, A., *Believing in the Church* (London, 1981)

Hay, Denys, *The Church in Italy in the Fifteenth Century* (Cambridge, 1977)

Haye, John de la, *Biblia Maxima* (Paris, 1660)

Heath, R., *Anabaptism from its rise at Zwickau to its fall at Münster, 1521–36* (London, 1895)

Heath, T. H., 'Logical Grammar and Grammatical Logic and Humanism in Three German Universities', *Studies in the Renaissance*, 18 (1971)

Henry, D. P., *The Logic of St Anselm* (Oxford, 1967)

Herren, M. W. (ed.), *The Sacred Nectar of the Greeks* (London, 1988)

Hillerbrand, H. J., *Christendom Divided* (New York, 1971)

Hilperin, H. A., *Rashi and the Christian Scholars* (Pittsburgh, 1963)

Holeczeck, H., *Humanistische Bibelphilologie als Reformproblem bei Erasmus von Rotterdam, Thomas More und William Tyndale* (Leiden, 1975)

Honselmann, K., 'Wimpinas Druck der Ablassthesen Martin Luthers 1528 (nach einem der 1517 von Luther ausgegebenen Texte) und Luthers frühe Aussagen zur Verbreitung seiner Ablassthesen', *Zeitschrift für Kirchengeschichte*, 97 (1986), 189–204

Hooker, M., 'ΠΙΣΤΙΣ ΧΡΙΣΤΟΥ', *New Testament Studies*, 35 (1989)

House of Bishops of the Church of England, The, *The Nature of Christian Belief* (London, 1986)

Hudson, A., *The Premature Reformation* (Oxford, 1988)

Hurley, M., '*Scriptura Sola*: Wyclif and his Critics', *Traditio*, 16 (1960), 275–352

Iserloh, E., 'Das Tridentinesche Messopferdekret zu der Kontroverstheologie der Zeit', *Il Concilio de Trento e la Riforma Cattolica* (Rome, 1965)

The theses were not posted (London, 1968)

Jardine, L., 'Lorenzo Valla and the Intellectual Origins of Humanistic Dialectic', *Journal of the History of Philosophy*, 15 (1977), 143–64

Jayne, S., *John Colet and Marsilio Ficino* (Oxford, 1963)

Jedin, H., *Seripando, Papal Legate at the Council of Trent*, tr. F. C. Eckhoff (St Louis, Miss., 1947)

Katholische Reform und Gegenreformation (Freiburg, 1967); tr. in *Reformation and Counter-Reformation, History of the Church*, ed. H. Jedin et al., vol. 5 (London, 1980)

Joachimsen, P., *Loci Communes: Eine Untersuchung zur Geistesgeschichte des Humanismus und der Reformation, Jahrbuch der Luthergesellschaft*, 8 (1926)

Johnson, L. T., *Decision-Making in the Church* (Philadelphia, 1983)

Jonge, H. de, 'Novum Testamentum a Nobis Versum: the Essence of Erasmus' Edition of the New Testament', *Journal of Theological Studies*, 35 (1984), 394–414

Kalkoff, P., 'Die Prädikanten Eberlin und Kettenbach', *Archiv für Reformationsgeschichte*, 25 (1928), 128–50

Kaminsky, H., *A History of the Hussite Revolution* (Berkeley and Los Angeles, 1967)

Kink, R., *Geschichte der Kaiserlichen Universität zu Wien* (Vienna, 1854)

Klug, E. F., *From Luther to Chemnitz* (Grand Rapids, Michigan, 1971)

Kristeller, P., *Il Pensiero Filosofico di Marsilio Ficino* (Florence, 1953)

'Humanism and Scholasticism in the Italian Renaissance', *Studies in Renaissance Thought and Letters* (Rome, 1955), 553–84

Kropatscheck, F., *Das Schriftprincip in der lutherischen Kirche, 1: Die Vorgeschichte. Das Erbe des Mittelalters* (Leipzig, 1904)

Lamping, A. J., *Ulrichus Velenus (Oldrich Velensky) and his Treatise against the Papacy*, Studies in Mediaeval and Reformation Thought, 19 (Leiden, 1976)

Landgraf, A., 'Zur Methode der biblischen Textkritik im 12 Jahrhundert', *Biblica*, 10 (1929)

Lathbury, T., *A History of the Convocation of the Church of England* (London, 1842)

Lane, A. N. S., 'Calvin's Doctrine of Assurance', *Vox Evangelica* II (1979), 32–54

Lau, F. and Bizer, E., *A History of the Reformation in Germany to 1555*, tr. B. A. Hardy (London, 1969)

Leff, G., *Bradwardine and the Pelagians* (Cambridge, 1957)

Heresy in the Later Middle Ages (Manchester, 1967), 2 vols.

'The Apostolic Ideal in Later Mediaeval Ecclesiology', *Journal of Theological Studies*, 18 (1967), 58–82

Lloyd-Jones, G., *The Discovery of Hebrew in Tudor England: a third language* (Manchester, 1983)

Löhse, B., 'Luther und die Autorität-Roms im Jahre 1518', in *Christian Authority: Essays Presented to Henry Chadwick*, ed. G. R. Evans (Oxford, 1988)

Lourdaux, W. and Verhelst, D. (eds.), *The Bible and Mediaeval Culture* (Louvain, 1979)

Lubac, H. de, *Corpus Mysticum*, 2nd ed. (Paris, 1939)

Exégèse médiévale (Paris, 1959), 2 vols.

McConica, J. M., 'Humanism and Aristotle in Tudor Oxford', *English Historical Review*, 94 (1979), 291–317

McCready, W. D. M., 'Papalists and Anti-Papalists', *Viator*, 6 (1975), 241–74

McDonough, T. M., *The Law and the Gospel in Luther* (Oxford, 1963)

McGrath, A., *Iustitia Dei* (Cambridge, 1986), 2 vols.

The Intellectual Origins of the European Reformation (London, 1987)

McNeil, D., *Guillaume Budé and Humanism in the Reign of Francis I* (Geneva, 1975)

Margolin, J. C., *Quatorze années de bibliographie érasmienne (1936–49)* (Paris, 1959); *Douze années ... (1950–61)* (Paris, 1963); *Neuf années ... (1962–70)* (Paris, 1971)

Massner, J., *Kirchliche Uberlieferung und Autoritat im Flaciuskreis* (Berlin/Hamburg, 1964)

Maxcey, C. E., *Bona Opera* (Nieuwkoop, 1980)

Meerhoff, K., *Rhétorique et poétique au xvie siècle en France* (Leiden, 1986)

Meier, L., 'On the Ockhamism of Martin Luther at Erfurt', *Archivum Franciscanum Historicum*, 43 (1950), 4–15

Miles, L., *John Colet and the Platonic Tradition* (London, 1962)

Minnis, A. J., *Mediaeval Theory of Authorship* (London, 1984)

Montclos, J. de, *Lanfranc et Bérengar* (Louvain, 1971)

Morrall, J. B., 'Ockham and Ecclesiology', in *Medieval Studies Presented to Aubrey Gwynn*, ed. J. A. Watt et al. (Dublin, 1961)

Mozley, J. F., *Coverdale and his Bibles* (London, 1953)

Oberman, H. A., *Forerunners of the Reformation* (London, 1967)

Masters of the Reformation, tr. D. Martin (Cambridge, 1981)

O'Connell, M. R., *Thomas Stapleton and the Counter Revolution* (Yale, 1964)

Oehler, K., 'Der Consensus Omnium', *Antike und Abendland*, 10 (1961), 103–29

Olin, J. C., *Christian Humanism in the Reformation: Selected Writings of Erasmus* (New York, 1965)

O'Malley, C. D., 'Some Renaissance Panegyrics of Aquinas', *Renaissance Quarterly*, 27 (1974), 174–92

Ong, W. J., *Ramus, Method and the Decay of Dialogue* (Cambridge, Mass., 1958)

O'Rourke Boyle, M., *Erasmus on Language and Method in Theology* (Toronto, 1977)

'Fools and Schools: Scholastic Dialectic, Humanist Rhetoric; from Anselm to Erasmus', *Medievalia et Humanistica*, N.S. 13 (1985)

Østergaard-Nielsen, H., *Scriptura Sacra et Viva Vox, Forschungen zur Geschichte und Lehre des Protestantismus*, 10 (Munich, 1957)

Overfield, J. H., *Humanism and Scholasticism in Late Mediaeval Germany* (Princeton, N.J., 1984)

Ozment, S., *The Age of Reform, 1250–1550* (Yale, 1980)

Padley, G. A., *Grammatical Theory in Western Europe, 1500–1700: the Latin Tradition* (Cambridge, 1976), *Trends in Vernacular Grammar* 1 (Cambridge, 1985)

Parker, T. H. L., *Calvin* (London, 1975)

Payne, J. B., 'Erasmus and Lefevre d'Étaples as Interpreters of Paul', *Archiv für Reformationgeschichte*, 65 (1974), 54–83

Pesch, C., *Institutiones Propaedeuticae ad Sacram Theologi* (Freiburg, 1924)

Polman, P., *L'élément historique dans la controverse religieuse du xvie siècle* (Gembloux, 1932)

Poschmann, B., *Penance and the Anointing of the Sick*, tr. F. Courtenay (Freiburg, 1964)

Power, David N., *The Sacrifice we Offer* (Edinburgh, 1987)

Preus, J. S., *From Shadow to Promise* (Cambridge, Mass., 1969)

Rattenbury, J. E., *The Eucharistic Hymns of John and Charles Wesley* (London, 1948)

Reuter, K., *Das Grundverständnis der Theologie Calvius* (Neukirchen, 1963)

Ritter, G., *Studien zur Spätscholastik*, 2 (Heidelberg, 1922, repr. 1975)

Rumscheidt, H. M., *Revelation and Theology, an Analysis of the Barth–Harnack Correspondence of 1923* (Cambridge, 1972)

Rupp, G., *Patterns of Reformation* (London, 1969)

Ruysschaert, J., 'Les manuels de grammaire latin composés par Pomponio Leto', *Scriptorium*, 8 (1954), 98–107

'A propos des trois premières grammaires latines de Pomponio Leto', *Scriptorium*, 15 (1961), 68–75

Sabbadini, R., *Le scoperte dei codice latini e greci nel secolo xiv e xv* (Florence, 1905, repr. 1967), 2 vols.

Il metodo degli umanisti (Florence, 1920)

Sanday, W., *Inspiration* (London, 1896)

Schmitt, C. B., 'Towards a Reassessment of Renaissance Aristotelianism', *History of Science*, 11 (1973)

Schuessler, H., 'Sacred Doctrine and the Authority of Canonistic Thought on the Eve of the Reformation', in *Reform and Authority in the Mediaeval and Reformation Church*, ed. G. F. Lyttle (Washington, 1981)

Schwarz, W., *Principles and Practice of Biblical Translation* (Cambridge, 1955)

Schwiebert, E. G., *Luther and his Times* (St Louis, Miss., 1950)

Sikes, J. G., *Peter Abailard* (Cambridge, 1932)

Smalley, B., 'The Gospels in the Paris Schools in the Late Twelfth and Early Thirteenth Centuries', *Franciscan Studies*, 28 (1979), 230–55, and 29 (1980), 298–369

The Study of the Bible in the Middle Ages, 3rd ed. (Oxford, 1983)

Southern, R. W., *Robert Grosseteste* (Oxford, 1986)

Starnes, de Witt T., *Robert Estienne's Influence on Lexicography* (Austin, Texas, 1963)

Steinmetz, B. C., 'Hermeneutic and Old Testament Interpretation in Staupitz and the Young Martin Luther', *Archiv für Reformationgeschichte*, 70 (1979), 24–58

Stephens, W. P., *The Theology of Huldrych Zwingli* (Oxford, 1986)

Stevens, H. J., 'Lorenzo Valla and Isidore of Seville', *Traditio*, 31 (1975)

Stock, Brian, *The Implications of Literacy* (Princeton, 1983)

Strange, R., *The Catholic Faith* (Oxford, 1986)

Strauss, G., *Luther's House of Learning* (Baltimore, 1978)

Stump, E., *Boethius: De Differentiis Topicis* (Ithaca, Ill., 1978)

Suenens, Cardinal, *Co-responsibility in the Church*, tr. F. Martin (London, 1968)

The Suenens Dossier, ed. J. de Broucker (Dublin, 1970)

Sykes, S. (ed.), *Authority in the Anglican Communion* (Toronto, 1987)

Synave, P. and Benoit, B., *Prophecy and Inspiration* (New York/Rome/ Paris/Tournai, 1961)

Tavard, G. V., 'A Forgotten Theology of Inspiration: Nikolaus Ellenbog's Refutation of "Scriptura Sola"', *Franciscan Studies*, 15 (1955), 106–22

Tentler, Thomas N., *Sin and Confession on the Eve of the Reformation* (Princeton, N.J., 1977)

Thomas, H., *Short-Title Catalogue of Books Printed in Spain and of Spanish Books Printed Elsewhere in Europe, before 1601, Now in The British Museum* (London, 1921)

Thorndike, L., *University Records and Life in the Middle Ages* (Columbia, New York, 1975)

Thurian, Max (ed.), *Churches Respond to BEM* (Geneva, 1986–), vols. 1–

Tillard, J. M. R., 'Recognition of Ministries; what is the real question', *One in Christ*, 21 (1985), 31–9
Todd, J. (ed.), *Problems of Authority* (London, 1962)
Torrance, T. F., *The Hermeneutics of John Calvin* (Edinburgh, 1988)

Ullman, B. L., *Studies in the Italian Renaissance* (Rome, 1955)
Unzue, J. L. de Orella y, *Respuestas católicas a Las Centurias de Magdeburgo, 1559–88* (Madrid, 1976)

Vasoli, C., *La dialettica e la retorica dell'umanesmo* (Milan, 1968)
Verkamp, B. J., *The Indifferent Mean* (Ohio, 1977)
Vetter, P., *Die Religionsverhandlungen auf dem Reichstag zu Regensburg 1541* (1889)
Vignaux, P., *Justification et prédestination au xive siècle* (Paris, 1934)
  Luther, Commentateur des Sentences, Études de Philosophie Médiévale (Paris, 1935)
Villoslada, Conrad, 'La Universidad de París durante los estudios de Francisco de Vitoria, O.P. (1507–33)', *Analecta Gregoriana*, 14 (Rome, 1938)

Wicks, J., 'The Lutheran *Forma Ecclesiae*', in *Christian Authority: Essays Presented to Henry Chadwick*, ed. G. R. Evans (Oxford, 1988)
Wilks, M., *The Problem of Sovereignty in the Later Middle Ages* (Cambridge, 1963)
Williams, G. H., *The Radical Reformation* (London, 1962)
Wisloff, C. F., *Abendmal und Messe* (Berlin, 1969)

Yarnold, E., 'ARCIC on Justification', *The Month*, 71 (February 1987)

Zappen, James P., 'Aristotelian and Ramist Rhetoric in Thomas Hobbes's *Leviathan*', *Rhetorica*, 1 (1983), 65–91
Zoubov, V., 'Autour des *Quaestiones super Geometriam Euclidis* de Nicholas Oresme', *Mediaeval and Renaissance Studies*, 6 (1968), 150–71

Index

Cajetan, Tomás de Vio 54
Calfhill, James 256
call 126
Calvin, Jean 4, 16, 19, 29, 33, 40,
50, 59, 64, 67, 68, 76, 83, 87, 91,
93, 94, 97, 99, 110, 116, 126,
130, 133, 134, 136, 137, 144,
145, 146, 150, 152, 154, 157,
161, 169, 172, 173, 175, 187,
220, 223, 233, 244, 249, 255,
267, 271, 273, 275, 276, 278,
279, 280, 285, 289, 290
Cambridge, University of 45, 111
Canon 38, 70
canon law 78, 234
Carlstadt 210
Carmelites 43
Carolingian churches 164
Carolingian period 84, 151,
190, 244
Carolingian precedents 209
Carranza, Sancho 44
Carthusians 243
Caspar 158, 159, 274
Cassiodorus 20
Castro, de 168
catholicity 283
Caubraith, Robert 91
cause and effect 193
Celaya, Juan de 91
celebration 172
Celtic churches 164
ceremonies 172, 280, 282
Chalcedon, Council of 256
chalice 221
charitas formata 30
charity 120, 133
Charles V, Emperor 275
Chemnitz, Martin 2, 3, 4, 52, 84, 271
chimaera 130, 154
Christ 5, 8, 11, 12, 13, 23, 31, 42,
52, 59, 62, 65, 70, 73, 79, 81, 94,
111, 117, 124, 129, 131, 132,

133, 134, 135, 140, 145, 152,
154, 155, 156, 162, 168, 174,
175, 176, 177, 180, 185, 187,
188, 190, 210, 218, 224, 229,
232, 237, 241, 248, 255, 262,
265, 289, 291
as Head 200, 232, 234, 237
as Lord 1, 7, 224
body of 181
death of 173, 174
merits of 129, 191, 192
mystical body of 214
Christ's soul 182
Christ-centredness 5
Christianus of Stavelot 260
Christology 4, 11
Chrysoloras, Manuel 39
Chrysostom 74, 179, 187
Church 78, 79, 80, 94, 103, 115,
144, 145, 146, 150, 162, 163,
171, 175, 185, 186, 191, 199,
201, 202, 205, 208, 209, 211,
216, 220, 224, 225, 226, 227,
231, 232, 234, 236, 238, 241,
245, 246, 248, 250, 252, 253,
257, 258, 261, 262, 263, 269,
270, 279, 281, 283, 287, 289,
290, 292
ancient 73
and state 202, 207
as witness and keeper 45, 71
attendance 200
authority 282
authority of 143
care 162
constitutions of 199
early 161, 162, 165, 227
Holy Catholic 115
institutional 203, 261, 269
invisible 286
local 213, 221, 227
membership 199
of God 225

Plato 40, 262
plenitude of power 202
poenitentia 152, 157
poetry 16
Polyglot Bible 44, 46
Pope 10, 11, 41, 78, 79, 205, 209, 213, 216, 212, 231, 232, 234, 235, 236, 245, 248, 256, 272, 276, 280, 289; *and see* Papacy
Porphyry 81, 82
poverty 216
power 2, 12, 37, 137, 144, 145, 154, 163, 164, 168, 169, 171, 184, 189, 212, 218, 219, 223, 230, 232, 246
  spiritual 208
  temporal 208, 212
power of the keys 162, 163, 164, 165, 168, 203, 236, 247, 280, 286
power-struggle 117, 238, 241
powerlessness 117, 134
prayer 11, 12, 13, 154
preaching 10, 37
predestination 106, 119, 121, 137, 139
prelates 229
presence 179
priests 12, 110, 118, 143, 162, 164, 165, 170, 175, 184, 185, 192, 218, 221, 247
  priesthood 170, 171, 175, 187, 219, 223
  priesthood of all believers 187, 218, 220
  priestly ministry 165, 168
primacy 236, 248
princes 162, 163, 206, 213, 232
Priscian 81, 82
private judgement 18, 285
processions 11
pronouncements 241
pronunciation 50
proofs 38

prophets 73
propitiation 174, 175, 177, 187, 189
  propitiatory sacrifices 192
propositiones 19
propositions 168
propriety of usage 131
Protestants 1, 28, 65, 86, 127
providence 207
province 284
public penance 161
punishment 161, 162, 165, 190
purgatory 8, 12, 13
Puritans 65
Pythagoras 263

quaestio 100, 101
quick and the dead, the 174
quickening 134, 135
Quintilian 32, 49

radicals 149, 210
Ramus, Peter 92
rational animal 96
Ratisbon, Colloquy of (1541) 4, 12, 28, 30, 70, 73, 76, 78, 88, 94, 103, 133, 158, 159, 182, 242, 270, 273, 274, 275, 276, 280
real presence 180
reason 112
reasoning 1, 89, 241
reception 253, 256, 258
reconciliation 2, 141, 148, 158, 165, 167, 176, 179, 187, 189, 277; *and see* forgiveness
rectus ordo 128, 129, 207
recusants 77
Reformation 14, 18, 89
Reformed, the 289
Reformed tradition 261
reformers 33, 103, 145
regeneration 135, 216
regulae 19
relics 5, 13